The Diné Hogan

Over the course of their history, the Navajo (Diné) have constructed many types of architecture, but during the 20th century, one building emerged to become a powerful and inspiring symbol of tribal culture. This book describes the rise of the octagonal stacked-log hogan as the most important architectural form among the Diné.

The Navajo Nation is the largest Indian reservation in the United States and encompasses territory from within Arizona, New Mexico, and Utah, where thousands of Native American homes, called hogans, dot the landscape. Almost all of these buildings are octagonal. Whether built from plywood nailed onto a wood frame or with other kinds of timber construction, octagonal hogans derive from the stacked-log hogan, a form which came to prominence around the middle of the last century. The stacked-log hogan has also influenced public architecture, and virtually every Diné community on the reservation has a school, senior center, office building, or community center that intentionally evokes it. Although the octagon recurs as a theme across the Navajo reservation, the inventiveness of vernacular builders and professional architects alike has produced a wide range of octagonally inspired architecture. Previous publications about Navajo material culture have emphasized weaving and metalwork, overlooking the importance of the tribe's built environment. But, populated by an array of octagonal public buildings and by the hogan – one of the few Indigenous dwellings still in use during the 21st century – the Navajo Nation maintains a deep connection with tradition. This book describes how the hogan has remained at the center of Diné society and become the basis for the most distinctive Native American landscape in the United States.

The Diné Hogan: A Modern History will appeal to scholarly and educated readers interested in Native American history and American architecture. It is also well suited to a broad selection of college courses in American studies, cultural geography, Native American art, and Native American architecture.

Lillian Makeda writes about the architecture and interior design of the American Southwest from her home in western New Mexico. Her work has appeared in *The Architectural Review, Buildings and Landscapes, Journal of the Southwest, Society of Architectural Historians Archipedia*, and *Kiva: Journal of Southwestern Anthropology and History*. She recently completed a Getty/ACLS postdoctoral fellowship in the history of art and is presently working on her next book, which will focus on the Santa Fe style of interior design.

Routledge Research in Architecture

The *Routledge Research in Architecture* series provides the reader with the latest scholarship in the field of architecture. The series publishes research from across the globe and covers areas as diverse as architectural history and theory, technology, digital architecture, structures, materials, details, design, monographs of architects, interior design and much more. By making these studies available to the worldwide academic community, the series aims to promote quality architectural research.

Curated in China
Manipulating the City through the Shenzhen Bi-City Biennale of Urbanism\
Architecture 2005–2019
Monica Naso

Urban Labyrinths
Informal Settlements, Architecture, and Social Change in Latin America
Pablo Meninato and Gregory Marinic

Architectural Exaptation
When Function Follows Form
Alessandro Melis, Telmo Pievani and Jose Antonio Lara-Hernandez

Theorizing Built Form and Culture
The Legacy of Amos Rapoport
Kapila D. Silva and Nisha A. Fernando

Artistic Migration
Reframing Post-War Italian Art, Architecture and Design in Brazil
Aline Coelho Sanches

The Diné Hogan
A Modern History
Lillian Makeda

For more information about this series, please visit: www.routledge.com/
Routledge-Research-in-Architecture/book-series/RRARCH

The Diné Hogan
A Modern History

Lillian Makeda

LONDON AND NEW YORK

Designed cover image: Ben Wittick, Courtesy Palace of the Governors Photo Archives (NMHM/DCA), #048998.

First published 2024
by Routledge
4 Park Square, Milton Park, Abingdon, Oxon OX14 4RN

and by Routledge
605 Third Avenue, New York, NY 10158

Routledge is an imprint of the Taylor & Francis Group, an informa business

© 2024 Lillian Makeda

The right of Lillian Makeda to be identified as author of this work has been asserted in accordance with sections 77 and 78 of the Copyright, Designs and Patents Act 1988.

All rights reserved. No part of this book may be reprinted or reproduced or utilised in any form or by any electronic, mechanical, or other means, now known or hereafter invented, including photocopying and recording, or in any information storage or retrieval system, without permission in writing from the publishers.

Trademark notice: Product or corporate names may be trademarks or registered trademarks, and are used only for identification and explanation without intent to infringe.

British Library Cataloguing-in-Publication Data
A catalogue record for this book is available from the British Library

Library of Congress Cataloging-in-Publication Data
Names: Makeda, Lillian, author.
Title: The Diné hogan : a modern history / Lillian Makeda.
Description: Abingdon, Oxon ; New York, NY : Routledge, 2024. |
   Series: Routledge research in architecture | Includes bibliographical
   references and index.
Identifiers: LCCN 2023058588 (print) | LCCN 2023058589 (ebook) |
   ISBN 9781032552576 (hardback) | ISBN 9781032556857 (paperback) |
   ISBN 9781003431770 (ebook)
Subjects: LCSH: Hogans—Navajo Nation, Arizona, New Mexico &
   Utah—History. | Navajo architecture.
Classification: LCC E99.N3 M35 2024 (print) | LCC E99.N3 (ebook) |
   DDC 728/.3730899726—dc23/eng/20240123
LC record available at https://lccn.loc.gov/2023058588
LC ebook record available at https://lccn.loc.gov/2023058589

ISBN: 978-1-032-55257-6 (hbk)
ISBN: 978-1-032-55685-7 (pbk)
ISBN: 978-1-003-43177-0 (ebk)

DOI: 10.4324/9781003431770

Typeset in Times New Roman
by Apex CoVantage, LLC

Contents

Preface	*viii*
Acknowledgments	*xi*

	Introduction: What Is a Hogan?	**1**
1	**Anthropology Villages and the Diné Hogan, 1890–1950**	**19**

The 1893 World's Columbian Exposition in Chicago 20
The 1902 and 1911 Alvarado Indian Villages 25
*The 1904 Louisiana Purchase International Exposition in
St. Louis 29*
The 1905 Indian Village at the Grand Canyon 32
*The 1906 Indian Crafts Exhibition at Eastlake Park in
Los Angeles 35*
*The 1909 United States Land and Irrigation Exposition in
Chicago 37*
The 1915–1916 Panama-Californic Exposition in San Diego 38
The 1915 Panama-Pacific Exposition in San Francisco 41
Mesa Verde National Park, 1925–1942 45
The 1933–1934 Century of Progress Exposition in Chicago 49
The 1936 Texas Centennial Exposition in Dallas 50
The 1948–1949 Chicago Railroad Fair 52
*Epilogue: The Discover Navajo Pavilion at the 2002 Winter
Olympics in Salt Lake City 54*

2	**"Improving" the Hogan**	**66**

*Governmental Efforts to Encourage Permanent Homes,
1868–1900 66*
*Model Homes for Native Americans: The Omaha Cottages at
Hampton Institute 68*

vi *Contents*

Native American Architecture and the Indian Boarding
   Schools 70
The Sanitation Issue 70
Louisa Wetherill's "Big Hogan" 75
Reassessing the Relationship Between the Hogan and
   Disease 78
Model Hogans at Schools on the Navajo Reservation,
   1922–1931 79
The Federal Government and Native American Architecture,
   1925–1932 82
Model Hogans and the Presbyterian Mission to the Navajo 84

3 Route 66 and Diné Architecture 92

Interpreting Route 66 Hogans 94
Navajo Rug Stands 95
Trading Posts and the Diné Hogan 97
Navajo-Inflected Architecture Along Route 66 99
Route 66 and the Jacobs Family 103
New Uses for the Diné Hogan 108
The Stacked-Log Hogan Becomes a Roadside Icon 112

4 The Indian New Deal 129

John Collier 129
Mayers, Murray & Phillip 132
The Soil Erosion Control Experiment Station in Mexican
   Springs 133
Practice Hogans on the Navajo Reservation 143
Hogans for Diné Nurse's Aides 151

5 Jacob Morgan and John Collier: Ideology and the Navajo Hogan 162

Schools for the Diné Before 1933 162
Native American Architecture for Native American Day Schools 165
Jacob C. Morgan 169
A Political Controversy 174
John Collier and Diné Architecture, 1937–1945 178

6 The Stacked-Log Hogan Becomes an Architectural Type 189

Model and Type 190
The Navajo House of Religion, 1929–1937 191
The Navajo Nation Council Chamber, 1934–1935 196

Contents vii

*John Carl Warnecke's Projects for the Navajo Nation,
    1958–1977 198*
*Education and Tribal Self-Determination: Rough Rock
    Demonstration School and Navajo Community College 203*
*The Navajo Hogan and Public Architecture During the 1970s
    and 1980s 207*
*Studio Southwest: The Navajo Nation Museum and New Schools
    for the Diné 208*
*Leon Shirley: Public Housing for the Diné and a Senior Center
    for Twin Lakes 212*
Dyron Murphy: A Diversity of Hogan-Inspired Designs 215
*Creating a Diné Sacred Place: The Senator John Pinto Library
    in Shiprock, 2009–2011 218*

Conclusion: The Stacked-Log Hogan Becomes a Cultural Icon   226

Illustration Credits   *231*
Index   *235*

Preface

The Navajo Nation covers more than 27,000 square miles of the southwestern United States, where thousands of hogans (the hogan is the traditional dwelling of the tribe) dot the countryside. There are few towns of any size, and the biggest, Tuba City (*Tó Naneesdizí*), Arizona, contains only about 9,000 people. But despite being large and sparsely populated, the Navajo reservation is unified by its architecture. Octagonal hogans abound, and almost every community possesses at least one public building with an octagonal plan. There is a considerable degree of variety in this architecture, but over the last two decades, I have come to realize that it can be traced back to one particular building – the *hooghan dah diitł 'ini* (stacked-log hogan).

Many places around the world feature recent architecture based on older vernacular paradigms that have been reconfigured to serve modern uses. Some architects have duplicated entire buildings and then adapted them for radically different and even transgressive ends. For example, during the first part of the 20th century, the French colonial government in Bamako, Mali, reproduced a *butabu* mosque to house the city's central market building (Figure P.1).

Others have taken an alternative approach: they focus on parts of buildings and rearrange them to create new and unprecedented designs. During the mid-20th century, the Egyptian architect Hassan Fathy became famous for combining catenary vaults from Nubia and courtyard plans from medieval palaces in Cairo to produce a regional style derived from the country's vernacular traditions. The British architects Edwin Lutyens and Herbert Baker selected elements from India's Buddhist, Hindu, and Mughal buildings to develop an architectural idiom for the imperial capital in New Delhi (1912–1931). In the chapters that follow, it will become clear that in Navajoland, both design strategies are much in evidence. In some situations, architects have produced literal translations of the hogan, while in others, they have abstracted the hogan's key elements and reworked them to generate entirely new buildings.

On the Navajo reservation, hogan-inspired architecture expresses Diné identity on an even larger scale. All hogans are aligned with the tribe's sacred mountains located at the four cardinal points: *Sis Naajiní* (Blanca Peak in Colorado) to the east, *Tsoodsił* (Mount Taylor in New Mexico) to the south, *Dook'o'oosłííd*

Figure P.1 Postcard of the central market building in Bamako, Mali, c. 1930s.

(the San Francisco Peaks in Arizona) to the west, and *Dibé Nitsaa* (Mount Hesperus in Colorado) to the north. Consequently, any building that is based on the hogan reinforces a specifically Diné landscape, or "ethnoscape." In his book, *Myths and Memories of the Nation*, historian Anthony Smith emphasized the existential importance of ethnoscapes, and observed:

> What is at stake is an historic and poetic landscape, one imbued with the culture and history of a group, and vice versa, a group part of whose character is felt by themselves and outsiders to derive from the particular landscape they inhabit, and commemorated as such in verse and song.
>
> (150)

Ethnoscapes provide human beings with a connection to place, and they can be found everywhere, from the Nazca Desert to the West Bank to the Australian Outback, where the song lines of aboriginal peoples create an environment rich with myth and meaning. The Diné ethnoscape is always present in any kind of hogan architecture.

The inventiveness of vernacular builders and professional architects alike has ensured a wide range of octagonally inspired architecture across Navajoland. But what really compelled me to write this book is the dramatic contrast between the poetry encoded within these buildings and the banality of so much of this country's built environment. I am not an expert on Diné ceremonialism, and this

x *Preface*

book has little to say about the hogan's role during religious rituals. But as an architectural historian, I can tell you about how the Diné have adapted this building to modernity while maintaining its connection with tradition. In the pages of this book, you will learn how the hogan has remained at the center of Diné society and become the basis for the most distinctive Native American landscape in the United States.

Reference List

Smith, Anthony. *Myth and Memories of a Nation.* New York: Oxford University Press, 1999.

Acknowledgments

I would like to thank everyone who helped to make this book happen. Peter Nabokov, John R. Stein, and Christopher Curtis Mead have been tremendously supportive, and their good energy has sustained me through the twists and turns along the way. The authors who have contributed to my thinking through their work are too numerous to mention, but I would like to especially thank Donald L. Parman, Stephen C. Jett and Virginia E. Spencer, Howard Bahr, and Thomas Arthur Repp for their scholarly excellence and the inspiration they have provided. With the publication of her book, *Contemporary Native American Architecture,* in 1996, Carol Herselle Krinsky led the way in establishing this subject as a field of study for others, like me, to follow. Carol's book is brilliant, and her generosity, kindness, and grace have brightened my life considerably.

The work for this book has included research visits to over 30 archives, and I have been reminded again and again that some of the finest people that one will ever encounter are archivists and librarians. I hesitate to single anybody out but would like to acknowledge Allan Lagumbay, Pamela Casey, the archivists at the Graduate Theological Union in Berkeley, Andrea Hanley, the librarians at the Harvard University Archives, Ann-Mary Lutzick, Dylan Rosenlieb, Margo Warnecke, the archivists at the National Archives in Denver and Riverside, and Scott Williams. And although she has now passed, I feel a great debt to Octavia Fellin, the founder of the special collections and archives at the public library in Gallup, New Mexico.

Dave Stuart read a manuscript draft of this book and offered comments that have shaped it. The Getty Foundation, the Office of the New Mexico State Historian, the National Park Service, the Huntington Library, the University of New Mexico, and the Rockefeller Archive Center have provided essential funding. I would also like to thank the following people for their kind assistance: Betty Jacobs; Craig Arnold and Karen Veneziano; Dyron Murphy; Leon Shirley and Matthew Shirley; the M.L. Woodard family; Harvey Leake; David Sloan; Wallace O. Chariton; Alexa Roberts; Rebecca Stoneman Washee; Charles Yanito; Eddie Lee; John McCarrell; Rich Friedman; Dave Dekker, Del Dixon, and the staff at Studio Southwest; Richard K. Begay; Ted Jojola; Emerald Tanner; Ellen Brennan; Ed Hackley; Wade Campbell; Arthur Krim; Robert Campanile; Joanne MacLean and Gene S. Carlson of the North Adams Historical Society; Chris Wilson; Judy and Philip Tuwaletstiwa; Manny Wheeler; Klara Kelley; Bev Davis and Shan Guadagnoli; Bruce Burnham; Al Grieve; Jean and Douglas Dejolie; Amos Thompson and the staff of the Seba Dalkai Boarding School; Elizabeth Dickey; Randy Eubank; Ruth Roessel; and Taft Blackhorse.

Introduction

What Is a Hogan?

Three years ago, one of my Diné neighbors began constructing a hogan. I live on the edge of the Navajo reservation, near Gallup (*Na'nízhoozhí*), New Mexico, and watched it go up as I drove by her property on the way to town. The Navajo hogan can take several different forms, but nowadays, the most common is the octagonal *tsineheeshjíí' bee hooghan*, which translates as "lumber hogan" (made of commercial lumber) (Figure 0.2).[1]

Across the Navajo Nation, the largest Indian reservation in the United States, I would estimate there are between two and three thousand lumber hogans, and this was the form my neighbor chose to build.

One day, there was a crowd at the construction site, and I stopped by to see what was going on. A builder was there who specializes in hogans, and he was busy installing the ring connecting the eight timbers that would support the hogan's pyramidal roof. The rest of the one-room structure comprised a wood frame clad with oriented strand board. It enclosed about 300 square feet, and with labor volunteered by family and friends, my neighbor could pay for the hogan's construction, even on a very tight budget.

In a region where poverty is endemic, the ability to build economically is crucial. McKinley County, where we live, is one of the poorest counties in the nation. Good jobs are hard to find, and when we last spoke, my neighbor was living in a mobile home and training to become a nursing assistant. But having a hogan is very important to her. There is no Navajo "church" as such, and all Diné religious ceremonies, to a greater or lesser degree, center on the hogan. Although it was not yet complete, her family had already used it as the site for a *kinaaldá*, the Diné puberty ritual for young women.[2] And once the hogan was finished, my neighbor was planning to hold her wedding there.

Fifty years ago, the most common hogan on the reservation was the *hooghan dah diitł'ini* (stacked-log hogan) which was often roofed with a corbelled dome (Figure 0.3).[3] Although the lumber hogan is constructed more frequently today, the stacked-log hogan remains the most important architectural form among the Diné. Over the last century or so, it has profoundly shaped the built environment of the Navajo Nation, and it serves as the most common symbol for "home" in Navajo visual culture.

DOI: 10.4324/9781003431770-1

2   Introduction

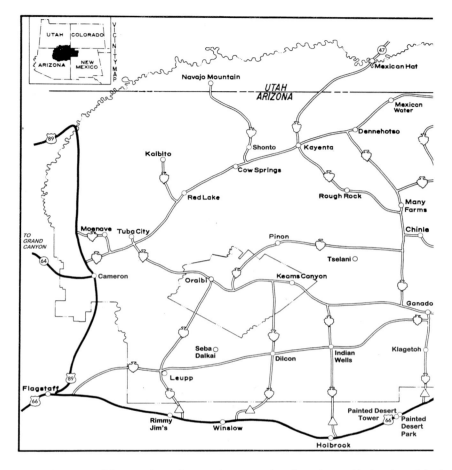

Figure 0.1 Map of the Navajo Nation, c. 1950. Locations have been added to the original map, and places that did not exist in 1950 have been italicized (note that the map is not to scale).

Nowadays, US Route 491 (formerly Highway 666) heading north from Gallup passes by an impressive array of hogans, almost all of them octagonal in shape. There are lumber hogans with pyramidal roofs and stacked-log hogans with corbelled domes. But there are also many stacked-log hogans with pyramidal roofs, some of which are actually lumber hogans clad with log siding. These hybridized forms signify a connection between the lumber hogan and the stacked-log hogan, and it is clear to me that the lumber hogan with a pyramidal roof is the most recent form of the stacked-log hogan with a corbelled dome.

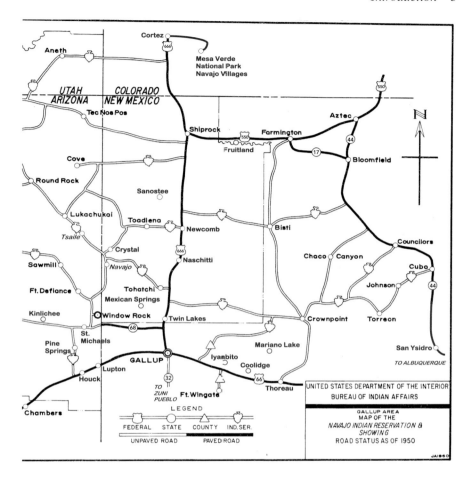

The origins of the stacked-log hogan are ancient, although the building as it exists today likely dates from the 19th century. In 1900, the stacked-log hogan was a rarity; in fact, the first published description of one did not appear until 1893. But during the early decades of the 20th century, there was a significant shift in the way the Diné chose to live. Hogan architecture is variable, and there is room in this book for only an abbreviated account of it.[4] But much of what makes the story you are about to hear so fascinating is its improbability. From a position of relative obscurity, the stacked-log hogan emerged from a diverse range of hogan forms to become a symbol in Diné culture and the dominant architectural presence on the Navajo reservation during the years after World War II.

4   Introduction

Figure 0.2 *Tsineheeshjíí' bee hooghan* (lumber hogan) with a pyramidal roof, model by Dyron Murphy Architects.

"Hogan" is the Anglicized version of the word *hooghan*. Father Berard Haile, an authority on the Navajo language, derived *hooghan* from *hoo-*, which means "place," and *-ghan*, which means "home." In modern parlance, the combination of the two stems, "place home," refers only to human dwellings.[5] Frank Mitchell, a Diné medicine man active during the mid-20th century, explained, "Hogan means habitation, a place where people are living, such as a tent, open shack, or under a tree – any place that is somebody's home. Hogan also means structure."[6] But after living in the Navajo country for 15 years or so, I've observed that many Diné maintain a much more circumscribed understanding of the hogan. Of special significance is its role in Navajo traditional religion. In 1981, during hearings before Congress, Roman Bitsuie, a Diné witness, testified:

> The traditional Navajo house – the hogan – bears little in common with the Anglo-American concept of a home. It is far more than just a place to eat and sleep. It is the site of all Navajo ceremonies, and its ritualistic purpose and

Figure 0.3 Hooghan dah diitł 'íní (stacked-log hogan) with a corbelled dome, photograph of Diné Tsosé's hogan by Simeon Schwemberger, c. 1905.

usages are described in great detail in the myths. During certain ceremonies, the hogan becomes the correlate of a church.

In fact, Bitsuie continued, "the hogan is the primary place of worship and the physical manifestation of sacred space."[7] More recently, I asked Taft Blackhorse, a Diné friend, how he would define a hogan. Blackhorse is a certified court interpreter and works for the movie industry as an advisor on Navajo language and culture. He told me it is possible to hold more than one definition of the hogan and that he agrees with both Mitchell *and* Bitsuie.

The Diné have constructed many different kinds of hogans over the years, although the archaeological research, historic documents, and photographs that form our primary sources for understanding the building can be highly problematic. For centuries, the Diné moved seasonally to provide plentiful water and grazing for their flocks of sheep. This lifestyle did not lend itself to constructing permanent, monumental architecture, and the archaeological remains of early Navajo buildings are often minimal, if they exist at all. Most documents about the Diné dating from before the mid-19th century offer only cursory descriptions of tribal culture. And few photographers ventured into Navajoland before the 1890s.[8] Their personal biases – be it towards hogans that appeared especially primitive or created a picturesque composition – complicate any effort to use their work as a foundation for generalizing what the Diné were building as a group.

6   *Introduction*

By 1890, anthropologists had begun the effort to systematize Diné architecture. In "Navajo Dwellings," an article published that year, Alexander Stephen wrote that the Navajo had "six distinct forms of summer shelter," constructed from various combinations of wooden uprights and tree boughs and sometimes even incorporating living trees.[9] These buildings serve largely as shade structures, and the Diné continue to construct some of them much as Stephen described in 1890. Often called "summer hogans," they tend to be informal and ephemeral. Although summer hogans are still a fixture on the reservation, this book will be mostly concerned with the second category of Diné architecture featured in Stephen's article: the winter hogan.

Stephen mentioned there were six varieties of winter hogan and described the *hooghan 'atch'į' adeez'á* (conical forked-pole hogan) as "the typical dwelling" among the Navajo. The forked-pole hogan is the earliest hogan form noted in the archaeological record and chronicled in historic documents. Examples dating from the 18th century have survived in the northwestern part of New Mexico, and in 1788, the Spanish soldier Vizente Troncoso gave a detailed description of its architecture.[10] The basic structure of a forked-pole hogan is very specific, and many versions of the Diné House Blessing Ceremony describe its sacred origins.[11] Three large poles directed north, west, and south are placed in a tripod formation, and two more are then set on the tripod so that they create an east-facing entrance. Timbers and then earth are stacked against this framework to complete the building (see Figure 0.4).

The forked-pole hogan is commonly referred to as the "male hogan" in contemporary Diné culture. Although examples of this form may vary in size and with regard to minor details, such as the length of the entrance area, the depth of the outer layer of earth, and the proximity of the smoke hole to the tripod, the basic five-pole configuration is obligatory and shared by them all.

The forked-pole hogan fell from use as a dwelling during the 1950s, as the Diné increasingly opted to build different versions of the "female hogan," or *hooghan nímazí* (round hogan).[12] One of the most important female hogan forms is the *tsé bee hooghan* (stone hogan) (Figure 0.5).

This form is defined by its stone walls, which can be carefully constructed with finely hewn blocks or laid with uncoursed rubble; the range is virtually limitless. The stone hogan is much more common in areas where there are few trees, and archaeological evidence indicates that it was in use during the first part of the 18th century, if not earlier.[13]

The *hooghan bijáád hólóní* (hogan with legs) is often referred to as the "many-legged hogan" (Figure 0.6).[14]

The trabeated structure of this hogan is based on four or more vertical uprights upon which roof beams are placed to create the framework for a ceiling. It is typical to lean a series of timbers against the roof beams to create the walls for the building, and although a flat roof is common, other roof structures are possible. Its shape is usually round, subrectangular (rectangular with rounded corners), or polygonal.

Cosmos Mindeleff, author of "Navaho Houses" (1898), the first detailed treatment of the subject, described only two kinds of winter hogans: the forked-pole and the many-legged, which he described as a special hogan for holding the *Yei Bichei*, a religious ceremony requiring a large space.[15] But as we shall see in the

Introduction 7

Figure 0.4 Hooghan 'ałch'į' adeez'á (conical forked-pole hogan), photographed in St. Michaels, Arizona, by Simeon Schwemberger, c. 1905.

8 Introduction

Figure 0.5 Tsé bee hooghan (stone hogan), photographed in northwestern New Mexico in 2015.

next chapter, the same form was being used to construct dwellings by at least the first decade of the 20th century. Like the forked-pole and stone hogans, the many-legged hogan has been dated to the 18th century or earlier.[16]

The *náneeskáál hooghan* (slender objects were set upright in a circle hogan) is more typically known as the palisaded hogan.[17] The walls of the palisaded hogan are constructed from vertical timbers placed perpendicular to the ground. It is a relatively uncommon form of the female hogan, and the three examples discussed in this book are illustrated in Figures 1.14, 3.8, and 3.11.

The *hooghan yistł'óní* (woven hogan) is also known as the corbelled-log hogan (Figure 0.7a).[18]

Structurally, this hogan can be described as a corbelled dome. It is assembled by arranging tiers of logs on top of each other such that each successive tier is oriented diagonally to the one below it (Figure 0.7b). As the dome increases in height, the logs cantilever inward, creating a closed structure. Although the corbelled-log hogan is seldom constructed today, the corbelled dome is commonly found on female hogans. The photograph in Figure 0.7c shows a corbelled dome atop a many-legged hogan, and other female hogans may also feature corbelled domes.

Archaeologists have documented corbelled domes in the American Southwest dating to at least 1,500 years ago. During the Los Pinos Phase (1–400 CE),

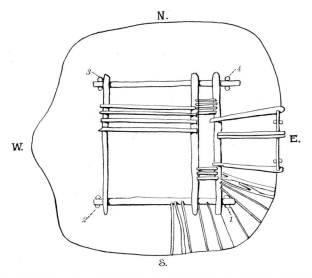

Figure 0.6 Hooghan bijááá hólóní (hogan with legs), plan view and rendering of a *Yei Bichei* house with a flat roof dating from the mid-1890s, originally published in Mindeleff, "Navajo Houses."

Indigenous peoples in northwestern New Mexico erected buildings similar to corbelled-log hogans, and they also built corbelled domes on other kinds of architecture.[19] The remains of corbelled domes have also been found atop kivas at a number of locations associated with the Chacoan Civilization, including Chaco Culture National Historical Park (c. 1050–1150 CE), Aztec Ruins National Monument (c. 1100–1200 CE), and Mesa Verde National Park (c. 1050–1300 CE).[20]

10 Introduction

a.

b.

c.

Figure 0.7 Images of corbelled construction in Diné hogan architecture: a. *Hooghan yistł'óní* (woven hogan) photographed in eastern Arizona in 2022; b. Model of a corbelled dome; and c. Construction of a corbelled dome on a many-legged hogan, photographed in Shonto, Arizona by Elizabeth Hegemann in 1930.

Did the Diné draw from these sources as inspiration, or did they invent the corbelled dome anew? Determining the structure's origin is of great interest because corbelled domes rarely appear in the architecture of the New World. Vernacular examples in the Mediterranean Region include adobe corbelled domes in Syria and the masonry corbelled domes of Italian *trulli* and Maltese *giren*.[21] The Roman historian Vitruvius described dwellings in Colchis (ancient Georgia) with wooden corbelled roofs, and the form has subsequently been recorded across Turkey, the Caucasus, Iran, Afghanistan, and into the Hindu Kush.[22] As common as the corbelled dome may be in Europe and Asia, there is little to indicate its widespread presence in the pre-Columbian Americas, even though corbelled arches and corbelled vaults are frequently found in Puuc Maya architecture. And in case you are wondering, the spiraling construction of the Inuit iglu is better described as arcuated rather than corbelled. Research on the architecture of most Native American groups remains in its early stages, but as things stand now, Diné buildings appear to contain the only Indigenous examples of the corbelled dome constructed in the Western Hemisphere since 1300.

Determining whether a building is a corbelled-log hogan or a stacked-log hogan can be challenging. According to Stephen C. Jett and Virginia E. Spencer, authors of the standard reference on hogan architecture, "a complete gradation exists between hogans of these two types."[23] The crucial factor is whether the building's walls are interwoven like a basket or whether they are divided into separate sections constructed from parallel logs lying directly on top of each other. Stacked-log hogans in New Mexico have been firmly dated to the 1840s.[24] One of the earliest photographs was taken by Ben Wittick during the early 1880s (Figure 0.8).

Figure 0.8 An early *hooghan dah diitł 'íní* (stacked-log hogan), photographed by Ben Wittick, c. 1880–1885.

12   *Introduction*

Several aspects of this building evoke the forked-pole hogan: The walls sweep back from the entrance all the way to the rear, and timbers jut out from around the top. But at the far-right corner of the building, the logs are notched, a construction technique known as corner-timbering that almost certainly derives from the architecture of other ethnic groups in the American Southwest.[25] The vestibule recalls similar structures in forked-pole hogans, but in this case, the entrance has a door constructed from sawn planks, indicating the use of metal tools. The building illustrates the transition in hogan architecture that would culminate in the decline of the forked-pole hogan and the emergence of the stacked-log hogan as an iconic form among the Diné today.

The process by which this happened was gradual. Alexander Stephen published the first description of a stacked-log hogan in 1893, and Washington Matthews' 1897 book, *Navajo Legends,* contains what is probably the first published photograph, although the building he depicted bears little resemblance to the stacked-log hogan photographed by Simeon Schwemberger around 1905 in Figure 0.3.[26] By 1910, the Franciscan Fathers at the Catholic mission in St. Michaels, Arizona, who authored the *Ethnologic Dictionary of the Navaho Language,* claimed the stacked-log hogan was "occasionally built in mountainous and other districts where timber is available."[27] In 1930, Dane and Mary Roberts Coolidge published *The Navajo Indians,* which includes a chapter describing their research on the hogan. The Coolidges provided the historical background and a drawing of eight different dwellings, including the stacked-log hogan, which they described as "the modern hohrahn." They were clear that it was not the most popular hogan form in Navajoland, but they noted, "such houses are rapidly supplanting the older forms wherever timber is plentiful."[28] Other authors writing during the 1930s concurred there was a direct relationship between the availability of lumber and the proportion of stacked-log hogans, and in 1944, the anthropologists Alexander and Dorothea Leighton wrote that the stacked-log hogan had become "the common type of hogan in the wooded areas" of Navajoland.[29]

It is difficult to assess how popular the form was elsewhere across the reservation, but two surveys conducted in the mid-1930s are suggestive. During the summer of 1937, John M. Corbett spent six weeks investigating a 1,000-square-mile area around Chaco Canyon on the eastern side of Navajoland, a region that has few timber resources. Working with translator Fred Yazzi, Corbett documented 150 hogans and organized the winter hogans into six different categories.[30] They included the following:

- 47 stone hogans with a corbelled roof
- 33 log hogans with either partial or complete corbelling[31]
- 28 many-legged hogans with a corbelled roof
- 13 square hogans constructed from logs
- 12 square hogans constructed from stone
- 11 hogans that did not fit into any of the other categories

Clearly, in 1937, the stone hogan was the most popular form within this area, and the number of many-legged hogans was almost equal to the number of corbelled-log and stacked-log hogans.

Gordon B. Page spent two years traveling around the Navajo country while working for the US Soil Conservation Service during the mid-1930s.[32] In an article published in 1937, he presented an analysis of several hogans at eight locations around Navajoland.[33] He concluded, "There appears to be no outstanding type of structure, but rather a general plan, which is followed in construction, using whatever materials happen to be most accessible to the builder." Page described Diné architecture as embracing a variety of forms, none of which were more numerous than the others.

But as the pages that follow will demonstrate, during the same period, the stacked-log hogan was fast emerging as the building of choice for representing Diné identity in other contexts. In Chapter 1, we will track this development by analyzing the hogans constructed in anthropology villages at world's fairs and along the Santa Fe Railway in the American Southwest. Beginning in the 1890s and continuing until the mid-20th century, governmental and commercial entities funded exhibits with full-size hogans where Diné lived and performed. A variety of objectives motivated the people who sponsored the villages, such as promoting tourism and affirming the legitimacy of Manifest Destiny. But in almost every instance, the exhibits were also intended to educate Euro-Americans about Native American culture. Diné were hired to construct the hogans at most of the anthropology villages, and the buildings offer a glimpse into the architectural forms that were common on the reservation.

Meanwhile, several different elements of American society were actively taking steps to change the Diné hogan. In Chapter 2, we will examine the efforts of religious groups and the federal Indian office to assimilate Indigenous peoples into mainstream American society by "improving" their architecture. During the early 20th century, model hogans became an important tool for promoting healthful building practices among the Diné. Tuberculosis and trachoma (an affliction of the eye that causes blindness) were widespread, and the consensus among the medical community and the populace at large was that dust serves as a vehicle for transmitting illness. The hogan, which was typically plastered with mud and constructed without a floor, was seen as unsanitary by many Euro-Americans. A few reformers tried to modestly alter the hogan, rather than change it in any significant way. But others were much more interested in persuading the Diné to live in houses, and the octagonal stacked-log hogan, which bears a resemblance to a log cabin, emerged as an acceptable compromise.

In Chapter 3, we will explore how entrepreneurs used the hogan to promote their businesses along Route 66, which followed the southern boundary of the reservation. Most of these individuals were Euro-American, although this chapter also includes a section about Diné rug dealers. As automobile traffic increased along Route 66 during the 1920s and 1930s, new hogan architecture appeared. The construction of the Gallup Inter-Tribal Ceremonial hogan in 1930 on a lot between Route 66 and the railway line proved to be a pivotal event. Although a variety of different hogan forms appeared along the roadside during this period, the Ceremonial's single (and later double) stacked-log hogan was especially influential. By the mid-1930s, stacked-log hogans along Route 66 and at locations across the nation had been transformed into a variety of different commercial enterprises.

14   *Introduction*

In 1933, John Collier, a former Native American rights activist, became the federal commissioner of Indian Affairs. Chapter 4 describes the hogans that federal relief programs administered by Collier constructed across the Navajo Nation. Soil erosion was an issue of grave concern during the 1930s, and the government's efforts to restore the productiveness of the reservation gave rise to an enormous federally funded land-use project covering millions of acres. Within months after Collier was appointed, a 67-square-mile area around Mexican Springs (*Naakai Bito'í*), New Mexico, became the center of this effort. Collier and his colleagues planned the Soil Erosion Control Experiment Station in Mexican Springs to be a model landscape for the Diné. During the fall of 1933, the New York architectural firm of Mayers, Murray & Phillip, in collaboration with John Collier's son, architect Charles Collier, developed a design for an octagonal stacked-log hogan dormitory to house Diné workers in Mexican Springs. The Office of Indian Affairs eventually constructed a village with eleven hogans at the center of the experiment station. In opting for the stacked-log hogan, the designers found a form that expressed the government's utopian vision and identified Mexican Springs as unequivocally "Navajo." For locations outside of Mexican Springs, Mayers, Murray & Phillip produced a plan for a different octagonal hogan. As we have seen, arid regions within the reservation have a preponderance of stone hogans, while areas that are forested have tended to favor log construction. The building designed by the architects – an octagonal stone hogan with a corbelled dome – synthesized regional differences into one form. There were practical reasons to use a single design across the reservation, but it is likely that Collier was also seeking to promote a sense of tribal identity among the Diné.

Chapter 5 analyzes how the Navajo hogan crystallized the ideological differences between Collier and the Diné leader, Jacob Morgan. In 1938, Morgan, a Christian Reformed missionary, became the first popularly elected chairman of the Navajo Nation Tribal Council. An enthusiastic proponent of assimilation, Morgan believed the tribe should reject their cultural traditions and fully embrace "the American way of life." When Collier proposed building schools in hogans, Morgan became incensed. He fully understood the relationship between the hogan and traditional Navajo religion, and a diatribe he published in 1924 became the first architectural history of the hogan written by a Navajo. To Morgan, a devout Christian, the hogan posed a threat because it symbolizes the Diné ritual landscape and serves as the site – "the medicine lodge" – for the performance of traditional ceremonies. The fight between Morgan and Collier continued for years and illustrates the symbolic power of the hogan among the Diné. Collier, who resigned in 1945, never gave up his efforts to promote traditional Diné culture and build hogans for children attending Diné schools. Similarly, Morgan maintained his opposition to hogan architecture on the Navajo reservation until he stepped down as chairman in 1942.

Over the last century or so, architects have designed a variety of large-scale public buildings based on the octagonal form of the stacked-log hogan. Two types (or typologies) have proven to be especially useful: the octagon and the corbelled dome. Chapter 6 traces the history of these buildings, beginning with the Navajo

Introduction 15

House of Religion (now the Wheelwright Museum) in Santa Fe and concluding with a discussion of several recent designs by the Diné architects Hemsley Lee, Leon Shirley, David Sloan, Dyron Murphy, and Richard K. Begay.

A Note on Orthography and Spelling

There was no standard system of orthography for the Navajo language during much of the period surveyed by this book. In the pages that follow, I have reproduced Navajo words as they were originally printed in historic sources, and as a result, the text includes variations in the orthography of those words. Today, most publications use the orthography devised by Robert W. Young and William Morgan during the late 1930s and early 1940s. But even so, variations in spelling are common, especially in Navajo place-names, and I have tried to employ the spellings that appear with the most regularity in popular usage.[34]

Notes

1 Robert W. Young and William Morgan, *The Navajo Language: A Grammar and Colloquial Dictionary* (Albuquerque: University of New Mexico Press, 1980), 459.
2 For more about the *kinaaldá*, see Charlotte Frisbie, *Kinaaldá: A Study of the Navaho Girl's Puberty Ceremony* (Salt Lake City: University of Utah Press, 1967).
3 Young and Morgan, *The Navajo Language*, 459. Another Navajo name for this hogan is *tsin* ([*dah*] *diitł' in*) *bee hooghan.* See Stephen C. Jett and Virginia E. Spencer, *Navajo Architecture: Forms, History, Distributions* (Tucson: University of Arizona Press, 1981), 80, 210; The Navajo Social Studies Project, *How We Live Now – And Long Ago* (Albuquerque: Bureau of Indian Affairs, 1970), 22.
4 If the reader is interested in a more detailed account, the standard reference on the subject is Jett and Spencer, *Navajo Architecture*.
5 See Charlotte Johnson Frisbie, "The Navajo House Blessing Ceremonial: A Study of Cultural Change" (PhD diss., University of New Mexico, 1971), 19–20; and Berard Haile, *A Stem Vocabulary of the Navaho Language*, vol. I (St. Michaels, AZ: St. Michaels Press, 1950–1951), 171.
6 Quoted in Frisbie, *Kinaaldá*, 100.
7 Quoted in Ninibah Hufford, "Land as Holy," in *By Executive Order: A Report to the American People on the Navajo-Hopi Land Dispute*, ed. Edgar S. Cahn (Citizens Advocate Center, 1982), 384.
8 For more on this topic, see James G. Faris, *Navajo and Photography* (Salt Lake City: University of Utah Press, 2003).
9 Alexander M. Stephen, "Navajo Dwellings," *Our Forest Children* 4, no. 4 (July 1890): 223. For more on Stephen, see Louis A. Hieb, "Alexander M. Stephen and the Navajos," *New Mexico Historical Review* 79, no. 3 (Summer 2004): 353–395.
10 Donald Worcester, "Early History of the Navaho Indians" (PhD diss., University of California, 1947), 220.
11 See, for example, the versions transcribed in Frisbie, "The Navajo House Blessing Ceremonial," Appendix B.
12 Young and Morgan, *The Navajo Language*, 459. Publications that describe the division of the hogan into male and female forms include Broderick Johnson, ed., *Grandfather Stories of the Navahos* (Rough Rock, AZ: Rough Rock Press, 1974); Chester Hubbard, *Hooghan Haz'ą́ągi Bó Hoo' Aah—The Learning of That Which Pertains to Home* (Tsaile, AZ: Navajo Community College Press, 1977); and Shirley Begay and Horace Spencer, *Hooghan Baahane'—A Book About the Hogan* (Rough Rock, AZ: Navajo Curriculum Center, 1982).

16 *Introduction*

13 Jett and Spencer, *Navajo Architecture*, 99–101. The examples cited by Jett and Spencer were dated to the Gobernador Phase (1696–1770), an archaeological period associated with Gobernador Polychrome ceramics.

14 Young and Morgan, *The Navajo Language*, 459. The form is also referred to as *hooghan bijáád łani*, Jett and Spencer, *Navajo Architecture*, 64–66, 69–71.

15 Cosmos Mindeleff, "Navaho Houses," in *Seventeenth Annual Report of the Bureau of American Ethnology, 1895–1896*, ed. J.W. Powell (Washington, DC: Government Printing Office, 1898), 509–514.

16 Jett and Spencer, *Navajo Architecture*, 65. The example cited by Jett and Spencer was dated to the Gobernador Phase (1696–1770).

17 Jett and Spencer, *Navajo Architecture*, 67–69, 71–72.

18 Young and Morgan, *The Navajo Language*, 459; Jett and Spencer, *Navajo Architecture*, 74–77, 80. Other names for the *hooghan yistł'óní* include *tsin náastl'ingo [bee] hooghan* ([with]-circularly-piled-logs hogan) or *hooghan dijoolí* (globular hogan).

19 Jett and Spencer, *Navajo Architecture*, 75.

20 Neil Judd, *The Architecture of Pueblo Bonito*, Smithsonian Miscellaneous Collections 147, no. 1 (Washington, DC: Smithsonian Institution, 1964); Gustaf Nordenskiöld, *Cliff Dwellers of the Mesa Verde, Southwestern Colorado, Their Pottery and Implements*, trans. D. Lloyd Morgan (Stockholm: P.A. Norstedt & Söner, 1893); Thomas C. Windes, "The Chacoan Court Kiva," *Kiva* 79, no. 14 (Summer 2014): 337–379; Jett and Spencer, *Navajo Architecture*, 79. Note that Judd and Windes refer to corbelling as "cribbing."

21 Monumental examples include the subterranean corbelled domes on tholos tombs like the Treasury of Atreus at Mycenae, Greece. For more details, see L. Rovero and U. Tonietti, "Structural Behaviour of Earthen Corbelled Domes in Aleppo's Region," *Materials and Structures* 45 (2012): 171–184; and Michael Fsadni, *The Girna: The Maltese Corbelled Stone Hut*, trans. Louis J. Scerri (Malta: Dominican Publication, 1992).

22 Alev Erarslan, "A Traditional Wooden Corbelled Dome Construction Technique from Anatolia: The Eastern Anatolian Tandoor House with Its Wooden 'Swallow-Dome' Type of Roof," *Journal of Asian Architecture and Building Engineering* 21, no. 4 (2022): 1276.

23 Jett and Spencer, *Navajo Architecture*, 78.

24 Jett and Spencer, *Navajo Architecture*, 77.

25 Jett and Spencer, *Navajo Architecture*, 78.

26 A.M. Stephen, "The Navajo," *American Anthropologist* 6, no. 4 (October 1893): 350; Washington Matthews, *Navaho Legends* (Boston: Houghton Mifflin Co., 1897), 14.

27 The Franciscan Fathers, *An Ethnologic Dictionary of the Navaho Language* (St. Michaels, AZ: Franciscan Fathers, 1910), 333.

28 Dane Coolidge and Mary Roberts Coolidge, *The Navajo Indians* (Boston: Houghton Mifflin Company, 1930), 83.

29 Jett and Spencer, *Navajo Architecture*, 218; Alexander H. Leighton and Dorothea C. Leighton, *The Navaho Door* (Cambridge, MA: Harvard University Press, 1944), plate caption.

30 A copy of Corbett's report on the survey, "Navaho House Types in the Chaco Canyon and Its Environs," is located in 90MSS.914, LA. He later published a summary of the survey in John M. Corbett, "Navajo House Types," *El Palacio* 47, no. 5 (May 1940): 97–107.

31 On page 105 of the article about the survey that Corbett wrote for *El Palacio* in 1940, he stated that the hogans in this category were corbelled-log hogans, but a photograph illustrating this category in the survey report is actually a stacked-log hogan. I can only conclude that Corbett did not distinguish between corbelled-log hogans and stacked-log hogans during his field research and that he grouped them together as one category.

See Corbett, "Navaho House Types in the Chaco Canyon and Its Environs," Illustration V, Figure 2.

32 Obituary of Col. Gordon B. Page, *Albuquerque Journal*, March 23, 1999.

33 The locations were "Tolani Lakes on the west, Denehotso and Kayenta on the north, Naschiti [sic] on the east, Gallup and Mariana [sic] Lake to the south, and Steamboat Canyon and Canyon de Chelly in the central portion." See Gordon B. Page, "Navajo House Types," *Museum Notes* [Museum of Northern Arizona] 9, no. 9 (March 1937): 47–48.

34 For details about the development of an orthography for the Navajo language, see Robert W. Young, "Written Navajo: A Brief History," in *Advances in the Creation and Revision of Writing Systems,* ed. Joshua A. Fishman (The Hague, Netherlands: Mouton & Co., 1977), 459–470.

Reference List

Archival Sources

Laboratory of Anthropology Archives, Santa Fe, New Mexico. Cited as LA.

Published Sources

Coolidge, Dane, and Mary Roberts Coolidge. *The Navajo Indians*. Boston, MA: Houghton Mifflin Company, 1930.

Corbett, John M. "Navajo House Types." *El Palacio* 47, no. 5 (May 1940): 97–107.

Erarslan, Alev. "A Traditional Wooden Corbelled Dome Construction Technique from Anatolia: The Eastern Anatolian Tandoor House with Its Wooden 'Swallow-Dome' Type of Roof." *Journal of Asian Architecture and Building Engineering* 21, no. 4 (2022): 1275–1303.

The Franciscan Fathers. *An Ethnologic Dictionary of the Navaho Language*. St. Michaels, AZ: Franciscan Fathers, 1910.

Frisbie, Charlotte. *Kinaaldá: A Study of the Navaho Girl's Puberty Ceremony*. Salt Lake City: University of Utah Press, 1967.

Hegemann, Elizabeth Compton. *Navaho Trading Days*. Albuquerque: University of New Mexico Press, 1963.

Hufford, Ninibah. "Land as Holy." In *By Executive Order: A Report to the American People on the Navajo-Hopi Land Dispute*, edited by Edgar S. Cahn. Citizens Advocate Center, 1982.

Jett, Stephen C. "The Navajo in the American Southwest." In *To Build in a New Land: Ethnic Landscapes in North America*, edited by Allen G. Noble, 331–344. Baltimore: Johns Hopkins University Press, 1992.

Jett, Stephen C., and Virginia E. Spencer. *Navajo Architecture: Forms, History, Distributions*. Tucson: University of Arizona Press, 1981.

Judd, Neil. *The Architecture of Pueblo Bonito*. Smithsonian Miscellaneous Collections 147, no. 1. Washington, DC: Smithsonian Institution, 1964.

Leighton, Alexander H., and Dorothea Leighton. *The Navaho Door: An Introduction to Navaho Life*. Cambridge, MA: Harvard University Press, 1944.

Matthews, Washington. *Navaho Legends*. Boston: Houghton, Mifflin and Co., 1897.

Mindeleff, Cosmos. "Navaho Houses." *17th Annual Report of the Bureau of American Ethnology, 1895–1896*, Part 2. Washington, DC: Government Printing Office, 1898.

The Navajo Social Studies Project. *How We Live Now – And Long Ago*. Albuquerque: Bureau of Indian Affairs, 1970.

18   *Introduction*

Nordenskiöld, Gustaf. *Cliff Dwellers of the Mesa Verde, Southwestern Colorado, Their Pottery and Implements*. Translated by D. Lloyd Morgan. Stockholm: P.A. Norstedt & Söner, 1893.

Obituary of Col. Gordon B. Page. *Albuquerque Journal*, March 23, 1999.

Page, Gordon B. "Navajo House Types." *Museum Notes* [Museum of Northern Arizona] 9, no. 9 (March 1937): 47–49 plus plates.

Stephen, Alexander M. "Navajo Dwellings." *Our Forest Children* 4, no. 4 (July 1890): 223.

———. "The Navajo." *American Anthropologist* 6, no. 4 (October 1893): 345–362.

Windes, Thomas C. "The Chacoan Court Kiva." *Kiva* 79, no. 4 (Summer 2014): 337–379.

Worcester, Donald. "Early History of the Navaho Indians." PhD diss., University of California, 1947.

Young, Robert W., and William Morgan. *The Navajo Language: A Grammar and Colloquial Dictionary*. Albuquerque: University of New Mexico Press, 1980.

1 Anthropology Villages and the Diné Hogan, 1890–1950

During the 19th century, a new phenomenon – the anthropology village – became an indispensable attraction at world's fairs in the United States and Europe. An anthropology village recreates a landscape – typically originating from a colonized region – and fills it with the Indigenous people who would characteristically live there. Performers not only dwell in the simulated landscape, they also carry out their everyday activities as if it were truly their home. The first of the great expositions to display colonized individuals in living exhibits was the 1867 Paris Exposition Universelle.[1] In the years that followed, anthropology villages also appeared at American expositions, where they were presented as an opportunity for Euro-Americans to learn about Native American culture. The sponsors of the villages typically sought to achieve other objectives as well, such as promoting the assimilation of Indians into mainstream American culture, boosting tourism, and affirming the legitimacy of Manifest Destiny. The educational aspirations of Native American anthropology villages meant that academic anthropologists were often closely involved with organizing these highly politicized exhibits.

Designed with an eye towards entertaining casual visitors rather than engaging serious students, the anthropology villages discussed in this chapter simplified Native American culture. It is no coincidence that Walt Disney's visit to the 1948 Chicago Railroad Fair with its American Indian anthropology villages and "Wild West" amusements became one of the inspirations for the creation of Disneyland.[2] Rather than represent tribal lifeways in all their complexity, anthropology villages portrayed them in terms that a wide audience would find easily understandable. The imperative to condense entire civilizations into a few quickly comprehended "view-bites" affected every aspect of the anthropology village. Consequently, the buildings in these artificial settings usually contained a limited number of examples to represent a much more sophisticated body of architecture.

Since the 1890s, when American expositions began to include Diné architecture, anthropology villages have offered a shorthand version of the hogan. Rather than represent the hogan's diversity, anthropology villages established iconic forms that could be readily associated with the tribe. Although the Diné who performed at the 1893 World's Columbian Exposition in Chicago and the 1904 World's Fair in St. Louis built male (forked-pole) hogans, various forms of the female hogan became predominant in anthropology villages during the first decade of the 20th

DOI: 10.4324/9781003431770-2

20 *Anthropology Villages and the Diné Hogan, 1890–1950*

century. Navajos built many-legged hogans at the Santa Fe Railway's anthropology village in Albuquerque in 1902 and at Antonio Apache's Indian Crafts Exposition in Los Angeles in 1906, and a Diné crew built a many-legged hogan and a palisaded hogan at the Panama-California Exposition in San Diego in 1915–1916.

But the stacked-log hogan was destined to become the most common hogan form in Native American anthropology villages. Two stacked-log hogans were constructed for the Santa Fe Railway's anthropology village at the Grand Canyon in 1905 and for the 1915 Panama-Pacific Exposition in San Francisco. The stacked-log hogan served as the principal hogan form in the anthropology village at the 1933 Century of Progress Exposition in Chicago, and by mid-century, it had emerged as an architectural signature for the Diné. Anthropology villages – sponsored by state and corporation alike – illustrate the development of the hogan's iconography and the rise of the stacked-log hogan.

The 1893 World's Columbian Exposition in Chicago

Between May 1 and October 30, 1893, 27.5 million people visited the first world's fair in Chicago, making it the largest American exposition of the 19th century.[3] There had been Native American anthropology villages at previous fairs, but as historian Robert A. Trennert has documented, in Chicago, "for the first time, significant numbers of living Indians, carrying out their daily activities, were viewed by the public."[4] At least 13 different attractions featured performances by Native Americans, including the "Outdoor Ethnographical Exhibit" – the anthropology village sponsored by the federal government where a group of Diné lived in a hogan and performed for visitors.

The main gate to the fair channeled visitors into the Court of Honor, the heart of the White City, so named for its monumental neoclassical architecture clad in white staff (a type of plaster). The anthropology village was situated on the banks of a lagoon known as the South Pond, immediately to the south of the Court of Honor (Figure 1.1).

Here, a series of buildings – together comprising a cultural landscape – illustrated a distinctly Eurocentric history of the Americas. The exhibits evoked a narrative of mythic proportions, one of "discovery," colonization, and the "progress" brought about by contact with Euro-American culture. The "discovery" of the continent was symbolized by a replica of the Convent of Santa María de la Rábida, dramatically located on a promontory next to the Court of Honor. The convent, located in in Palos de la Frontera, Spain, is closely associated with Christopher Columbus's first voyage across the Atlantic in 1492, and the replica contained memorabilia associated with Columbus. To the south of the convent's replica was the federal government's Model Indian School, exemplifying the progress brought by the coming of the Europeans.[5] The school linked the "civilization" signified by the convent with the series of exhibits highlighting precontact Indigenous culture further along the edge of the South Pond.

The anthropology village, to be discussed in more detail shortly, was located to the south of the Indian School on a long, narrow site covering approximately two to three acres (Figure 1.2).[6]

Figure 1.1 View towards the South Pond, looking south, 1893 World's Columbian Exposition in Chicago. The buildings from left to right are the Convent of Santa María de la Rábida, the Model Indian School (encircled by the fair's railway line), the "Outdoor Ethnographical Exhibit" (hidden behind the Model Indian School), and "The Ruins of Yucatán" and "The Cliff Dwellers" (visible in the distance). To the right is the Agriculture Building, which was part of the Court of Honor.

Figure 1.2 The "Outdoor Ethnographical Exhibit," looking southwest, 1893 World's Columbian Exposition in Chicago.

Adjoining the village to the east was a log cabin where Euro-Americans demonstrated "carding and weaving and other home occupations of the pioneers, illustrating the early life of the white race on this continent."[7] "The Ruins of Yucatán," a

22   *Anthropology Villages and the Diné Hogan, 1890–1950*

group of life-size, papier-mâché reproductions of Puuc Maya buildings from Central America, was just south of the anthropology village. And "The Cliff Dwellers," a five-story, 1/10-scale reproduction of Colorado's Battle Mountain Rock, was just south of "The Ruins." "The Cliff Dwellers" contained human remains and a variety of artifacts associated with the Chacoan Civilization that once dominated parts of the American Southwest.

Frederic Ward Putnam, head of Harvard University's Peabody Museum and chief of the Department of Ethnology at the World's Columbian Exposition, organized the anthropology village. Contemporary accounts differ as to how many different tribal groups appeared there, and the population fluctuated during the six months that the fair was open. Recent research, however, indicates that participants included Cree, Haida, Kwakiutl, and Inuit from Canada and Alaska; Iroquois, Chippewa, Lakota, Menominee, Penobscot, Winnebago, Passamaquoddy, Crow, Choctaw, Chiricahua Apache, Diné, Zuni, Hopi, and Coahuila from the United States; Papago and Yaqui from the US/Mexico borderlands; and representatives of several groups from British Guiana.[8] The tracks of the fair's elevated railroad ran alongside these exhibits and looped around the Model Indian School.

The architectural highlights of the village included an impressive group of Northwest Coast plank buildings and sculptures, with a 40-foot Haida house and totem pole, as well as "a Tsimshian heraldic column, Bella Coola memorial columns, Salish house posts, and two Tlingit poles."[9] Representatives of the Penobscot constructed three tipis and a rectangular building with a pitched roof covered in birch bark. The Iroquois built a group of bark-covered structures, including a longhouse, a stockade, and four circular and rectangular dwellings.[10] Nearby, there was also a circular thatched dwelling sponsored by the British government inhabited by Indigenous people from British Guiana.[11]

Putnam hired a staff of over 100 people to find artifacts and hire performers for the archaeological and ethnological exhibits.[12] His agent for the Diné and Apache was a young man named Antonio Apache. On August 4, 1892, Putnam wrote to Antonio about his plans for the Diné exhibit at the anthropology village:

> All I can do is to have about five who will live together in a Hogan (although it may be possible to have two Hogans) and as I stated before I wish for you to secure a good silver worker and a good weaver among the number as well as a good basket and bottle maker. While we might procure wood for the house at the north [at the exposition], it will be difficult to get just the right kind and it seems to me it will be best to have the house built in the Navajo country and then taken down, carefully packed, and sent to Chicago by freight, that it may be reconstructed there. You will see that the Indians who come have all the fixings for the house as well as their loom and material for making their various objects. We want everything as purely Indian as possible.[13]

Five Diné performers arrived in late June 1893 with three women (Marietta, Kimizin [or Kimizra], and Chiquita) and two men (Peshloki and Cheeno) from Fort

Defiance, Arizona.[14] They included two weavers and one silversmith, and their expenses were paid by the State of Colorado.[15]

Hubert Howe Bancroft's *Book of the Fair*, a classic account of the exposition, includes a photograph showing a skin-covered tipi captioned "Quarters of the Navajos."[16] This is puzzling since there is little evidence to indicate that the Diné have ever lived in skin-covered dwellings. To add to the confusion, in another section of the text, Bancroft describes the building in the anthropology village as "a log hut covered with sod."[17] But contemporary newspaper accounts help to resolve this discrepancy. The June 27 issue of the *Inter Ocean*, a Chicago newspaper, related that a newly arrived group of five Diné were housed in "buffalo-hide tepees," while on the following day, the *Chicago Tribune* described their dwelling as "a small conical tent made of painted skins."[18] If the construction materials for the hogan were shipped by freight, as requested by Putnam, they may not have reached Chicago until after the Diné performers set up residence in the village. By July 9, the *Inter Ocean* reported that the Diné group was living in "a hut built of logs and shaped like a farmyard ash hopper turned upside down."[19] An ash hopper of the period was a conical structure made of large timbers, and the account almost certainly refers to a forked-pole hogan.

A series of models illustrating the construction of a forked-pole hogan were on display in the Smithsonian exhibit at the US Government Building, and they offer further evidence that the Diné dwelling in the anthropology village was indeed a forked-pole hogan (Figure 1.3).

And there may ultimately have been more than one Diné building at the anthropology village. A newspaper article in early July described the presence of a "Navajo hogan and summer house," the summer house probably being a summer hogan.[20]

Performers at the anthropology village demonstrated a number of traditional arts and crafts, and the Diné were among those who offered items for sale on site. Putnam's instructions to Antonio Apache specified how this would be arranged:

> You state that the [federal Indian] Agents would send things to Chicago for sale. I think that everything they could send would be sold, but they must entrust the material to some one individual to sell it under my direction. One of the Navajos coming would be the best person to be entrusted with that work. They could furnish him with a list of all the material which they send, stating the lowest price at which each article is to be sold; then we can add to the price after we see what other things are on the grounds for sale. The Navajo so entrusted with the things would sell them from his own house.[21]

But the anthropology village was intended to be more than just a backdrop for the display of arts and crafts; the intent was to present a comprehensive picture of Native American life. Indigenous people lived at the village, preparing meals, maintaining their homes, and performing music and dances for the visitors to the fair.[22]

Life at the anthropology village was challenging at times. The Diné group was homesick and subject to circumstances far beyond the ordinary. They were

24   Anthropology Villages and the Diné Hogan, 1890–1950

NAVAJO LODGE

Figure 1.3 Exhibit illustrating the construction of a conical forked-pole hogan in the US Government Building, 1893 World's Columbian Exposition in Chicago.

prohibited from using a stove to keep their hogan warm "because it did not represent the native mode of life," and they were forced to tolerate curious fairgoers, who did not always respect their privacy.[23] According to a local newspaper, at least one incident necessitated the intervention of Antonio Apache:

> Well-informed and scrupulously polite, he did the other day have his courteous nature so overtaxed that he administered, though urbanely, a stinging rebuke to a woman who persisted in tearing away the curtain or "portieres" to the doorway of the hogan, while the Indians were at dinner, and peering in at them "to see," as she expressed it, "how Indians eat." Identifying her by the glasses she wore, Antonio turned and calmly remarked: "Madam, if I were to come to your residence on Beacon street, pull apart the shutters of a window, and stare in at you, you'd scream or exclaim, 'What a rude savage!'"[24]

As a symbol of Indigenous America, the anthropology village related to the cultural landscape around it on many levels. Paired with the Convent of Santa Maria de la Rábida, it represented America on the brink of conquest. Juxtaposed with the elevated railroad and the log cabin architecture of Euro-American pioneers nearby, it symbolized the settlement of the American frontier. For fair planners, the most explicit

Anthropology Villages and the Diné Hogan, 1890–1950 25

contrast was intended to be with the Model Indian School, but the plan envisioned by Thomas J. Morgan, commissioner of Indian Affairs, went awry, for the school was one of the least popular attractions at the exposition.[25] The effort to promote the assimilation of Indigenous peoples into mainstream American society had to compete with the popularity of Buffalo Bill's Wild West, which for the duration of the fair occupied a 13-acre encampment just outside the fair's main gate. The interest in Native American culture coincided with "The Closing of the American Frontier," a phenomenon famously articulated at the exposition by historian Frederick Jackson Turner.[26]

Ultimately, the anthropology village, not the Model Indian School, emerged as a persuasive argument for Native American assimilation. On October 13, 1893, 14 Diné, accompanied by federal Indian Agent Edwin H. Plummer, left Gallup, New Mexico, for the fair. The trip was funded by the Santa Fe Railway and the Indian Rights Association, a private organization actively promoting assimilation.[27] In Chicago, the Diné stayed at the anthropology village while they toured the city.[28] By all accounts, the experience had a powerful effect. Plummer later recounted that Peshoki and Hosteen Deete Sahghy were astonished at what they witnessed. Hosteen Bagota recalled, "The headmen were ashamed of their hogans after seeing the houses the white men lived in."[29] Two of the three chiefs who journeyed to Chicago became resolutely in favor of schooling Native American children.[30] During the 1880s, members of the tribe were devastated when several Diné students died while attending off-reservation boarding institutions.[31] But the visit to Chicago in 1893 led to what Commissioner Morgan described as an "awakening of the Navajos" and a change of attitude towards Euro-American schools ensued.[32]

The 1902 and 1911 Alvarado Indian Villages

During the 1880s, the Santa Fe Railway began marketing its newly established passenger service through the Southwest by publicizing the region's Native American culture. In 1884, the Atlantic and Pacific Railroad, a partner of the Santa Fe, cosponsored the exhibit sent by Arizona Territory to the World's Industrial and Cotton Centennial Exposition in New Orleans. The exhibit contained examples of Diné textiles and extolled the railway's easy accessibility to pre-Columbian ruins and the Pueblos at Zuni and Hopi.[33] During the 1890s, the Santa Fe published promotional literature describing the Southwest as a place characterized by exotic peoples and unparalleled natural beauty. Santa Fe Railway employee C.A. Higgins began producing a series of informative booklets about the route through the Southwest and placed magazine advertisements for the railroad that focused on Native American culture. Finally, in 1899, as historian Michael Zega has noted, "Higgins's Indian campaign grew into a full-blown marketing strategy," with the railway's advertising efforts including calendars featuring Native American imagery and traveling lecturers accompanied by lantern slides.[34]

The business relationship between the Fred Harvey Company and the Santa Fe Railway began in 1876 when Fred Harvey signed a contract to provide food for passengers at the train station in Topeka, Kansas. In 1901, when Harvey died, the company had grown from a chain of lunch counters to a nationally known

26   *Anthropology Villages and the Diné Hogan, 1890–1950*

enterprise overseeing 47 restaurants, 30 railway dining cars, and 15 hotels.[35] By that point, the railroad's Indian-themed advertising had set the stage for Harvey's family to expand into another arena: selling Native American art to passengers on the Santa Fe.

The Harvey Company established its new Indian Department at the Alvarado Hotel in Albuquerque. The hotel, designed in the Mission Revival style by Santa Fe Railway architect Charles Whittlesey, was completed in 1902. The Indian Department occupied several buildings in and near the hotel that together comprised the first great example of the Harvey Company and Santa Fe Railway's "stationside 'world's fairs.'"[36]

For passengers heading west to Los Angeles, the attractions began several hundred feet before reaching the Alvarado as the train passed by an anthropology village, to be described shortly. Upon stopping at the hotel, travelers would have had the opportunity to visit the Alvarado's Indian Museum (or Collection Building) which occupied a central location on the train platform in front of the hotel's main court. Inside were "many ethnological specimens, classified by tribes, illustrating the life and customs of the western Indians, past and present."[37] The museum helped situate the Indian Department as an authority on Native American art and as a source for the most exclusive objects on the market. Indeed, during the years that followed, the Indian Department would become a supplier of rare and expensive American Indian art to museums, as well as to some of the country's wealthiest collectors.

The Indian and Mexican Building was located to the south of the museum. During those periods when a train was stopped along the platform, Native American vendors gathered in front of the entrance to sell weavings and other handmade objects to travelers. The rooms inside the building, which included many similar items for purchase, were designed by Mary Jane Elizabeth Colter. Colter furnished the main display areas with Arts and Crafts–style tables, settles, and benches, and the décor illustrated how Native American art could contribute to contemporary home design. Shoppers could also visit a workroom in the building, where Native American artisans demonstrated their skills. Weavers, silversmiths, ceramicists, basket makers, and artisans working in leather, cloth, and horsehair all exhibited their artistry in this space "cunningly wrought" to resemble a summer hogan.[38]

Some of the Native Americans who worked in the Indian and Mexican Building lived in full view of passing trains at "a model village" north of the Alvarado Hotel (Figure 1.4).

The village was designed by Herman Schweizer, manager of Harvey's Indian Department, "who spent considerable time and labor in constructing [it] according to his ideas."[39] The architecture of the village took shape over the course of several months. On November 29, 1902, a local newspaper reported, "The building of an adobe [building] on the industrial Indian village site will be begun today. This will make the second dwelling on the site, the first, a winter hogan, was erected some time ago." The winter hogan was a forked-pole hogan and housed two Diné artisans, Alejandro, who made quirts and other items from horsehair, and a rug weaver (presumably his wife).[40]

Anthropology Villages and the Diné Hogan, 1890–1950 27

Figure 1.4 Postcard of the first Alvarado Indian Village, c. 1905, looking west.

Then in February 1903, three Diné constructed "the most unique building that has been erected in Albuquerque." The *Albuquerque Citizen* related the following:

> The hogan is shaped like a bee hive [sic], the top being a cone shape with a hole in the top. A fire is built in the center of the hogan and the Indians sleep with their feet to the fire. It is built entirely of mountain cedar, the posts being stood upright and the cracks filled in with adobe.[41]

This building, the second winter hogan on the site, was a many-legged hogan (located to the right in Figure 1.4). The forked-pole hogan stood for several years but not for long. By 1908, the architecture of the Indian Village comprised the many-legged hogan, along with the adobe building constructed in 1902 and a flat-roofed wooden building walled with vertical planks.[42]

Some of the most famous Diné of the period resided at the Alvarado Indian Village between 1902 and its demolition, c. 1911. Many of them came from Ganado (*Lók'aah Niteel*), Arizona, through an arrangement with Lorenzo Hubbell, who operated a trading post there and oversaw the largest trading network in Navajoland. Diné from Ganado who worked for Fred Harvey included Miguelito, a medicine man who in later life appeared in three classic ethnographies by anthropologist Gladys Reichard.[43] Asdzaa Łichíí, more commonly known as Elle of Ganado, and her husband, Tom, also lived there. Publicized as "the best blanket weaver among the Navajos," Elle became famous for creating a blanket for President Theodore Roosevelt and presenting it to him personally when he stopped at the Alvarado in

May 1903. Oft-photographed with celebrities and frequently pictured in advertising literature, Elle was "the most recognizable icon for the Harvey/Santa Fe portrayal of the Indian Southwest."[44]

The Diné architecture at the Indian Village appeared in a variety of publications. A booklet by anthropologist George Pepper documented a healing ritual led by Miguelito for Tom of Ganado that took place in an Indian Village hogan in 1904.[45] Several postcards produced by Fred Harvey pictured Elle sitting in front of the many-legged hogan with two children. The most popular of these later inspired images on trading cards produced by the Fleer Bubblegum Company and Belgium's De Beukelaer cookie company. By 1908, newspapers and magazines in the US and Great Britain were using pictures of the many-legged hogan to illustrate the history of architecture. Photographs in the *Los Angeles Herald, The Pacific Monthly*, and the London-based serial *The Reliquary and Illustrated Archaeologist* juxtaposed the many-legged hogan at the village with Albuquerque's cityscape in the background, captioned with the title, "The Old and the New."[46]

In 1911, the construction of a new warehouse for a large mercantile business compelled the demolition of the 1902 village, and a set of new buildings were constructed on a site immediately to the south (Figure 1.5).

The village, again designed by Schweizer, included two hogans.[47] A local newspaper reported Schweizer's "double purpose" of "exciting the curiosity of the sightseeing tourist" and housing the Native American demonstrators who worked in the Alvarado Indian Building.[48] Like the 1902 village, the 1911 village was located

Figure 1.5 Postcard of the second Alvarado Indian Village, looking northwest, with, from left, a conical forked-pole hogan, a stacked-log hogan, and a Pueblo-style building.

Anthropology Villages and the Diné Hogan, 1890–1950 29

less than a hundred feet from the railroad tracks. An L-shaped adobe building of two stories dominated the new location; the *Albuquerque Journal* described it as follows:

> an exact replica of the quaint homes to be found in the ancient pueblos of Isleta and Santa Domingo, Laguna, and Acoma, and all the other famous cities of this remarkable people to be easily reached from Albuquerque.[49]

To the west of the adobe building stood a large octagonal stacked-log hogan and a tall forked-pole hogan.[50]

In the publicity surrounding the new village, much was made of the "primitive" aspects of its architecture. The construction methods were wholly traditional, and the everyday life of the Native Americans who lived there was intended to reflect an earlier era. As a local newspaper observed about the adobe building:

> No modern frills of existence such as beds or other furniture have been allowed in the house, with its smooth walls and floors and other artistic fireplaces [sic]. In primitive fashion they unroll their blankets and sleep on the floor as did their forefathers.[51]

The Fred Harvey Company encouraged tourists to stop by and "see a real Indian house and the Indians living therein in real Indian fashion."[52] A contemporary image taken in front of the forked-pole hogan suggests that the village was also open for sightseers to "play Indian" with the performers who worked at the Alvarado (Figure 1.6).[53]

The 1904 Louisiana Purchase International Exposition in St. Louis

The world's fair in St. Louis in 1904 was the largest American exposition to date and drew nearly 20 million visitors.[54] Like the 1893 fair in Chicago, the US government sponsored a Native American village as part of an array of exhibits under the auspices of the fair's Department of Anthropology. WJ McGee, the chair of the department, conceived a large outdoor group of dwellings he called "The Anthropology Villages and Indian Village" and located them on a hill within the fairgrounds. McGee explicitly designed the villages to "represent human progress from the dark prime to the highest enlightenment, from savagery to civic organization, from egoism to altruism."[55]

It is likely that many visitors would have inferred an "upward course of human development" from the contrast between the villages and the "Ivory City" of cream-colored Beaux-Arts buildings at the center of the fair.[56] But McGee also arranged the buildings within the exhibit in a sequence to elucidate his conception of cultural progress. The path ascending Indian Hill passed by dwellings associated with a variety of different ethnic groups and terminated at the top of the hill, where the fair's Model Indian School, a three-story, eclectically styled building with Italianate, Classical, and Mission Revival accents, was located.[57]

30   *Anthropology Villages and the Diné Hogan, 1890–1950*

Figure 1.6 Two Native American performers and a tourist in front of the conical forked-pole hogan at the second Alvarado Indian Village, c. 1915.

By designing the Model Indian School as the largest structure in the anthropology village and placing it atop Indian Hill, McGee and his colleagues created a powerful evocation of Manifest Destiny. The building's interior was divided by a passageway with arts and crafts demonstrators arrayed along one side and boarding school students from around the country displaying their newly learned skills along the other. Visitors were intended to view the demonstrators as emblematic of an archaic past and the students as symbols of a future in which Indians would become fully assimilated and self-supporting members of American society.

Anthropology Villages and the Diné Hogan, 1890–1950 31

The Indian Village followed a D-shaped plan with the Indigenous architecture arranged in a semi-circle facing the Model Indian School and a "frontier sutlery" (or trading post). According to ethnohistorians Nancy Parezo and Don Fowler, the "Indian groups were interspersed, reflecting the supposed evolution of housing styles."[58]

Around 200 Native Americans had gathered to perform at the Indian Village as of June 1, and by the fair's end on December 1, more than 400 had officially registered.[59] Samuel M. McCowan, who supervised the Indian Exhibit under McGee's direction, recorded that the tribes included Osage (Wajaji); Chippewa; Dakota; Jicarilla Apache; Santa Clara Pueblo; Pomo; Acoma Pueblo; Wichita; Pawnee; Cheyenne; Arapaho; Maricopa; Pima; and Kickapoo, as well as Diné.[60]

McCowan's official report describes three hogans in the Indian Village, although it does not specify their style. A writer for *Scientific American* had this to say about the Diné buildings:

> Next to the Maricopa dwellings one sees two small, conical, earth-covered houses of the kind that were built by the Navahos. These consist of a framework of willow poles covered with grass sod. Compared with some of the other native homes, they are small and uncomfortable.[61]

A contemporary photograph shows a group of Diné constructing one of these buildings, a forked-pole hogan (Figure 1.7).

As the photograph indicates, the fair's intramural railway passed nearby the village so that the exhibit was on view for visitors on foot and traveling by train. In his official report, McGee noted that the hogans were ritually blessed:

> [the Diné] were housed in habitations of native type known as hogans, i.e., earth-lodges, in which the soil is heaped over a framework of timbers and a sheathing of shrubbery, the entire process of building being conducted in accordance with an elaborate ritual.[62]

At least 23 Diné from Fort Defiance, Arizona, worked at the Indian Village in St. Louis. Parezo and Fowler have found records for five families (the Begays, the Good Lucks, the Joses, the Peshlakais, and the Taos family) as well as two individuals (Frank Smith and Hotine Tsosie).[63] Mrs. Taos taught visitors how to make frybread and tortillas near the hogans, while Diné weavers and metalsmiths performed within the Model Indian School.[64] Contemporary observers recorded that the Indian Village site was plagued by "ankle-deep mud" for several months and that the sanitary conditions were appalling.[65] Disease was rampant, and nerves wore thin when fairgoers peeped through doors and openings to view the occupants who lived in the dwellings. Countering these negative experiences, many Native Americans at the fair traveled around St. Louis, met new people, and in several instances, made substantial amounts of money. Even though McGee's plan for the exhibit was overtly racist and the living conditions were abysmal, many Native Americans chose to stay, and as historian John Troutman has argued, for them,

Figure 1.7 Diné building a conical forked-pole hogan, 1904 Louisiana Purchase Exposition in St. Louis. The intramural railway line is visible in the background.

the Indian Village ended up being "a multiplex juxtaposition of distress, disease, adventure, and economic success."[66]

The 1905 Indian Village at the Grand Canyon

In 1905, the Santa Fe Railway in association with the Fred Harvey Company opened a large resort on the South Rim of the Grand Canyon. The resort's centerpiece was and remains El Tovar, a 100-room hotel inspired by Swiss chalet and Norwegian villa architecture and designed by Charles Whittlesey, the architect of the Alvarado.[67] Hopi House, located to the east along the canyon's rim, is a multistory reproduction of a Native American Pueblo, primarily designed by Mary Colter.[68] It formerly served as a residence for Native American artisans who worked at the Grand Canyon and still contains salesrooms with Native American arts and crafts on display. Although now demolished, several hogans were once located to the south of Hopi House, where they housed Diné performers and provided an additional setting for weavers and silversmiths to demonstrate their skills. The arrangement of the buildings repeated the theme established by the Santa Fe and Fred Harvey at the Alvarado in Albuquerque, with a large hotel located near salesrooms featuring Native American demonstrators and an anthropology village situated nearby. While Hopi House has been well documented, the hogans at the Grand Canyon have received scant attention. The artisans who lived in Hopi House moved out in 1936, and it seems likely that the hogans were abandoned around the same time.[69]

In its earliest iteration, the Diné encampment at the Grand Canyon consisted of two buildings, each a stacked-log hogan with partially corbelled walls (Figure 1.8).

Herman Schweizer, who directed the construction of the anthropology villages at the Alvarado, also played a central role in setting up the village at the Grand Canyon. A letter he wrote to trader Lorenzo Hubbell dating from 1904 expressed his desire that the hogans appear primitive and lacking in modern conveniences. Schweizer requested the buildings be furnished without stoves and directed the Diné to cook their meals with handcrafted ceramic pots. Silversmiths were to use "a regular Navaho forge, perhaps a piece of steel rail or whatever there may be that is homemade and a homemade bellows."[70] In 1905, Elle and Tom of Ganado lived in one of the hogans, while Elle worked on her loom inside Hopi House.[71] The area around the hogans was used as an outdoor workshop for Diné metalworkers, at least when weather permitted.[72]

Figure 1.8 Postcard of Navajo hogans, 1905, looking east, Grand Canyon National Park.

34 *Anthropology Villages and the Diné Hogan, 1890–1950*

By 1922, the anthropology village had several new buildings, each of them an example of a stacked-log hogan (Figure 1.9). Photographs from the 1920s and 1930s indicate that in later years, the hogans dating from 1905 fell into ruin, while the newer hogans housed Diné performers.

Author and etiquette doyenne Emily Post toured the hogans at the Grand Canyon in 1915 while traveling cross-country to the West Coast. Her account of the visit attests that the Harvey Company was actively promoting the village as an opportunity to see the Diné and learn about their culture. According to Post:

> The Navajo huts – *hogans* they are called – are made of logs and twigs plastered with mud, not all over like an icing, but merely in between the logs as a mortar. They have no openings except a low door that you have to stoop to enter, and a smoke hole in the center of the domelike roof. Inside, if the ones at Grand Canyon are typical, as they are supposed to be, they are merely one room with a fire burning in the center and blankets spread around the edge of the floor close under the slanting walls. Personally I feel rather embarrassed on being told to look in upon a group of swarthy figures who contemplate the intrusion of their privacy in solemn silence.[73]

Did the Fred Harvey Company encourage the Diné to build stacked-log hogans at the Grand Canyon, or did Herman Schweizer give the performers free rein to

Figure 1.9 Grand Canyon Village, with Navajo hogans in the foreground and El Tovar Hotel and Hopi House in the background, looking west, photographed by Emery Kolb, c. 1930–1940.

Anthropology Villages and the Diné Hogan, 1890–1950 35

construct whatever they wanted? We cannot be sure, but the sightseers who visited the hogans at this most popular of tourist destinations would have received the impression that the stacked-log hogan was the "typical" Navajo dwelling. What is more, newspaper and magazine articles used photographs of the anthropology village at the Grand Canyon to represent the Diné hogan, similar to the way pictures of the many-legged hogan at the Alvarado appeared in many diverse contexts.[74]

The 1906 Indian Crafts Exhibition at Eastlake Park in Los Angeles

During the years following the World's Columbian Exposition in Chicago, Antonio Apache led a colorful life, and newspapers across the nation covered his activities in detail. In 1897, he helped to organize a Native American anthropology village at the New England Sportsman Show.[75] In 1899, Antonio made preparations to take a group of Apache to the 1900 Exposition Universelle in Paris.[76] It is unclear whether these plans materialized, but we do know that in 1900, he was in Buffalo, New York, attempting to organize a concession at the 1901 Pan-American Exposition "to exhibit Indians as seen in their native villages."[77]

In September 1905, Antonio met with Henry E. Huntington of the Pacific Electric Railway and persuaded him to extend a loan for $50,000 and provide a 15-acre site to build a permanent "Indian Crafts Exhibition."[78] Antonio envisioned "a model Indian village," where Native Americans could "ply their respective peculiar vocations" and "learn such lessons of industry as will be communicated to their offspring and tend to elevate the succeeding generations."[79] The site near Eastlake Park would be easily accessible to visitors who could travel from central Los Angeles by the Pacific Electric Railway in a matter of 20 minutes.[80] The Exhibition was incorporated in April 1906 and then opened the following December with 38 Native American men and women living on site.[81]

Seeking to fill his "ethnological exposition" with authentic architecture, Antonio traveled to Alaska, where he secured a Haida totem pole, as well as an authentic Haida plank house.[82] There were also Pueblo-style buildings, tipis, and Navajo hogans.[83]

Antonio distributed advertising cards that illustrated the Diné who performed at the Exhibition. One depicts "Navajo Camps" with two female hogans forming the backdrop for a silversmith and a weaver sitting at an enormous loom (Figure 1.10). The hogans are covered with earth, and it is difficult to determine whether they are corbelled-log, stacked-log, or many-legged forms.

There is a striking resemblance between this card and the scene in the photograph in Figure 1.8, which was widely distributed as a postcard. Both images depict two female hogans of the same size, similarly arranged and viewed from the same perspective. But as it happens, the Diné encampment at Antonio's village looked nothing like the anthropology village at the Grand Canyon (Figure 1.11).

The Diné in Los Angeles lived in two large many-legged hogans. One had a flat roof and was covered with tarps at the time it was photographed for Figure 1.11, while the other had a corbelled dome. It seems likely that the advertising card in Figure 1.10 was seeking to draw on the fame and reputation of the Santa Fe Railway's anthropology village to attract tourists to visit and shop at the Indian Crafts

36   *Anthropology Villages and the Diné Hogan, 1890–1950*

Figure 1.10 Advertising card for the Indian Crafts Exposition, Los Angeles, c. 1907.

Figure 1.11 Navajo hogans at the Indian Crafts Exhibition, photographed by Warren C. Dickerson in 1907.

Exhibition.[84] By December 1911, the Indian Crafts Exhibition had closed to be replaced by a movie studio and a zoo, owned by the movie producer William N. Selig.[85]

The 1909 United States Land and Irrigation Exposition in Chicago

The 1909 US Land and Irrigation Exposition took place at the Chicago Coliseum from November 20 to December 4. Popularly known as "The Land Show," it was billed as "the greatest Exposition that has been held in Chicago since the World's Fair."[86] One of the purposes for the event was to encourage Euro-Americans to settle in the southern and western regions of the US. Exhibits presented information about farming and publicized the opportunities that irrigation and reclamation projects were making possible.[37] Eleven Diné traveled to Chicago to take part in the Santa Fe Railway exhibit, including Elle and Tom of Ganado, Mr. and Mrs. Nee-yo Bigay, and Mr. and Mrs. Nas-tin Washi, along with five children.[88]

The *Chicago Tribune* reported that the group would be demonstrating weaving and silversmithing, but the paper devoted even more space to the construction of a full-size hogan inside the Coliseum (Figure 1.12).[89]

Figure 1.12 The Navajo exhibit at the 1909 Chicago Land Show, with Elle of Ganado weaving at left and her husband, Tom, standing in front of the exhibit's hogan.

38 *Anthropology Villages and the Diné Hogan, 1890–1950*

According to the *Tribune*, "The process of creating a ho-gan [sic] like the one which now stands complete, consists of making a dome of logs and twigs and then slapping nice soft mud over the interstices." The article featured a series of caricatures with a portrait of Elle and a picture of "Bigay at Work on the Indian Hut," a many-legged hogan, possibly with a corbelled dome.[90] Navajo rugs covered the floor of the display, which also featured "both ancient and modern pottery made by the different tribes of New Mexico, articles used in the ceremonial dances and other things that will be of great interest."[91]

The 1909 Land Show marked the first time the Santa Fe Railway sponsored an anthropology village at a major exposition. The Diné group, along with the Native American art and architecture on display, portrayed the Southwest as a fascinating destination for both tourists and settlers alike. The *Tribune* even used the hogan to promote the attraction of going "back to the land" and reported that the Diné enjoyed seeing Chicago, "even though they have decided that life in a hut of twigs is preferable to existence in a crowded city."[92]

The 1915–1916 Panama-California Exposition in San Diego

The official opening of the Panama Canal on August 15, 1914, inspired two American world's fairs the following year – the Panama-California Exposition in San Diego and the Panama-Pacific Exposition in San Francisco. In January 1912, the US Senate held hearings to establish the scope of each of the events. Colonel David Charles Collier, the director-general of the San Diego exposition, suggested that the two fairs could complement each other, explaining:

> Our idea is to show the progress of civilization from the time of the prehistoric Mayas, Zapotecs, Aztecs, and Incas down to the present time. We want to give an idea of prehistoric conditions and precivilized conditions in the United States and then let them go to San Francisco and contrast what was with what is.[93]

The anthropology exhibits at the Chicago and St. Louis fairs had played upon an evolutionary theme, but Collier promised (a bit disingenuously perhaps) that the San Diego exhibit would be the first to adopt "a scientific standpoint" under the supervision of "trained scientists of national and international reputation."[94]

In August 1913, Collier traveled to Chicago to meet with Edward Payson Ripley, president of the Santa Fe Railway, about financing a living exhibit at the fair.[95] According to the *San Diego Union*, Ripley pledged over a quarter of a million dollars to build an anthropology village where hundreds of Native Americans would live and demonstrate "the art baskets, the pottery, the blankets, the beaten silver ware that has won fame for the makers all over the world."[96]

Ripley turned to the Fred Harvey Company to develop the exhibit, which soon became known as "The Painted Desert." The design was a collaborative effort

Anthropology Villages and the Diné Hogan, 1890–1950 39

involving Harvey's Indian Department, with Herman Schweizer, Mary Colter, and the department's head, J.F. Huckel, making important contributions, assisted by Kenneth Chapman, an art historian and archaeologist based in Santa Fe.[97] The model of the village made by Colter divided the 6 1/2–acre site into two contrasting areas to the east and west, each with distinctive cultural and geographical features (Figure 1.13).

The village was bisected by a large structure that combined artificial "rocky outcrops" with full-scale replicas of architecture from the Western Pueblos at Acoma, Zuni, and Hopi. The "Pueblos" faced eastward onto a plaza containing two kivas. The plaza was bounded to the south by a replica of the North House at Taos Pueblo, to the north by a trading post with items for sale, and to the east by the entrance to the village. The rear (west) side of the structure containing the Western Pueblo replicas featured a simulated rock wall with alcoves displaying "Anasazi ruins." It overlooked a wild desert landscape with Diné hogans and Apache wikiups. The anthropology village was planned for a location on the north side of the exposition at the end of the fair's midway, known as "The Isthmus."

When it became clear that Schweizer could not be spared to manage "The Painted Desert," Edgar Hewett, the fair's director of exhibits, recommended Jesse Nusbaum to supervise construction of the village. Nusbaum combined an impressive background in pre-Columbian archaeology with a wide range of practical building experience. While a college student, he had worked as a photographer for Hewett at the Mesa Verde archaeological site in southwestern Colorado, later to become a national park. After graduation, he was hired to oversee the reconstruction and remodeling of New Mexico's first capitol, the Palace of the Governors in Santa Fe. During 1910 and 1911, he participated in archaeological expeditions to Central America, where he photographed Quiriguá, Copán, and other archaeological sites. Back in the States, he worked on the restoration of Balcony House ruin at Mesa Verde in collaboration with his father, an experienced contractor. In 1921, Nusbaum became the first archaeologist hired by the National Park Service, and in 1929, he would be appointed the first director of the Laboratory of Anthropology in Santa Fe. As we shall see later in this chapter, Nusbaum became directly involved with building anthropology villages at Mesa Verde National Park and planning the anthropology village at the 1933–1934 Century of Progress Exposition in Chicago.

According to Schweizer, the goal of "The Painted Desert" was "to reproduce a true representation of Indian life and to depict their mode of living at home."[98] On September 8, 1914, Schweizer wrote to Lorenzo Hubbell in Ganado, requesting, "three men to go to San Diego to build about four hogans." The material for the hogans was to be shipped by rail and ready for the men when they arrived.[99] In early October, six Diné arrived in San Diego from Gallup, New Mexico. The group included Nuntah Beah and Miguelito, who took time off from work at the Alvarado to come with one of his wives and two of his daughters.[100]

Nuntah Beah and Miguelito built two winter hogans for the exhibit (see Figure 1.14). One was a many-legged hogan resembling the hogan at the 1902 Alvarado Indian village. The other hogan was a palisaded hogan with a corbelled dome.

40 *Anthropology Villages and the Diné Hogan, 1890–1950*

Figure 1.13 Model of "The Painted Desert" for the 1915–1916 Panama-California Exposition in San Diego (north is up). The exhibit's hogans are located at bottom left.

Figure 1.14 Nuntah Beah and Miguelito building a *náneeskáál hooghan* (palisaded hogan) for "The Painted Desert" (looking east). The exhibit's many-legged hogan is at left, and a summer hogan covered with boughs is at right.

Miguelito and Nuntah Beah also built a summer hogan. The guidebook for the exhibit noted that a Diné medicine man would be using one of the hogans as "the Medicine Lodge," where he would create sand paintings.[101]

The Panama-California Exposition opened on January 1, 1915, and closed two years later, on December 31, 1916.[102] "The Painted Desert" would become the largest and most elaborate anthropology village originating from the American Southwest ever to be staged. As we shall see, the railroad and Fred Harvey would maintain a relationship with Santa Fe's professional archaeology community for many years, but world events and financial problems would prevent them from collaborating on another anthropology village until the 1948 Chicago Railroad Fair.

The 1915 Panama-Pacific Exposition in San Francisco

The Panama-Pacific Exposition in San Francisco attracted enormous crowds and, by its close, had drawn nearly 19 million visitors. Only the previous world's fairs in Chicago in 1893 and St. Louis in 1904 recorded larger attendance figures.[103] As in San Diego, the Santa Fe Railway's anthropology village was located along the exposition's midway, called "The Zone." William F. Sesser, a photographer and

42   *Anthropology Villages and the Diné Hogan, 1890–1950*

artist, led the design team for the railroad's exhibit, known as "The Grand Canyon of Arizona Replica" (Figure 1.15).

Sesser had previously created exhibits for major expositions and worked for the Santa Fe Railway, taking publicity photographs in the Southwest.[104] At the world's fair in Chicago in 1893, he collaborated with artist Walter W. Burridge on a cyclorama – "The Volcano of Kilauea" – an enormous 54′ by 412′ painting hung cylindrically to create a space visitors could enter for a three-dimensional, immersive experience.[105] The Santa Fe's concession in San Francisco also included large-scale paintings, but they illustrated a series of views from the South Rim of Grand Canyon. The paintings, totaling 450,000 square feet of canvas, along with flora and stuffed fauna from the Southwest, depicted seven scenes that passengers observed from an electric train.[106] Although the Santa Fe Railway supervised "The Grand Canyon of Arizona Replica," it turned the exhibit's anthropology village over to Fred Harvey's Indian Department to manage.[107]

The electric train and the tableaux recreating the Grand Canyon were located behind the entrance building which, like the Alvarado, was designed in the Mission Revival style. On the left, or west side of the building, a kiosk sold tickets to visitors who could then climb a stairway to the anthropology village located on top of the roof (Figure 1.16).

Native Americans from Zuni, Hopi, and Acoma Pueblos, as well as Supai and Diné performed in the village. A magazine article published by the railroad in July 1914 estimated that 20 families would be employed at the exhibit. As performers, they would be "making baskets, blankets, pottery, beadwork and baking bread from cornmeal ground by the hand process in use for hundreds of years by these Indians."[108]

The route through the anthropology village wound along the top of the building by replicas of Native American Pueblos and a small Spanish mission church. After passing these buildings, visitors approached "a grotto," where Diné weavers and metalsmiths worked, and then encountered two examples of a stacked-log hogan anchoring the east side of the exhibit (Figure 1.17).

The exhibit's pamphlet described the anthropology village and noted:

> The greatest care and pains have been taken to adhere rigidly to the absolute truth in the building of this village. For example, the Navajo Hogans were built from old logs, dwarf pine trunks, and old cedar trunks from the reservation.[109]

A close look at the hogans in San Francisco reveals they bear a marked resemblance to the hogans built at the Grand Canyon in 1905. Not only was the architecture virtually identical but the two buildings were also arranged in a similar way (see Figure 1.8). The Santa Fe Railway's "Grand Canyon of Arizona Replica" at the Panama-Pacific Exposition not only reinforced the "authenticity" of the Diné encampment at the real Grand Canyon but it also offered the first appearance of a stacked-log hogan at a world's fair, one that would serve as a harbinger of things to come.

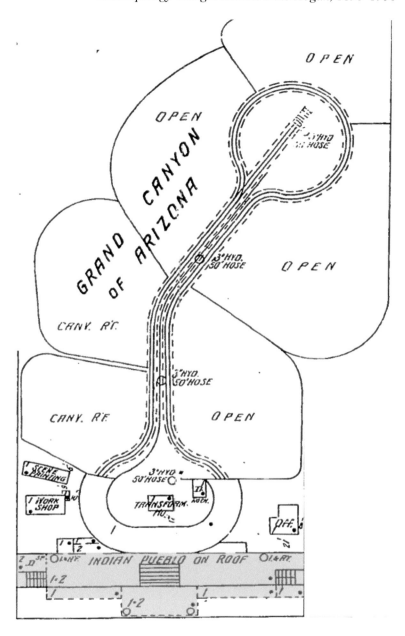

Figure 1.15 Sanborn Fire Insurance Map of "The Grand Canyon of Arizona Replica," 1915 Panama-Pacific Exposition in San Francisco (north is up and the entrance building is shaded). The Indian Village occupied the roof of the entrance building on the south side of the exhibit along The Zone. The railway embarked from within the entrance building and then looped past the seven tableaux, recreating sights along the South Rim of Grand Canyon.

Figure 1.16 The entrance building to "The Grand Canyon of Arizona Replica" and the Indian Village, looking northwest, 1915 Panama-Pacific Exposition in San Francisco.

Figure 1.17 The Navajo hogans at "The Grand Canyon of Arizona Replica," looking northeast, 1915 Panama-Pacific Exposition in San Francisco.

Mesa Verde National Park, 1925–1942

In 1921, the National Park Service appointed Jesse Nusbaum to be the first superintendent of Mesa Verde National Park, a job which would draw upon his broad background in archaeology, construction management, and Native American culture. Soon after taking up this position, Nusbaum, along with his wife, Aileen, began work on a set of Pueblo-Spanish Revival designs for the new National Park Service buildings at Mesa Verde.[110] Nusbaum hired Diné work crews to build roads and to expand the park's infrastructure, and the men inspired him to organize a separate construction project: a small village featuring Diné hogans. Thus, the park's earliest architecture, comprising several Pueblo-inspired buildings and a group of Navajo dwellings, became an analog for the exhibit Nusbaum had helped to build in San Diego.

Nusbaum's monthly reports first mention the Diné crews in September 1922.[111] Later, in 1923, he hired Sam Ahkeah as an interpreter and foreman for the Navajo employees at the park.[112] Ahkeah would continue working at Mesa Verde each summer season until 1941, when he began a brilliant political career that led to his appointment in 1946 as chairman of the Navajo Nation Tribal Council, a position he held until 1954.[113]

In 1925, Nusbaum began working to create an anthropology village for the Diné work crews. In April, he wrote National Park Service (NPS) landscape architect Daniel R. Hull about the village and explained:

> $750 was allotted for the construction of four "Hogans" (regulation Indian homes of the Navaho type) where the unmarried men and those without family will be kept. I did not submit a plan of this for the reason that I could not ascertain from the Indians just what four types they would erect. They have erected four different types of Hogans, each one of which represents a particular and widely used type on the reservation and they make a most interesting display. We have not figured costs as yet but the total will approximate $275 to $300 for the four. They are in a group on the rim of Spruce Canyon about one-quarter mile from camp, segregated yet within convenient distance of visitors who may wish to see the Indians' homes and how they live. These four units will house all but the Indian foreman.[114]

The four dwellings included a forked-pole hogan and a many-legged hogan (Figure 1.18). There was also a stacked-log hogan.[115]

NPS Director Horace Albright's 1929 book, *"Oh, Ranger!": A Book about the National Parks*, included a description of the anthropology village at Mesa Verde:

> [Nusbaum] employs Navahoes in the work of maintaining the park roads and trails. These Navajo men have their wives and children with them and park visitors are privileged to see a real Navaho village in the park. There are always Navaho women weaving blankets, others doing camp work, and usually there is a baby or two to lend more interest to the scene.[116]

46 *Anthropology Villages and the Diné Hogan, 1890–1950*

Figure 1.18 The first Navajo Indian Village at Mesa Verde National Park, photographed by George L. Beam, c. 1925. Jesse Nusbaum and an unidentified man stand in front of a many-legged hogan and by a conical forked-pole hogan.

After remarking on the magnificent ruins at the center of Mesa Verde, Albright continued:

> Mesa Verde Park is also one of the best places to go to see modern Indians, but how much more interesting is a place like this park where one can see the civilization and culture of tribes that have disappeared, as well as that of those who are still in the flesh![117]

In 1935, the NPS Branch of Plans and Design began preparations for another Navajo village at Mesa Verde to be constructed by the Civilian Conservation Corps (CCC), a federal relief program initiated as part of the New Deal (Figure 1.19a).

Located around a loop were 12 hogans, a comfort station, and a "Yeibitchai Area" for dances. The preliminary sketch of the village shows plans and elevations for two octagonal "family" hogans measuring 9 1/2′ on each side and containing 735 square feet (Figure 1.19b–c). The design can best be described as a masonry version of a many-legged hogan (which is traditionally constructed in wood). Each building was provided with an east-facing entrance, skylight, and an attached rustic shade structure, while the interior included a living room, kitchen, bedroom, and bathroom. Although primarily derived from Diné architecture, the NPS architects also included several elements drawn from Native American Pueblo buildings. The ceiling of each "family" hogan was to be constructed of 4″-diameter *savinos* (peeled logs), and the flat roof – hidden behind a parapet – was to be drained by *canales* (scuppers), features more typical in Pueblos.[118] By the end of September 1936, two "family" hogans had been completed for Sam Ahkeah's family and for the Lee family, and by the end of September 1937, a combination latrine and toilet building had been added to the village.[119] The latrine's exterior was similar to the exterior of the two family hogans, although the building included a cupola providing illumination and ventilation.

In 1937, Betty Franke, the wife of an NPS employee, published an article about the Diné families at Mesa Verde who still resided at the old Navajo Indian Village:

> They live in the park much as they do on the reservation. The little group of hogans is over on the rim of Spruce Tree Canyon, only a quarter of a mile from our own residential area. In the summer outdoor cooking fires are used and the women set their looms up under the trees. At night the men sing and dance, practicing for the Yeibichais and Squaw Dances that they will attend on the reservation. We have grown to love the sound of the clear, high calls in their songs, and the thump of moccasined feet on the resonant earth. We listen for it and it is as natural as the voices of the coyotes and owls; it is a part of the life of the Mesa Verde.[120]

During the years before the dissolution of the CCC in 1942, NPS architects prepared two more plans for hogans to house workers in the new Navajo Indian Village. Both designs were circular and constructed from stone masonry, with each building accommodating four single men. The first of these designs was 25′ in diameter and roofed with a corbelled dome (Figure 1.19d).[121] Two hogans of this type were completed by the end of September 1937. The second design was 20′ in diameter and covered with a 2 1/2″–thick, reinforced-concrete dome surrounded by a parapet (Figure 1.19e). Two examples were finished during May 1942 to become the last of the seven hogan-style buildings at the village.[122]

Although the 1925 anthropology village at Mesa Verde featured four traditional forms of the Navajo hogan constructed by the Diné who lived in them, the buildings designed by the NPS Branch of Plans and Design pursued a different set of goals. NPS architects, working from afar, began by creating a hogan in 1935 that combined Navajo and Pueblo elements, followed by another design that more closely resembled a traditional stone hogan. This shift may have been a consequence of Jesse Nusbaum's return as superintendent of the park at the beginning of 1936 and reflected his interest in building authentic forms of Navajo architecture. But after Nusbaum's departure in 1939, the NPS produced a third hogan design requiring less labor to build than the other hogans in the new anthropology village. The decision to change the design may well have been the result of budget constraints and the downsizing of the CCC after the beginning of World War II.

48 *Anthropology Villages and the Diné Hogan, 1890–1950*

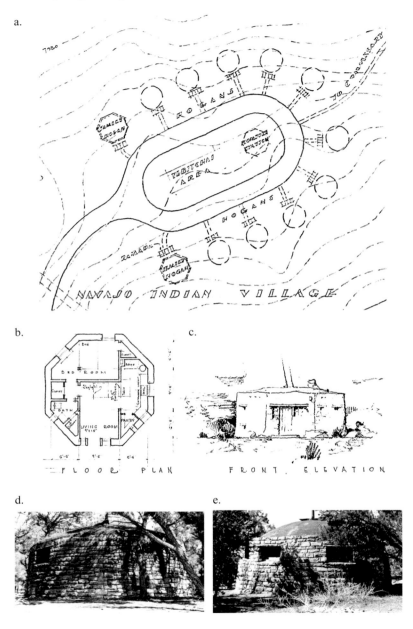

Figure 1.19 The second Navajo Indian Village at Mesa Verde National Park: a. Site plan for the village, dated July 22, 1935; b and c. Front elevation and plan of the two family hogans at the village, dated July 22, 1935; d. The second hogan design for the village (1936–1937) photographed in 1937; e. The third hogan design for the village (1941–1942), photographed in 1951.

Anthropology Villages and the Diné Hogan, 1890–1950 49

The 1933–1934 Century of Progress Exposition in Chicago

The Century of Progress Exposition honored Chicago's centennial anniversary and attracted nearly 50 million visitors during the two seasons it was open.[123] Fay-Cooper Cole, an anthropologist with the University of Chicago, directed the fair's social science division and supervised the anthropological exhibits. Cole was determined that the exhibits should include an anthropology village, and he formulated a plan which included several tribal encampments arranged around a replica of a Mayan temple.[124] Some of the groups were to be sponsored by western railroad companies, including the Great Northern, the Southern Pacific, and the Canadian Pacific. Cole hoped that the Santa Fe Railway would finance and coordinate the performers at the anthropology village representing tribes from the Southwest.[125]

In April 1932, W.H. Simpson, head of advertising for the Santa Fe, contacted Fred Harvey's Indian Department and began a lively correspondence about organizing the anthropology village at the exposition.[126] Herman Schweizer was not enthusiastic. He noted that while the Indian Department had "pioneered in this game" with the exhibit at the 1909 Land Show in Chicago, times had changed. Authors claiming to be experts on Native American art had become commonplace, and "where there used to be a handful of curio dealers there are now hundreds with myriads of filling stations and camp grounds along the highways selling curios, and sometimes using an Indian or two as a ballyhoo." Native Americans were performing for the public more than ever, and Schweizer continued, "I can't get away from the feeling that this thing of Indian shows to put it bluntly, has become 'a little common.'"[127]

Schweizer consented to serve as an advisor for the anthropology village in Chicago, although he refused to manage it, and so Simpson recommended that Cole contact Nusbaum.[128] Nusbaum convened a planning meeting at Cole's behest, and by June 8, 1932, Nusbaum, Simpson, and Schweizer had compiled an itemized budget for the construction of a "minimum of four Navajo hogans, one pueblo structure to house Pueblo Indians [and] one pueblo structure combined [with a] small trading post and manager's quarters."[129] Nusbaum, however, declined to manage the Indian groups in Chicago.[130]

As the Depression unfolded, financial problems began to complicate matters for the Santa Fe Railway and for Cole. Between April 23 and June 1, 1932, the Santa Fe Railway's stock dropped by 50%.[131] By September, Cole was proposing to increase the revenue generated by the anthropology village with pageants and other ticketed performances. He also suggested that the Indian groups defray some of their expenses by bringing items produced offsite to sell at the fair.[132] Schweizer and J.F. Huckel, head of the Indian Department, were alarmed by these developments, and in November 1932, Huckel wrote to Simpson, outlining several reasons why Cole's "commercialized plans" would "tend strongly to detract from the dignity and importance of any Indian exhibit made by the Santa Fe Railroad."[133]

By April 1933, it was becoming clear that the Santa Fe Railway was not going to support the Southwest Indian encampment in the anthropology village.[134] On April 24, a little more than a month before the fair was scheduled to begin, Cole wired Nusbaum requesting help. He had drummed up the financial backing

50 *Anthropology Villages and the Diné Hogan, 1890–1950*

he needed for the village from a group of local businessmen but needed to find a manager along with a group of Native American performers.[135] Nusbaum recommended Wick Miller, an Indian trader from San Ysidro, New Mexico, on the east side of the Navajo reservation.[136]

Miller managed and toured with a company of Diné and Indians from Zia and Jemez Pueblos, who gave demonstrations promoting Native American arts and crafts at department stores across the Eastern US. His trading post in San Ysidro included two stacked-log hogans, where a group of Diné lived and crafted rugs and jewelry.[137] Nusbaum wrote Cole, "Wick's Navajos are good old long hairs," who "have had little contact with our civilization and are splendid representatives."[138] Cole was persuaded and hired Miller to manage the trading post at the fair and coordinate the Diné and Pueblo performers at the exhibit.

When the Century of Progress Exposition opened on May 27, 1933, the anthropology village included the Native American architecture of four separate tribal groups located on a 3 1/2-acre site in the southern part of the fairgrounds.[139] At the north end of the village, the Northwest Coast display, which was uninhabited, included a plank house and totem poles. On the east side of the village, 50 Ho-Chunk (Winnebago) from the Standing Rock Reservation in Wisconsin lived in wigwams constructed from birch bark, elm bark, and reed, while next door, a group of tipis housed 36 Lakota from Pine Ridge, South Dakota. The village also contained a stadium for shows featuring performers including Chief Silvertongue, a Hoopa tenor from southern California, and Evergreen Tree, a voice artist from Cochiti Pueblo who imitated animals.[140] The trading post occupied the area next to the stadium and sold a variety of goods produced by the Indians working at the village. Behind the trading post stood a two-story, Pueblo-style building housing 32 Hopi performers (see Figure 1.20).

Twenty-nine people performed in the Diné encampment located at the southwest corner of the village, and the Navajo architecture they occupied represented a significant change from fairs in the past.[141] While the Diné at the World's Columbian Exposition in 1893 had lived in a forked-pole hogan and the Santa Fe Railway exhibit at the 1909 Chicago Land Show had featured a many-legged hogan, the encampment in 1933 was dominated by the stacked-log hogan. One large and two smaller examples were constructed along the side where spectators stood.[142]

There were also several shade structures, as well as a small many-legged hogan, but it was located to the rear and behind the other buildings in the exhibit. The architecture of the anthropology village at the Century of Progress Exposition signaled that the stacked-log hogan was becoming increasingly important among the Diné. And its central position within the Diné encampment suggests that it was gaining in symbolic significance as well.

The 1936 Texas Centennial Exposition in Dallas

The Texas Centennial Exposition opened on June 6, 1936, and 6 million people passed through its gates before it closed at the end of November.[143] The exposition's main site at Fair Park in Dallas covered 185 acres and became known for

Anthropology Villages and the Diné Hogan, 1890–1950   51

Figure 1.20 View of the Diné encampment in front of the "Pueblo" at the Indian Village, looking northwest, 1933–1934 Century of Progress Exposition in Chicago.

its extraordinary Art Deco architecture, designed by George Dahl in association with Paul Cret. New Mexico was the only state to sponsor its own pavilion, aside from Texas. In March 1936, the *Dallas Morning News* published an architectural rendering of the proposed New Mexico Building and explained that "one half of the structure will be a replica of a Spanish mission; the other will be fashioned after [the Palace of the Governors]."[144] Eventually, the plan to reproduce a Spanish mission was scrapped and a 2,000-square-foot replica of the Palace of the Governors was constructed as the main pavilion.[145]

The gardens around the building were planned to illustrate the state's "natural resources and every phase of ancient and modern industrial life."[146] As the landscape design evolved, exhibit organizers began to focus on promoting tourism, and the grounds eventually featured "a liberal mound of the famous White Sands [from White Sands National Monument]."[147] By April 1936, the scheme for the gardens had also come to include a Diné hogan enclosing the "New Mexico State Indian Exhibit" (Figure 1.21).

J. Marshall Drolet operated a trading post on the Navajo reservation in Naschitti (*Nahashch'idii*), New Mexico, and by the end of June, the *Southwest Tourist News* reported that he had arranged to build a hogan at the exposition with a weaver, a silversmith, and "a large collection of Indian arts and crafts" for sale.[148] According to local newspapers, the artisans were Isko Yazza (Small Weaver) and her husband, Etsitty Chincilli (Curlyheaded Silversmith).[149] Etsitty also created sand paintings under the *portal* of the exhibit's "Palace of the Governors."[150] Drolet's octagonal stacked hogan was constructed with large doors that opened out to reveal the interior. Strictly speaking, the exhibit was not an anthropology village, as it functioned solely as a

52 *Anthropology Villages and the Diné Hogan, 1890–1950*

Figure 1.21 "The New Mexico State Indian Exhibit," looking north, 1936 Texas Centennial Exposition in Dallas.

salesroom and as a setting for arts and crafts presentations. But the prominent role it played at the exposition in Dallas demonstrates that by 1936, the stacked-log hogan had emerged as the most potent architectural symbol of Diné culture.

The 1948–1949 Chicago Railroad Fair

According to historian Curtis L. Katz, "The Chicago Railroad Fair was born of postwar euphoria, civic boosterism, and the railroads' desire to secure a share of peacetime progress and prosperity."[151] Occupying 50 acres along the shores of Lake Michigan, the fair featured exhibits sponsored by 38 different railway companies, as well several businesses associated with the industry.[152] The main attraction was "Wheels a-Rolling," an historical pageant on an enormous scale featuring a group of historic trains and locomotives that steamed across a 450-foot-wide stage laid with railroad tracks.[153] The Santa Fe Railway's anthropology village was located near the entrance to the pageant's grandstand.

One hundred twenty-five Native Americans, including Diné, Hopi, Jemez, Zuni, Laguna, and Apache lived and performed at the Indian Village, which included 15 buildings spread across a three-acre site.[154] The centerpiece was a three-story imitation Pueblo. Nearby, there were two kivas and several Apache wikiups.

The map in the exhibit's interpretive guide (see Figure 1.22) illustrated several examples of Diné architecture. A many-legged hogan and an octagonal stacked-log hogan were planned to serve as dwellings, while a large octagonal stacked-log hogan was labeled as a "Navajo Medicine Lodge."

When the village was constructed, its architecture differed from the map. The dwellings included a highly stylized forked-pole hogan that towered above two

Anthropology Villages and the Diné Hogan, 1890–1950 53

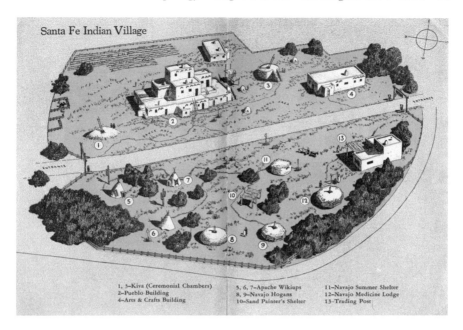

Figure 1.22 Map of the Santa Fe Indian Village, 1948–1949 Chicago Railroad Fair.

octagonal stacked-log hogans on either side of it (Figure 1.23).[155] And a many-legged hogan, rather than a stacked-log hogan, served as the "Navajo Medicine Lodge."[156] But in both the rendering and within the actual village, the stacked-log hogan served as the most prominent form, as at the 1933–1934 Chicago fair and the 1936 Dallas fair.

Aside from the winter hogans, there was also a summer hogan, which served as the "Sand Painter's Shelter." Unfortunately, the Windy City proved to be too much for demonstrations of sand painting; the medicine man hired for the village began several performances, "only to have his colored sands blown to the six directions."[157]

Two Pueblo-Spanish Revival-style buildings faced each other on the south side of the anthropology village. One was the Fred Harvey Trading Post, a shop where visitors could buy curios and view Native American art from the museum at the Alvarado in Albuquerque.[158] The other was the anthropology village's Arts and Crafts Building. Inside, fairgoers could view a curated exhibit of valuable Native American art from the Museum of New Mexico and the Laboratory of Anthropology in Santa Fe.[159] The Fred Harvey Indian Department had balked at sponsoring an anthropology village at the Century of Progress exposition 15 years earlier, but in 1948, the company was willing to participate in a highly commercialized fair exhibit. There were any number of reasons to account for this change of heart, but the presence of the Museum of New Mexico at the village was probably a factor. The objects housed in the Arts and Crafts Building imparted the cultural authority

54 *Anthropology Villages and the Diné Hogan, 1890–1950*

Figure 1.23 Still from a home movie taken at the 1948 Chicago Railroad Fair showing several of the Navajo hogans in the Santa Fe Indian Village.

the Fred Harvey Indian Department coveted and helped preserve the elite reputation it had sought for nearly 50 years.

Epilogue: The Discover Navajo Pavilion at the 2002 Winter Olympics in Salt Lake City

In February 2002, a multimillion-dollar pavilion called "Discover Navajo: People of the Fourth World" opened as part of the Winter Olympics in Salt Lake City. Unlike the other exhibits discussed in this chapter, "Discover Navajo" originated with the Diné. Occupying 15,000 square feet and enclosed by a circular tensile structure, "Discover Navajo" included an illustrated history of the tribe with colorful graphics, videos, fiber-optic displays, and models arranged around an octagonal stacked-log hogan (Figure 1.24).

The pavilion began as a project of the Navajo Nation Department of Tourism headed by Fred White. According to White, "Discover Navajo" was intended to publicize "the beauty of the land and the cultural experience" of the reservation. He additionally hoped that it would lead to new economic opportunities for the people who live in the Navajo Nation.[160] The design team for "Discover Navajo" was led by Ed Hackley, a non-Native who spent eleven months putting the exhibit

Figure 1.24 The octagonal stacked-log hogan from the Discover Navajo Pavilion at the 2002 Winter Olympics, now installed in the Explore Navajo Interactive Museum at Tuba City, Arizona.

plan together. During that time, he traveled the reservation to consult with tribal elders, Diné architects, including David Sloan and Donna House, and Diné historians, including Nancy Maryboy and David Begay. Six months before the pavilion was to open, Hackley previewed the design in front of a group of the tribe's most important leaders to secure their approval.[161]

The octagonal shape of the hogan set the pattern for the exhibits surrounding it, with the four cardinal directions each featuring a different cultural theme. Special displays focused on weaving and World War II's Navajo Code Talkers, but the hogan was the centerpiece of the pavilion. Constructed by a Diné team, including Wally Brown and Cesar and Ellouise Paredes, the building was elevated so that visitors walked upward to see it.[162] The tribe's oral narratives relate that the Diné ascended through several different worlds to arrive at this, the Glittering World, and the walk upwards within the pavilion was intended to offer a similar experience. Inside the stacked-log hogan – a powerful symbol and iconic representation of the Navajo home – visitors could listen to teachings about sacred traditions and learn about the hogan's mythic origins.[163]

At the world's fairs in Chicago and St. Louis, Diné architecture was represented by the male (forked-pole) hogan, a form dating back to at least the 18th century.

56 *Anthropology Villages and the Diné Hogan, 1890–1950*

But new building practices developed on the reservation during the late 19th and early 20th centuries, and the hogans constructed at the Alvarado Hotel in Albuquerque and at the Grand Canyon reflected those practices. Larger female hogans supplanted the male hogan as the primary dwelling type, and by 1925, when Diné employees at Mesa Verde designed and built an anthropology village for the park, three of the four hogans were female hogans.

Although there are a variety of different female hogans, during the 1930s, the stacked-log hogan became the predominant form at exhibits featuring Diné architecture. The earliest versions of the stacked-log hogan at anthropology villages were rounded and lacked a distinctly polygonal shape. But by 1936, the octagonal form had become the iconic example of Navajo architecture, and it has now become the primary symbol for "home" among the Diné.

Notes

1 Paul Greenhalgh, *Ephemeral Vistas: The Expositions Universelles, Great Exhibitions and World's Fairs, 1851–1939* (Manchester: Manchester University Press, 1988), 85.

2 Leonard Mosley, *Disney's World* (New York: Stein and Day, 1985), 216–218; Karal Ann Marling, "Disneyland, 1955: Just Take the Santa Ana Freeway to the American Dream," *Smithsonian Studies in American Art* 5, nos. 1–2 (1991): 180; and Richard Snow, *Disney's Land: Walt Disney and the Amusement Park that Changed the World* (New York: Scribner, 2019), 25–33.

3 See John E. Findling and Kimberly D. Pelle, eds. *Encyclopedia of World's Fairs and Expositions* (Jefferson, NC: McFarland & Company, Inc. Publishers, 2008), 414.

4 Robert A. Trennert, Jr., "Fairs, Expositions, and the Changing Image of Southwestern Indians, 1876–1904," *New Mexico Historical Review* 62, no. 2 (April 1987): 133.

5 For more about the Model Indian School, see Christopher T. Green, "A Stage Set for Assimilation: The Model Indian School at the World's Columbian Exposition," *Winterthur Portfolio* 51, nos. 2–3 (Summer/Autumn 2017): 95–133.

6 Rossiter Johnson, ed., *A History of the World's Columbian Exposition*, vol. II (New York: D. Appleton, 1897), 315.

7 John J. Flinn, *Official Guide to the World's Columbian Exposition* (Chicago: The Columbian Guide Company, 1893), 55.

8 Johnson, *A History of the World's Columbian Exposition*, vol. III, 429; Hubert Howe Bancroft, *The Book of the Fair*, vol. II (Chicago: The Bancroft Company Publishers, 1895), 663; Melissa Rinehart, "To Hell with the Wigs! Native American Representation and Resistance at the World's Columbian Exposition," *American Indian Quarterly* 36, no. 4 (Fall 2012): 408; and Flinn, *Official Guide to the World's Columbian Exposition*, 55.

9 Ira Jacknis, "Northwest Coast Indian Culture and the World's Columbian Exposition," in *The Spanish Borderlands in Pan-American Perspective*, vol. III of *Columbian Consequences*, ed. David Hurst Thomas (Washington, DC: Smithsonian Institution Press, 1991), 98.

10 Daniel Dorchester, Superintendent of Indian Schools, in Thomas J. Morgan, *Annual Report of the Commissioner of Indian Affairs, 1893* (Washington, DC: Government Printing Office [hereafter abbreviated as GPO], 1893), 394.

11 Flinn, *Official Guide to the World's Columbian Exposition*, 55.

12 David R.M. Beck, *Unfair Labor? American Indians and the 1893 World's Columbian Exposition in Chicago* (Lincoln: University of Nebraska Press, 2019), 32.

13 Frederic Ward Putnam to Antonio Apache, August 4, 1892, Box 31, FWP-HU.

Anthropology Villages and the Diné Hogan, 1890–1950 57

14 See "Savage Life Illustrated," *The Inter Ocean* [Chicago, IL], June 27, 1893, and "Before Colon Came," *The Inter Ocean* [Chicago, IL], July 9, 1893. According to Robert A. Trennert, one of the Diné men was known as "Navajo Jake," a silversmith from Fort Wingate. See "Fairs, Expositions and the Changing Image of Southwestern Indians, 1876–1904," 136.

15 Dorchester, in Thomas J. Morgan, *Annual Report of the Commissioner of Indian Affairs, 1893,* 395.

16 Bancroft, *The Book of the Fair*, vol. II, 645.

17 Bancroft, *The Book of the Fair*, vol. II, 663.

18 See "Savage Life Illustrated" and "Three Navahoe Indians Arrive," *Chicago Tribune*, June 28, 1893. Although the title of the *Tribune* article refers to three individuals, the article mentions five.

19 "Before Colon Came." An ash hopper is used to collect ash for soapmaking.

20 "World's Fair Gossip." *Rocky Mountain News* [Denver, CO], July 10, 1893.

21 Frederic Ward Putnam to Antonio Apache, August 4, 1892, Box 31, FWP-HU.

22 Rosemarie Bank, "Representing History: Performing the Columbian Exposition," *Theatre Journal* 54, no. 4 (December 2002): 594.

23 Trennert, "Fairs, Expositions, and the Changing Image of Southwestern Indians, 1876–1904," 139–140.

24 "Before Colon Came," *The Inter Ocean* [Chicago, IL], July 9, 1893.

25 Robert A. Trennert, Jr., "Selling Indian Education at World's Fairs and Expositions, 1893–1904," *American Indian Quarterly* 11, no. 3 (Summer 1987): 210.

26 Turner's "Frontier Thesis" was presented at the annual meeting of the American Historical Society on July 12, 1893, in Chicago during the Columbian Exposition.

27 Henry Fritz, *The Movement for Indian Assimilation, 1860–1890* (Philadelphia: University of Pennsylvania Press, 1963), 199.

28 Lieutenant Edwin H. Plummer, in Indian Rights Association, *The Eleventh Annual Report of the Executive Committee of the Indian Rights Association, 1893* (Philadelphia: Office of the Indian Rights Association, 1894), 18; Trennert, "Fairs, Expositions and the Changing Image of Southwestern Indians, 1876–1904," 140.

29 US Board of Indian Commissioners, *Annual Report of the United States Board of Indian Commissioners, 1894* (Washington, DC: GPO, 1895), 30–31.

30 Plummer, in Indian Rights Association, *The Eleventh Annual Report of the Executive Committee of the Indian Rights Association, 1893,* 19.

31 Garrick Bailey and Roberta Glenn Bailey, *A History of the Navajos: The Reservation Years* (Santa Fe: School of American Research Press, 1986), 65.

32 Thomas J. Morgan, "Report of the Commissioner of Indian Affairs," in *Annual Report of the Secretary of the Interior, 1893,* ed. Hoke Smith (Washington, DC: GPO, 1894), 5.

33 Trennert, "Fairs, Expositions and the Changing Image of Southwestern Indians, 1876–1904," 132.

34 Michael Zega, "Advertising the Southwest," *Journal of the Southwest* 43, no. 4 (Autumn 2001): 281.

35 Keith L. Bryant, Jr., *History of the Atchison, Topeka and Santa Fe Railway* (Lincoln: University of Nebraska Press, 1974), 121.

36 Marta Weigle, "From Desert to Disney World: The Santa Fe Railway and the Fred Harvey Company Display the Indian Southwest," *Journal of Anthropological Research* 45, no. 1 (Spring 1989): 121.

37 Fred Harvey Company, *The Indian and Mexican Building, Albuquerque, N.M.*, 17th ed. (Albuquerque, c. 1919), CSWR.

38 Fred Harvey Company, *The Alvarado, A New Hotel at Albuquerque, New Mexico* (Fred Harvey/Santa Fe Railway, 1908), private collection of Alexa Roberts.

39 "After Indian Fashion," *Albuquerque Citizen*, February 13, 1903.

58   *Anthropology Villages and the Diné Hogan, 1890–1950*

40   "Adobe Building – On the Site of the Indian Industrial Village," *Albuquerque Weekly Citizen*, November 29, 1902; "They Are Going Home – Navajo Blanket Weavers Will Return to the Reservation," *Albuquerque Citizen*, November 7, 1902.

41   "After Indian Fashion."

42   See Sanborn's Fire Insurance Map, Albuquerque+July+1908,+Sheet+10. Some images of the village show a corral and building constructed from vertically placed boards on the north side of the many-legged hogan. See PA 2006.25.46 and PA 2006.31.39, Nancy Tucker Collection, Albuquerque Museum.

43   *Spider Woman: A Story of Navajo Weavers and Chanters* (1934), *Navajo Shepherd and Weaver* (1936), and *Navajo Medicine Man: Sandpaintings and Legends of Miguelito* (1939).

44   Kathleen L. Howard, "Weaving a Legend: Elle of Ganado Promotes the Indian Southwest," *New Mexico Historical Review* 74, no. 2 (April 1999): 127–128.

45   George H. Pepper, *An Unusual Navajo Ceremony* (Hampton, VA: Hampton Institute, 1905).

46   See John L. Cowan, "The Dawn of Architecture," *The Reliquary and Illustrated Archaeologist* 14 (1908): 106; John L. Cowan, "Evolution of Architecture," *The Los Angeles Herald,* May 3, 1908; and John L. Cowan, "Two More Stars for Old Glory," *The Pacific Monthly* 22, no. 3 (1909): 222.

47   On April 1, 1912, Herman Schweizer wrote to trader Lorenzo Hubbell, "Last year you sent here an old Indian to help us build the Hogan," and requested information to include on a postcard featuring a picture of the man. Letter located in Box 37, HTP-UA.

48   "Navajo Hogans for Red Brethren – Harvey System to Have Typical Indian Village Along Railroad Between Central and Copper Avenues," *Albuquerque Journal*, May 5, 1911.

49   "Quaint Pueblo Indian Homes – Local Arts and Crafts Center," *Albuquerque Journal*, June 22, 1911.

50   Historic photos located in Scrapbook 6–21–18, Box 11, FH-UA, show the stacked-log hogan in more detail.

51   "Quaint Pueblo Indian Homes."

52   "Quaint Pueblo Indian Homes."

53   By 1951, the village seems to have disappeared. See Sanborn Fire Insurance map Albuquerque+1942-Feb.+1951,+Sheet+2.pdf (which shows no trace of the village).

54   The fair, which covered 1,272 acres, opened on April 30 and closed on December 1. See Findling and Pelle, *Encyclopedia of World's Fairs and Expositions*, 415.

55   Quoted in Robert Rydell, *All the World's a Fair* (Chicago: University of Chicago, 1984), 162.

56   Astrid Böger, "St. Louis, 1904," in Findling and Pelle, *Encyclopedia of World's Fairs and Expositions*, 172.

57   The building's three-story section occupied a footprint measuring 40′ by 208′ to total an estimated 24,960 square feet. A large auditorium also extended from the building's rear.

58   Nancy J. Parezo and Don D. Fowler, *Anthropology Goes to the Fair: The 1904 Louisiana Purchase Exposition* (Lincoln: University of Nebraska Press, 2007), 103.

59   Parezo and Fowler, *Anthropology Goes to the Fair*, 103.

60   S.M. McCowan, "Resumé of Government's Indian Exhibit," in WJ McGee, Report of the Department of Anthropology to Frederick J.V. Skiff, Director, Universal Exposition of 1904, Division of Exhibits, May 10, 1905, 118, LPEC-MHS.

61   "Native Dwellings at the St. Louis Exposition," *Scientific American* 91, no. 13 (September 24, 1904): 217–218. A photograph in the collections of the Missouri History Museum (N40211) also shows two wooden structures and a tent as part of the encampment.

62   WJ McGee, "Report of the Department of Anthropology to Frederick J.V. Skiff, Director, Universal Exposition of 1904, Division of Exhibits," May 10, 1905, 110, LPEC-MHS.

Anthropology Villages and the Diné Hogan, 1890–1950 59

63 Parezo and Fowler, *Anthropology Goes to the Fair*, 406.

64 Parezo and Fowler, *Anthropology Goes to the Fair*, 120–124. See also Robert A. Trennert, "A Resurrection of Native Arts and Crafts: The St. Louis World's Fair, 1904," *Missouri Historical Review* 87, no. 3 (1993): 274–292.

65 Edw. Anthony Spitzka to McGee, October 6, 1904, quoted in John William Troutman, "'The Overlord of the Savage World': Anthropology, the Media, and the American Indian Experience at the 1904 Louisiana Purchase Exposition" (Master's thesis, University of Arizona, 1997), 30.

66 Troutman, "The Overlord of the Savage World," 66.

67 W.H. Simpson, *El Tovar: A New Hotel at Grand Canyon* (Fred Harvey Company, n.d.), 9, collection of the author.

68 For more about the architecture of Hopi House, see Amanda Zeman, "Preservation and Repatriation: American Indian Sacred Objects and National Historic Landmarks at Grand Canyon National Park" (Master's thesis, Cornell University, 2003).

69 Zeman, "Preservation and Repatriation," 89.

70 Herman Schweizer to J.L. Hubbell, November 17, 1904, Box 36, HTP-UA.

71 Kathleen L. Howard and Diana F. Pardue, *Over the Edge: Fred Harvey at the Grand Canyon and in the Great Southwest* (Tucson, AZ: Rio Nuevo Publishers, 2016), 71.

72 See PICT 000–742, WK-CSWR.

73 Emily Post, *By Motor to the Golden Gate* (New York: D. Appleton and Company, 1916), 184–185.

74 See, for example, John L. Cowan, "Playing Cadmus to the Navajos," *Overland Monthly* 58, no. 4 (October 1911): 330; and John L. Cowan, "The 'Good Indian' of the Future," *The Christian Herald,* June 17, 1908: 491.

75 Trennert, "Fairs, Expositions, and the Changing Image of Southwestern Indians, 1876–1904," 141.

76 "To Take Indians to Fair," *Inter-Ocean* [Chicago, IL], February 7, 1899.

77 "Apache Plans to Bring Big Chiefs," *Buffalo* [NY] *Courier*, May 23, 1900; "Assurances that the Display at the Buffalo Exposition will be a Record Breaker," *Buffalo* [NY] *Commercial*, May 18, 1900.

78 Kathleen L. Howard, "Creating an Enchanted Land: Curio Entrepreneurs Promote and Sell the Indian Southwest, 1880–1940" (PhD diss., Arizona State University, 2002), 160–161; "Antonio Apache Is in Pendleton," *East Oregonian*, December 30, 1905; "Redskins Show Peaceful Arts," *Los Angeles Herald*, December 7, 1906.

79 "Indian Village Idea of Antonio Apache," *Los Angeles Times*, September 10, 1905.

80 "Antonio Apache is in Pendleton." Eastlake Park later became known as Lincoln Park.

81 C.R. Curry, *Biennial Report of the Secretary of State of the State of California for the 56th and 57th Years*, beginning July 1, 1904, and ending June 30, 1906 (Sacramento: WW Shannon, Superintendent State Printing, 1906), 71; "Redskins Show Peaceful Arts."

82 Howard, "Creating," 161n4. Antonio described the attraction as an "ethnological exposition" on an advertising card in which he was pictured under a shade structure, or *chaha'oh,* dressed as a Diné silversmith. For more, see Trennert, "Fairs, Expositions, and the Changing Image of Southwestern Indians, 1876–1904," 135.

83 Howard, "Creating," 162.

84 Curteich, one of the largest postcard-manufacturing companies in the US, was producing a postcard with the same scene and entitled "Navajo Families in Front of Their Hogans" as late as 1943 (3B-H1394).

85 "Lions Coming Here for Picture Poses," *Los Angeles Express*, December 11, 1911.

86 Advertisement on p. 9 of the *Chicago Tribune*, November 12, 1909.

87 "Land and Irrigation Exposition," *Conservation* 15, no. 6 (June 1909): 376; "A National Land Exposition in Chicago," *Conservation* 15, no. 11 (November 1909): 719; "Call O' the Farm Lure to City Men," *Chicago Tribune*, November 20, 1909.

60 *Anthropology Villages and the Diné Hogan, 1890–1950*

88 "Showing a Heap Big Town to a Heap of Heap Curious Indians," *Chicago Tribune*, November 21, 1909.
89 "Navajos Feature of 'Tribune' Show," *Chicago Tribune*, November 16, 1909.
90 "Showing a Heap Big Town."
91 "Navajos Feature of 'Tribune' Show."
92 "Navajos Feature of 'Tribune' Show."
93 David C. Collier, in US Senate, *The Panama-Pacific and the Panama-California Expositions: Hearings Before the Committee on Industrial Expositions* (Washington, DC: GPO, 1912), 11.
94 David C. Collier, in US Senate, *The Panama-Pacific and the Panama-California Expositions*, 11.
95 Richard W. Amero, *Balboa Park History*, Chapter 7, at www.balboaparkhistory.net; "Indian Tribes will be Brought to Exposition," *San Diego Union*, August 21, 1913.
96 "Indian Tribes Will Be Brought to Exposition."
97 Herman Schweizer to Jesse Nusbaum, July 19, 1921, 93 NP2.058, LA. J.F. Huckel was Fred Harvey's son-in-law and a founder of the Indian Department.
98 "New Mexico Indian Life to be Shown at Exposition," *San Diego Union*, December 14, 1914.
99 Herman Schweizer to J.L. Hubbell, September 8, 1914, Box 37, HTP-UA
100 See "Indians at Work on Exhibit for Exposition," *San Diego Union*, October 6, 1914, and "Navajo Indians Take Joy Jaunt," *San Diego Union*, October 12, 1914.
101 *Painted Desert Exhibit, San Diego Exhibition* [exhibit guide] (Fred Harvey/Santa Fe Railway, 1915).
102 Findling and Pelle, *Encyclopedia of World's Fairs and Expositions,* 415.
103 The fair opened on February 20 and closed on December 4, 1915; it was located on a 635-acre site along San Francisco Bay. See Findling and Pelle, *Encyclopedia of World's Fairs and Expositions*, 415.
104 [Local News], *St. Joseph* [Michigan] *Saturday Herald*, July 12, 1902; "The Santa Fe Exhibit," *Threshermen's Review and Power Farming* [St. Joseph, Michigan] 24, no. 5 (May 1915): 62.
105 Trumbull White, *The World's Columbian Exposition* (Philadelphia: P.W. Ziegler, 1893), 578–579. The exhibit was also mounted at the 1898 Trans-Mississippi International Exposition in Omaha and the 1901 Pan-American Exposition in Buffalo.
106 *Grand Canyon of Arizona Replica, Panama-Pacific International Exposition, San Francisco* [exhibit guide] (Santa Fe Railway, 1915).
107 Herman Schweizer to J.F. Huckel, May 13, 1932, 1933-FAC.
108 "The Grand Canyon of Arizona at Panama-Pacific Exposition," *The Santa Fe Magazine* 8, no. 8 (July 1914): 50; "The 'Zone'," *Los Angeles Times*, April 4, 1915.
109 *Grand Canyon of Arizona Replica, Panama-Pacific International Exposition, San Francisco*.
110 For more about Mesa Verde's Pueblo-Spanish Revival architecture, see Laura Soullière Harrison, *Architecture in the Parks: National Historic Landmark Theme Study* (Washington, DC: National Park Service, 1986), 211–228.
111 Jesse Nusbaum, "Superintendent's Report for September 1922," September 10, 1922, Box 6, HR-MEVE.
112 "Transcript of Jesse L. Nusbaum Interview by Herbert Evison," December 9, 1962, 14, Box 3, RT/JLN-MEVE.
113 Elvon L. Howe, "The Sachem of Shiprock," *The Rocky Mountain Empire Magazine* [insert in *The Denver Post*], March 2, 1947: 4–7, mimeo located in Box 1, RT/JLN-MEVE.
114 Jesse L. Nusbaum to D[aniel] R. Hull, April 28, 1925, Box 9, HR-MEVE.
115 Another photograph, taken at the park between 1926 and 1927, shows Ahkeah dancing with two other Diné men and Nusbaum's stepson, Deric, in front of a stacked-log

Anthropology Villages and the Diné Hogan, 1890–1950   61

hogan. The photograph, N-57, is in the Western History Collection at the Denver Public Library.

116 Horace M. Albright and Frank J. Taylor, *"Oh, Ranger!": A Book about the National Parks* (Stanford: Stanford University Press, 1929), 85.

117 Albright and Taylor, *"Oh, Ranger!"* 85–86.

118 See MEVE 307 3052 and MEVE 307 3052A, eTIC.

119 "ECW Balance Sheets," Box 2, and "Job no. 34," Box 6, CCC-MEVE.

120 Betty Franke, "Our Navaho Neighbors," *Mesa Verde Notes* 7, no. 1 (March 1937): 3.

121 "Job no. 98," Box 6, CCC-MEVE.

122 The designer is listed as "K. Saunders." See "Job No. 182," Box 7, CCC-MEVE.

123 John E. Findling, "Chicago 1933–1934," in Findling and Pelle, *Encyclopedia of World's Fairs and Expositions*, 270. Between May 27 and November 12, 1933, the fair had 27.3 million visitors, and between May 29 and October 31, 1934, 21.1 million visited the exposition which occupied a 427-acre site along Lake Michigan (Findling and Pelle, *Encyclopedia of World's Fairs and Expositions*, 416).

124 The temple would ultimately be a full-size replica of the Nunnery at Uxmal, Mexico.

125 W.J. Black, Passenger Traffic Manager to J.F. Huckel, May 14, 1932, 1933-FAC.

126 W.H. Simpson to Herman Schweizer, April 14, 1932, 1933-FAC.

127 Herman Schweizer to W.H. Simpson, April 26, 1932, 1933-FAC.

128 Herman Schweizer to J.F. Huckel, May 3, 1932, 1933-FAC; Fay-Cooper Cole to Jesse Nusbaum, June 4, 1932, 89 LA3.044b, LA.

129 Fay-Cooper Cole to Jesse Nusbaum. June 4, 1932, 89 LA3.044b, LA; "Preliminary Estimates, Pueblo-Navajo Group Provided by Santa Fe Railway," June 7, 1932, 1933-FAC.

130 Jesse Nusbaum to Fay-Cooper Cole, June 10, 1932, 89 LA3.044b, LA.

131 Jesse Nusbaum to Fay-Cooper Cole, June 1, 1932, 89 LA3.044a, LA.

132 Fay-Cooper Cole to W.H. Simpson, September 1, 1932, 1933-FAC.

133 J.F. Huckel to W.H. Simpson, November 5, 1932, 1933-FAC.

134 On April 27, 1933, Nusbaum wrote to Cole, "I have not yet been able to get Herman Schweitzer [sic], but my feeling is that the show that he would like to see put on, which would be in accordance with the Santa Fe-Fred Harvey past shows, would be on a basis that your sponsors would not care to undertake," 89 LA3.044b, LA. For more about Cole's last-minute efforts to organize the exhibit, see Abigail Markwyn, "'I Would Like to Have This Tribe Represented': Native Performance and Craft at Chicago's 1933 Century of Progress Exposition," *American Indian Quarterly* 44, no. 3 (Summer 2020): 329–361.

135 [Fay-Cooper] Cole to Jesse Nusbaum [telegram], April 24, 1933, 89 LA3.044b, LA.

136 Jesse L. Nusbaum to Fay-Cooper Cole, April 27, 1933, 89 LA3.044b, LA.

137 "Wick Miller, Friendly Indian Trader, and His Post for Pueblo Indians," *School Arts* 30, no. 7 (March 1931): 467–468.

138 Jesse L. Nusbaum to Fay-Cooper Cole, April 27, 1933, 89 LA3.044b, LA.

139 James O'Donnell Bennett, "Indian Villages at Fair Weave Bit of Old Days," *Chicago Sunday Tribune*, July 30, 1933.

140 "Some Wisdom and Wisecracks from the Indian Village," *Official World's Fair Weekly* (week ending June 17, 1933): 7–8.

141 "Some Wisdom and Wisecracks from the Indian Village," 6; [advertisement for arts and crafts exhibit at Marshall Field's department store], *Chicago Tribune*, December 5, 1932.

142 These buildings are visible in an aerial photograph (vmc38140) located in the collections of the Walter P. Reuther Library, Wayne State University.

143 Stephen G. Snyder and James H. Charleton, "National Historic Landmark nomination, Texas Centennial Exposition Buildings, Dallas, Dallas County, Texas," 1986 [National Register of Historic Places #86003488], section 8, page 2.

62 *Anthropology Villages and the Diné Hogan, 1890–1950*

144 "New Mexico to Have Own Building at Fair," *Dallas Morning News*, March 17, 1936. For more about the Palace of the Governors and its architectural importance as a symbol of New Mexico, see Chris Wilson, *The Myth of Santa Fe* (Albuquerque: University of New Mexico Press, 1997), 125–128.
145 According to "Old Palace Replica," *Albuquerque Journal*, May 6, 1936, the building was set to measure 82′ × 25′.
146 "New Mexico to Exhibit Indian Wares," *Gallup* [NM] *Independent,* February 28, 1936.
147 Ollie Lansden, "Enjoys Centennial – Times Society Editor Writes of Visit to Dallas Celebration," *El Paso Times*, August 10, 1936. A large pile of white sand is visible on the side of the "Palace of the Governors" in an aerial photo (PA2008–5–177) in the collections of the Dallas Public Library.
148 "Reservation News," *Southwest Tourist News*, June 30, 1936. For more about Drolet's trading post, see Klara Kelley and Harris Francis, *Navajoland Trading Post Encyclopedia* (Window Rock: Navajo Nation Department of Heritage and Historic Preservation, 2018), 269–270.
149 "Synthetic Indians Meet Real Ones," *Dallas Morning News*, June 29, 1936, and see also "Navajo at Dallas Shun Publicity to Surprise of Press," *Southwest Tourist News*, July 28, 1936.
150 "Sand Painter Prays for Rain," *Dallas Morning News*, June 18, 1936.
151 Curtis L. Katz, "The Last Great Railroad Show," *Trains* 58, no. 8 (August 1998): 60.
152 Katz, "The Last Great Railroad Show," 60–61.
153 For more details, see "Big Pageant Will Depict Rail History," *Chicago Tribune*, July 20, 1948.
154 "Villages Form Interesting Part of Lake Front Show" and "Members of Six Tribes Live in Indian Village," *Chicago Tribune*, July 20, 1948.
155 "Chicago Railroad Fair Color Home Movies, 1948" (Periscope Film #34452).
156 An image of this building is located at http://rgusrail.com/ilcrf.html
157 John L. Sinclair, "Museum of New Mexico Exhibit at Chicago Railroad Fair," *El Palacio* 55, no. 8 (August 1948): 229.
158 *Santa Fe Railway Indian Village, Chicago Railroad Fair* [exhibit guide] (Santa Fe Railway, 1948).
159 "Members of Six Tribes Live in Indian Village."
160 Quoted in Mary Perea, "Olympic Exhibit to Offer Trip Through History with Navajo," *Los Angeles Times*, August 12, 2001.
161 Ed Hackley, telephone conversation with author, June 30, 2022.
162 Nathan J. Tohtsoni, "Final Touches put on Winter Olympics Display," *Navajo Times*, January 24, 2002.
163 Ed Hackley, *Discover Navajo: People of the Fourth Word* [promotional booklet] (self-published), collection of David Sloan.

Reference List

Archival Sources

1933 Chicago Exposition Papers, Fray Angélico Chávez Library, Museum of New Mexico, Santa Fe. Cited as 1933-FAC.
CCC Program Records, MEVE 71372, Mesa Verde National Park Archives, Colorado. Cited as CCC-MEVE.
Center for Southwest Research and Special Collections, University of New Mexico, Albuquerque. Cited as CSWR.
Frederic Ward Putman Papers, Harvard University Archives, Cambridge, Massachusetts. Cited as FWP-HU.

Anthropology Villages and the Diné Hogan, 1890–1950 63

Fred Harvey Collection (AZ 326), Special Collections, University of Arizona Libraries, Tucson, Arizona. Cited as FH-UA.

Historic Records and Central Files, Series 001.03, MEVE 78525, Mesa Verde National Park Archives, Colorado. Cited as HR-MEVE.

Hubbell Trading Post Papers (AZ 375), Special Collections, University of Arizona Libraries, Tucson, Arizone. Cited as HTP-UA.

Laboratory of Anthropology Archives, Santa Fe. Cited as LA.

Louisiana Purchase Exposition Company Files, Series 3, Subseries 11, Missouri Historical Society, St. Louis. Cited as LPEC-MHS.

National Park Service Electronic Technical Information Center. Cited as eTIC.

Rosemary Talley/Jesse L. Nusbaum Papers, Series 001, Correspondence and Photographs, File Units 001–015, MEVE 96900, Mesa Verde National Park Archives, Colorado. Cited as RT/JLN-MEVE.

William Keleher Collection, Center for Southwest Research, University Libraries, University of New Mexico. Cited as WK-CSWR.

Published Sources

Albright, Horace M., and Frank J. Taylor. *"Oh, Ranger!": A Book about the National Parks*. Stanford, CA: Stanford University Press, 1929.

Amero, Richard W. *Balboa Park History* Located online at www.balboaparkhistory.net.

Bailey, Garrick, and Roberta Glenn Bailey. *A History of the Navajos: The Reservation Years*. Santa Fe: School of American Research Press, 1986.

Bancroft, Hubert Howe. *The Book of the Fair*, vols. I and II. Chicago: The Bancroft Company Publishers, 1895.

Bank, Rosemarie. "Representing History: Performing the Columbian Exposition." *Theatre Journal* 54, no. 4 (December 2002): 589–606.

Beck, David R.M. *Unfair Labor? American Indians and the 1893 World's Columbian Exposition in Chicago*. Lincoln: University of Nebraska Press, 2019.

Broggie, Michael, *Walt Disney's Railroad Story: The Small-Scale Fascination that Led to a Full-Scale Kingdom*. Pasadena, CA: Pentrex, 1997.

Cowan, John L. "The Dawn of Architecture." *The Reliquary and Illustrated Archaeologist* 14 (1908): 105–114.

———. "The 'Good Indian" of the Future." *The Christian Herald,* June 17, 1908: 491, 493.

———. "Playing Cadmus to the Navajos." *Overland Monthly* 58, no. 4 (October 1911): 327–333.

———. "Two More Stars for Old Glory." *The Pacific Monthly* 22, no. 3 (September 1909): 215–232.

Curry, C.F. *Biennial Report of the Secretary of State of the State of California for the 56th and 57th Years,* beginning July 1, 1904, and ending June 30, 1906. Sacramento: W.W. Shannon, Superintendent State Printing, 1906.

"The Cyclorama." *Scientific American* 55, no. 19 (November 6, 1886): 296.

Dexter, Ralph W. "Putnam's Problems Popularizing Anthropology." *American Scientist* 54, no. 3 (September 1966): 315–332.

Findling, John E., and Kimberly D. Pelle, eds. *Encyclopedia of World's Fairs and Expositions*. Jefferson, NC: McFarland & Company, Inc. Publishers, 2008.

Flinn, John J. *Official Guide to the World's Columbian Exposition*. Chicago: The Columbian Guide Company, 1893.

Franke, Betty. "Our Navajo Neighbors." *Mesa Verde Notes* 7, no. 1 (March 1937): 3–6.

Fritz, Henry E. *The Movement for Indian Assimilation, 1860–1890*. Philadelphia: University of Pennsylvania Press, 1963.

"The Grand Canyon of Arizona at Panama-Pacific Exposition." *The Santa Fe Magazine* 8, no. 8 (July 1914): 49–50.

64   Anthropology Villages and the Diné Hogan, 1890–1950

Grand Canyon of Arizona Replica, Panama-Pacific International Exposition, San Francisco [exhibit guide]. Santa Fe Railway, 1915.

Greenhalgh, Paul. *Ephemeral Vistas: The Expositions Universelles, Great Exhibitions and World's Fairs, 1851–1939*. Manchester: Manchester University Press, 1988.

Howard, Kathleen L. "Weaving a Legend: Elle of Ganado Promotes the Indian Southwest." *New Mexico Historical Review* 74, no. 2 (April 1999): 127–154.

———. "Creating an Enchanted Land: Curio Entrepreneurs Promote and Sell the Indian Southwest, 1880–1940." PhD diss., Arizona State University, 2002.

Howard, Kathleen L., and Diana F. Pardue. *Over the Edge: Fred Harvey at the Grand Canyon and in the Great Southwest*. Tucson, AZ: Rio Nuevo Publishers, 2016.

Indian Rights Association. *Annual Report of the Executive Committee of the Indian Rights Association, 1893.* Philadelphia, PA: Office of the Indian Rights Association, 1894.

Jacknis, Ira. "Northwest Coast Indian Culture and the World's Columbian Exposition." In *The Spanish Borderlands in Pan-American Perspective,* edited by David H. Thomas, 91–118. *Columbian Consequences,* vol. III. Washington, DC: Smithsonian Institution Press, 1991.

Johnson, Rossiter, ed. *A History of the World's Columbian Exposition*, 4 vols. New York: D. Appleton, 1897.

Katz, Curtis L. "The Last Great Railroad Show." *Trains* 58, no. 8 (August 1998): 58–67.

King, Margaret. "The Theme Park: Aspects of Experience in a Four-Dimensional Landscape." *Material Culture* 34, no. 2 (2002): 1–15.

"Land and Irrigation Exposition." *Conservation* 15, no. 6 (June 1909): 376.

Marling, Karal Ann. "Disneyland, 1955: Just Take the Santa Ana Freeway to the American Dream." *Smithsonian Studies in American Art* 5, nos. 1–2 (1991): 168–207.

Morgan, Thomas J. *Annual Report of the Commissioner of Indian Affairs, 1893*. Washington, DC: GPO, 1893.

Mosley, Leonard. *Disney's World*. New York: Stein and Day, 1985.

"A National Land Exposition in Chicago." *Conservation* 15, no. 11 (November 1909): 719.

Official Guide to the Louisiana Purchase Exposition at the City of St. Louis, State of Missouri, April 30th to December 1st, 1904. St. Louis: The Official Guide Co., 1904.

Painted Desert Exhibit, San Diego Exhibition [exhibit guide]. Fred Harvey/Santa Fe Railway, 1915.

Parezo, Nancy J., and Don D. Fowler. *Anthropology Goes to the Fair: The 1904 Louisiana Purchase Exposition*. Lincoln: University of Nebraska Press, 2004.

Pepper, George H. *An Unusual Navajo Ceremony*. Hampton, VA: Hampton Institute, 1905.

Post, Emily. *By Motor to the Golden Gate*. New York: D. Appleton and Company, 1916.

Rinehart, Melissa. "To Hell with the Wigs! Native American Representation and Resistance at the World's Columbian Exposition." *American Indian Quarterly* 36, no. 4 (Fall 2012): 403–442.

Rydell, Robert. *All the World's a Fair*. Chicago: University of Chicago, 1984.

Santa Fe Railway Indian Village, Chicago Railroad Fair, Summer 1948 [exhibit guide]. Santa Fe Railway, 1948.

Sinclair, John L. "Museum of New Mexico Exhibit at Chicago Railroad Fair." *El Palacio* 55, no. 8: 227–230.

Smith, Duane A. *Mesa Verde National Park: Shadows of the Centuries*. Lawrence: University Press of Kansas, 1988.

Smith, Hoke, ed. *Annual Report of the Secretary of the Interior, 1893*. Washington, DC: GPO, 1893.

Snow, Richard. *Disney's Land: Walt Disney and the Amusement Park that Changed the World*. New York: Scribner, 2019.

"Some Wisdom and Wisecracks from the Indian Village." *Official World's Fair Weekly* (week ending June 17, 1933): 7–8.

Trennert, Robert A., Jr. "Fairs, Expositions, and the Changing Image of Southwestern Indians, 1876–1904." *New Mexico Historical Review* 62, no. 2 (April 1987): 127–150.

Anthropology Villages and the Diné Hogan, 1890–1950 65

———. "Selling Indian Education at World's Fairs and Expositions, 1893–1904." *American Indian Quarterly* 11, no. 3 (Summer 1987): 203–220.

Troutman, John William. "'The Overlord of the Savage World': Anthropology, the Media, and the American Indian Experience at the 1904 Louisiana Purchase Exposition." Master's thesis, University of Arizona, 1997.

US Board of Indian Commissioners. *Annual Report of the United States Board of Indian Commissioners, 1894*. Washington, DC: GPO, 1895.

US Senate. *The Panama-Pacific and the Panama-California Expositions: Hearings Before the Committee on Industrial Expositions*. Washington, DC: GPO, 1912.

Weigle, Marta. "From Desert to Disney World: The Santa Fe Railway and the Fred Harvey Company Display the Indian Southwest." *Journal of Anthropological Research* 45, no. 1 (Spring 1989): 115–137.

White, Trumbull. *The World's Columbian Exposition*. Philadelphia: P.W. Ziegler, 1893.

"Wick Miller, Friendly Indian Trader, and His Post for Pueblo Indians." *School Arts* 30, no. 7 (March 1931): 467–468.

Zega, Michael. "Advertising the Southwest." *Journal of the Southwest* 43, no. 4 (Autumn 2001): 281–315.

Zeman, Amanda. "Preservation and Repatriation: American Indian Sacred Objects and National Historic Landmarks at Grand Canyon National Park." Master's thesis, Cornell University, 2003.

2 "Improving" the Hogan

During the late 19th and early 20th centuries, the federal government, Native American rights organizations, and religious groups worked to "improve" Diné architecture. Some sought to persuade the Diné to live in houses in order to assimilate the tribe into mainstream American society. Others argued that the hogan contributed to diseases such as tuberculosis and trachoma. By the 1920s, reformers increasingly came to promote the "model hogan" as an important tool for encouraging healthful building practices. All of the model hogans surveyed in this chapter were female hogans and incorporated features from Western-style houses in the US. But increasingly, the stacked-log hogan became the form of choice for experimentation and innovation in Diné-inflected architecture.

Governmental Efforts to Encourage Permanent Homes, 1868–1900

The Long Walk to Bosque Redondo (known to the tribe as *Hwéeldi*) began as an elaborate scheme to convert the Diné into self-reliant farmers. But it ended in catastrophe. Of the 11,000 Navajo who departed for southeastern New Mexico Territory beginning in 1864, only 6,800 returned in 1868. To Brigadier General James H. Carleton, the 40-square-mile reserve along the Pecos River seemed to offer the ideal location for transforming the tribe into a peaceful agrarian community. But the problems that beset Carleton's plan proved to be overwhelming. Efforts to farm the land failed abysmally, and disease and malnutrition took a great toll.

During the Bosque Redondo period, the federal government began to consider the value of "improved" dwellings for the Navajo. In 1867, Theodore H. Dodd, the US Indian Agent at Bosque Redondo, reported, "Some of the Indians have built very fair adobe houses, and were it not for their superstitious fears of living in a house in which one has died they all would soon have comfortable homes."[1] Dodd was one of the earliest of many observers to report that the fear of ghosts among the Diné frequently led members of the tribe to abandon buildings.[2]

In 1868, the imprisonment at Bosque Redondo came to an end. After the Diné moved back to their homeland in northwestern New Mexico and northeastern Arizona, the federal government began a campaign to persuade them to build dwellings to be occupied on a permanent basis. When President Ulysses S. Grant established the federal Board of Indian Commissioners in 1869, he directed its

DOI: 10.4324/9781003431770-3

members to work towards "civilizing" the Indians.[3] In their first official report, the Board responded to Grant with the details of a plan that would come to be known as "assimilation." Assimilation would lead to new policies, such as ending the payment of cash annuities to the tribes, promoting the creation of private property, English language classes, and Christian evangelizing. The government hoped this would indoctrinate Native Americans with the elements of Euro-American culture and make them self-sufficient.[4] Persuading the Diné to establish a single residence rather than moving from place to place would be key to this process.

In 1873, L. Edwin Dudley, superintendent of Indian Affairs for New Mexico, declared the Diné "should be brought to prefer permanent abodes instead of their hogans, and be taught how to construct them."[5] During the same decade, government officials began to promote milled lumber as integral to the type of dwellings that would induce the Diné to settle. In 1876, US Indian Agent Alex G. Irvine reported:

> Another great need is that of a saw-mill, to furnish lumber for the use of the agency, as well as to provide doors and windows for the use of the Indians in their dwellings. They would build a better class of homes than the hogan, now used by them, if lumber were within their reach, and they would not be so ready to abandon them as they now are, which would be one great step toward making them settled in their habits.[6]

By 1885, US Indian Agent John H. Bowman recorded that "the more progressive of the tribe" were disregarding the death taboo and building houses. Like his predecessors, he held a dim view of the traditional Navajo "rude shelters, built of brush, stones, and sticks, or dirt" and asserted that "fixed habitations" "will do much to hold them in the right path."[7] Bowman's statements revealed a fundamental ignorance of the difficulties permanent dwellings would pose to people who must keep their livestock on the move in an arid environment.

But some federal officials understood the conflict between a transhumant lifestyle and the "civilizing" influence of Euro-American–style houses. The government established a sawmill in Fort Defiance (*Tsé Hootsooí*), Arizona, in 1889, but even the availability of milled lumber could not overcome the more pressing issue of where the Diné would water their animals. In 1900, US Indian Agent G.W. Hayzlett noted:

> The Indians are making more and better improvements than heretofore in the way of building houses. They are furnished with all the lumber they need from the Government sawmill. Many of them come in and tell that they want to put up houses and begin to live like white people, and ask to be furnished with beds and cook stoves, of which so far we have none for issue. One great difficulty in keeping these people located in their houses is the fact that they have to move about from place to place in order to find feed and water for their flocks.[8]

68 *"Improving" the Hogan*

A reliable water supply would remain elusive across the reservation for years to come, and a sedentary lifestyle would only become possible with the decline of the Navajo livestock economy during the mid-20th century.

Model Homes for Native Americans: The Omaha Cottages at Hampton Institute

During the 19th century, a reform movement developed that profoundly influenced the role of the family home in American culture. Historian Gwendolyn Wright has traced the origins of this movement to the 1830s, when books and articles began representing the home "as a stronghold of traditional values and a refuge from the frenzy of city life."[9] Architectural pattern books became increasingly popular. These texts – designed for professional and amateur audiences alike – offered ideas and guidance about how to build and furnish houses.[10] By the 1840s and 1850s:

> Architects who aspired to a more professional status, ministers with an interest in family counseling, feminists who sought to improve the position of women within the family, promoters of tract and benevolence societies who wished to spread Christianity, and almanac and magazine editors who hoped to capitalize on the popular middle-class fascination with self-help and self-improvement schemes all joined in a massive promotional effort to create a new ideal for the American family home.[11]

Many influential authors, including Alexander Jackson Downing and Catherine Beecher, promoted the idea that homes could serve as an instrument of social reform.[12] Thus, designing a house became more than a matter of aesthetics or self-expression; domestic architecture became a means for making the world a better place.

The reformers who worked to assimilate Native Americans during the late 19th century reflected a cultural climate in which morality and the home were intertwined. One approach to "improving" dwellings on Indian reservations was to build model houses for Native Americans to imitate. Model homes were certainly constructed for other populations in the US during the late 19th century. By 1855, a model tenement had been erected in New York City and a "Workingman's Model Home" was located within a few yards of the Native American anthropology village at the 1893 World's Columbian Exposition in Chicago.[13] But model homes were deemed a particularly powerful tool for acculturating an Indigenous population that was largely illiterate and far removed from mainstream Euro-American society.

The earliest model homes for Native Americans were built in 1883 under the guidance of Alice Fletcher at Hampton Institute, a boarding school for African Americans and Native Americans in Virginia.[14] Fletcher first visited the Omaha Reservation in Nebraska in 1881, and in the autumn of the following year, she helped bring two Omaha families to live at Hampton. There, she supervised the construction of two clapboard-clad cottages, each possessing a rectangular plan with three rooms.[15] According to an article in the school's newspaper, the cottages were meant to do the following:

> furnish an effective object lesson to the students, and teach them how comfortable and attractive a house can be put up at small expense. At the same time they also give such an insight, it is hoped, into true homekeeping as cannot fail to do good.[16]

Twenty-three Omaha, Sioux, Winnebago, and Oneida families lived in the cottages and participated in the family program at Hampton before it ended in 1891.[17] As part of her campaign for Native American assimilation, Fletcher created an exhibit on "Indian Civilization" for the 1884 New Orleans Cotton and Industrial Exposition. The pictorial materials in the exhibit offered several variations on the theme of "before and after."[18] It began with a picture of an Omaha earth lodge and ended with a picture of one of Hampton Institute's "Omaha Houses."[19] Another image showed a tableau that architectural reformers would repeatedly return to in subsequent decades, namely, "The Civilization of the Home" (see Figure 2.1).

In the picture, "progress" on a successful farm that had been worked for ten years by an Omaha family has been illustrated with, from left to right, a large hayrick, a log outbuilding, and a clapboard-clad wood-frame house.[20] Many of the photographs in the exhibit were reproduced and described in Fletcher's book *A*

Figure 2.1 An Omaha Indian farm, from *A Historical Sketch of the Omaha Tribe of Indians in Nebraska* by Alice Fletcher

70 *"Improving" the Hogan*

Historical Sketch of the Omaha Tribe in Nebraska (1885), where they reached an even wider audience.

Native American Architecture and the Indian Boarding Schools

Native American boarding schools also employed other methods to condition students to prefer Euro-American–style houses. In some instances, school newspapers published articles that belittled Indigenous architecture. In the May 16, 1913, issue of *The Carlisle Arrow*, published by the Native American boarding school at Carlisle, Pennsylvania, Joseph Broker, a Chippewa student, wrote that "contact with a higher civilization has prompted [the Indian] to abandon his primitive home for a better one – a home he never dreamed of in his earlier days." The author went on to describe an "ideal" home: a two-story house with four bedrooms, a bathroom, lots of closets, and "plenty of light and ventilation." The issue also included photographs of four Euro-American–style wood-frame homes belonging to Carlisle graduates.[21] The following year, an issue of *The Red Man*, another Carlisle publication, featured a cover showing a Native American man hard at work notching logs for a cabin (see Figure 2.2).

Sioux artist Lone Star (William H. Dietz) created the illustration called "The Indian Home Builder." It includes a domical Indian dwelling in the background, but the picture's emphasis is on the cabin's construction, and the message it conveys is that the man has made the right choice in leaving his Native American heritage behind.

American Indian boarding schools sometimes reinforced this message in more theatrical ways. In February 1913, the Phoenix Indian School entered five floats in a parade at the Aztec Sun Fête, an event celebrating the first anniversary of Arizona's statehood.[22] A series of four floats represented several tribes from Arizona and featured the traditional dwellings of those groups. The Apache float included a student "sitting peacefully" in front of a reproduction of a *ki*. A structure made of "weeds and sticks" stood atop the Pima (Akimel O'odham) and Papago (Tohono O'odham) float, while the Hopi float included an imitation pueblo. The Diné float was draped with blankets and included a stacked-log hogan surrounded by weavers and metalsmiths (see Figure 2.3).

The Indian School's fifth and final float was labeled "The New Way" and included students "engaged in crafts of skill." The school newspaper, *The Native American,* reported the float "was not so gay in coloring as the others but there was an atmosphere of thorough-going industry about it that speaks well for the Indian of tomorrow."[23] Taken as a group, the Phoenix Indian School floats proclaimed the gospel of assimilation in no uncertain terms: Native American culture (including the hogan) is a thing of the past, and "good" Indians of the future will eschew the ways of their forebears and adopt the customs of mainstream American society.

The Sanitation Issue

As we have seen, during the years after the Diné returned from Bosque Redondo, certain sectors of American society regarded the hogan as an obstacle to

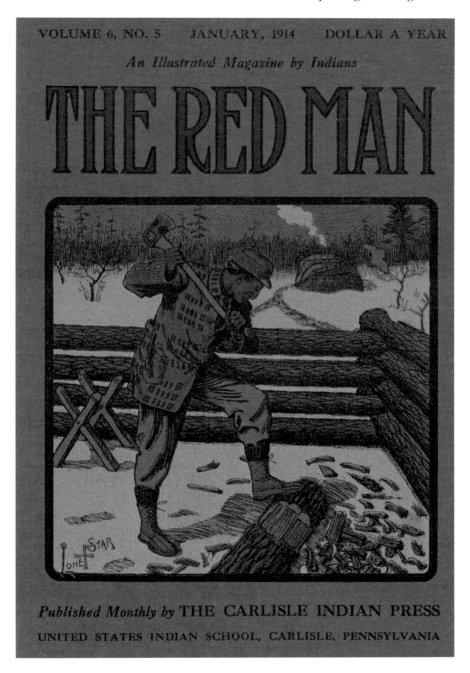

Figure 2.2 Cover of the January 1914 issue of *The Red Man,* Lone Star (William H. Dietz), artist.

72   "Improving" the Hogan

Figure 2.3 Postcard with floats from the Aztec Sun Fête, Phoenix, Arizona, February 1913.

"*Improving" the Hogan* 73

assimilation. But Native American architecture also came under fire for another reason: as a possible source of disease.[24] As historian Nancy Tomes has documented, the concept of "sanitary science" influenced popular attitudes towards illness during the late 19th and into the early 20th centuries. Sanitary science maintains that good health is dependent upon living in homes that are clean, well-aired, and free from the noxious gases associated with faulty plumbing.[25] Many afflictions, including tuberculosis, were termed "house diseases" because it was thought they derived from homes that were dirty and lacked ventilation. It is true that in the late 19th century, medical practitioners were increasingly embracing the "germ theory" – the idea that microbes cause illness.[26] But as sanitation science encountered the germ theory in public discourse, the result was a new approach that continued to argue against dirt and close environments but chiefly because they were thought to harbor germs. Many Native American dwellings rely on earthen construction and contain few openings. These buildings were particularly vulnerable to the criticisms lodged by individuals concerned about improving health on the reservations.

Two early critiques of the poor sanitation in Diné hogans were published in 1904. The February issue of *Home Mission Monthly* included an article entitled "A Navajo Hōghän," which describes the dwelling of an elderly Diné woman.[27] The author, missionary Josephine Brodhead, argued that the living conditions inside the hogan had contributed to the death of its occupant. Of particular note were the open fire, "which filled the hut with smoke so that one's eyes smarted," the bed, which consisted of "an old sheepskin spread on the ground," and a general lack of cleanliness. The article includes two photos: one features a forked-pole hogan similar to the Diné woman's home and the other, a rectangular one-room building with a chimney, which is described as the "Home of Navajo Policeman, showing contrast with the ordinary hōghän" (see Figure 2.4).

To Brodhead, the architecture of the forked-pole hogan justified her appeal for money so that "the children of to-day may know something better for their bodies, souls, and spirits."[28]

During the same year, Dr. Charles J. Logan, agency physician for the Diné, reported, "The principle diseases among them are tuberculosis, due to heredity, and their way of living; rheumatism, due to exposure; and diseases of the eye, due to sand-laden winds and the method of heating their habitations."[29] Although Logan did not elaborate on whether "their way of living" referred to behavioral or environmental factors, he held Diné architecture partially to blame for "diseases of the eye." These afflictions would have included trachoma, which if left untreated, leads to blindness. According to historian Robert A. Trennert, tuberculosis and trachoma were the two diseases reaching epidemic levels among the Diné during the early years of the 20th century.[30] Like tuberculosis, trachoma is caused by bacteria and is transmitted by human secretions; its source was identified as a microorganism in 1907, and in 1938, the federal government discovered that the disease could be healed with sulfanilamide.[31] It is likely that Josephine Brodhead emphasized the hogan's open fire in her article because she also saw it as contributing to chronic eye problems.

74   "Improving" the Hogan

A NAVAJO HŌGHÁN, NEW MEXICO

HOME OF NAVAJO POLICEMAN, SHOWING CONTRAST WITH
THE ORDINARY HŌGHÁN.

Figure 2.4 Illustrations from "A Navajo Hōghän" by Josephine Brodhead.

With few exceptions, during the early decades of the 20th century, the Indian Service continued to treat tuberculosis as a "house disease" which could be prevented by making homes "sanitary." In 1912, President William Howard Taft submitted a message on Indian Affairs to Congress in which he commented on Native American dwellings, writing:

> There are on certain reservations hundreds of Indian homes without either openable windows, floors, or provision for ventilation; and it is on these very reservations that tuberculosis is rife. This is a house disease and thrives best under conditions found in such homes.[32]

President Taft's address likely prompted R.G. Valentine, the commissioner of Indian Affairs, to mail copies of an article entitled "Sanitary Homes for Indians" to the superintendents overseeing the country's Indian reservations.[33] The article was accompanied by a letter asserting, "No question in the Indian Service is of more vital importance than the one discussed in the article in question."[34] The article's author, Edgar B. Meritt, criticized one-room cabins and shacks, as well as traditional Native American dwellings. In their stead, he recommended several model homes for which he provided photographs and plans. The simplest contained two rooms arranged on a "dogtrot" plan, while the most elaborate was a two-story house featuring diamond-paned window sashes with six rooms, a basement, and a sleeping porch.

Louisa Wetherill's "Big Hogan"

In August 1913, former president Theodore Roosevelt traveled to the Wetherill Trading Post, located on the Navajo reservation in Kayenta (*Tó Dínéeshzhee'*), Arizona. There, he prepared for a pack trip to Rainbow Bridge, one of the largest natural bridges in the world. The outing was part of a longer trek across Arizona that included a visit to the mesa-top villages on the Hopi Reservation and a mountain lion hunt on the North Rim of the Grand Canyon. The Wetherill Trading Post was only a staging point, but Roosevelt was so impressed by his stay that he wrote about it in the monthly magazine, *The Outlook*.[35]

Although the ride to Rainbow Bridge was led by John Wetherill, Roosevelt also described his conversations with John's wife, Louisa. Louisa Wade Wetherill was renowned for her mastery of the Navajo language and for the close friendship she maintained with the Native Americans who frequented the post.[36] She was fascinated by the Indigenous cultures of northern Arizona; she collected oral narratives from the Diné and assembled a significant ethnobotanical collection. According to Roosevelt, "Mrs. Wetherill was not only versed in archaeological lore concerning ruins and the like, she was also versed in the yet stranger and more interesting archaeology of the Indian's own mind and soul."[37]

76   *"Improving" the Hogan*

In *The Outlook*, the former president expounded his ideas about Indian education. He spoke against the kinds of homes that Alice Fletcher had promoted, arguing, "The Indian should be encouraged to build a better house; but the house must not be too different from his present dwelling, or he will, *as a rule*, neither build it nor live in it."[38] As an alternative, Roosevelt presented a different kind of model home, conceived by Louisa Wetherill, that he argued would be much more likely to succeed:

> One of her hopes is to establish a "model hogan," an Indian home both advanced and possible for the Navajos now to live up to – a half-way house on the road to higher civilization, a house in which, for instance, the Indian girl will be taught to wash in a tub with a pail of water heated at the fire; it is utterly useless to teach her to wash in a laundry with steam and cement bathtubs and expect her to apply this knowledge on a reservation.[39]

Roosevelt was so convinced by Louisa Wetherill's idea for a "half-way house," he even included an appeal for contributions to pay for it. The article, which included an enthusiastic review of the accommodations in Kayenta, helped to make the trading post famous.

Roosevelt's ringing endorsement of Louisa Wetherill's "model hogan" almost certainly prompted donations to help with its construction, although in 1921, the building was still in the planning stages.[40] But by the fall of 1923, the "Big Hogan" had become a reality. According to William Dory, who wrote about it for the magazine, *Natural History*:

> There is crying need on the reservations generally for more physicians, nurses, and hospitals. Wide Navajo land has but few. Mr. and Mrs. Wetherill have built a "big hogan" as an infirmary, and also as an example of what a hogan might be, where Navajo could cook over an open fire, as usual, yet have more room to keep their belongings neatly and a chimney to prevent injury to the eyes from smoke. Mrs. Wetherill said they liked it very much.[41]

The hogan, which was located on the north side of the trading post, was a large female hogan, plastered with earth and roofed with a corbelled dome (see Figure 2.5).

An article by Marda Mackendrick in the June 1923 issue of *Sunset* magazine profiled Louisa Wetherill. In "'Mother' of the Navajos," Wetherill maintained that trachoma was attributable to smoke and argued that the chimney was an aid to good health. She reiterated the importance of model hogans and argued that Diné students should be given an education that would prepare them for life on the reservation:

> Don't send them to far-off schools to learn things of no use to them. Give them home teachers who will show them how to live healthily in their hogans, not try to force them in one inadequate step from primitive life to modern efficiency. Make the hogan "the half-way house on the road to civilization." The rest will follow.[42]

"Improving" the Hogan 77

Figure 2.5 Louisa Wetherill's "Big Hogan," Kayenta, Arizona, c. 1920s.

During the same year, the Eastern Association on Indian Affairs published a bulletin called *Medical Problems of our Indian Population*. The bulletin reprinted a speech by Frederick L. Hoffman, a statistician, and it signaled an important change in public attitudes towards the Diné hogan. Hoffman observed:

> The housing question on Indian reservations and settlements calls in many directions for radical changes and reforms. There are reasons for believing that some of the old native houses as, for illustration, the "hogan" on the Navaho reservation is better adapted to the Indian's needs in his present state of civilization than the frame building of modern construction.[43]

Hoffman added that the hogan "could be improved upon decidedly in the light of a careful study of the Indian's habits and needs." But his position significantly revised the statements of earlier reformers who had urged the abandonment of traditional forms of Native American architecture. The bulletin, published by one of the largest Indian rights organizations in the country, affirmed a more broad-minded approach that would become increasingly influential over the next few years.

78 *"Improving" the Hogan*

Reassessing the Relationship Between the Hogan and Disease

In June 1926, Secretary of the Interior Hubert Work commissioned a privately funded organization, the Institute for Government Research, to survey the economic and social condition of American Indians.[44] The Institute's director, W.F. Willoughby, selected Lewis Meriam to lead a team of nine experts on a wide array of topics relating to Indian affairs. For seven months, the group traveled across the country and investigated the living conditions of Native Americans. Their comments and analysis were subsequently combined into a document known as the Meriam Report, which was presented to Secretary Work in February 1928.

In the report's chapter on health, Herbert R. Edwards, medical field secretary for the National Tuberculosis Association, wrote that the federal government "has recognized two great health problems, probably the outstanding two, namely tuberculosis and trachoma."[45] Amongst the factors he listed as influencing health, Edwards included "Environment" and commented on several aspects he found to be particularly troubling. The first was the cleanliness of Indian homes, which he attributed to water being in short supply. Edwards also described overcrowding as "a serious problem," aggravated by conditions where "whole family groups sleep on the ground and privacy is unknown." But he added that some types of Native American architecture compensated for this issue, noting:

> For the most part, the dwellings in the Southwest are of a temporary nature, the hogan, wickiup, tepee or tent. That the primitive dwellings are temporary is in one sense a great blessing, for they are abandoned lightly and new clean ones constructed elsewhere, thus curtailing the spread of disease, which even so is inevitable under the existing conditions of overcrowding.[46]

He concluded that "scarcity of water, overcrowding, lack of adequate ventilation, careless disposition of sewage, and exclusion of sunshine are almost universal in the typical Indian dwelling."[47]

Meriam's group also endorsed a 1924 report by Florence Patterson – a nurse working for the Red Cross – that described health conditions on Indian reservations in the Southwest.[48] In 1928, Patterson appeared before a Senate subcommittee and testified, "health conditions are serious, and the measures and methods used in improving these conditions are in no way comparable with the provisions made for the protection of health generally in the United States."[49] But her evaluation of the Diné hogans that she visited in the Western Navajo and Hopi jurisdictions in Arizona was resoundingly positive. Patterson recounted the observations she had made in 1924 and remarked:

> The Navajo had a very distinctive type of home known as the hogan, which was constructed of logs and covered with mud on the exterior. It was built in the shape of a dome with a circular opening in the top which acted as both window and chimney. This type of dwelling seemed to be

very satisfactory as far as a 1-room home as primitive as this could be. It was warm, fairly well ventilated, and allowed for the escape of the camp-fire smoke, and admitted both light and sunshine. Across the desert, these homes look like small mounds of dirt which were often miles apart and miles from a road.[50]

Mary Louise Mark, a professor of sociology at Ohio State University, authored the section on "Family and Community Life and the Activities of Women" in the Meriam Report.[51] Mark commented that the most common "primitive dwellings" among Indians in the United States were the Diné hogan, the Apache wikiup, and "the brush or cactus house of the less progressive Pimas and Papagos."[52] Mark considered Pueblo buildings to be more sophisticated and described them as a "development from an earlier civilization." Among other Native American tribes, she noted, "the tent, the nondescript shack usually of rough lumber, and the log house have generally replaced the earlier dwellings."[53]

Mark's analysis paid particular attention to overcrowding. "Room congestion" was exacerbated by traditional cultural patterns in which homes were shared with extended family members and friends, people slept on the ground, and long-term guests were common. The Meriam Commission visited 366 Native American homes and found that 54.5% averaged two or more persons per room, 32.8% averaged three of more persons per room, 23.2% averaged four or more persons per room, 16.9% averaged five or more persons per room, and 11.5% averaged six or more persons per room. In these environments, Mark argued that "cleanliness and order" were a challenge to maintain.[54] In fact, she acknowledged that the circumstances facing homemakers frequently ranged from difficult to impossible. Water, for example, was often scarce and had to be hauled from a distance.

But Mark did not recommend abandoning traditional Native American dwellings for Euro-American–style houses. While she did suggest that "homes could be enlarged by the building of other rooms," she also acknowledged the importance of tribal traditions. In a long passage weighing the advantages and disadvantages of "congestion," Mark reasoned:

> The Indian's wider sense of close relationship as well as his feeling of responsibility for all the members of his clan and race may be a fundamental spiritual necessity even though it results in crowding his home with relatives and friends and making it anything but a place of peace and quiet.[55]

For Mark, the deciding factor was not assimilation but rather, the general well-being of Native Americans.

Model Hogans at Schools on the Navajo Reservation, 1922–1931

Between 1909 and 1935, the Navajo reservation was divided into six administrative jurisdictions, with five separate Navajo agencies as well as an agency for the Hopi reservation.[56] In 1912, when Samuel Stacher received a copy of Edgar

80 *"Improving" the Hogan*

Meritt's article, "Sanitation in Indian Homes," from Commissioner of Indian Affairs R.G. Valentine, he had been serving as superintendent of the Eastern Navajo Agency, based in Crownpoint (*T'iis Ts'óóz Nídeeshgiizh*), New Mexico, for only three years. Stacher responded to Valentine that he was making every effort to persuade the Indians within the agency to aspire to the architecture "of the best houses by the progressive whites in the country."[57] But ten years later, Stacher filed a report on "Home Building" to the Office of Indian Affairs (OIA) that was much more pragmatic about the conditions facing the Diné he had been appointed to oversee. In a passage offering a rare glimpse into the domestic arrangements of the Navajo living in western New Mexico during the early 1920s, he wrote:

> The pastoral people of the desert are nearly always concerned about range and water for their herds and these necessities compel them to move about and live a sort of semi-nomadic life, living in the warmer weather in a hastily constructed shelter made of boughs and in the winter each family may have several hogans in different localities to which they move as water, range and climatic conditions may require, so that the construction of substantial houses has not concerned many of the Indians. He makes use of the material at hand, with perhaps no outlay of money or but little. The hogan is well ventilated and serves the Indians' purpose.

But Stacher insisted he was doing what he could to implement the OIA's housing policies, especially with regard to improving Native American health. As evidence, he described the model hogan that he and his staff had created:

> We equipped a hogan with beds, table, cupboard, benches and have mentioned the desirability of getting up from the floor and eating from a table while sitting on bench or chair and keeping food from flies.

But the furnishings in the model hogan had proved impractical for the Diné, and he continued:

> The Indians say that the average hogan is not large enough to accommodate this equipment and have room for the average family. There are quite a number who now have cook stoves or heaters, and beds, with the stoves their [sic] is no smoke in the hogan to irritate or aggravate eye trouble. Beautification of exterior premises cannot receive attention by trees and lawn planting as there is no water near the Indian home as he must haul water often from long distance.

Stacher concluded with an observation that at first might seem unimportant, writing:

> The Navahoes like to have pictures displayed on the walls of their humble homes but further than this the contours of the hogans do not permit of much decoration.[58]

"Improving" the Hogan 81

But this detail confirms that straight walls were not yet typical in 1922 and that hogans constructed with them – such as the stacked-log hogan – had yet to attain a significant presence in the eastern part of the reservation.

The 1920s were a time of great change, judging from Stacher's report on "Constructive Accomplishments," filed in 1926. That year, a new model hogan was added to the boarding school in Crownpoint. Unlike the earlier model hogan, which had been adapted from an existing structure, this building was constructed from the ground up with "materials on hand." It included utensils and "a fireplace, stove, cupboard, bed, table." The hogan was used for teaching home economics at the school, and Stacher claimed that "many Indians have viewed this home and are copying same for themselves."[59]

By mid-1927, the boarding school at the Northern Navajo Agency's headquarters in Shiprock (*Tsé Bit'a'í*), New Mexico, possessed "an improved hogan" that could be loaded onto a wagon to serve as a mobile exhibit.[60] But the most radically designed model hogan of this era was constructed in 1928 on the grounds of the boarding school at Leupp (*Tółchíí' Kooh*), Arizona. As early as May 1926, the school was holding classes in first aid in a model hogan equipped with simple medical supplies.[61] By the following year, the school's superintendent, W.O. Roberts, had constructed another hogan for teaching cooking and sewing.[62] The building was a hexagonal stacked-log hogan plastered with earth. Like the example at Crownpoint, it contained furniture, including benches, a chest, a cupboard, and a makeshift table made from a board placed on boxes. All of the furnishings were created by students. According to Roberts, his intention was to give them training they could use when they returned to their homes on the reservation.

In July 1927, John G. Hunter was appointed superintendent of the Leupp Navajo Agency in Arizona. While in Leupp, Hunter's greatest achievement would be to initiate the Navajo chapter system, the primary form of local governance among the Diné.[63] But by the end of February 1928, Hunter had also supervised the construction of the most innovative model hogan to date. While other Navajo superintendents had used hogans primarily to demonstrate new furnishings and equipment, this building was meant to be an object lesson in architecture. According to a local newspaper, its walls were of rock, "instead of brush and adobe as the old hogans were made," a fireplace replaced the smoke hole, and it had two rooms rather than one.[64] Hunter's hogan integrated traditional Diné building techniques with Euro-American elements in an entirely new way.

By November 1931, the Mapel Public School, located south of Gallup, had completed a hogan dormitory so that Diné children could stay and continue their education during the winter months when transportation from their homes was difficult. A local telephone company supplied the logs for the building, Diné parents helped to put it up, and the remaining construction expenses (which were "slight") were financed by Euro-Americans living in the school district. Mrs. F.O. Shepard, the teacher who directed the project, described the dormitory as "a model hogan" and explained:

we hope that the reservation Indians may find the arrangement so interesting that they will add to their comfort and sanitation by applying the same principle of arrangement in their own hogans.[65]

82   *"Improving" the Hogan*

The hogan was a hexagonal stacked-log hogan and covered 519 square feet, with "large airy double windows" located in each of its 14-foot-long sides. The interior was divided into three rooms: a living room and kitchen area occupied half of the space, while separate bedrooms for six girls and six boys were located in the other half. Three fireplaces – one for each room – opened out of a central chimney and provided heat for the building. Shepard did not identify the hogan's sanitary aspects, but they likely included the air circulation provided by windows and a separate kitchen that helped keep insects and rodents away from sleeping areas. The fireplaces would have channeled smoke out of the building's interior and helped to ventilate the building.

The Federal Government and Native American Architecture, 1925–1932

But while schools in and around the Navajo reservation were working to "improve" the hogan, the Office of Indian Affairs in Washington was rather less open-minded about traditional Native American architecture. In 1926, the government sent out a 32-page booklet entitled *Plans and Specifications for Indian Homes and Improvements* to reservations across the country. The booklet featured buildings constructed between 1923 and 1926 on the Kiowa reservation in Oklahoma.[66] All of the houses were single-story, Craftsman-style bungalows, ranging in size from two to six rooms. The booklet also included plans for a poultry house, outhouse, and several barns.

Although the booklet offered no rationale for encouraging Indians to construct these buildings, in his annual report for 1928, Commissioner of Indian Affairs Charles H. Burke explained "that substantial houses, well ventilated and constructed, with due regard to sanitary requirements, are the best preventives against disease and the highest incentive to good morals and industrial advancement." He specifically mentioned his hopes for the Navajo reservation and voiced his expectation "that the next five years will show a rapid change from the present dirt hogan to a class of homes of which the Navajos may well be proud."[67]

By March 1929, Edgar B. Meritt had been appointed as the assistant commissioner of Indian Affairs. That month, Meritt, who had authored "Sanitary Homes for Indians" in 1912, sent out a circular letter to Indian agency superintendents recommending that they use *Plans and Specifications for Indian Homes and Improvements* as a guide for new construction on the reservations. He claimed, "the health, education, and economic conditions of a family are materially improved by having a home."[68] In 1933, Meritt came very close to becoming Franklin Delano Roosevelt's commissioner of Indian Affairs. But his attitude towards Native American architecture exemplified an "old-school" assimilationism that would place him firmly in the crosshairs of John Collier. Collier, who was appointed as commissioner in April of that year, laid his competition to rest by aggressively attacking Meritt.[69] And as we shall see in Chapter 4, under Collier, the federal Office of Indian Affairs initiated a program for building model hogans that would embrace traditional Diné architecture while also seeking to "improve" it.

"Improving" the Hogan 83

In 1929, President Herbert Hoover appointed Charles J. Rhoads and J. Henry Scattergood to succeed Burke and serve as co-commissioners.[70] The pair worked to implement many of the reforms recommended by the Meriam Report, and they were widely viewed as heralding a new day in Indian policy. In their annual report for 1931, Rhoads and Scattergood discussed the efforts made by home extension agents to address sanitation and nutrition in Indian homes and specifically mentioned the successes they had achieved in persuading Native Americans to use chairs and beds and eat on tables.[71] In their annual report for 1932, a section on "Home Extension Work" opened by declaring:

> In conducting home extension work the field staff has endeavored to keep in mind the cultural values of the past. In order to avoid the disintegration of family life by the introduction of our own culture and practices too rapidly, the introduction of new materials is in terms of their culture with only very small elements of our own.[72]

The sensitivity displayed in the report was nothing short of revolutionary and represented a reversal of earlier assimilative policies.

Following the creation of the Meriam Commission in 1926, several other efforts were made to examine the living conditions of Native Americans. John Collier was instrumental to the passage of a congressional resolution in February 1928 leading to a series of investigations and hearings that were recorded in a document entitled *Survey of Conditions*.[73] The survey, which began in 1928 and ended in 1943, eventually produced thousands of pages of text organized into 41 separate parts.[74] Part 18 took place on the Navajo reservation during April and May 1931, when a subcommittee of the Senate Committee on Indian Affairs held hearings at 13 different locations in Arizona and New Mexico.

On several occasions during the hearings, Senator Burton Wheeler inquired about the availability of lumber for building Euro-American–style houses. At Fort Defiance, Arizona, he questioned John G. Hunter, who had left the Leupp Navajo Agency to become superintendent of the Southern Navajo Agency at the beginning of 1929. After Hunter stated that most Diné lived in hogans, Senator Wheeler asked, "Do most of these Indians, or do many of the Indians want better homes?" Hunter answered, "I would say at least 75 percent of them want better homes. Probably the percentage is greater than that."[75] Senator Wheeler equated "better homes" with wood-frame construction, and he proposed that the government sawmill provide free milled lumber "for the purpose of building better homes."[76] Later during the same day, Senator Wheeler remarked:

> A 2-room house would be better than a hogan. It does seem to me that if you can supply timber to the Indians to build homes with and let them build the houses themselves or help them to build the houses, you ought to do everything possible in order to let them have the lumber.

84   *"Improving" the Hogan*

Figure 2.6 The Kinlichee Chapter House dedication ceremony, Kinlichee, Arizona, 1931, photographed by Donald E. Harbison.

When he was told that that timber was plentiful and that the Diné could have logs planed at a nearby sawmill, Senator Wheeler instructed Hunter, "Explain that to them and get them to build their houses and see if you can get others to explain it to them, too."[77]

In May 1931, Hunter readily agreed with Senator Wheeler that the Diné should be encouraged to build houses and declared that "better homes" would increase the Diné self-respect and "develop their pride and improve other conditions that relate to their welfare."[78] Hunter's desire to encourage Euro-American–style "better homes" on the reservation may have inspired the housing exhibit constructed for the 1931 dedication of the Kinlichee (*Kin Łichíí'*) Chapter House in Arizona (see Figure 2.6). Chapter houses on the Navajo reservation serve as a place for chapter organizations and other community groups to meet.

In the exhibit, three different hogans were arranged in a row with the "earliest form at left" (a forked-pole hogan), followed by a corbelled hogan plastered with mud, and a "modern" octagonal stacked-log hogan, with a corbelled dome. To the right of the three hogans was the chapter house, a rectangular log building with a hipped roof. The object lesson here seems to have been that the chapter house represented the most advanced form of architecture and one that should be emulated.

Model Hogans and the Presbyterian Mission to the Navajo

The federal employees who worked in Navajoland during the Interwar Period were caught between the realities of life on the reservation and the policies laid down by their superiors in Washington. During the late 1920s, Superintendent Billie P. Six worked to persuade the Indians living in the Northern Navajo Agency to build "new sanitary homes," but he was unable to disguise his pessimism about the prospects for success. In his annual report for 1929, he observed:

> The Navajo Hogan will probably remain on this reservation for many, many years. It is a very convenient mode of living as far as the Indian is concerned, and I find that even the Indians who have constructed good houses leave those houses during certain periods of the year to live in their hogans. Not until it becomes possible to convert the Navajo Indians from a pastoral to an agricultural people will it be possible to induce them to discontinue living in the hogans.[79]

Christian missionaries who worked on the reservation found themselves in a similar predicament. The Presbyterian Church was among the earliest Christian denominations to evangelize among the Diné. In 1868, the Presbyterians founded a mission in Jewett, New Mexico, and the following year, they sponsored the first teacher to work at the reservation's first government school in Fort Defiance.[80] In 1901, a more centrally located site for the mission was established at Ganado, Arizona. Dr. Clarence Salsbury arrived there in 1927 to embark on a long career that would bring him national attention as the founder of the first nursing school for Native American women.[81] In 1937, Salsbury published an article in which he dismissed the hogan as a "hut" and associated it with poor health.[82] But several years earlier, during the fall of 1932, the mission constructed an octagonal stacked-log hogan for Diné visitors to stay overnight (see Figure 2.7).

Figure 2.7 A guest hogan at the Ganado Presbyterian Mission, Ganado, Arizona, c. 1934.

86 *"Improving" the Hogan*

The *Ganado News Bulletin* – the mission's newsletter – described the building as "a model hogan, with a fireplace and windows, plastered inside and very neatly formed and framed by a former schoolboy."[83] The lumber for the building had been milled, and the dirt covering the roof was contained with a fascia that extended outward to create an overhanging eave. Constructed by a young Diné man who had received a boarding school education, the hogan represented a work of hybrid architecture in almost every regard.

In April 1934, the *Bulletin* reported on the construction of a second model hogan by the church, this one at the mission's branch in Tselani (*Tsé Łání*), Arizona. The building, another stacked-log hogan, was constructed by 40 Diné men and equipped with two windows and a stove. According to the author of the article, "This hogan, besides being a shelter for overnight guests should help the people to see how they can improve their own hogans and make them more comfortable with things that they can easily make."[84]

Clearly, there were still many people who would have preferred the Diné live in Euro-American–style homes. As we have seen, much of the opposition to the hogan arose from longstanding misconceptions about the nature of diseases like tuberculosis and trachoma. Other criticisms revealed a prejudice against dwellings that differed from the houses favored by mainstream American society. But by the early 1930s, it was apparent that the Diné hogan had survived and was not going to fade away. What is more, the stacked-log hogan was well on its way to becoming the basis for further developments in hogan architecture.

Notes

1 Theo. H. Dodd, in Charles E. Mix, "Annual Report on Indian Affairs by the Acting Commissioner," in Orville H. Browning, *Annual Report of the Secretary of the Interior* (Washington, DC: GPO, 1867), 201.

2 For more background on "the fear of living in a house in which one has died," described by Dodd, see Stephen C. Jett and Virginia E. Spencer, *Navajo Architecture: Forms, History, Distributions* (Tucson: University of Arizona Press, 1981), 28.

3 Ulysses S. Grant, in US Board of Indian Commissioners, *Annual Report of the United States Board of Indian Commissioners* (Washington, DC: GPO, 1870), 5.

4 *Annual Report of the United States Board of Indian Commissioners*, 9–10.

5 L. Edwin Dudley, in Edw. P. Smith, "Report of the Commissioner of Indian Affairs," in *Annual Report of the Secretary of the Interior,* ed. Columbus Delano (Washington, DC: GPO, 1873), 635.

6 Alex G. Irvine, in J.Q. Smith, "Report of the Commissioner of Indian Affairs," in *Annual Report of the Secretary of the Interior*, ed. Zachariah Chandler (Washington, DC: GPO, 1876), 514.

7 John H. Bowman, in J.D.C. Atkins, *Annual Report of the Commissioner of Indian Affairs, 1885* (Washington, DC: GPO, 1885), 154.

8 G.W. Hayzlett, in William A. Jones, *Annual Report of the Commissioner of Indian Affairs, 1900* (Washington, DC: GPO, 1900), 192.

9 Gwendolyn Wright, *Moralism and the Model Home: Domestic Architecture and Cultural Conflict in Chicago, 1873–1913* (Chicago: University of Chicago Press, 1980), 9.

10 Dell Upton, "Pattern Books and Professionalism: Aspects of the Transformation of Domestic Architecture in America, 1800–1860," *Winterthur Portfolio* 19, no. 2/3 (Summer–Autumn 1984): 108.

"Improving" the Hogan 87

11 Clifford Edward Clark, Jr., *The American Family Home: 1800–1960* (Chapel Hill: University of North Carolina Press, 1986), 15.
12 Upton, "Pattern Books and Professionalism," 127–128, and Clark, *The American Family Home*, 28. See also Dolores Hayden, *The Grand Domestic Revolution: A History of Feminist Designs for American Homes, Neighborhoods, and Cities* (Cambridge, MA: MIT Press, 1981).
13 David Handlin, *The American Home: Architecture and Society, 1815–1915* (Boston: Little, Brown and Company, 1979), 70; Wright, *Moralism and the Model Home*, 152.
14 In later years, Fletcher would become a highly influential ethnographer of Native American culture, but during the early 1880s, she focused her considerable energy on Indian policy reform and the promotion of assimilation.
15 E.G. [Elaine Goodale], "Incidents of Indian Life at Hampton," *Southern Workman* 13, no. 3 (March 1884): 32; J.R. [Josephine Richards], "Indian Incidents – Our Indian House Warming," *Southern Workman* 13, no. 4 (April 1884): 43; "Indian School," *Southern Workman* 13, no. 6 (June 1884): 68. The authors of these articles are identified in W. Roger Buffalohead and Paulette Fairbanks Molin, "'A Nucleus of Civilization': American Indian Families at Hampton Institute in the Late Nineteenth Century," *Journal of American Indian Education* 35, no. 3 (Spring 1996): 67.
16 "Indian School."
17 Buffalohead and Molin, "A Nucleus of Civilization," 59, 71.
18 Joan Mark, *A Stranger in Her Native Land: Alice Fletcher and the American Indians* (Lincoln: University of Nebraska Press, 1988), 109; Jane E. Simonsen, *Making Home Work: Domesticity and Native American Assimilation in the American West, 1860–1919* (Chapel Hill: University of North Carolina Press, 2006), 81–85. According to Mark and Simonsen, the exhibit included 16 photographs, two pen-and-ink drawings, and a map (which showed the progress of allotment on the Omaha Reservation).
19 Alice Fletcher, *Historical Sketch of the Omaha Tribe of Indians in Nebraska* (Washington, DC: Judd & Detweiler, 1885), 2, 12.
20 This picture was "#11 of the Exhibit." See Fletcher, *Historical Sketch of the Omaha Tribe of Indians in Nebraska*, 8–9.
21 Joseph Henry Broker, "Home Building for Indians," *The Carlisle Arrow* 9, no. 36 (May 16, 1913): 15 (photographs); 18–19.
22 "All Arizona Celebrates First Anniversary of Statehood on Broad Streets of Capital," *Arizona Republic*, February 15, 1913.
23 "Aztec Sun Fête," *The Native American* [Phoenix Indian School] 14, no. 8 (February 22, 1913): 115–116.
24 See, for example, Ely Samuel Parker's comments on Winnebago dwellings in "Report of the Commissioner of Indian Affairs," in *Annual Report of the Secretary of the Interior*, ed. Jacob D. Cox (Washington, DC: GPO, 1869), 472.
25 Nancy Tomes, *The Gospel of Germs: Men, Women, and the Microbe in American Life* (Cambridge, MA: Harvard University Press, 1998), 8, 57.
26 Tomes, *The Gospel of Germs*, 5–6.
27 Josephine Phelps Brodhead, "A Navajo Hōghän," *Home Mission Monthly* 18, no. 4 (February 1904): 84–85. *Home Mission Monthly* was published by the Woman's Executive Committee of Home Missions of the Presbyterian Church.
28 Brodhead, "A Navajo Hōghän," 84–85.
29 Charles J. Logan, in Reuben Perry, "Report of School Superintendent in Charge of Navaho Agency," in William A. Jones, *Annual Reports of the Department of the Interior, Fiscal Year Ended June 30, 1904 – Indian Affairs, Part I. Report of the Commissioner and Appendixes* (Washington, DC: GPO, 1905), 142.
30 Robert A. Trennert, *White Man's Medicine: Government Doctors and the Navajo, 1863–1955* (Albuquerque: University of New Mexico Press, 1998), 100.
31 Robert A. Trennert, "Indian Sore Eyes: The Federal Campaign to Control Trachoma in the Southwest, 1910–1940," *Journal of the Southwest* 32, no. 2 (Summer 1990): 142.

88 *"Improving" the Hogan*

32 William Howard Taft, in Robert G. Valentine, "Report of the Commissioner of Indian Affairs," in *Reports of the Department of the Interior for the Fiscal Year Ended June 30, 1912*, vol. II (Washington, DC: GPO, 1913), 22.

33 Edgar B. Meritt, "Sanitary Homes for Indians," *The Red Man* 4, no. 10 (June 1912): 439–450.

34 R.G. Valentine, "Circular 678 – Sanitary Homes for Indians," Box 9, E. Navajo CCF-NARA-R.

35 Theodore Roosevelt, "Across the Navajo Desert," *Outlook* 105 (October 11, 1913): 309–317.

36 Mary Apolline Comfort, *Rainbow to Yesterday: The John and Louisa Wetherill Story* (New York: Vantage Press, 1979), 74, 174.

37 Roosevelt, "Across the Navajo Desert," 316.

38 Roosevelt, "Across the Navajo Desert," 315. The emphasis is original to Roosevelt's article.

39 Roosevelt, "Across the Navajo Desert," 316.

40 In June of that year, Evelina C. Verplanck sent money to Louisa Wetherill for the project; Evelina C. Verplanck to Mrs. Wetherill, June 29, 1921, collection of Harvey Leake.

41 William Dory, "Navajo Land," *Natural History* 23, no. 5 (September–October 1923): 505.

42 Marda Mackendrick, "'Mother' of the Navajos," *Sunset* 50, no. 6 (June 1923): 61–62.

43 Frederick L. Hoffman, *Medical Problems of Our Indian Population*, Eastern Association on Indian Affairs, Inc., Bulletin No. 6 (Eastern Association on Indian Affairs, 1925), SAR.

44 Lewis Meriam, et al., *The Problem of Indian Administration* (Baltimore: Johns Hopkins Press, 1928), vii.

45 Meriam, et al., *The Problem of Indian Administration*, 192.

46 Meriam, et al., *The Problem of Indian Administration*, 219–220.

47 Meriam, et al., *The Problem of Indian Administration*, 220.

48 Randolph C. Downes, "A Crusade for Indian Reform, 1922–1934," *The Mississippi Valley Historical Review* 32, no. 3 (December 1945): 347.

49 Florence Patterson, "A Study of the Need for Public-Health Nursing on Indian Reservations" [Exhibit no. 143], in US Senate, Committee on Indian Affairs, Subcommittee on Senate Resolution 79, *Survey of Conditions of the Indians in the United States* [*SOC*], Part 3, December 12–13, 1928, and January 7–10 and 14–17, 1929 (Washington, DC: GPO, 1929), 1001.

50 Patterson, "A Study of the Need for Public-Health Nursing on Indian Reservations," in *SOC*, Part 3, 977.

51 Francis Paul Prucha, *The Great Father: The United States Government and the American Indians*, vol. II (Lincoln: University of Nebraska Press, 1984), 809n37.

52 Meriam, et al., *The Problem of Indian Administration*, 553.

53 Meriam, et al., *The Problem of Indian Administration*, 553.

54 Meriam, et al., *The Problem of Indian Administration*, 555, 561–562.

55 Meriam, et al., *The Problem of Indian Administration*, 567.

56 The jurisdictions included the Hopi Agency (1899, originally called the Moqui reservation), administered from Keams Canyon, Arizona; the Western Navajo Agency (1901), administered from Tuba City, Arizona; the Southern Navajo Agency (1903, also known as the Navajo Agency), administered from Fort Defiance, Arizona; the Northern Navajo Agency (1903, also known as the San Juan Agency), administered from Shiprock, New Mexico; the Leupp Navajo Agency (1908), administered from Leupp, Arizona; and the Eastern Navajo Agency (1909, also known as the Pueblo Bonito Agency), administered from Crownpoint, New Mexico. For details and a map showing the agency boundaries, see Garrick Bailey and Roberta Glenn Bailey, *A History of the Navajos: The Reservation Years* (Santa Fe, NM: School of American Research Press, 1986), 107–108.

57 "Superintendent to Commissioner of Indian Affairs [Circular #678 – Sanitary Homes for Indians]," October 24, 1912, Box 9, E. Navajo CCF-NARA-R.

"Improving" the Hogan 89

58 "Superintendent to Commissioner of Indian Affairs [Cir.1819 – Ind[ustrial]-Program]," November 9, 1922, Box 12, E. Navajo CCF-NARA-R.

59 "Circular 2518, Constructive Accomplishments, 1926," Box 14, E. Navajo CCF-NARA-R.

60 Charles H. Burke, *Extracts from the Annual Report of the Secretary of the Interior Fiscal Year 1927 Relating to the Bureau of Indian Affairs* (Washington, DC: GPO, 1927), 10.

61 "Leupp School Girls Demonstrate First Aid," *Coconino Sun*, May 21, 1926.

62 "Navajo Maidens at Leupp Now Being Given Practical Training in Household Arts," *Coconino Sun*, February 11, 1927; "Leupp Navajo Indians Have Achievement Day," *Coconino Sun*, June 10, 1927.

63 Aubrey W. Williams, Jr., *Navajo Political Process* (Washington, DC: Smithsonian Institution Press, 1970), 1.

64 "Leupp Indians to Plant Thousands Irrigated Acres," *Winslow* [AZ] *Daily Mail*, February 28, 1928.

65 "Model Navajo Hogan Erected for a School," *Albuquerque Journal*, November 6, 1931.

66 Charles H. Burke, *Extracts from the Annual Report of the Secretary of the Interior Fiscal Year 1927 Relating to the Bureau of Indian Affairs*, 16; *Plans and Specifications for Indian Homes and Improvements* (Chilocco, OK: Chilocco Indian Agricultural School, 1926), Box 46, E. Navajo CCF-NARA-R.

67 Charles H. Burke, *Extracts from the Annual Report of the Secretary of the Interior Fiscal Year 1928 Relating to the Bureau of Indian Affairs* (Washington, DC: GPO, 1928), 19.

68 Edgar B. Meritt, "Circular No. 2563 – Home Improvements, Repair and Upkeep," March 9, 1929, Box 15, E. Navajo CCF-NARA-R.

69 Lawrence C. Kelly, "Choosing the New Deal Indian Commissioner: Ickes vs. Collier," *New Mexico Historical Review* 49, no. 4 (1974): 283.

70 Prucha, *The Great Father*, vol. II, 923. J. Henry Scattergood was technically the assistant commissioner, but both men signed the office's reports together.

71 Charles J. Rhoads and J. Henry Scattergood, *Annual Report of the Commissioner of Indian Affairs* (Washington, DC: GPO, 1931), 18.

72 Charles J. Rhoads and J. Henry Scattergood, *Annual Report of the Commissioner of Indian Affairs* (Washington, DC: GPO, 1932), 14.

73 For more on Collier's role in the passage of the resolution, see Kenneth R. Philp, *John Collier's Crusade for Indian Reform, 1920–1954* (Tucson: University of Arizona Press, 1977), 82–84.

74 Prucha, *The Great Father*, vol. II, 812–813.

75 US Senate, Committee on Indian Affairs, Subcommittee on Senate Resolution 79, *Survey of Conditions of the Indians in the United States* [*SOC*], Part 18, April 27–30 and May 15–20, 1931 (Washington, DC: GPO, 1932), 9158. The hearings at Fort Defiance were held on May 16.

76 *SOC*, Part 18, 9159.

77 *SOC*, Part 18, 9265.

78 *SOC*, Part 18, 9158–9159.

79 B.P. Six, "Circular 2570 – Annual Report, 1929," *Roll 93*, SANSR-NARA-NAB.

80 Michael J. Warner, "Protestant Missionary Activity Among the Navajo, 1890–1912," *New Mexico Historical Review* 45, no. 3 (1970): 213–214, 223.

81 See, for example, Webb Waldron, "Big White Medicine Man," *Christian Century* 58 (October 15, 1941): 1271–1273, and Oren Arnold, "Sagebrush Surgeon," *Saturday Evening Post* 217, no. 21 (November 18, 1944): 16–17, 67, 69, 70. The Sage Memorial Hospital School of Nursing at Ganado was listed as a National Historic Landmark in 2009.

82 Clarence Salsbury, "Christ Comes to the Navajo," *Missionary Review of the World* 60 (February 1937): 76.

83 "Our Hogan," *Ganado News Bulletin*, 4, no. 1 (January 1933): 3, GNBC-UA.

84 E.P., "A Need Supplied," *Ganado News Bulletin* 5, no. 2 (April 1934): 2, GNBC-UA.

90 *"Improving" the Hogan*

Reference List

Archival Sources

Eastern Navajo Central Classified Files, RG 75, Records of the BIA, National Archives and Records Administration, Riverside, California. Cited as E. Navajo CCF-NARA-R.

Ganado News Bulletin Collection, University of Arizona Libraries, Special Collections, Tucson, Arizona. Cited as GNBC-UA.

School for Advanced Research Archives, Santa Fe, New Mexico. Cited as SAR.

Superintendent's Annual Narrative and Statistical Reports from Field Jurisdictions of the Bureau of Indian Affairs, 1907–1938, Record Group 75, Records of the BIA, National Archives Microfilm Publications, Microfilm Publication M1011, 1975, National Archives and Records Administration. Cited as SANSA-NARA-NAB.

Published Sources

Atkins, J.D.C. *Annual Report of the Commissioner of Indian Affairs, 1885*. Washington, DC: GPO, 1885.

"Aztec Sun Fête." *The Native American* [Phoenix Indian School] 14, no. 8 (February 22, 1913): 115–116.

Bailey, Garrick, and Roberta Glenn Bailey. *A History of the Navajos: The Reservation Years.* Santa Fe, NM: School of American Research Press, 1986.

Brodhead, Josephine Phelps. "A Navajo Hóghän." *Home Mission Monthly* 18, no. 4 (February 1904): 84–85.

Broker, Joseph Henry. "Home Building for Indians." *The Carlisle Arrow* 9, no. 36 (May 16, 1913): 18–19.

Browning, Orville H., ed. *Annual Report of the Secretary of the Interior, 1867*. Washington, DC: GPO, 1867.

Buffalohead, W. Roger, and Paulette Fairbanks Molin. "'A Nucleus of Civilization': American Indian Families at Hampton Institute in the Late Nineteenth Century." *Journal of American Indian Education* 35, no. 3 (Spring 1996).

Burke, Charles H. *Extracts from the Annual Report of the Secretary of the Interior Fiscal Year 1927 Relating to the Bureau of Indian Affairs*. Washington, DC: GPO, 1927.

———. *Extracts from the Annual Report of the Secretary of the Interior Fiscal Year 1928 Relating to the Bureau of Indian Affairs.* Washington, DC: GPO, 1928.

Chandler, Zachariah, ed. *Annual Report of the Secretary of the Interior, 1876.* Washington, DC: GPO, 1876.

Clark, Clifford Edward, Jr. *The American Family Home: 1800–1960*. Chapel Hill: University of North Carolina Press, 1986.

Comfort, Mary Apolline. *Rainbow to Yesterday: The John and Louisa Wetherill Story*. New York: Vantage Press, 1979.

Cox, Jacob D., ed. *Annual Report of the Secretary of the Interior, 1869.* Washington, DC: GPO, 1869.

Delano, Columbus., ed. *Annual Report of the Secretary of the Interior, 1873.* Washington, DC: GPO, 1873.

Dory, William. "Navajo Land." *Natural History* 23, no. 5 (September–October 1923): 487–505.

Downes, Randolph C. "A Crusade for Indian Reform, 1922–1934." *The Mississippi Valley Historical Review* 32, no. 3 (December 1945): 331–354.

E.G. [Elaine Goodale]. "Incidents of Indian Life at Hampton." *Southern Workman* 13, no. 3 (March 1884): 32.

Fletcher, Alice. *Historical Sketch of the Omaha Tribe in Nebraska*. Washington, DC: Judd & Detweiler, 1885.

Handlin, David. *The American Home: Architecture and Society, 1815–1915*. Boston: Little, Brown and Company, 1979.

"Improving" the Hogan 91

Jett, Stephen C., and Virginia E. Spencer. *Navajo Architecture: Forms, History, Distributions*. Tucson: University of Arizona Press, 1981.

J.R. [Josephine Richards]. "Indian Incidents – Our Indian House Warming." *Southern Workman* 13, no. 4 (April 1884): 43.

Jones, William A. *Annual Report of the Commissioner of Indian Affairs, 1900*. Washington, DC: GPO, 1900.

———. *Annual Report of the Department of the Interior, Fiscal Year ended June 30, 1904—Indian Affairs, Part I, Report of the Commissioner and Appendixes*. Washington, DC: GPO, 1905.

Kelly, Lawrence C. "Choosing the New Deal Indian Commissioner: Ickes vs. Collier." *New Mexico Historical Review* 49, no. 4 (1974): 268–288.

Mackendrick, Marda. "'Mother' of the Navajos." *Sunset* 50, no. 6 (June 1923): 61–62.

Mark, Joan. *A Stranger in Her Native Land: Alice Fletcher and the American Indians*. Lincoln: University of Nebraska Press, 1988.

Meriam, Lewis, et al. *The Problem of Indian Administration*. Baltimore: Johns Hopkins Press, 1928.

Meritt, Edgar B. "Sanitary Homes for Indians." *The Red Man* 4, no. 10 (June 1912): 439–450.

Prucha, Francis Paul. *The Great Father: The United States Government and the American Indians*, 2 vols. Lincoln: University of Nebraska Press, 1984.

Rhoads, Charles J., and J. Henry Scattergood. *Annual Report of the Commissioner of Indian Affairs, 1931*. Washington, DC: GPO, 1931.

———. *Annual Report of the Commissioner of Indian Affairs, 1932*. Washington, DC: GPO, 1932.

Roosevelt, Theodore. "Across the Navajo Desert." *Outlook* 105 (October 11, 1913): 309–317.

Salsbury, Clarence. "Christ Comes to the Navajo." *Missionary Review of the World* 60 (February 1937): 75–80.

Simonsen, Jane E. *Making Home Work: Domesticity and Native American Assimilation in the American West, 1860–1919*. Chapel Hill: University of North Carolina Press, 2006.

Tomes, Nancy. *The Gospel of Germs: Men, Women, and the Microbe in American Life*. Cambridge, MA: Harvard University Press, 1998.

Trennert, Robert A. "Indian Sore Eyes: The Federal Campaign to Control Trachoma in the Southwest, 1910–1940." *Journal of the Southwest* 32, no. 2 (Summer 1990): 121–149.

———. *White Man's Medicine: Government Doctors and the Navajo, 1863–1955*. Albuquerque: University of New Mexico Press, 1998.

Upton, Dell. "Pattern Books and Professionalism: Aspects of the Transformation of Domestic Architecture in America, 1800–1860." *Winterthur Portfolio* 19, no. 2/3 (Summer–Autumn 1984): 107–150.

US Board of Indian Commissioners. *Annual Report of the United States Board of Indian Commissioners, 1869*. Washington, DC: GPO, 1870.

US Senate, Committee on Indian Affairs, Subcommittee on Senate Resolution 79. *Survey of Conditions of the Indians in the United States*, Part 3. December 12–13, 1928, and January 7–10, and 14–17, 1929. Washington, DC: GPO, 1929. Cited as *SOC*, Part 3.

———. *Survey of Conditions of the Indians in the United States*, Part 18. April 27–30 and May 15–20, 1931. Washington, DC: GPO, 1932. Cited as *SOC*, Part 18.

Warner, Michael J. "Protestant Missionary Activity Among the Navajo, 1890–1912." *New Mexico Historical Review* 45, no. 3 (1970): 209–232.

Williams, Aubrey W., Jr. *Navajo Political Process*. Washington, DC: Smithsonian Institution Press, 1970.

Wright, Gwendolyn. *Moralism and the Model Home: Domestic Architecture and Cultural Conflict in Chicago, 1873–1913*. Chicago: University of Chicago Press, 1980.

3 Route 66 and Diné Architecture

In March 1947, the French philosopher Simone de Beauvoir boarded a bus in Los Angeles and headed east along Route 66. Several days later, she passed by Petrified Forest National Monument in northern Arizona.[1] In her book, *America Day by Day*, Beauvoir recorded:

> Now and then, there is a shack along the road where they sell petrified wood. Big billboards announce solemnly: "In 5 miles, petrified wood." "In 4 miles, authentic petrified wood." "In 3 miles, your last chance for petrified wood." And indeed, the bus stops.[2]

The "shack" where Beauvoir's bus stopped was a curio store/gas station/café called the Painted Desert Park (see Figure 3.1).

She noted "the great round slices of petrified wood" outside the store and a tall viewing platform to the building's rear. But Beauvoir did not mention two of the most unusual features at the Painted Desert Park: a polygonal building with a pyramidal roof dating from the late 1920s and a round stone hogan constructed around 1940.[3]

The polygonal building closely resembled an earlier work of architecture called the Onset Wigwam (1893–1894) in Onset Bay, Massachusetts (see Figure 3.2). The Native American architecture of Onset Bay's native Mi'kmaq peoples inspired the designer of the Wigwam, Mary Weston, to give a wood-frame building an octagonal shape and a pyramidal roof.[4] According to an article published in the *Boston Globe* in 1896:

> It is a circular structure built of wood, and with a high roof to copy as near as possible the birch wigwam of the red men. The aim and object of this building is to furnish a meeting place for a band of believers in the power of the spirits of the departed to return to earth and do good here.[5]

The peaked roof of the Onset Wigwam resembles the conical wigwam traditionally built by the Mi'kmaq.[6] But the building also evokes other types of Native American architecture such as the Plains tipi, which had been widely publicized by Buffalo Bill's Wild West and similar traveling shows during the late 19th century.

DOI: 10.4324/9781003431770-4

Route 66 and Diné Architecture 93

Figure 3.1 The Painted Desert Park, Petrified Forest National Monument, Arizona, looking northeast, photographed by Leslie J. Hansen in 1956.

Figure 3.2 Postcard of the Onset Wigwam, Onset Bay, Massachusetts (postmarked 1907).

94   *Route 66 and Diné Architecture*

The clapboard-clad Onset Wigwam combined Euro-American and Native American architecture in a way that was new and unusual. Similarly, the polygonal building at the Painted Desert Park was a very early example of the Indian-inflected architecture that would become commonplace on Route 66 along the southern border of Navajoland during the 1930s. For the Jacobs family who constructed it, the building's rounded form and peaked roof represented something that was broadly "American Indian."

In 1940, when Charlie and Loretta Jacobs built a round stone hogan at the Painted Desert Park, they added a specifically Diné sensibility to the business's roadside façade. Other small-time entrepreneurs around Navajoland also built hogans and used them as shops, lodging for tourists, or simply to catch the eye of passing motorists. But during the 1930s, one building proved to be especially adaptable to new kinds of architecture along Route 66, the major highway connecting Los Angeles with Chicago and points east. For nearly 250 miles – from Flagstaff, Arizona, to Grants, New Mexico – the stacked-log hogan created a cultural landscape that was identifiably and uniquely Diné.

Interpreting Route 66 Hogans

There were several reasons why entrepreneurs along Route 66 might have chosen to build hogans. Some roadside hogans were examples of "programmatic architecture." Historian David Gebhard coined this term to describe the imaginative buildings that sprang up along American roads during the 1920s and 1930s, a period when more and more people were acquiring automobiles.[7] Los Angeles, the western terminus of Route 66, was especially known for the fantastic imagery of places like the Brown Derby restaurant (1926) and Graumann's Chinese Theatre (1927). The architecture of these establishments offered an element of playfulness and surprise that attracted passing motorists. Most programmatic architecture was associated with the service industry, which sought to increase sales by offering customers the opportunity to eat, drink, shop, stay overnight, or watch a movie in a fairy-tale environment.

Roadside hogans also cater to "ethnic tourism," which derives from curiosity about Indigenous cultures.[8] Hogans at businesses along Route 66 were often open and accessible to travelers who were interested in exploring Native American dwellings. At some places, Diné weavers and silversmiths occupied the hogans where visitors could watch them work. While ethnic tourism could certainly be educational, it also promised the *frisson* of fear and excitement that many non-Natives seem to experience when encountering the "Wild West" and its original inhabitants, the American Indians. Given the fact that hogans were relatively cheap to build, they became an attractive means to entice travelers to pull over and stop.

Hogans could additionally serve as a kind of logo, indicating that a roadside business sold Navajo-made goods. Historian Catherine Gudis has brilliantly described the transformation of the American landscape during the 1920s when car ownership became increasingly commonplace across the country. "Automobility" led to larger and more graphic advertising signs that depended less on textual messages and more on simple images that could be quickly grasped and understood. Hogans were well suited to this "aesthetics of speed" due to their size and their unique appearance. As we shall see, the stacked-log hogan with a corbelled dome was especially well suited to serve as an icon along Route 66. Even from afar or when weather or darkness impaired the ability to see, the distinctive profile of the stacked-log hogan conveyed an unblinking recognition that the building was Navajo.[9]

Navajo Rug Stands

After the National Old Trails Road became Route 66 in 1926, highway departments across the country worked to upgrade its surface and improve driving conditions. As the road became a major thoroughfare, roadside businesses took advantage of the new sales market it presented. Many of the small-scale entrepreneurs along the southern boundary of Navajoland in eastern Arizona and western New Mexico were Euro-American, but some were Diné.

In 1931, the "Navajo Hogan de Ugie," also known as "The House of Navajo Rugs," was constructed in Lupton, Arizona, just west of the New Mexico–Arizona state line. The name of the shop was derived from *diyogí*, the Navajo word for "rug." According to the *Gallup* [New Mexico] *Independent*, the store was "the first retail marketing attempt by Indians," and the Diné operated it as a cooperative. The manager, a Euro-American named Frank Reynolds, oversaw a line of merchandise consisting of products made by Navajo artisans. The newspaper described the hogan as "one of the largest ever built on the reservation," and it contained a fireplace constructed from pieces of petrified wood.[10]

Diné families who lived near the highway also established commercial ventures selling rugs and other Native American art. As Beauvoir headed east from the Painted Desert Park in 1947, she noticed:

> More numerous than gas stations, booths displaying Navajo rugs appear one after another. "In 3 miles, Navajo rugs." "Motorists, don't miss the Navajo rugs 6 miles ahead." A solitary Indian watches over brightly colored weavings hanging from wires. Are there enough people in all of America to buy so many rugs?[11]

By the time Beauvoir visited the Southwest in 1947, Native American artisans had been peddling their wares at train stations along the Santa Fe Railway line for many years. But as automobile traffic increased along Route 66 through Navajoland, vendors also became a common sight by the road.[12] Two photographs I have collected over the years help give an idea of what these small Diné businesses looked like when Beauvoir's bus rode by. In an image dating from 1941, a woman stands in front of an octagonal stacked-log with a sign announcing, "Weaver at Work" (see Figure 3.3).

The hogan was larger than most vernacular hogans of the period and had windows, but the builder used traditional techniques to construct its dirt roof and walls of rough-hewn logs chinked with adobe. In the photograph, the building's rustic architecture offers a striking contrast to the geometrical abstraction of the Ganado-style rug displayed on its walls. The use of Navajo rugs as a form of architectural ornament along the road became increasingly common during the 20th century, and many businesses dealing in Native

96   Route 66 and Diné Architecture

Figure 3.3 A roadside hogan used for selling rugs, photographed in 1941.

Figure 3.4 A roadside rug stand along Route 66, photographed c. 1955.

American arts and crafts employed colorful murals of Navajo textiles to decorate their exteriors.

Around 1955, a group of tourists heading west on Route 66 snapped another photograph of a Navajo rug stand (see Figure 3.4).

The stand could be identified by a large sign printed with the words, "Navajo Rugs." A shade structure, also called a *chaha'oh*, located at the front gate, probably served as the point of sale, and two hogans, each a polygonal stacked-log hogan, stood to the west of it. A square building with a pitched roof and another *chaha'oh* were positioned further back from the highway. Two horses hitched to a wagon created from an old automobile chassis are also visible in the photograph.

During the early 1960s, Route 66 was replaced by Interstate 40 and the highway was widened through eastern Arizona. This resulted in the removal, or "taking," of land along the road, and several rug stands were demolished. The records for an Arizona Highway Department survey conducted in 1962 identify the locations of eight different rug stands along a five-mile stretch of Route 66 extending eastward from Houck. All but one of the eight stands included a round or polygonal hogan.[13]

Three of the eight rug stands were situated on tribal lands, and the detailed appraisals for those properties are now located within the archives of the Navajo Nation Land Department. Like the example pictured in Figure 3.4, they each comprised several buildings. One of the sites included three rectangular buildings occupying 1,242 square feet, while the second site had a rectangular building, a palisaded hogan measuring 56' in circumference, and an L-shaped building containing a sales stand, adding up to 1,456 square feet. The third and smallest site included two rectangular buildings along with an octagonal stacked-log hogan measuring 7' on a side and constructed from railroad ties for a sum total of 1,130 square feet. The amount of signage at each business varied. The takings listed by the appraisers at the first rug stand included no signs and at the second rug stand included two 2' × 6' signs. The third rug stand, which featured two 2' × 6' signs and two 6' × 10' signs, would have been especially conspicuous from Route 66.[14]

Trading Posts and the Diné Hogan

The earliest Navajo trading posts date from shortly after 1868, when the reservation was first established. While some trading posts have historically provided a wide range of services, others have been little more than a place to barter for basic foodstuffs. Ethnohistorians Klara Kelley and Harris Francis, authors of the *Navajoland Trading Post Encyclopedia,* offer a definition of Navajo trading posts as "retail stores that offer general merchandise for local products or money, including through secured or unsecured debt."[15] By 1930, there were as many as 150 posts serving roughly 10,000 Diné across the greater Four Corners region. Each of them sold goods in exchange for currency or for items such as wool, weaving, metalwork, hides and pelts, piñon nuts, and livestock. As the Great Depression unfolded, several factors led to the decline of the trading post system. Greater mobility due to automobiles and better roads as well as the rise of a cash economy decreased Navajo dependence on trading posts, and ultimately, the people living on the reservation came to rely on the wider markets existing at border towns such as Gallup and Farmington. Despite the central role they once played in Diné life, only a handful of the old trading posts remain in operation today. While some former trading post buildings have been transformed into convenience stores, the majority of Navajoland's trading posts have either fallen derelict or been demolished.[16]

The architecture of most early trading posts was simple and intended for functionality rather than aesthetic value, but a notable exception is the Tuba Trading Post (see Figure 3.5).

Figure 3.5 The Tuba Trading Post, Tuba City, Arizona, photographed by Burton Frasher in 1934.

In 1905, the Babbitt Brothers Trading Company constructed a two-story octagonal brick building at Tuba City (*Tó Naneesdizí*), Arizona, following a plan conceived by Samuel Preston, a managing partner with the firm.[17] When Sharlot Hall – Arizona's first and only territorial historian – visited Tuba City in July 1911, she described the post as follows:

> built of gray stone in the octagonal shape of a Navajo hogan; there are no windows in the sides, but on top where the opening in a hogan would be there are a great many windows set in an octagonal skylight.[18]

Hall wrote that the building's entrance "carries out the hogan idea," probably because it resembles the vestibule-like feature found on the east side of forked-pole hogans. Samuel Preston worked at the trading post until 1917, and Hall spoke at length with him during her visit. It may very well be that Hall associated the post's appearance with hogan architecture based on what Preston had told her about his ideas for its design.[19]

But Frank McNitt, author of *The Indian Traders* (1961), the first scholarly study of trading posts, attributed the trading post's design to the fashion for octagonal houses that spread across the US during the mid-19th century. Orson Squire Fowler originated it with his book *A Home for All*, first published in 1848. In the 1850s, a variety of pattern books and agricultural journals featured plans for octagonal homes, and *A Home for All* was reissued in numerous editions as late as the 1880s.[20] The movement continued to influence domestic architecture until the 1920s, and around 560 octagonal houses have been documented across the nation.[21] One example, the Dr. Warren D. Day House (1877), a single-story brick octagonal house, was built in northern Arizona at Prescott, the territorial capital, where Preston may have visited.[22] It is also possible that Preston, who was born in Kentucky, was familiar with octagonal houses from his time out east, where many examples featured cupolas like the Tuba Trading Post.[23] Whatever its origins, the Tuba Trading Post would remain the only large-scale octagonal building on the Navajo reservation until the Navajo Nation Council Chamber was completed in 1935.

Although the Tuba Trading Post wielded little if any architectural influence across the reservation, another type of trading post building, the guest hogan, was the ancestor of many roadside hogans along Route 66. It is difficult to determine when trading posts began to include accommodations for Navajo customers to stay overnight. According to McNitt:

When the guest hogan was introduced, and where and by whom, is entirely uncertain. The oldest of Navaho traders spoke of Indians coming to their posts in journeys of a day or two, or even more. But provision for their shelter appears to be fairly recent, perhaps from the late 1880s or early 1890s.[24]

In "Navaho Houses" (1898), the first book-length publication about Diné architecture, Cosmos Mindeleff included the earliest firsthand description of a trading post hogan that I have encountered. In that instance, the trader supervised a Navajo crew who built the guest hogan.[25] In 1934, agricultural economist Bonney Youngblood led a team of researchers who visited more than 100 trading posts in and around the Navajo reservation. The group collected detailed information about the guest accommodations at 50 of those posts and found that 43 had hogans "for the use of Indians coming from a distance to trade."[26] McNitt, who published his classic account of Navajo trading posts in 1962, noted that traders typically hired Diné to construct guest hogans. The buildings would likely have resembled other hogans on the reservation, but functionally, they were "with no counterpart in Indian or white society."[27]

Navajo-Inflected Architecture Along Route 66

As we saw in the first chapter, the Santa Fe Railway initiated the hogan's conversion from dwelling to commercial space in 1902 at the Alvarado's anthropology village in Albuquerque. But as automobile traffic increased during the 1920s, it was inevitable that trading posts along the highways bounding the Navajo reservation would also develop new uses for the hogan. An early example of this type of appropriation, dating from 1926, was located 20 miles east of Gallup at Crafts del Navajo (see Figure 3.6).[28]

The proprietors of Crafts del Navajo, Berton and Rebecca Staples, originated from Vermont and moved to New Mexico in 1916.[29] In 1926, the Staples established Crafts del Navajo at a place they named "Coolidge" along Route 66 and close by the Santa Fe Railway's main line. According to Frank McNitt:

The Staples trading post, if it may be called that, probably could have been conceived only by an imaginative easterner. Certainly no other trader in the

Figure 3.6 Postcard of Crafts del Navajo in Coolidge, New Mexico (text on back is dated September 3, 1926).

Southwest up to that time, even on moonshiny dream, blueprinted such an establishment. Faintly resembling the restored Palace of the Governors in Santa Fe, which today no longer resembles its old self, Staples' building had a long running porch of upright posts and horizontal *vigas* separating two adobe rooms each measuring twenty-five by fifty feet.[30]

Crafts del Navajo was an extraordinary endeavor and not least because of the anthropology village the Staples established in front of it. In 1927, the *Winslow Mail* reported that Crafts del Navajo was "surrounded" by hogans, "in which live and work several families of Navajos, in one an expert silversmith, in another a rug weaver, and other craftmen [sic], all busily occupied at their work."[31] Two of the hogans were open for visitors to enter and watch the artisans.[32] Each of the hogans was a stacked-log hogan, constructed with either logs or railroad ties.

In the late 1920s, Berton Staples began conducting publicity tours with a trio of Diné artists, including a silversmith, a weaver, and a medicine man who created ceremonial dry paintings for spectators. The composition of the groups changed, but they included silversmiths Da Pah, Pishliki Yazza, Kinnie Begay, and Hosteen Begay Peshlakai; weavers Yanabah, Ahennabah, Tanabah, and Yil Habah; and medicine men Haskanaya, Dineh Chili Bitsui, and Hastiin Klah.[33] Da Pah worked during the tourist season at Crafts del Navajo, where he was photographed inside one of the hogans for a popular postcard printed around 1930 (see Figure 3.7).[34]

In 1932, Crafts del Navajo continued to exhibit weavers and silversmiths working at the hogans in front of the porch.[35] But that year, a different type of hogan appeared at the Staples' post: Leland Wyman, a medical doctor and anthropologist,

Figure 3.7 Postcard of Da Pah working inside one of the hogans at Crafts del Navajo, c. 1930.

and his wife, Paula, built a hogan for their personal use on the property. Berton Staples was quoted in the *Gallup Independent* as stating that the hogan was the first of what he anticipated would become "a summer colony of those who wish to study Navajo Indian lore."[36] During this period, Crafts del Navajo was attracting an elite clientele. Visitors included nationally known celebrities such as Will Rogers; connoisseurs of Native American art, including Charles de Young and Ruth C. Elkus; and scholars, like anthropologist Gladys Reichard, who wrote *Spider Woman*, her classic account of Navajo weaving, while in residence at Crafts del Navajo.[37]

Wyman's stacked-log hogan was constructed by Harry Boyd, a Diné trader from Smith Lake, New Mexico.[38] According to Charlotte Frisbie, who interviewed Wyman in 1967:

> It was of the crib-work variety, being constructed with railroad ties. A stone fireplace was on the west wall facing the door in the east and a niche was built in over the mantle piece. Both the floor and roof were cement; the door was wooden, and the fireplace chimney was stone. The roof lacked a smokehole, and a kitchenette containing a wood stove and stovepipe, was added to the side. A flagstone strip was placed outside of the hogan on the west side, with a bench on it, to enable the occupants to watch sunsets.[39]

The hogan's non-traditional elements included a fireplace, a kitchen extension, and the use of concrete as a construction material. Haskanaya, one of the medicine men who toured with Staples, conducted the House Blessing Ceremony for the hogan in August 1932.[40]

Between August 1932 and February 1933, Anna Wilmarth Ickes, a politician and author, and her husband, Harold, secretary of the interior from 1933 to 1946 under the Roosevelt and Truman administrations, built a "summer home (hogan style)" at Coolidge.[41] Later, in April 1937, Gouverneur and Ruth Wightman Morris moved to Crafts del Navajo.[42] Gouverneur Morris was a noted author, while Ruth was a writer, bullfighter, airplane pilot, and "one of America's first female race car drivers."[43]

In October 1937, Gouverneur Morris published "Trading Post" in the *Saturday Evening Post*, one of America's most popular magazines.[44] The story captured a slice of life at Crafts del Navajo.[45] Morris's fictionalized account described the trading post as including a main house where five visitors were staying and a cottage which housed two more. Like Berton Staples, the post's owner "was away lecturing on Navaho handicrafts," while "three of the guests in the main house were professors out to study the ways of the Navaho and make solemn, almost holy, work of it."[46] By the beginning of 1938, the Morrises had moved into a Diné hogan on the property, the third and probably the last to be built in the artist's colony at Coolidge.[47]

Lupton sits along the boundary between New Mexico and Arizona in an area of dramatic cliffs and spires featuring a range of colorful geological strata. From the late 1920s onward, businesses there served a mostly tourist clientele and included hogan architecture as a draw.[48] The businesses included the Navajo Hogan De Ugie and the Stateline Trading Post.

The post, owned by brothers Jake and Leroy Atkinson, had three hogans, including a stacked-log hogan constructed from logs, a polygonal stacked-log hogan built from square beams, and a palisaded hogan. In Figure 3.8, a postcard published

Figure 3.8 Postcard of the Stateline Trading Post, photographed by Burton Frasher on June 5, 1941.

during the early 1940s, a group of Diné with several small children stand by a shade structure, or *chaha'oh*. A loom has been mounted underneath it, and the group probably includes one or more weavers. The open door of the middle hogan suggests that it was accessible for tourists to look inside.

Route 66 and the Jacobs Family

The largest anthropology village in Navajoland was located at the Navajo Indian Village, which was completed around 1940 on Route 66 west of Chambers, Arizona (Figure 3.9).

The owners, Charlie and Loretta Jacobs, were part of an extended family, including Charlie's uncle Harry E. "Indian" Miller, who operated several properties along Route 66. The Navajo Indian Village was the second roadside business owned by Charlie and Loretta. It was located 22 miles east of the Painted Desert Park, where Simone de Beauvoir stopped in 1947.[49]

The Painted Desert Park was established by Paul Jacobs, who met and married Betty, a Diné woman, while she was working there. Paul sold the business to his brother, Bill, who in turn sold it to their mother, Julia Grant Miller, who sold it to her third son, Charlie, in 1940.[50] As we saw at the beginning of this chapter, the stone hogan that Charlie and Loretta constructed at the Painted Desert Park was connected to a "Native American" polygonal building with a pyramidal roof and the main store. At the Navajo Indian Village, the main store building was constructed from the three conjoined hogans at the center of Figure 3.9.

Figure 3.9 Postcard of the Navajo Indian Village in Chambers, Arizona, photographed by Burton Frasher, c. 1940.

104 *Route 66 and Diné Architecture*

A large hexagonal stacked-log hogan walled with 13-foot-long bridge timbers and topped with a hexagonal glass cupola was located at the front of the store. Glass panels inserted between the timbers on the three sides facing Route 66 further illuminated the hogan and added visual interest to its exterior.[51] The roof was decorated with several Native American murals, including a large thunderbird painted in orange, yellow, and blue. A set of elk antlers and two upright petrified tree trunks marked the front entrance which was surrounded by great roundels of petrified wood and sandstone slabs carved with pre-Columbian petroglyphs (cut out and removed from their original locations).[52] The store's middle stacked-log hogan was also hexagonal. It was crowned with a square glass cupola and constructed from logs measuring 10′ on each side. The rear hogan was originally a large polygonal stacked-log hogan built from squared timbers. During the early 1940s, the Jacobs lived in the stone hogan on the left side of Figure 3.9. Later, the store building was altered to incorporate new living quarters for the Jacobs. The rear hogan was replaced with a stone hogan, and another stone hogan was added to the west to produce an L-shaped building comprising four hogans that combined the Jacobs' store and residence.

The tall *chaha'oh* pictured on the right side of Figure 3.9 was located next to the highway. The front of the Painted Desert Park featured a similar structure during the early 1940s.[53] The *chaha'oh* at the Navajo Indian Village was hung with Navajo rugs and decorated with colorful wooden katsinas, Native American motifs, and signs identifying the "Indian Village" and "Desert Art Supply." The "desert art" marketed by the Navajo Indian Village included "sands of the Painted Desert in picture bottles and paper weights" as well as petrified wood.[54] Charlie Jacobs specialized in cutting and marketing petrified wood, and the landscape of the Navajo Indian Village was filled with it. Small pieces were displayed on tables under the *chaha'oh*, large chunks served as fencing, and rows of even larger pieces occupied a space to the west of the *chaha'oh*. Tall vibrantly painted katsinas, some nearly 20′ tall, were set along Route 66.

According to ethnohistorian Thomas Arthur Repp, the Navajo Indian Village "was founded around one central idea: that Navajo families, invited from the reservation, might set up permanent residence on its grounds and thereby create a new and viable community." During the research for his book *Route 66: Romance of the West*, Repp discovered that members of six different families resided at the village, including "Big Maggie" Nez, her grandson Eddie Lee, Pony Roanhorse and his wife, and Jimmy House. Nez was a silversmith and Roanhorse worked in gold, but the rugs were purchased from elsewhere, and the village did not typically include weavers or their looms. The Diné lived in hogans that they owned and almost certainly built or commissioned other Diné to build.[55]

The different Diné dwellings at the Navajo Indian Village transformed it into an architectural museum. Along with examples of the stacked-log hogan and the stone hogan, there was a palisaded hogan, a many-legged hogan, and rectangular homes constructed from logs and stone. As a group, the buildings

Route 66 and Diné Architecture   105

demonstrated the diversity of Navajo architecture in a manner that was rare for roadside businesses.[56]

During the early 1950s, Route 66 was rerouted to the south, bypassing the Navajo Indian Village, and by March 1952, the Jacobs had obtained land to relocate the business along the highway's new alignment.[57] Then in August 1953, Charlie and Loretta Jacobs embarked on a new enterprise located about a mile west of the Painted Desert Park on an inholding within Petrified Forest National Monument. They called it the Painted Desert Tower (Figure 3.10).[58]

The buildings at the Painted Desert Tower were cheaply constructed and framed with wood covered by composition roofing paper. The Jacobs never expected the business to endure because here, too, Route 66 was being realigned and moved to the south. The couple's primary purpose was to compel the National Park Service to purchase the property, which was within the boundaries of the monument. As the monument's superintendent, Fred Fagergren wrote shortly before the Painted Desert Tower opened, "It appears there is no way to eliminate this eye-sore without buying the land, which it appears is the nature behind the establishing of the trading post."[59]

The business's most prominent feature was a 40-foot-tall observation tower, but it also included a large *chaha'oh* measuring 30' wide and 60' long where Charlie Jacobs displayed petrified wood and stowed the tools he used to cut and polish it.[60] Although the architecture of the Painted Desert Tower was intended to be ephemeral and easy to transport to the new alignment should the need arise, the Jacobs invested in the construction of two octagonal lumber hogans. One contained a cistern, measured 6' on a side, and had an earthen roof, while the other, a storage building, measured 12' on a side and had a pyramidal galvanized iron roof with a cupola.[61] In 1957, the Jacobs succeeded in selling their land within Petrified Forest National Monument to the National Park Service. They were among the few roadside proprietors in the area to survive the realignment and subsequent construction of Interstate 40 without sustaining great financial hardship.

Another roadside entrepreneur, Arthur Beasley, built hogans to house two petrified wood shops in eastern Arizona, both called Wonderview Wood. Beasley married a Diné woman, Anna Yellowhorse, and his son, Frank Yellowhorse, later owned another roadside business at Lupton. Wonderview Wood had two different sites because the realignment of Route 66 forced the Beasleys to move to a new location.[62] During the 1940s, they built a heptagonal hogan to serve as their first store west of Houck (Figure 3.11).

The hogan was a palisaded hogan with a painted, pyramidal, asphalt-covered roof. Petrified wood was the primary item handled by the Beasleys, and large roundels along with tables filled with smaller pieces were arranged around the building.[63] In the 1950s, they rebuilt their business at a new site nearer to Lupton in two conjoined hogans. The hogans were clad with vertically mounted, board-and-batten siding painted in red and yellow and topped with two domes.[64]

The V.J. Holmes Trading Post in Bluewater, New Mexico, adapted the stacked-log hogan and transformed it into two different buildings (Figure 3.12).

106 *Route 66 and Diné Architecture*

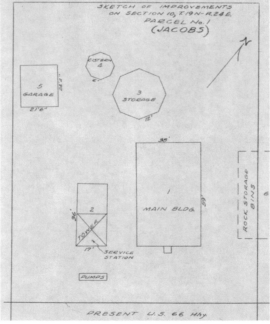

Figure 3.10 Plan and view of the Painted Desert Tower, Petrified Forest National Monument, Arizona, looking northwest from Route 66, 1957. The octagonal building marked "3" in the diagram is visible at right in the photograph.

Route 66 and Diné Architecture 107

Figure 3.11 Snapshot of the Wonderview Hogan, near Houck, Arizona (text on the back is dated July 27, 1946).

Figure 3.12 Postcard of the V.J. Holmes Trading Post, Bluewater, New Mexico, photographed by Burton Frasher on June 26, 1940.

108 *Route 66 and Diné Architecture*

The main entrance to the trading post building was in a rectangular building with a shed roof sloping to the rear. Two octagonal hogans with pyramidal roofs adjoined the central block, creating wings on either side. According to Repp, one of these hogans served as a residence for the Holmes family.[65] A third hogan, similar to the other two, stood apart and served as the trading post's "Rug Room." A photograph taken in 1940 shows the interior of this hogan filled with Navajo rugs, as well as weavings from Mexico and Hispanic textiles from the Rio Grande Valley in New Mexico.[66] Other types of Native American art, including baskets, painted gourds, and a beaded dress were also for sale. Horizontally mounted log slab siding helped to unify the trading post and outhouses with the stacked-log hogans. In Figure 3.12, the buildings have been draped with a variety of different kinds of weavings. The juxtaposition of rough, unpeeled logs with the sophistication displayed by these geometrically patterned textiles created the "rough/refined" aesthetic favored by many entrepreneurs along Route 66.

New Uses for the Diné Hogan

The Route 66 entrepreneurs who repurposed hogans to become salesrooms for Navajo art did not venture far from the building's original function. But during the 1930s, the landscape along the highway began to include hogan architecture designed for radically new uses. An early example of this kind of architectural adaptation was the headquarters building for the Gallup Inter-Tribal Indian Ceremonial, an annual event established in 1923 showcasing Native American culture. In 1930, the Inter-Tribal Indian Ceremonial Association built a new headquarters out of railroad ties donated by the Santa Fe Railway. The building, a domed, heptagonal stacked-log hogan with an earth-covered roof, was located on a narrow lot between Route 66 and the railroad's main line between Chicago and Los Angeles (see Figure 3.13).[67]

Herbert C. Yenne, the association's secretary, suggested the idea for the hogan, and M.L. Woodard, publisher of the *Southwest Tourist News*, proposed that a *chaha'oh* be constructed nearby where Navajo artisans could work "for the edification of the tourists."[68] During the summer of 1930, a weaver and silversmith worked under the *chaha'oh*, and "the hogan attracted hundreds who passed through on the train during the 10 minute stops."[69] By 1933, the hogan was also being used to house the Gallup Chamber of Commerce, the United Indian Traders Association, and Woodard's newspaper.

In 1936, the building was expanded with a rectangular bay to the south and connected to an octagonal hogan, also constructed from railroad ties. Although the hogans were primarily used to provide services for tourists, various civic groups used the rooms for meetings and small exhibitions were held there.[70] El Navajo, a large hotel managed by the Fred Harvey Company, was located about 300′ to the east across a space called Santa Fe Plaza, which was used for Native American dances and public events such as band concerts.[71] Later, in 1955, the *Gallup Independent* reported that

Figure 3.13 Postcard of the Gallup Inter-Tribal Ceremonial Hogans, c. late 1940s.

the Ceremonial Hogan, "one of the best-known offices of any organization in America," had been given "a new look" that matched the paint on the Santa Fe locomotives: The logs at the corners were painted in silver and red, and the roof was finished with a silver-colored, presumably aluminum-asphalt coating.[72]

In 1934, James Lowery Rush built a gas station on the south side of Route 66 east of Gallup (Figure 3.14).[73]

Rush had previously worked as a trader and as a government employee with the Southern Navajo Agency under Superintendent John G. Hunter. While with the government, Rush had been assigned as a field-worker to help establish Navajo chapters within Hunter's jurisdiction.[74] By spring 1934, he was also charged with organizing Navajo artisans to travel to fairs and festivals to demonstrate weaving and metalsmithing.[75] As an entrepreneur in Gallup, Rush constructed two conjoined hexagonal hogans to create the Hogan Station. The wood-frame building was clad with horizontally mounted unpeeled log slabs.

Initially, the focus of the Hogan Station was servicing motor vehicles and selling Texaco products. But it soon diversified. By 1937, the rear hogan was being billed as "the Indian Room," and advertisements in the local newspaper promoted "tasty sandwiches and good coffee served both day and night in this cozy room beside the open fire." The room was rented out for special events and club meetings, and on Monday nights, a "reservations-only" Mexican dinner was served in "El Hogan."[76] The photograph in Figure 3.14 shows a rectangular booth with slab siding mounted with a sign reading, "Indian Arts & Crafts." Boughs have been

Figure 3.14 The Hogan Station, Gallup, New Mexico, photographed by Tom Mullarky, c. 1940.

placed along its top in an effort to create the appearance of a *chaha'oh*. By 1941, the Hogan Station had a cabin available for rent, and during World War II, it expanded into the grocery business.[77]

In 1937, the State of New Mexico initiated a plan to build several ports of entry along its borders with funding provided by the Works Progress Administration, a federal New Deal program. The buildings were to be "Indian-type structures" in the Pueblo-Spanish Revival style with the exception of the port near Gallup, which newspapers reported "will be modeled from a Navajo hogan."[78] By the end of 1937, however, the hogan idea had been nixed, and a new "Pueblo style" port of entry was set to be constructed six miles west of Gallup.[79] On the other side of the state line, however, the Arizona inspection station at Lupton did adopt a Navajo architectural idiom, and an article in the May 30, 1954, issue of the *Arizona Republic* observed that it "looks more like an Indian hogan than a state-operated department" (Figure 3.15).[80]

The octagonal building resembled the masonry hogans built by the Office of Indian Affairs during the 1930s (see Chapter 4). The timber used for the port of entry was shaped into rectangular blocks, the walls were neatly squared off at each corner, banks of windows illuminated the interior, and the roofing was contained by a fascia, creating a rim around the perimeter of the hogan.

Route 66 and Diné Architecture 111

Figure 3.15 The inspection station at Lupton, Arizona, as it appeared in the *Arizona Republic* on May 30, 1954. The caption reads, "Earl Blackwell, assistant chief inspector at Lupton, checks truck of J.S. Slatton, trading post owner."

During the late 1920s, Harry and Hope Locke established Meteor Station at the southeast corner of the junction between Route 66 and the road to Meteor Crater in Arizona.[81] The couple sold gas and meteorite fragments to customers there, but Harry Locke's interest in meteorites and Meteor Crater impelled him to construct a more impressive work of architecture to the east that became known as the Meteor Crater Observatory. In 1933, James "Rimmy Jim" Giddings leased and took over Meteor Station from the Lockes. He operated the business for another ten years, until his death in 1943.[82] Rimmy Jim's carried basic supplies for travelers, including Texaco gasoline, groceries, candy, cigarettes, soft drinks, beer, wine, and liquor, as well as automobile parts and accessories.[83] Around 1939, Rimmy Jim added overnight accommodations to his business.[84]

Figure 3.16 The hogans at Rimmy Jim's, near Meteor Crater, Arizona, photographed by Burton Frasher on September 1, 1939.

The hogans in Figure 3.16 are arranged in a row on the corner between Route 66 and the road south to Meteor Crater. They include two variations of the stacked-log hogan. At the far right is a heptagonal stacked-log hogan with its entrance facing north towards Route 66. It is larger than the other five hogans, and its log walls are visible through the stucco that has been applied to it. The remaining five hogans all face east, in the manner traditional to Navajo hogans. Their octagonal shape is readily apparent from the sharply defined corners of each building, making them facsimile versions of the stacked-log hogan. It is difficult to ascertain how they were constructed because they have each been plastered from top to bottom, probably with gunite (also known as shotcrete), a type of concrete sprayed on with a hose. The hogans were noted during the mid-1940s when Jack Rittenhouse was researching *A Guide Book to Highway 66* (1946), the first published mile-by-mile description of tourist facilities along the route.[85] As simple as these buildings were, they contained the essential elements necessary for Rittenhouse and other travelers to recognize a Navajo hogan: a polygonal shape and a domical roof.

The Stacked-Log Hogan Becomes a Roadside Icon

Beginning in the late 1920s, several entrepreneurs built hogan-inspired architecture beyond the Four Corners area where the Navajo reservation is located. The earliest examples I have come across were part of "Indian-themed" cultural landscapes. Among the various hogan forms we have seen, only one – the stacked-log hogan – appeared repeatedly in these landscapes, signifying its emergence as an icon that embodied "Navajoness."

Route 66 and Diné Architecture   113

In 1871, William Jackson Palmer and his associates with the Denver and Rio Grande Railroad founded Colorado Springs, Colorado. The following year, they established Manitou Springs, located five miles to the southwest.[86] The two towns were originally intended as resort destinations along the railway line south from Denver and they occupy a landscape of great natural beauty. Dominating the view to the west lies the summit of Pike's Peak, while Garden of the Gods, a public park featuring unusual rock formations, is situated in the area between the two municipalities.

The tourism industry in and around Manitou Springs during the late 19th and early 20th centuries employed Native American theming to great effect. "Manitou" is an Algonquian word referring to "a pervasive supernatural force."[87] Manitou's eight mineral springs were all named after Indian tribes, and among its higher-end guesthouses was the Navajo Hotel (1872), located next to Navajo Geyser and built in the Queen Anne style. A tourist attraction called the Manitou Cliff Dwellings is located just north of Manitou Springs and features a group of pre-Columbian ruins transported from western Colorado. The ruins, which contain about 100 rooms, were installed between 1904 and 1907, and by 1910, Native American artisans and dancers were living on-site in a replica of Taos Pueblo, while Diné performers were housed in hogans nearby.[88]

In 1915, the Hidden Inn, a Pueblo-Spanish Revival-style curio store and tea shop was constructed at the north end of Garden of the Gods. The Hidden Inn probably inspired Curt Goerke, a local entrepreneur, to commission architect T. Charles Gaastra to design a Pueblo-Spanish Revival building containing a museum, curio shop, and ticket office for the west side of Garden of the Gods in 1924.[89] It was never completed, but one of Goerke's employees, Charles Strausenback, subsequently established his own business at Garden of the Gods in a three-story Pueblo-Spanish Revival building resembling Gaastra's design. Strausenback had previously worked for the Fred Harvey Company's Indian Department as a buyer.[90] By the time he built his trading post, the juxtaposition of Diné with Pueblo architecture had become a trademark of the Santa Fe Railway's anthropology villages described in Chapter 1. In a publicity postcard, a painting of the main store building appears with a Kewa-style subterranean kiva and a stacked-log hogan while Pike's Peak rises from the background (Figure 3.17).

The Garden of the Gods Curio Company opened in June 1929. Strausenback engaged a family from Santa Clara Pueblo and five Diné, including Hosteen Goodluck and his family, to live in two hogans at the store – a stacked-log hogan and a building shaped like a truncated cone constructed from large logs.[91]

In 1935, shortly after Strausenback's opened, Caesar Gheno and Nicholas Fontecchio opened the Navajo Hogan, a restaurant and bar on the north side of Colorado Springs (Figure 3.18).

Fontecchio worked as a labor organizer for the United Mine Workers, and his experiences with the Diné while on the road in the Southwest may have led to his interest in building hogan architecture.[92] Gheno and Fontecchio collaborated with John Aaron, "a well-known carpenter and builder," to complete the design.[93]

The west hogan, closest to the street, was constructed in 1935. The "Navajo" identity of the building was signaled by its polygonal exterior and by an octagonal

114 *Route 66 and Diné Architecture*

Figure 3.17 Two postcards from Strausenback's Trading Post, Garden of the Gods, Colorado. The back of the bottom postcard identifies the woman as Lupita Naranjo of Santa Clara Pueblo.

Route 66 and Diné Architecture   115

Figure 3.18 Postcard of the Navajo Hogan, Colorado Springs, c. 1940s. The bottom image shows the log ceiling in the building's dodecagonal section.

116 *Route 66 and Diné Architecture*

corbelled-log ceiling on its interior, constructed of hand-hewn native pine.[94] The builders decided to create a pyramidal rather than a traditional domed roof, and thus, when a second stacked-log hogan was added in 1940, it was possible to build a connecting rectangular bay and merge its pitched roof with both hogans. The east hogan was larger, and its corbelled-log ceiling was dodecagonal. Double-hogans during this period were very rare, and it seems likely that conjoined hogans in and around the Navajo reservation such as the Gallup Inter-Tribal Ceremonial headquarters had some influence over the design in Colorado Springs.

Several decades earlier, in 1875, author and Indian rights activist Helen Hunt Jackson had made her home in Colorado Springs. While there, she wrote *A Century of Dishonor* (1881), one of the first scholarly histories documenting the relationship between Native Americans and the federal government.[95] Then in 1884, Jackson published the book that would establish her as a figure of lasting renown: *Ramona*. Jackson originally wrote *Ramona* to raise public awareness of the hardships endured by Native Americans, but after the novel was released, readers began responding to it on a much more personal level. The story, which is set in California during the 1850s, relates the tragedies and triumphs of the half–Native American and half-Scots title character.

Although the book is a work of fiction, many readers came to believe that Ramona had been a historic figure, and within a few years after the book's release, several of the key sites within the story materialized as actual locations in southern California, including "Ramona's Home" in San Gabriel and "Ramona's Marriage Place" in San Diego.[96] As we shall see, the romance and fantasy that came to be associated with *Ramona* also helped to generate an Indian-themed cultural landscape centered in Hemet, San Jacinto, and Soboba Hot Springs, all located within a 25-square-mile area in the San Jacinto Valley east of Los Angeles.

One of the events leading to the popularity of Native American–inspired architecture in the valley was the first presentation, in 1923, of *The Ramona Pageant*, a play based on *Ramona*. The pageant, held in an outdoor amphitheater outside Hemet, became an annual event that is still held every spring. Then in 1924, the year after the pageant was first presented, John and Tillie Althouse commissioned architect Robert Stacy-Judd to design a new resort for Soboba Hot Springs located on the Althouses' 320-acre ranch.[97] In October 1927, Edgar Lloyd Hampton described the project in the *New York Times Sunday Magazine*:

> The plan in its entirety includes at least fifty cottages. When these are completed they will tell, in the shape of human abodes, the entire story of the American aborigine, from the Tree Dwelling and Cliff Dwelling periods down to the more elaborate structures of the Pueblos and the beginning of the world-famous California Mission type of home. It is probably the first time that any one has ever attempted to tell the racial story of any country in a series of related structures and it is the first time that American Indian designs have ever been adapted to a hotel group.[98]

Stacy-Judd took a significant degree of artistic license with his designs for Soboba, but when *Los Angeles Times* columnist Lee Shippey visited in 1931, he pronounced

Route 66 and Diné Architecture   117

it "the most beautiful health resort, to our mind, in Southern California." He praised the Althouses and credited them with the idea to use Native American architecture as an inspiration. Shippey remarked:

> Robert Stacy Judd of Los Angeles was the architect employed to work out those plans and he did such an effective job of it that the towns of San Jacinto and Hemet have followed the lead set by Soboba Springs and the most noticeable and artistic buildings in them were inspired by these buildings at Soboba.[99]

In March 1930, the *Los Angeles Times* featured a pictorial with an image of the resort at Soboba Hot Springs combined with several photographs of new architecture in San Jacinto and Hemet. The pictorial was entitled "Ramona Pageant Affects Architecture of San Jacinto and Hemet," and an accompanying article maintained:

> Since the inception of the outdoor play in 1923, the tendency in much of the new construction is to follow the Indian motif of architecture, with the idea of preserving for posterity the atmosphere and romance which is glorified in the play by Helen Hunt Jackson's novel, *Ramona*.[100]

Many of the new buildings, such as the Soboba Theatre (1927), were completed in the Pueblo-Spanish Revival style.[101] But San Jacinto and Hemet were not trying to imitate Santa Fe, New Mexico, which had adopted the Pueblo-Spanish Revival as an architectural idiom in 1912.[102] Rather, in the San Jacinto Valley, "the Indian motif" took a variety of forms. Some buildings, like the San Jacinto Drug Store and the San Jacinto Museum, were eclectically styled to appear rustic or in ruins. The drugstore was covered with unfinished boards and ornamented with a row of sticks and animal skins, while a totem pole was placed in front of its main entrance.[103] The museum, which was located across the street from the Soboba Theatre, was faced with a random-rubble veneer and large asymmetrical openings to make it appear like a work of pre-Columbian architecture (Figure 3.19).

One of the openings was surmounted by a stone sculpture resembling Chaac, a Central American rain god frequently carved on the walls of Mayan temples. A line of vertically placed boughs created a jagged profile along the building's cornice and reinforced the building's prehistoric ambience. Next door was a Pueblo-Spanish Revival building containing the San Jacinto Chamber of Commerce and a bakery, followed by a camera shop housed in an imitation tipi.

All of these buildings, or at least their "Native American" façades, have now disappeared. The only significant relic remaining from the American Indian building craze that captured San Jacinto Valley during the 1930s is "The Hogan," located in downtown San Jacinto, catty-corner from the buildings in Figure 3.19.

Alice Flanders constructed The Hogan as an octagonal stacked-log hogan with a creased dome. The postcard in Figure 3.20 shows the main entrance decorated by Navajo rugs and flanked by two rusticated stone walls displaying smaller Native American art objects. The window awnings were painted with Native American

118 *Route 66 and Diné Architecture*

Figure 3.19 Postcard of downtown San Jacinto, California, photographed by Burton Frasher, c. 1940.

Figure 3.20 Postcard of The Hogan, San Jacinto, California, c. 1935.

symbols, while a large katsina-like sculpture stood by the building's chimney. By 1940, there was a Pueblo-Spanish Revival building next door containing a watch shop.

The Hogan sold "curios, examples of the art of Indian painters, sculptors and other creators, blankets, rugs, footwear and most attractive of all, a large carefully selected stock of Indian jewelry."[104] The items were mostly Pueblo or Diné in origin, although Flanders also carried sombreros and Chimayo rugs and jackets from the Rio Grande Valley. The interior was decorated with chile ristras and ears of corn, further identifying The Hogan with the Southwest.[105]

Flanders made annual trips to New Mexico and Arizona to buy items for the business and to attend "fiestas, ceremonial observances and dances."[106] In October 1936, the year that the shop opened, a local newspaper described Flanders as an "authority on arts and crafts of Indians of the Southwest," and she gave a public talk about her experiences visiting the Gallup Inter-Tribal Ceremonial.[107] The influence of the architecture around Gallup on Flanders' shop seems undeniable.

The Ceremonial drew visitors from across the nation, and Edna Hallahan, a resident of East Charlemont, Massachusetts, also attended it regularly during the 1930s. In 1932, she and her husband, William, built Indian Plaza, which included two Diné hogans, where Navajo employees made and sold arts and craft items.[108] Charlemont, like Manitou Springs, Colorado Springs, and San Jacinto, was associated with an Indian-themed environment, in this case, Massachusetts' Mohawk Trail.

The Mohawk Trail officially opened in October 1914 as a scenic highway and followed an ancient trace laid down by the Indigenous peoples of the region. In its earliest 20th-century incarnation, the Mohawk Trail ran for 15 miles between West Charlemont and North Adams. But over time, it expanded, and in 1922, Wilfred French wrote that it was popularly regarded to stretch between Greenfield and Williamstown for 43 miles.[109] By the 1920s, there were several attractions along the Mohawk Trail playing upon a Native American theme, including the Wigwam (1914), a restaurant and curio shop east of North Adams; the Totem Trading Post (c. 1920) at Cold River; as well as the Indian Village (c. 1920s), which featured birch-bark wigwams.[110]

The main store at Indian Plaza was a simple rectangular, flat-roofed building featuring protruding beams and clad with vertical boards (Figure 3.21).[111]

In 1933, Mrs. Hallahan employed two Diné men – Frank Barboane and Nelson Bodie – to travel from the reservation to work for her. Barboane was a weaver and sand painter, while Bodie, his nephew, was a silversmith. According to an article in the June 29 issue of the *North Adams Transcript*:

Once at Charlemont they proceeded to make themselves perfectly at home by building for themselves a "hogan," or low hovel of logs and poles the top of which is covered with earth, such as they and their ancestors have lived in since time immemorial.[112]

120   *Route 66 and Diné Architecture*

Figure 3.21 Indian Plaza, Charlemont, Massachusetts. The top postcard shows the large hogan (at right) constructed in 1933 by Frank Barboane and Nelson Bodie before it was destroyed by a flood in 1938. The bottom postcard shows the small hogan they built, which survived the flood.

The hogan was a polygonal stacked-log hogan, constructed from horizontally stacked lengths of milled lumber.[113] The newspaper continued:

> Miss Hallahan also had them build a larger hogan for use as a showroom in which to display their handiwork and also a large assortment of other Indian

Route 66 and Diné Architecture   121

handiwork which she brought with her from the West. And it was the building of this second hogan which brought much perturbation to Frank and Nelson, for in it all the accepted rules of hogan building were violated.[114]

The problems with the building were as follows:

> In the first place, Miss Hallahan wanted the entrance toward the main highway. This, explained Frank, was impossible. No one could live in a hogan in which the entrance did not face the rising sun. She tried to explain to him that no one was going to live in it, that it was for display purposes only. Finally, under protest, Frank and Nelson did as directed. Then their, to their minds, unreasonable employer insisted upon such unorthodox things as windows in the sides of the hogan. Then to cap it all, the usual opening in the center of the circular roof had to be covered up. With silent and foreboding shakes of the head the two Indians did as directed, but they still eye the monstrosity askance.[115]

In 1934, Mrs. Hallahan returned from New Mexico with an artisan who had recently been on tour with Berton Staples: Da Pah (see Figure 3.7).[116] Da Pah came with his wife, Estan-Chi, a weaver, and their 6-year-old granddaughter, Ah-He-He-Bah, who performed dances and helped her grandmother to prepare wool.[117] According to a local newspaper, the family served as a tourist attraction and lived in the small hogan that Barboane and Bodie had built in 1933.[118]

Like Alice Flanders, Edna Hallahan gave public talks on the Indians of the Southwest.[119] And each spring, she and her husband traveled from Massachusetts to bring back a group of Native American artisans. In 1935, four members of San Ildefonso Pueblo were in residence at the Indian Plaza. A young woman from Taos Pueblo came in 1937 to work for the Hallahans, but Da Pah and his grandson, Louis (who performed dances), soon became a regular fixture at the business each summer.[120]

In 1938, a flood damaged Indian Plaza, and it had to be rebuilt.[121] The large hogan was replaced with a significantly taller octagonal building topped by a cupola. But a small hexagonal stacked-log hogan survived. Pictured in Figure 3.21, it had a roof constructed from asphalt roofing material stretched over a wood frame and was located at the west end of Indian Plaza. By the mid-1940s, colorful Navajo rugs were painted on its sides, and a sign clearly identified it as a "Navajo Hogan."

Why did the stacked-log hogan become the most popular choice for roadside architecture along Route 66 and in locations farther afield? The main reason was that the stacked-log hogan was the most distinctive and easily identifiable form of the Navajo hogan. The conical shape of the forked-pole hogan bears a strong resemblance to a tipi. And although other female hogans could be roofed with a corbelled dome (a uniquely Diné construction during the 20th century), the clearly articulated polygonal shape of the stacked-log hogan (emphasized by the building's corner timbering) made it easy to recognize. The concrete-encased hogans at Rimmy Jim's demonstrated that little else was necessary to render a building "Navajo."

122 *Route 66 and Diné Architecture*

The log walls and domical roof of the stacked-log hogan would also have felt familiar to people who were acquainted with log cabins and domed buildings, like the US Capitol. Since the mid-19th century, the log cabin has become firmly ensconced in this country's popular imaginary. In fact, the building's association with several US presidents – most notably Abraham Lincoln – has established it as a veritable institution. The stacked-log hogan – neat, contained, and drawing on positive associations with mainstream American culture – made an unusual building more approachable and attractive to prospective patrons and customers.

Finally, the polygonal shape of the stacked-log hogan made it easy to conjoin and adapt to create larger and more complicated buildings. As we shall see, this particular aspect would contribute to the role the stacked-log hogan would play during the Indian New Deal and help make it an important influence on the design of contemporary public architecture on the Navajo reservation.

Notes

1 Petrified Forest National Monument became Petrified Forest National Park in 1962.
2 Simone de Beauvoir, *America Day by Day*, trans. Carol Cosman (London: Phoenix, 1998), 184.
3 Thomas Arthur Repp, *Route 66: The Romance of the West* (Lynnwood, WA: Mock Turtle Press, 2002), 120.
4 Bernardine Rose Angelo, "Beckoning the Red Man's Spirit: Exploring the Boundaries of Gender, Race, Sacred and Commercial Spaces at the Wigwam Spiritualist Temple, Onset, Massachusetts, 1880–1913" (Master's thesis, University of Massachusetts – Boston, 2010), 9.
5 "Onset's Wigwam," *Boston Globe*, July 26, 1896.
6 Peter Nabokov and Robert Easton, *Native American Architecture* (New York: Oxford University Press, 1989), 63.
7 David Gebhard, introduction to *California Crazy and Beyond: Roadside Vernacular Architecture*, by Jim Heimann (San Francisco: Chronicle Books, 2001), 8.
8 Stephen C. Jett, "Culture and Tourism in the Navajo Country," *Journal of Cultural Geography* 11, no. 1 (1990): 86.
9 Catherine Gudis, *Buyways: Billboards, Automobiles, and the American Landscape* (New York: Routledge, 2004), 68.
10 "Navajos Build Hogan to Sell Own Products at State Line," *Gallup Independent*, August 10, 1931.
11 Beauvoir, *America Day by Day*, 185.
12 See, for example, Kenneth Chapman, "Indian Pottery by the Roadside," *Indians at Work* 4, no. 4 (October 1, 1936): 23–26.
13 Arizona Highway Department, Right of Way Map of Holbrook – Lupton, Interstate Highway 40 (US 66), Sec. Cedar point – 3 Hogans, April 26, 1962, RF-NNLD.
14 Appraisal for various portions of T21N-R29E, T22N-R29E and T22N-R30E in Apache County, 2–3, RF-NNLD.
15 Klara Kelley and Harris Francis, *Navajoland Trading Post Encyclopedia* (Window Rock, AZ: Navajo Nation Heritage and Historic Preservation Department, 2018), xiii.
16 Lillian Makeda, "*Navajoland Trading Post Encyclopedia* by Klara Kelley and Harris Francis" [review], *Kiva* 87, no. 3 (Fall 2021): 377–378.
17 Kelley and Francis, *Navajoland Trading Post Encyclopedia*, 413.
18 Sharlot Hall, *Sharlot Hall on the Arizona Strip: A Diary of Journey Through Northern Arizona in 1911*, ed. C. Gregory Crampton (Flagstaff, AZ: Northland Press, 1975), 39,

Route 66 and Diné Architecture   123

quoted in Pat Stein, "Tuba Trading Post, Coconino County, Arizona," October 1996 [National Register of Historic Places listing #96001362], section 7, page 2.

19 Hall, *Sharlot Hall on the Arizona Strip*, 39; Kelley and Francis, *Navajoland Trading Post Encyclopedia*, 413.

20 Rebecca Lawin McCarley, "Orson S. Fowler and a Home for All: The Octagon House in the Midwest," *Perspectives in Vernacular Architecture* 12 (2005): 54–55.

21 McCarley, "Orson S. Fowler and a Home for All," 49–50.

22 Stein, "Tuba Trading Post," section 8, page 5.

23 McCarley, "Orson S. Fowler and a Home for All," 57.

24 Frank McNitt, *The Indian Traders* (Norman: University of Oklahoma Press, 1962), 78n7.

25 Cosmos Mindeleff, "Navaho Houses," *17th Annual Report of the Bureau of American Ethnology, 1895–1896*, Part 2 (Washington, DC: GPO, 1898), 499.

26 Bonney Youngblood, "Navajo Trading," in US Senate, Committee on Indian Affairs, Subcommittee on Senate Resolution 79, *Survey of Conditions of the Indians in the United States*, Part 34 (Washington, DC: GPO, 1937), 18036, 18042, 18045.

27 McNitt, *The Indian Traders*, 78.

28 This postcard is postmarked September 3, 1926.

29 The actual date of the move varies according to the source.

30 McNitt, *The Indian Traders*, 237.

31 "Artistic Resort Being Completed at Coolidge, N.M.," *Winslow [AZ] Daily Mail*, May 15, 1927.

32 "Crafts del Navajo, Resort of New Mexico, Abounds in Lore," *Winslow Daily Mail*, September 1, 1927.

33 See M.L. Woodard, "The Navajo Goes East," *New Mexico Highway Journal*, March 1931: 14; "Navajo Group Displays Handiwork Here Today," *Muscatine [IA] Journal and News-Tribune*, February 28, 1931; Harry E. Shuart, "New Mexico Goes to the 'World's Fair'," *New Mexico*, July 1934: 10–12; "Indian Workers and Handicraft Articles Draw Large Crowds," *Gallup Independent*, October 28, 1937. For more on Hastiin Klah, see Franc Johnson Newcomb, *Hosteen Klah: Navaho Medicine Man and Sand Painter* (Norman: University of Oklahoma Press, 1964).

34 An example of one of these postcards in the author's collection is postmarked August 15, 1934.

35 "Advertisement [for Crafts del Navajo]," *Southwest Tourist News*, January 15, 1934.

36 "Hogan Dedicated for Boston Doctor," *Gallup Independent*, August 11, 1932.

37 Charlotte Whaley, *Alice Marriott Remembered* (Santa Fe: Sunstone Press, 2009), 99; McNitt, *The Indian Traders*, 238.

38 Charlotte Johnson Frisbie, "The Navajo House Blessing Ceremonial: A Study of Cultural Change" (PhD diss., University of New Mexico, 1970), 252n10.

39 Frisbie, "The Navajo House Blessing Ceremonial," 252n10.

40 Haskanaya's name was also spelled Haskanayah and Haske Nah-Yah.

41 "Today in New Mexico," *Albuquerque Journal*, February 28, 1933.

42 "Gouverneur Morris, Author, Will Live at Coolidge, N.M.," *Albuquerque Journal*, December 16, 1936; "Gouverneur Morris Picks Indian Trading Post for Locale of Short Stories," *Albuquerque Journal*, January 31, 1938. For more about the Morrises, see John A. Greenwald, *Wild Bird: The True Jazz Age Tale of Ruth Wightman Morris* (Monterey, CA: Hawk Tower Press, 2016), Kindle edition.

43 Greenwald, *Wild Bird*.

44 Gouverneur Morris, "Trading Post," *Saturday Evening Post*, October 30, 1937: 8–9, 74–75, 78.

45 "Trading Post Story in Saturday Post," *Southwest Tourist News*, October 28, 1937.

46 Morris, "Trading Post," 8.

47 "Society Flashes," *Albuquerque Journal*, January 26, 1938.

48 One of the earliest examples was the Three Hogans Trading Post, established three miles southwest of Lupton in 1928. For more details, see Kelley and Francis, 237–238,

124   *Route 66 and Diné Architecture*

and Repp, *Route 66*, 95, which includes a photograph of the business showing a large stacked-log hogan with a corbelled dome.

49 Court records and oral histories indicate that ownership of the Painted Desert Park and the Navajo Indian Village was complicated by a series of exchanges between members of the Jacobs family during the early 1940s.

50 Repp, *Route 66*, 120.

51 "Rural Property Report Card for 01–207–14–0002," June 23, 1966, gives a date of 1931 for the store, and "Appraisal of 01–207–14–0002," May 3, 1991, dates the store to 1934, ACA.

52 This description is based on a detailed photograph of the store entrance in the author's collection.

53 See Frasher Foto's postcard X8860, PPL.

54 Letterhead text on Charles H. Jacobs to United States Department of the Interior, May 25, 1995, PFNPA.

55 Repp, *Route 66*, 111; Eddie Lee, conversation with the author, October 22, 2009.

56 This list is based on an analysis of postcards and photographs in the author's collection.

57 "Superintendent's Report for March 1952," April 10, 1952, PFNPA.

58 "Superintendent's Report for August 1953," September 8, 1953, PFNPA.

59 "Superintendent's Report for March 1953," April 10, 1953, PFNPA.

60 H.B. Embach, "Appraisal Report for All of Section 10, T 19 N, R 24 E. S1/2 S1/2; NE1/4 SE1/4; E1/2 NE1/4 of Section 26, T 20 N, R 24 E, G.S.R.B.&M," March 21, 1957, 6. PFNPA.

61 Embach, "Appraisal Report for All of Section 10," 6.

62 This paragraph draws from Repp, *Route 66*, 105–107, 111–112.

63 Based on details in a photograph from author's collection.

64 Repp, *Route 66*, 107.

65 Repp, *Route 66*, 46.

66 Frasher Fotos postcard B9748, PPL.

67 "Ceremonial Committees Function; Hogan Headquarters on Plaza," *Gallup Independent*, July 25, 1930; "Hogan Roof Work," *Gallup Independent*, June 15, 1939.

68 "Hogan has Tourist Appeal," *Gallup Independent*, August 12, 1946.

69 "Ceremonial Sets Up in Hogan for Summer Offices," *Gallup Independent*, April 28, 1931.

70 "Work Shop Group Meets Wednesday," *Gallup Independent*, November 15, 1938; "Local Art Work Displayed at Hogan," *Gallup Independent*, June 9, 1942; "Hoofed Imprints Exhibited Here – Doctor's Navajo Find Shown at Hogan," *Gallup Independent*, June 30, 1939.

71 "Special Navajo Dance on Santa Fe Plaza Near Ceremonial Hogan Every Night," *Gallup Independent*, August 12, 1932; "Gamerco Band Plays on Santa Fe Plaza," *Gallup Independent*, August 25, 1934; "Band Plays Sunday," *Gallup Independent*, June 16, 1934.

72 "Ceremonial Gets Set for Big August Event," *Gallup Independent*, May 18, 1955.

73 "Obituary – J. Lowry Rush, Hogan Station," *Gallup Independent*, December 15, 1972. The Hogan Station was located about three miles from central Gallup near the Hogback, a geological formation on the city's east side.

74 Aubrey W. Williams, Jr., *Navajo Political Process* (Washington, DC: Smithsonian Institution Press, 1970), 35.

75 John G. Hunter to Irene Coonan, March 17, 1934, Box 19, NCCF-NARA-R.

76 Advertisement in the *Gallup Independent*, October 9, 1937: 4; "Harringtons Host the Bridgers," *Gallup Independent*, October 22, 1937; "Get-Together Dinner Held," *Gallup Independent*, November 17, 1937.

77 "For Rent – Furnished Cabin at Hogan Station [classified ad]," *Gallup Independent*, September 23, 1941: 3; "Eggs Potatoes Cash Wholesale Prices Hogan Station Grocery [advertisement]," *Gallup Independent*, October 11, 1943.

78 "Ports of Entry to Have Indian Type Buildings," *Clovis News-Journal*, June 19, 1937.

Route 66 and Diné Architecture 125

79 "Port of Entry to Have New Home," *Gallup Independent*, December 27, 1937; "FDR Approves Fund for New Entry Port," *Gallup Independent*, March 14, 1940.

80 "Sanders – Chambers – Lupton, Area Abounds in Trading Posts and Unique Open Pit Clay Mine," *Arizona Republic*, May 30, 1954.

81 This section relies on Repp's section about Meteor Station, later known as Rimmy Jim's in *Route 66: The Romance of the West*, 149–157.

82 "'Rimmy Jim' Giddings is Heart Victim," *Winslow Mail*, June 25, 1943.

83 Based on Frasher's Fotos postcard B9082, PPL, and an unnumbered Frasher's Fotos postcard in the Rimmy Jim's flat file, OTM.

84 Frasher's Fotos negative F1556z, PPL.

85 Reprint (Albuquerque: University of New Mexico Press, 1989), 99.

86 Carl Abbott, Stephen J. Leonard, and David McComb, *Colorado: A History of the Centennial State*, 4th ed. (Boulder: University Press of Colorado, 2005), 224.

87 Kathleen Bragdon, *The Columbia Guide to American Indians of the Northeast* (New York: Columbia University Press, 2001), 18.

88 "The Manitou Cliff Dwellers' Ruins in Cliff Dwellers' Cañon, Manitou" c. 1910, collection of the author.

89 "Goerke to Spend $30,000 in Development of West Garden of Gods as Scenic Spot," *The Sunday Gazette and Telegraph – Annual Edition*, March 2, 1924.T. Charles Gaastra was a Dutch architect who came to New Mexico from Chicago in 1918. He designed several New Mexico landmarks, including the Cassell Building (1921) and Bishop's Lodge (1928) in Santa Fe and the Monte Vista Elementary School (1930–1931) in Albuquerque.

90 Diana F. Pardue and Norman L. Sandfield, *Awa Tsireh: Pueblo Painter and Metalsmith* (Phoenix: Heard Museum, 2017), 73.

91 "Indians Transplanted to Garden of Gods in Strausenback's New Trading Post," *Colorado Springs Gazette*, June 9, 1929. The building shaped like a truncated cone is visible in an unprovenanced photo of Strausenback's trading post, collection of the author. An undated photo located in the collections of the Albuquerque Museum (PA2006.31.39) shows a similar building at the 1902 Alvarado Indian Village that may have influenced Strausenback.

92 Vicki Rottman, "Navajo Hogan, Colorado Springs, El Paso County, Colorado," September 1990 [National Register of Historic Places listing #90001420], section 8, page 2. In 1933, Gallup, New Mexico, was the site of a major effort to unionize coal miners, and a subsequent strike led to violence and garnered national attention. For more, see Harry R. Rubinstein, "The Great Gallup Coal Strike of 1933," *New Mexico Historical Review* 52, no. 3 (1977): 173–192.

93 Rottman, "Navajo Hogan, Colorado Springs," section 7, page 1.

94 Postcard text, postcard manufactured by Milton Company, c. 1950.

95 Kate Phillips, *Helen Hunt Jackson: A Literary Life* (Berkeley: University of California Press, 2003), 27.

96 Dydia Delyser, *Ramona Memories: Tourism and the Shaping of Southern California* (Minneapolis: University of Minnesota Press, 2005), 31.

97 Lee Shippey, "Lee Side o'L.A.," *Los Angeles Times*, May 20, 1931. For more on Robert Stacy-Judd, see David Gebhard and Anthony Peres, *Robert Stacy-Judd: Maya Architecture and the Creation of a New Style* (Santa Barbara, CA: Capra Press, 1993).

98 Edgar Lloyd Hampton, "In Aboriginal Homes We Now Can Live: California Recaptures the Architecture of America's Cave and Cliff Dwellers," *New York Times Magazine*, October 30, 1927: 12, 21.

99 Shippey, "Lee Side o'L.A."

100 "Buildings Hark to Early Days – Ancient Style Architecture Features Cities – American Indian Motif Used in Development – Homes Depict Atmosphere of Ancestral Period," *Los Angeles Times*, March 9, 1930.

101 "Theater of Indian Motif Inside and Outside: San Jacinto Playhouse Looks Like Home of Aborigines," *Los Angeles Times*, August 26, 1927. Other Pueblo-Spanish Revival

126   *Route 66 and Diné Architecture*

buildings in San Jacinto included Lloyd Record's Chrysler dealership and his Monte Vista Garage, as well as the First National Bank, San Jacinto Cleaners, and the O.S. Hofmann Building in San Jacinto. The Alessandro Hotel (1929), named after Ramona's ill-fated lover, and the Women's Club (c. 1930) were two more examples of the Pueblo-Spanish Revival style in Hemet. See "Indian Influence," *Hemet News*, April 19, 1940.

102   See Chris Wilson, *The Myth of Santa Fe* (Albuquerque: University of New Mexico Press, 1997), 122ff.

103   "Indian Influence."

104   *Life of Ramona and Alessandro If They Lived Today – A Pictorial Review of Riverside County – Golden Jubilee Edition* (San Jacinto Valley Register, 1938), collection of the author.

105   Based on Frasher Foto's postcard F759, PPL.

106   *Life of Ramona and Alessandro if They Lived Today*.

107   "Business Women Join District Meet at Hemet," *San Bernardino County Sun*, October 20, 1936.

108   In 1963, when William Hallahan sold the business, a newspaper article stated that he had been the proprietor for 31 years. See "Francis Keatings Buy Indian Plaza on Mohawk Trail," *North Adams Transcript*, June 5, 1963.

109   Wilfred French, "Through the Berkshires Over the Mohawk Trail," *Photo-Era Magazine* 49, no. 2 (August 1922): 76; *The Mohawk Trail – Historic Auto Trail Guide* (Brookline, MA: Muddy River Press, 2003), 1. For more on the Mohawk Trail, see Arthur Krim, "Mohawk Trail Rediscovered," *Society for Commercial Archeology Journal*, Spring 2002: 23–25.

110   *The Mohawk Trail – Historic Auto Trail Guide*, 33, 42; unprovenanced postcard, collection of the author.

111   Details based on a postcard in the author's collection.

112   "Navajo Indians Create Two-Man Town on Trail," *North Adams Transcript*, June 29, 1933.

113   The hogan was pictured in "Navajo Indians on the Mohawk Trail in Charlemont," *The Springfield Republican*, July 15, 1934.

114   "Navajo Indians Create Two-Man Town on Trail."

115   "Navajo Indians Create Two-Man Town on Trail."

116   "Indian Family Arrives in Town – Navajo Representatives at Trail Stand," *North Adams Transcript*, May 25, 1934.

117   "Holiday Event at Indian Camp – Unique Observance by Navajo Representatives," *North Adams Transcript*, June 29, 1934.

118   "Navajo Indians in Charlemont – Family of Three Attract Many Tourists at Casa del Navajo on Mohawk Trail," *Greenfield Daily Recorder-Gazette*, July 24, 1934.

119   "Varied Program for Women's Club – 35 Members in Attendance at Session," *North Adams Transcript*, January 24, 1935.

120   "Charlemont," *Springfield Republican*, August 5, 1937; "To Get Indians for Plaza Stand – William Hallahans Leave for Navajo Reservation," *North Adams Transcript*, April 21, 1938.

121   "Trader Topics," *Southwest Tourist News*, October 13, 1938.

Reference List

Archival Sources

Apache County Assessor's Office, St. Johns, Arizona. Cited as ACA.

Navajo Central Classified Files, RG 75, Records of the BIA, National Archives and Records Administration, Riverside, California. Cited as NCCF-NARA-R.

Petrified Forest National Park Archives. Cited as PFNPA.
Roads Files, Navajo Nation Land Department, Window Rock, Arizona. Cited as RF-NNLD.
Special Collections, Old Trails Museum, Winslow, Arizona. Cited as OTM.
Special Collections, Pomona Public Library, Pomona, California. Cited as PPL.

Published Sources

Abbott, Carl, Stephen J. Leonard, and David McComb. *Colorado: A History of the Centennial State*, 4th ed. Boulder: University of Colorado Press, 2005.

Angelo, Bernardine Rose. "Beckoning the Red Man's Spirit: Exploring the Boundaries of Gender, Race, Sacred and Commercial Spaces at the Wigwam Spiritualist Temple, Onset, Massachusetts, 1880–1913." Master's thesis, University of Massachusetts – Boston, 2010.

Beauvoir, Simone de. *America Day by Day*. Translated by Carol Cosman. London: Phoenix, 1998.

Bragdon, Kathleen. *The Columbia Guide to American Indians of the Northeast*. New York: Columbia University Press, 2001.

Carroll, Terry. "Gallup and Her Ceremonials." PhD diss., University of New Mexico, 1971.

Delyser, Dydia. *Ramona Memories: Tourism and the Shaping of Southern California*. Minneapolis: University of Minnesota Press, 2005.

French, Wilfred. "Through the Berkshires Over the Mohawk Trail." *Photo-Era Magazine* 49, no. 2 (August 1922): 74–82.

Frisbie, Charlotte Johnson. "The Navajo House Blessing Ceremonial: A Study of Cultural Change." PhD diss., University of New Mexico, 1970.

Gebhard, David. "Introduction." *California Crazy and Beyond: Roadside Vernacular Architecture*, by Jim Heimann, 6–17. San Francisco: Chronicle Books, 2001.

Greenwald, John A. *Wild Bird: The True Jazz Age Tale of Ruth Wightman Morris*. Monterey, CA: Hawk Tower Press, 2016.

Gudis, Cathering. *Buyways: Billboards, Automobiles, and the American Landscape*. New York: Routledge, 2004.

Hall, Sharlot. *Sharlot Hall on the Arizona Strip: A Diary of Journey Through Northern Arizona in 1911*. Edited by C. Gregory Crampton. Flagstaff, AZ: Northland Press, 1975.

Jett, Stephen C. "Culture and Tourism in the Navajo Country." *Journal of Cultural Geography* 11, no. 1 (1990): 85–107.

Kelley, Klara, and Harris Francis. *Navajoland Trading Post Encyclopedia*. Window Rock, AZ: Navajo Nation Heritage and Historic Preservation Department, 2018.

McCarley, Rebecca Lawin. "Orson S. Fowler and a Home for All: The Octagon House in the Midwest." *Perspectives in Vernacular Architecture* 12 (2005):

McNitt, Frank. *The Indian Traders*. Norman: University of Oklahoma Press, 1962.

Mindeleff, Cosmos. "Navaho Houses." *17th Annual Report of the Bureau of American Ethnology, 1895–1896*, Part 2. Washington, DC: GPO, 1898.

The Mohawk Trail – Historic Auto Trail Guide. Brookline, MA: Muddy River Press, 2003.

Morris, Gouveneur. "Trading Post." *Saturday Evening Post*, October 30, 1937: 8–9, 74–75, 78.

Nabokov, Peter, and Robert Easton. *Native American Architecture*. New York: Oxford University Press, 1989.

Pardue, Diana F., and Norman L. Sandfield. *Awa Tsireh: Pueblo Painter and Metalsmith*. Phoenix: Heard Museum, 2017.

Phillips, Kate. *Helen Hunt Jackson: A Literary Life*. Berkeley: University of California Press, 2003.

Repp, Thomas Arthur. *Route 66: The Romance of the West*. Lynnwood, WA: Mock Turtle Press, 2002.

Rittenhouse, Jack. *A Guide Book to Highway 66*. Albuquerque: University of New Mexico Press, 1989. First published 1946.

Rottman, Vicki. "Navajo Hogan, Colorado Springs, El Paso County, Colorado." September 1990. National Register of Historic Places listing #90001420.

128 *Route 66 and Diné Architecture*

Scott, Quinta. *Along Route 66*. Norman: University of Oklahoma Press, 2000.

Shuart, Harry E. "New Mexico Goes to the 'World's Fair.'" *New Mexico*, July 1934: 10–12.

Stein, Pat. "Tuba Trading Post, Coconino County, Arizona." October 1996. National Register of Historic Places listing #96001362.

US Senate, Committee on Indian Affairs, Subcommittee on Senate Resolution 79. *Survey of Conditions of the Indians in the United States*, Part 34. March 18 and 25, May 14–15 and 29, August 17–21, 1936. Washington, DC: GPO, 1937. Cited as *SOC*, Part 34.

Williams, Aubrey W., Jr. *Navajo Political Process*. Washington, DC: Smithsonian Institution Press, 1970.

Wilson, Chris. *The Myth of Santa Fe*. Albuquerque: University of New Mexico Press, 1997.

Woodard, M.L. "The Navajo Goes East." *New Mexico Highway Journal* (March 1931): 14.

4 The Indian New Deal

In 1933, Franklin Delano Roosevelt became president, and in his wake, a group of progressive intellectuals rose to positions of power within the federal government. Among those intellectuals was John Collier, who would serve until 1945 as the commissioner of Indian Affairs. On July 7, 1933, Collier addressed the Navajo Nation Tribal Council for the first time as a federal official. He opened by commending the Diné for their ability "to deal with the modern world in an efficient way while at the same time remaining truly Indian and faithful to the Indian traditions and to the great Indian ideals."[1] This theme – navigating between modernity and tradition by embracing both – had guided Collier's work for over 25 years. It would now underpin the government's commitment to funding the construction of Diné hogans on the reservation.

This chapter will examine three different building projects designed for the federal government by the architectural firm of Mayers, Murray & Phillip. The projects were constructed by Native American men who worked as part of locally based crews or who were enrolled in the Civilian Conservation Corps-Indian Division. The first project, dating from 1933, was a hogan village located in Mexican Springs (*Naakai Bito'í*), New Mexico. Mexican Springs was the site of an historic soil erosion control experiment station that later became known as "the birthplace of the Soil Conservation Service."[2]

In 1934, the Office of Indian Affairs (OIA) organized the construction of "practice hogans" for teaching home economics and improving health practices on the reservation. And during the same year, the government funded another project to build hogans for young Navajo women serving as nurse's aides. In the next chapter, we will examine Collier's day school/community center program and explore the debate over the new "hogan schools" he proposed for the Diné. By tracing the federally funded architecture constructed during the New Deal, it becomes clear that by the early 1930s, architects seeking to employ the Diné hogan for new uses found the octagonal stacked-log hogan to be an adaptable form carrying a high level of symbolic significance.

John Collier

John Collier was born in Atlanta in 1884. As a young man, he pursued studies in several intellectual disciplines, but ultimately, sociology emerged as his

DOI: 10.4324/9781003431770-5

major focus.³ As Collier matured, he became one of the many reformers of the age who expressed "the *gemeinschaft* grouse," the complaint "that industrialism had dissolved the fabric of community leaving alienation in its wake."⁴ For intellectuals like Collier, modernity was a mixed blessing; its many benefits seemed inextricably tied to societies dominated by rules and impersonal relationships. In 1907, he embarked on a career as a social worker among the immigrants of New York City. For the next twelve years, Collier worked to combat the fragmentation he saw in modern American society. He authored articles, gave speeches, organized public events, and initiated programs that promoted community-based decision-making and emphasized the value of traditional cultures.⁵

It was during the same period that Collier began to reflect on the role of educational institutions as agents of social change. In 1911, he began a program to develop public schools in New York City into "school community centers," where children and adults could meet after regular class hours. The program kept young immigrants off the streets and provided a space for cultural activities. At the conclusion of World War I, he left New York City to become the director of California's state adult

Figure 4.1 Chee Dodge, John Collier, Charles Collier, and Tom Dodge, 1933.

The Indian New Deal 131

educational program. Collier, who viewed the newly formed Soviet Union as "the most important single sociological experiment of our time," was targeted by a group of conservative entrepreneurs, and the funding for his position evaporated.[6]

Collier found himself adrift, but a trip to visit his old friend Mabel Dodge in Taos, New Mexico, led to an encounter that would prove transformative. In December 1920, he attended a Native American religious ceremony at Taos Pueblo and was shaken to the core. Collier discovered a culture that embraced the communal values he had been advocating throughout his career as a social worker, and he experienced a depth of emotion that vindicated his efforts to preserve ethnic traditions. As Kenneth Philp has observed, "Collier concluded that Pueblo culture, and tribal life in general, must survive, not only in justice to the Indian but in service to the white."[7]

In 1922, Collier became an American Indian rights activist sponsored by the General Federation of Women's Clubs.[8] He quickly turned his attention to New Mexico and brought all of his talents to bear on defeating the Bursum Bill, which jeopardized land grants to Pueblo Indians. Collier orchestrated an extensive campaign that brought him national recognition and established him as a central figure in the Native American rights movement. In 1923, he helped found a new organization, the American Indian Defense Association (AIDA), which subsequently became the most progressive of the major Indian reform groups in the US. Serving as the AIDA's executive secretary until 1933, Collier set out a far-reaching agenda that addressed a range of Native American issues, including religious freedom, land rights, economic development, reimbursable debt, health, and education.

In mid-1923, Collier traveled through the Navajo reservation for the first time.[9] Like Theodore Roosevelt before him, Collier stayed at the Wetherill Trading Post in Kayenta, Arizona. He met Louisa Wetherill and later described her as "the person with the most detailed and penetrating vision of the esthetic and mystic life of the Navajo."[10] Collier would have seen the "Big Hogan" during the visit, and the articles he published in *Sunset* and *Survey Graphic* about the trip outlined a "new Navajo program," which he credited to Mrs. Wetherill.[11] The program advocated the creation of community centers alongside model hogans, as Collier explained:

> Build all the field services around local community centers, placed about the reservation so that Navajos wherever they wander will be within ten or twenty miles of one of them. Locate there the medical work, the stock and farm education, the craft centers. Make each of these local headquarters into an experimental undertaking, trying out how to combine child education with adult education, book education with agriculture, trade with arts and crafts, and everything with health. Boarding schools will still be necessary, but they will be small institutions, the basis of community centers, and the Navajo children will live in outdoor structures in the nature of "model" hogans.[12]

As commissioner of Indian Affairs, Collier would later initiate the construction of model hogans at community centers across the Navajo reservation, but they would bear little resemblance to the "Big Hogan" in Kayenta.

132   *The Indian New Deal*

Mayers, Murray & Phillip

In August 1933, John Collier dispatched his oldest son, Charles, to New York City to find an architect to design new buildings for Native American reservations (see Figure 4.1). Charles Collier, who had recently earned an undergraduate degree in architecture, began by consulting Oliver La Farge. La Farge had a background in anthropology and, in 1930, had been awarded the Pulitzer Prize in fiction for *Laughing Boy*, a novel about the challenges experienced by boarding school students who returned to live on the Navajo reservation. In 1932, La Farge turned away from a promising academic career to become the president of the National Association of Indian Affairs, one of the country's most important Indian rights organizations.[13] La Farge was also probably tapped for help because his family included several prominent architects, including his father, C. Grant La Farge.

While in New York, Charles Collier interviewed several candidates for the contract with the OIA.[14] The group included Raymond Hood,[15] William J. Creighton,[16] Lawrence G. White of McKim, Mead, and White,[17] Arthur C. Holden,[18] Clarence Stein,[19] as well as the firm of Mayers, Murray & Phillip. John Collier and Secretary of the Interior Harold Ickes met with Hardie Phillip of Mayers, Murray & Phillip, and on August 19, the commissioner wired the architects with the news that their contract had been finalized.[20]

Francis L.S. Mayers, Oscar Harold Murray, and F. Hardie Phillip had previously worked together for architect Bertram Grosvenor Goodhue. Francis L.S. Mayers was born in Barbados and educated at McGill University in Montréal. He became Goodhue's office manager in 1914.[21] Oscar H. Murray was born in Gateshead, England, and educated at the Municipal School of Art and Technical School in Birmingham.[22] Hardie Phillip was born in Scone, Scotland, and educated in Edinburgh. He joined the office of architect Robert Lorimer in 1905 and rose to the level of assistant before departing the firm in 1910. Phillip spent two years working in the Federated Malay States (now part of Malaysia) and then immigrated to New York.[23]

An article about Goodhue's office published in 1922 offers a look at the various roles that Mayers, Murray, and Phillip played. While Mayers served as Goodhue's office manager, Murray and Phillip were among the four draftsmen employed by the office. In the article, Goodhue credited Murray with the design for the Rockefeller Memorial Chapel (1918–1928) at the University of Chicago, "a large church that is, perhaps, the most advanced and monumental piece of Gothic design that has ever come from here." Goodhue also noted that Phillip had trained with Robert Lorimer, "one of the four or five architects in the world who really understand Gothic." He praised Phillip's versatility and described him as "chiefly responsible" for the Church of St. Vincent Ferrer (1916–1918), an important example of the Gothic Revival style in Manhattan.[24]

After Goodhue's death in 1924, Mayers, Murray, and Phillip formed Bertram Grosvenor Goodhue Associates. The firm was renamed Mayers, Murray & Phillip by early 1929 and then dissolved in 1940, when each of the architects established his own practice. The early years of the partnership must have been almost unimaginably busy as the three men endeavored to complete the projects that had been underway when Goodhue died, including the Nebraska State Capitol (1922–1932), the Los Angeles

The Indian New Deal   133

Public Library (1924–1926), the Rockefeller Chapel at the University of Chicago, and the Honolulu Academy of the Arts (1922–1927). Mayers, Murray & Phillip also continued work that had begun in 1915 at the California Institute of Technology (a project that would not end until 1938) and at Oahu College in Hawaii.[25]

Goodhue's visit to Hawaii in 1917 had established connections that led to several commissions for Mayers, Murray & Phillip after his death. According to historian Daina Penkiunas, one of the most important was Hardie Phillip's Bank of Hawaii (1925–1927), which "began a new tradition in commercial building design in Honolulu."[26] Goodhue and Phillip together established a vocabulary of iconic elements that would come to identify a distinctive Hawaiian style. These elements included lava block masonry; stucco manufactured from locally sourced stone; a bonnet (or double-pitched hipped) roof covered with terracotta tiles; broad, overhanging eaves; window grilles, metal railings, and other types of ornamentation featuring vegetal patterns inspired by Hawaiian plants; and interior ceiling decorations based on traditional tapa (bark cloth) designs.[27]

Immediately after hiring Mayers, Murray & Phillip, John Collier contacted the superintendents of the country's Indian reservations to explain the rationale behind his choice:

> The firm has done noteworthy building in many parts of the world. Most interesting from our Indian standpoint are the Hawaiian buildings which were planned and supervised on the ground by Mr. Phillip. These buildings practically established an indigenous architecture for modern uses in the Islands. Native labor and native materials were used and native traditions were built on.[28]

Although native Hawaiian buildings and Navajo hogans are quite different, Collier viewed Phillip's success in creating "an indigenous architecture for modern uses" as excellent preparation for designing an idiom that would accommodate new functions while reflecting the tribal identity of American Indians.

The Soil Erosion Control Experiment Station in Mexican Springs

Soil erosion is a geological phenomenon that offers little cause for concern under normal circumstances. Whether initiated by water, wind, or other forces, the wearing away of the top layer of the earth's surface is a process that is natural and unceasing.[29] Excessive or "abnormal" soil erosion, however, can present a significant challenge, especially to farmers dependent on the fertility of the land.[30] Soil loss in the Eastern United States had become a problem as early as the mid-18th century. As historian Angus McDonald has documented, "many fields were becoming barren, farms had already been abandoned, and in the older, settled regions, erosion was more generally noticed."[31] But even though soil erosion was serious enough to merit discussion in the earliest book on American agriculture – Jared Eliot's *An Essay upon Field-Husbandry in New-England* (1748) – it would not be considered a major issue until the 1920s.[32] It was during those years that Hugh H. Bennett rose to prominence as a leader in the movement to prevent soil erosion across the US.

134　*The Indian New Deal*

Bennett – later to become the first director of the US Soil Conservation Service – began his career as a soil scientist in 1903. Working for the US Department of Agriculture (USDA), he performed surveys assessing soil conditions and noticed that erosion was taking a considerable toll on the farmlands that he visited.[33] In the years that followed, he concentrated his efforts on reducing soil erosion and raising awareness of the issue.[34] During the 1920s, he produced a series of publications for scholarly and lay audiences alike, culminating in *Soil Erosion: A National Menace* (1928), a USDA pamphlet coauthored with William Ridgely Chapline.[35] Thousands of copies were distributed across the US, and Bennett soon found he had created the public forum he had been seeking.[36]

While Bennett's plan for controlling soil erosion was multi-faceted in its approach, it relied on research about the conditions that aid and abet erosion. Facilities where scientific data could be gathered under controlled conditions were essential. Bennett engaged in a vigorous campaign to obtain funding for soil erosion control experiment stations. His efforts finally bore fruit in December 1928 when the House of Representatives adopted the Buchanan Amendment and appropriated $160,000 for soil erosion investigations.[37]

Bennett's new program was by no means the first to study of soil erosion in the US. His home agency, the USDA's Bureau of Chemistry and Soils, as well as state-based agricultural experiment stations, the US Forest Service, and even the Bureau of Public Roads had all been collecting information about the effects of erosion for years before the Buchanan Amendment's passage. But Bennett brought these disparate projects under one umbrella to create "the first national program of erosion research."[38]

As of mid-1932, ten soil erosion control experiment stations were in operation across the country with each location focusing on a different soil profile.[39] When funding became available through the New Deal's Public Works Administration (PWA) in 1933, Bennett found the means to build more experiment stations and begin research on the soils located within the Navajo reservation.

By late spring of 1933, John Collier had appointed his son, Charles, to serve in an official capacity as his personal representative. He would later write, "I knew, as Charles did, that severe wind and water erosion existed in the Southwest Indian reservations," and that a survey of soil conditions was necessary. Collier saw the declining viability of tribal lands as a threat to the growing populations who lived there, and he asked Charles to search for an individual to head up the survey. In due time, Charles located Hugh Bennett.[40]

Two hundred and fifty thousand dollars from the federally funded Emergency Conservation Work (ECW) program were on tap to support a unit of the Civilian Conservation Corps-Indian Division (CCC-ID) in building a soil erosion control experiment station. The CCC-ID was a unit of the CCC specifically designated for Native Americans, and it funded work on a wide range of projects within Indian reservations. Native American men of all ages could join, and the rules laying out the organization gave enrollees a great deal of flexibility. Some crews were set up so that men could stay at CCC-ID camps with their families, while others could live at home.[41]

On June 26, a committee chaired by Bennett met in Gallup to begin a tour to examine soil erosion on the reservation.[42] After traveling north to Shiprock, New Mexico, and then westward to Ganado, Arizona, Bennett and his colleagues

The Indian New Deal   135

selected a parcel of land northwest of Gallup in Mexican Springs.[43] The parcel, which was "as representative a cross section of the reservation as could be found," covered about 67 square miles.[44] Averaging five miles wide, it extended along a single watershed from the peaks of the Chuska Mountains eastward across Highway 666 (now US Route 491) into an area known as the Tohatchi Flats.

When Hugh Bennett led his survey team through the Navajo reservation, he witnessed a landscape that, from his perspective, was seriously eroded and in need of remediation.[45] The report that he and committee submitted on July 2, 1933, described the areas they had visited and warned:

> This is not a problem for future solution. It must be cared for at present. Much of the more productive land is lost or is approaching an irreparable condition. Because of the soil loss already sustained a large part of the better range probably cannot be restored to more than fifty to seventy-five percent of its former productivity.[46]

The sense of urgency in the report pervaded the presentation that Bennett gave to the Navajo Nation Tribal Council on July 7. His opening words – "The soil, the land is the most precious thing we have" – elevated the speech above conventional political rhetoric.[47] As he continued, he portrayed soil erosion as a national crisis and spoke of civilizations that had "disappeared from the earth because of this evil."[48] Having established the threat, Bennett outlined his plan for soil erosion control experiment stations on the Navajo reservation and described his proposal for a facility in Mexican Springs.

On July 8, 1933, the Tribal Council unanimously adopted a resolution "for the establishment and operation of an Erosion Control Station."[49] Two days later, on July 10, Richard Boke – a biologist and educator who had been designated as the project's manager – arrived in Mexican Springs.[50] After lengthy discussions on July 14, local residents, including Benny Tahe, Frank Cadman, and Frank Catron, "applied all their energies to securing the approval of the Navajo people concerned," and an agreement was reached on July 15 to begin building.

Boke and a CCC-ID crew began fencing the experiment station "almost immediately" afterwards.[51] During the months that followed, livestock were removed, and a 75-mile-long barbed-wire fence was completed by November 1.[52] In addition to the fence, the 130 CCC-ID enrollees working in Mexican Springs constructed check dams along the drainages within the station.[53] Check dams can take many forms, but essentially, they are "structures built in water channels and gullies to slow down the movement of water and give it more time to soak into the ground."[54] As late as February 1934, Boke would report that the erosion control work at the station consisted almost exclusively of clearing out livestock and constructing hundreds of check dams.[55]

When Hugh Bennett and his committee submitted their report about soil erosion on the Navajo reservation back in July 1933, they included an interesting stipulation:

> The station should be provided with attractive and comfortable staff quarters, a pleasantly arranged group of hogans for the Indians and such other structures as the director may recommend.[56]

136 *The Indian New Deal*

Walter C. Lowdermilk, the vice director of the Soil Erosion Service, took up the directive and arranged for Boke to build ten log hogans to house the CCC-ID crew. Thirty-six thousand dollars had been released from the PWA for construction purposes in Mexican Springs, and the money was applied to fund the hogans.[57]

Historic records indicate that two different groups each began working on a design for the hogans at about the same time.[58] On November 2, Charles Collier, acting as a special assistant to Bennett, requested a plan for the hogans from Mayers, Murray & Phillip. Meanwhile, on November 4, Lowdermilk wrote to Boke and asked him to prepare a drawing for a log hogan with a diameter of 20' and a sloping roof for shedding snow.[59]

The correspondence between architect Hardie Phillip and Charles Collier indicates a painstaking consideration of various aspects of the design, with special attention being paid to the hogans' corbelled-log roof, corner-timbering, adobe flooring, and light fixture arrangement, as well as the construction of the bunkbeds that were to line the walls of the hogans. Phillip altered the plan in accordance with Collier's suggestions and lightheartedly described his work as "the latest adventure in hogan design."[60]

Meanwhile, Walter Lowdermilk was moving ahead with his own plan for the hogans. He instructed the CCC-ID crew to proceed with felling trees and wrote Bennett, "we expect to use either paved or concrete floors and shakes for the roof. Mr. Boke has very cleverly trained the Indians to split shakes of the Pine trees, which will give us a very artistic roof for hogans."[61]

The architects mailed Phillip's hogan design to Mexican Springs on November 24.[62] By December 11, Lowdermilk reported to John Collier that the logs for the hogans were at the building site and that the foundations would soon be in place.[63] Shortly afterwards, Phillip sent Charles Collier a picture of the construction site showing a group of octagonal stacked-log hogans, each with a pyramidal roof (Figure 4.2a).

The picture was accompanied by a note from Phillip in which he commented on the request – perhaps made by Lowdermilk – that the architects withdraw their plan to employ corbelled-log roofs. Phillip's sense of humor was evident as he observed:

> most of the roofs are covered with boarding and the shingles are *beautifully* hand split and ready for the Delux [sic] surfacing. The reason why the hogan type roof was abandoned is that it "harbors and encourages too many bugs, lice, etc." Do nothing but enjoy the joke, and the irony of it all until I see you.[64]

In the end, the pyramidal roofs were given a rounded shape and covered with earth to make them look corbelled (see Figure 4.2b). Shingles are not typical roofing material in Navajo country, and the layer of earth gave the hogans a more traditional appearance. The roof's unusual structure was probably a compromise reached between the two teams of designers – Charles Collier and Hardie Phillip on the one hand and Walter Lowdermilk and Richard Boke on the other.

Eleven hogans were eventually built at the heart of Mexican Springs, creating a small village (Figure 4.3).

Ten of the hogans contained one room with concrete flooring and adobe-plastered interior walls. An eleventh log "double-hogan" was connected to a rectangular

The Indian New Deal 137

Figure 4.2 The hogans at the Mexican Springs Soil Erosion Control Experiment Station, Mexican Springs, New Mexico: a. Photo of hogans under construction, looking north, 1933; b. Photo of a completed hogan, looking east, c. 1935.

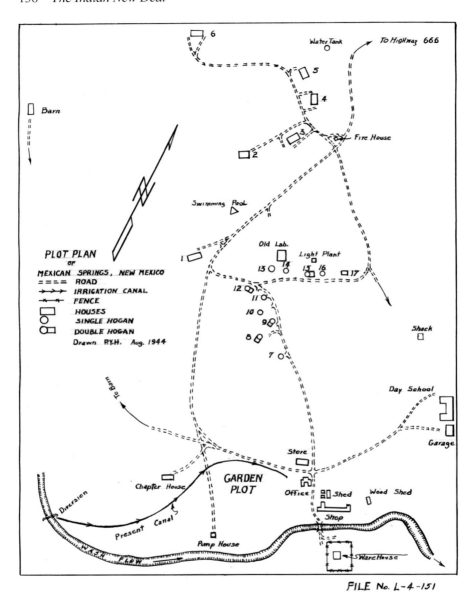

Figure 4.3 Plot Plan of the Mexican Springs Soil Erosion Control Experiment Station, August 1944. The hogans are numbered 7 through 17, and the Pueblo-Spanish Revival residences are numbered 1 through 6. The day school is located on the east side and the chapter house on the west side of the plan.

The Indian New Deal   139

building containing a kitchen. By the time the plot plan illustrated in Figure 4.3 was prepared in 1944, three more of the hogans had been enlarged with an attached building, presumably containing a kitchen. Two bathhouses, each with three showers and two toilets, provided additional facilities for the staff who lived in the hogans.[65] In March 1936, when Hardie Phillip toured the reservation to review the condition of the buildings his firm had designed, some of the hogans had been expanded with log-cabin-style garages. Phillip complained:

> These garages have tin roofs and on account of their location and relation to the main approach road, one looks down on top of these tin roofs. They look decidedly out of place and no relation whatsoever to the native architecture of the houses.[66]

The presence of the garages indicated that the hogans were no longer being occupied by members of the CCC-ID. When Charles J. Whitfield replaced Boke at the end of January 1934, the station's professional staff began to arrive, and some of them were immediately housed in the hogans.[67] E.R. Fryer, who became superintendent of the Navajo reservation on April 15, 1936, was among the employees who lived in the hogans. Donald S. Hubbell – later to become the experiment station's director – arrived on February 1, 1934, as its chief soil scientist and assistant director. He and his family lived in one of the hogans for two years.[68]

The hogan village was the first major architectural project in Mexican Springs, and it was almost certainly used to accommodate Euro-Americans working at the station because there were no other buildings available at the time.[69] By January 2, 1934, Soil Erosion Service officials had assembled a set of recommendations with regard to the next building phase.[70] The list included ten private residences, each with at least three bedrooms; a powerhouse; a large garage; an administration building; a bachelor's quarters to house ten men; and a warehouse.[71]

The need for a large laboratory facility and several multiroom residences to house Euro-American families explains why the architects employed the Pueblo-Spanish Revival style for the remaining architecture in Mexican Springs. Mayers, Murray & Phillip combined hogans to form larger buildings in their plans for hogan schools on the reservation to be discussed in detail in the following chapter. But the design was impractical for smaller buildings containing a variety of interior spaces.

By the fall of 1934, it was fast becoming clear that the construction costs for the first six private residences and the power plant would expend the entire PWA allocation.[72] In March 23, 1935, the Soil Erosion Service moved from the Department of the Interior to the USDA to become the Soil Conservation Service.[73] In May of that year, Acting Secretary of Agriculture M.L. Wilson petitioned Ickes for funding to build more residences and stressed, "At the present time, the staff of the Soil Erosion Service is living and working very largely in tents and hogans in a manner which very seriously interferes with the effectiveness of the work."[74] But the original plans for Mexican Springs were never to be completed. The only buildings added to the six houses built during 1934–1935 were a garage, warehouse, machine shop, powerhouse, and the administration building.[75]

140 *The Indian New Deal*

During the same period, federal employees and the architects were working to build a chapter house in Mexican Springs.[76] The earliest mention of this building occurs in a telegram dated November 7, 1933, from Richard Boke to Charles Collier.[77] By February 17, 1934, Charles Whitfield was in contact with Hardie Phillip about designing the new "community house."[78] Two days later, Charlies Collier also communicated with Phillip and reported that the "Indians are anxious to have it built and we would like to start soon."[79]

Whitfield specified an "octagonal hogan thirty feet in diameter" with space for 200 people. Details included a stage platform, two fireplaces, six windows, and one 3′ by 7′ door, facing east.[80] The controversy over the method used to roof the 11 residential hogans seems to have been revived during these discussions. Charles Collier sent Phillip a sketch plan of the proposed chapter house and was emphatic that it should have a corbelled-log roof. On February 26, 1934, Collier wrote Phillip:

> I hope that you will write a strong letter insisting that the roof be constructed in the hogan manner, rather than with two – by – four and boarding, and if they are not willing to do this they should make a standard rectangular chapter house with vegas [sic].[81]

The letter and accompanying drawing that Mayers, Murray & Phillip sent Charles Whitfield on March 9 would probably have pleased Charles Collier. Phillip wrote that the roof was "worked out on the lintel system used by the Indians in the building of their own hogans, and I hope that this type of construction will be adhered to."[82] But the chapter house that was dedicated on June 11, 1934, was not a hogan but rather, a rectangular log building with a large auditorium and two small rooms.[83]

According to an article published in the *Albuquerque Journal* on July 31, 1934, the new day school in Mexican Springs was to be a "hogan school" with buildings composed of conjoined hogans.[84] But the school that was completed by the following year was in the stripped Pueblo-Spanish Revival style that the architects employed for most of the Navajo reservation (the building is visible in the background of Figure. 4.2b). A similar style was used for the Mexican Springs Trading Post.[85]

Although a small community was materializing at the center of Mexican Springs, the building projects there were dwarfed by the scale of construction proceeding around the rest of the station. According to M.E. Musgrave, chief of range studies at the experiment station, the five-acre nursery in Mexican Springs cultivated plants that would "not only serve as soil-binders and -builders, but which would provide food for man or beast, or both." The site included a peach orchard, a one-acre lath canopy where seedlings could sprout, and a heeling bed for resting plants shipped from elsewhere. Trees, including willow and tamarisk, were planted along the banks of gullies. The foodstuffs grown at the station included varieties regularly consumed by Indigenous peoples in the Americas, such as honey locust pods, sumac berries, and hawthorn berries. By mid-February 1935, the federal program had added over 600,000 plants to the landscape in Mexican Springs.[86]

The Indian New Deal 141

During the first few years, "almost every conceivable erosion control measure was tried out, and silt and run-off were studied" at the experiment station.[87] The check dams that constituted the "bread and butter" of early engineering structures at the station were later used more selectively. By 1939, Bennett would report that jetties and drop (or chute) structures were being favored.[88] Other means were also being implemented to divert water away from gullies, thereby increasing the absorption of moisture by the soil. In Mexican Springs, earthen dikes, spreaders, and diversion dams were built for this purpose. Dikes and spreaders were typically smaller projects; while dikes were more permanent, spreaders could be constructed from inexpensive materials. Some comprised nothing more than woven wire faced with burlap bags to provide a fence-like barrier against onrushing water. The largest engineering structure at the station was the Norcross Dam, a rock-and-earth diversion dam extending 1,310′ across Mexican Springs Wash.[89] Constructed during early 1934, it redirected the wash's flow so that it could spread at a more gradual rate over the surrounding area.[90] But most of the projects in Mexican Springs were much more simple and easy to construct; the objective was to persuade people without an engineering background that they could build them too.

During the 1930s, Mexican Springs served as an attraction – a demonstration area of sorts – for Euro-Americans. High-ranking government officials came to eastern New Mexico to visit the experiment station as did private citizens like the poet Archibald MacLeish, who opined, "Here, the destiny of a nation is at stake."[91] But how did the Diné feel about it?

In 1936, a Senate subcommittee held a series of hearings in New Mexico and Arizona regarding a proposed boundary extension to the Navajo reservation. Fred Edsitty and Frank Cadman testified in Window Rock (*Tségháhoodzání*), Arizona, and John Dean Barney submitted a letter that was entered into the record.

Edsitty, the president of the Mexican Springs Chapter, stated, "I am much in favor of soil conservation."[92] Barney, the chapter's vice-president, also supported the experiment station in his letter, writing:

I and the people I represent want very much a permanent soil-conservation program for the reservation, as the soil is our life at present and is necessary to our life in the future. Due to abuse by our people, by our livestock, wind, and water, our land is all either blowing or washing away.[93]

But Frank Cadman expressed a very different point of view and said:

To my knowledge, the area that was first set aside by the present administration for the purpose of experimenting soil-conservation work – the area that I refer to is Mexican Springs – not much has developed there to brag about. I think mostly that the condition, the way things are now, is not only due to overgrazing but drought, and water is a thing we need; water is the main thing we should get. I think that the money that has been expended on soil erosion – putting dams in these arroyos, and stuff like that – that money has

142 *The Indian New Deal*

all been thrown away; it could very easily have been used for water development; then we would have water now.[94]

Cadman, who lived at the station, spoke about the problems created by keeping the gates to the station closed and explained that the fences there prompted him to stop working for the Soil Erosion Service.

During the 1930s, photographs of fences featured prominently in the publicity about the reservation's soil erosion control program. The federal government argued that fences were necessary to keep out livestock and demonstrate soil conservation practices. But for many Diné, the fences became a major source of hostility. On July 10, 1943, the Tribal Council voted to abolish Mexican Springs.[95] But although the measure passed 46–5, the Secretary of the Interior vetoed it.[96] Friction between the federal government and the Diné, as well as infighting between various tribal factions, would continue to prevent a satisfactory resolution to the issues created by the Mexican Springs Soil Erosion Control Experiment Station well into the 1950s.

In an interview conducted in 1970, E.R. Fryer, who served as the superintendent of the Navajo reservation between 1936 and 1942, discussed the history of Mexican Springs and reflected:

> The establishment of this area meant the dispossession, the taking out of use for at least a temporary period, of this whole vast acreage, and many people were deprived of their historic grazing lands and were naturally bitter. As the opposition developed to the program of conservation, Mexican Springs became the focal point of opposition, and chapter officers who had earlier seen great opportunities in the establishment of Mexican Springs and had aided the government's efforts there, who had sanctioned it, turned against the program until Mexican Springs became a bone of contention far beyond any useful purpose served by it.[97]

From the perspective of the Soil Erosion Service, the Navajo architecture in Mexican Springs declared "this is a Navajo place" and helped make the erosion control methods being demonstrated there more attractive to the Diné. But the government's best efforts could not overcome the resentment that Navajos felt about the enclosure of their land. Ironically, the "typical" Navajo dwelling around Mexican Springs was a round stone hogan.[98] But the architects who designed the experiment station were not seeking to imitate local vernacular styles. Mexican Springs was founded as a symbol of soil conservation on the Navajo reservation, and the federal government opted for an iconic form that rose above any sense of individuality – the stacked-log hogan with an imitation corbelled dome. Even the site plan of Mexican Springs emphasized the buildings' significance by lining the hogans along the main road through the station and placing them in a central position overlooking Mexican Springs Wash. But after the bitterness grew, Mexican Springs became a different type of symbol, representing the federal government's refusal to comply with the wishes of the Navajo people.

Practice Hogans on the Navajo Reservation

Although Diné boarding schools began to include model hogans during the 1920s, the federal government did not seriously address "improving" the hogan until John Collier became the commissioner of Indian Affairs in 1933. During the months following his appointment, Collier laid out his plans and obtained the funding to create a system of day school/community centers across the Navajo reservation that would enable children to attend classes while living at home. The $1,438,200 budget he obtained for building schools at the Pueblos and on the Navajo, Hopi, and Papago reservations across Arizona and New Mexico included a special appropriation: $18,000 for Federal Project (F.P.) 295 to be used for building "Home practice houses and hogans to be located at central day schools, chiefly in the Navajo area."[99] Ten years earlier, Collier had visited Louisa Wetherill's "Big Hogan" and published his vision for building model hogans at community centers across the reservation. That vision was about to become a reality.

The model hogans built on the Navajo reservation during the Indian New Deal were known by several different names, including "practice hogans," "demonstration hogans," "community hogans," and "home economics hogans." But they were all based on a plan originating with Mayers, Murray & Phillip. The architects were slated to oversee construction as well; however, Collier arranged to give the Diné who lived locally a more direct role in building the hogans. By the first week of June 1934, the OIA had released the architects from their contract for the practice hogans, although Collier requested that Mayers, Murray & Phillip supply blueprints "to insure the erection of structures harmonizing with the buildings being designed by you."[100] The architects agreed to serve in a reduced capacity; they determined the location of the practice hogans and then acted as consultants to the Indian crews.[101]

As it turned out, Mayers, Murray & Phillip produced an unprecedented design that synthesized two traditional female hogan forms (Figure 4.4).

Like the stacked-log hogan, the buildings were octagonal in plan, but like the stone hogan, the walls were constructed from masonry. In some cases, the roof of the practice hogans was constructed from corbelled logs, but in other examples, milled lumber was employed to create a pyramidal roof.

The OIA directed that some communities build single practice hogans, while in others, more money was allocated for the construction of a double-hogan consisting of two hogans connected by a small room in between (Figure 4.5).

Double-hogans are virtually nonexistent in the archaeological and historical records of the American Southwest, and the combination devised by Mayers, Murray & Phillip signaled another departure from tradition.[102] Given these differences from typical Diné forms, what exactly made these buildings "hogans"? Clearly, their form linked them to traditional architecture on the reservation. But equally as important, the hogans were all oriented so that the doorways were located on the east side of the building, even when that alignment disrupted a site plan's overall building arrangement.

As early as 1932, the Navajo boarding school at Fort Wingate (*Shash Bitoo*), New Mexico, was offering courses in home economics taught in a "typical hogan."[103] By mid-1934, Harold W. Foght, the school's superintendent, was finalizing plans for

Figure 4.4 The practice hogan at Iyanbito, New Mexico, looking south, c. 1935.

Figure 4.5 The double-hogan at Crystal, New Mexico, looking southeast, photographed by Milton Snow, c. 1935.

a much more elaborate set of home economics classrooms.[104] The government specifications called for a group of three hogans described as follows:

1) The simple, traditional hogan usually found on the Navajo reservation
2) A well constructed hogan larger and more practical than number one
3) One double hogan containing new arrangements and facilities not now found on the reservations but to be constructed for the purpose of inducing the young Indians now growing up to imitate this more satisfactory architecture when they return to the reservation[105]

The buildings were arranged in a sequence from left to right, beginning with the "traditional" example and ending with a building resembling the double-hogans that Mayers, Murray & Phillip had designed for the rest of the reservation. *Water! Grass! The Navajo's Eternal Quest*, a movie produced by the federal government and released in 1940, included a segment about the hogans at the Fort Wingate boarding school (Figure 4.6).

The "traditional hogan" at the boarding school was a stacked-log hogan, 18' in diameter. It contained a single dirt-floored, windowless room with a smoke hole ventilating an open fire.[106]

Figure 4.6 The three demonstration hogans at the Fort Wingate boarding school, Fort Wingate, New Mexico, as pictured in the film, *Water! Grass! The Navajo's Eternal Quest*, with, above, "the traditional hogan," and on the following page, "the well constructed hogan," and "the double hogan containing new arrangements."

146 The Indian New Deal

Figure 4.6 (Continued)

The second hogan was a modified stacked-log hogan, comprising two parts: an octagonal hogan, 23′ in diameter, with a rectangular room measuring 8′ × 12′ projecting from one side. Sawn logs imparted a neater appearance to its exterior. Rather than dirt, the floor was paved with flagstones set in cement, and the smoke hole in the roof was replaced by an oculus covered by a plate-glass window with a ventilator. Heat was provided by a fireplace, and two casement windows lit the main space. The attached rectangular room housed a separate kitchen containing a stove and storage space and included another door and an additional window. Like the "traditional" hogan, this building was constructed from logs and adobe, but a sheet of weatherproofing was inserted between the interior and exterior layers of its earthen roof.[107] Although the specifications didn't explain the reason for the "improvements," the roof ventilator and casement windows would have enhanced air circulation, the fireplace would have minimized smoke within the building, and the separate kitchen would have aided sanitation.

The third building was a double-hogan built from stone blocks. Each of the two octagonal hogans was 23′ in diameter and connected by a rectangular room measuring 6′ by 8′. The roofs were identical to the roof on the second hogan, as were the floors. One of the hogans was heated with a stove and the other one with a fireplace, and each had built-in seats along the walls. The kitchen and storage area were located in the connecting room which had its own window and door.[108]

According to the narrator of the segment about the Fort Wingate hogans in *Water! Grass! The Navajo's Eternal Quest*:

A tribal characteristic of the Navajo is his devotion to his dwelling, the circular, dirt-floored hogan. It has been his home since the beginning of his history, and he shows no inclination to change. To meet this persistence halfway, the reservation's better housing program centered at Fort Wingate is offering models with modern conveniences but with the same old round house walls.

In 1937, the school's newspaper reported that girls from the ninth grade at Fort Wingate lived in the first and second hogans, where they learned various home-making skills, including cooking, sewing, and laundering. The third hogan housed older girls from the school, where they further developed their proficiency without the day-to-day supervision of a teacher.[109] The full-size model hogans at the boarding school emphasized ventilation and separate food facilities as vital factors in keeping a home healthy. *Water! Grass! The Navajo's Eternal Quest* also includes a demonstration illustrating another change that the government perceived would improve sanitation in Diné homes: the use of furniture. The segment opens with a Euro-American man (presumably a teacher at Fort Wingate) gesturing towards three different tabletop models arranged in a sequence (Figure 4.7).

The first two buildings resemble the first two full-size hogans at Fort Wingate, while the third hogan has been replaced by an octagonal hogan with a pyramidal roof. Its sides are decorated with a gridded pattern, implying that the model has masonry walls. During the demonstration, the teacher lifts off the roof of the third – by

148 *The Indian New Deal*

Figure 4.7 A demonstration on constructing and equipping hogans at the Fort Wingate boarding school, c. 1940.

The Indian New Deal 149

implication the most advanced – example, which includes a table, a chair, a bench, a cupboard, and a stove vented by a fireplace (Figure 4.7). The narration amplifies the point the teacher is making and explains, "The Navajo family sits and sleeps on the ground and is no friend of furniture but such exhibits as these are creating curiosity which may bring social change."

The reforming attitude underlying the model hogan program at Fort Wingate also influenced the literature the OIA published for the new Navajo day school/ community centers. Collier conceived the day schools as "community centers," and the OIA used this term to refer to them during the first years after Collier's appointment as commissioner. But by the end of the 1930s, the comprehensive role that he had envisioned for the community centers diminished, and it became typical to call them "day schools."[110] In the pages that follow, these institutions will be called day school/community centers, a name which embraces all of their functions.

The OIA circulated information for the community workers, teachers, and staff who worked at the day school/community centers in a newsletter called *Community Center Naltsos*.[111] The first issue, published in September 1934, includes an article discussing sanitation in the hogan. It notes:

> Among the unsolved problems to be met by the New Deal to the Navajos is to decrease or eliminate affliction and great suffering due to trachoma and tuberculosis. In order to carry out this task, a few changes must be made to improve sanitary conditions in the homes of the Navajo people.[112]

The article recommends using furniture, and the newsletter includes drawings of several easily constructed pieces, including a bench, a tall cupboard, a table, and a stool (a plan for a bed was still in development). The author additionally advocates using pasteboard cartons for storage and explains the advantages of "some sort of a hardwood floor or preferably a baked glossy smooth, warm adobe floor such as the Pueblo Indians use at Santa Domingo." The final section addresses how to heat a hogan while minimizing the smoke and ash that cause eye irritation and endorses a coal-burning fireplace over the central fire found in most traditional hogans because the fireplace "is an effective means of ventilation."[113]

The second issue of *Community Center Naltsos*, published in October 1934, presented the practice hogans as a tool to persuade the Diné to improve their own hogans. The issue provides a detailed list of the equipment that each practice hogan should contain, including the following:

- A cellar for vegetables, fruit, meat, milk, and cheese
- Protected (covered) water barrels and pails with dipper and plenty of individual cups which have nail hooks for sun-hanging. Water goes from dipper to cup. No one drinks from the dipper
- An oven outside and outside grill
- A rack for sheepskins (used for sleeping)
- A rack for utensils
- Food cupboards – protected with wire fly screening and burlap

150 *The Indian New Deal*

- Funnels, scoop, fire shovel
- Hewn hogan doors with wrought iron hinges (hogans traditionally lack doors)
- Recesses in walls and ledge just under the roof, wooden harness hooks
- Fireplace flush with outside wall
- A flue for stove in second hogan (of a double-hogan)
- A screen for the hole in the roof
- Two milk goats and plans of saving fodder for winter
- An incinerator
- Latrines of stone, adobe, or lumber
- A bench for the hogan[114]

This equipment was intended to make the hogan a healthy place to live. Food storage and preparation were separated from sleeping and living areas to prevent contamination; screens and doors helped curb insects and rodents; furniture, racks, wall recesses, and hooks kept cooking utensils, bedding, and other materials off the floor; an incinerator and latrine controlled waste; the fireplace and flue together formed a heating source that did not generate ashes and smoke within the hogan; and the water barrel, dipper, and cup arrangement helped prevent the transmission of disease.

The fourth issue of the newsletter, published in June 1935, describes how the chapter at Dennehotso (*Denihootsoh*), Arizona, built a double-hogan for demonstrating home economics.[115] The project included extensive discussions between federal employees and Dennehotso's chapter officers leading to a signed agreement committing the chapter to construct the practice hogan within a three-to-four-week time period. The timber was harvested and hauled under the direction of the chapter president, who also oversaw the construction of the building's roof. The chapter vice-president supervised the quarrying and hauling of stone blocks and took charge of the building's masonry. The Indian Office expended $500 on materials for the project, and the labor was donated by local Diné.[116] As the article explains, the one constant shared by all of the community hogans across the Navajo reservation was the building's design: every project began by "securing [the] Architect's plan and blue print of Hogan" from the central office in Gallup, ensuring that all of the buildings would be identical.[117]

As of May 1, 1935, the budget for F.P. 295 included funding to construct five practice hogans in the Eastern Navajo jurisdiction, nine practice hogans in the Southern Navajo jurisdiction, six practice hogans in the Northern Navajo jurisdiction, and three practice hogans in the Western Navajo jurisdiction.[118] Some of this money was designated for boarding schools and paid for the construction of the three hogans at Fort Wingate, as well as for students to build practice hogans at the boarding schools in Crownpoint, Tohatchi (*Tó Haach'i'*), and Shiprock in New Mexico, and Fort Defiance, Tuba City, and Keams Canyon (*Lók'a'Deeshjin*) in Arizona.[119]

But as at Dennehotso, Diné adults also built practice hogans at day school/community centers across the reservation. On August 31, 1934, local Diné

The Indian New Deal   151

completed the first practice hogan in Navajoland at Iyanbito (*Ayání Bito'*), New Mexico (see Figure 4.7).[120] Over the next two to three years, 16 Diné chapters located across the reservation as far west as Navajo Mountain (*Naatsis'áán*), Utah, and as far east as Torreon (*Na'neelzhiin*), New Mexico, constructed practice hogans designed by Mayers, Murray & Phillip.[121] A few were single hogans, like the example at Iyanbito, but most were double-hogans.

Hogans for Diné Nurse's Aides

The federal government also supported the construction of hogans to house Diné nurse's aides at the day school/community centers. The nurse's aide program was founded on the idea that young Diné women with a boarding school education would be well-suited to provide health care on the reservation.[122] The project may have originated with Collier, but Sally Lucas Jean, the OIA's coordinator on Community Centers, was the person who implemented it.[123] In June and July of 1934, 98 students – all of them young Diné women – attended a health institute at Santa Fe, where they received "lessons in the care and prevention of trachoma, infant hygiene and first aid, as well as dental hygiene, social service problems and health teaching."[124] Two hogans with dirt roofs were built to serve as classrooms.[125]

By December 1934, the federal government had authorized 15 young Diné women to become nurse's aides, and $2,500 had been appropriated to build hogans for them to live in.[126] But by June 1935, only ten nurse's aides were stationed on the reservation.[127] That summer, 30 Diné women participated in the second health institute, but most of the students attended in preparation for careers in home economics or as registered nurses.[128] By the summer of 1936, Jean had been replaced by Edna Gerken, and the third health institute was organized for the teachers and Native American assistants who were serving as regular employees at the community centers, not for training nurse's aides.

By that time, according to Robert A. Trennert, "the nurse-aid concept had run its course," although the reasons for the program's failure are not entirely clear.[129] Budget shortfalls may have been an issue, but probably the most important factor was the opposition voiced by W.W. Peter, who became the Medical Director of the OIA's Navajo Area in May 1934. Peter was particularly interested in increasing the professionalism of the OIA's medical staff, and he expressed a "strong reluctance" about employing "poorly trained aids except as direct companions of registered nurses."[130]

As a result, only 15 nurse's aide hogans were constructed.[131] On February 7, 1935, E.J. Stenson, the special disbursing agent for the Southern Navajo jurisdiction, wrote to Dorothy Ellis, the OIA's associate supervisor of home economics, "we are assuming that these hogans will be built on the plan of half of the Home Economics hogan plans."[132] But the stone masonry hogans designed by Mayers, Murray & Phillip were relatively expensive and would have far exceeded the amount of money that was available. While some of the nurse aide hogans ended up as small versions of the single practice hogans on the reservations, as at Iyanbito (Figure 4.8), other locations ended up with a traditional stacked-log hogan, as at Sanostee (*Tsé 'Ałnáozt'í'*), New Mexico.

Figure 4.8 The nurse's aide hogan at Iyanbito, New Mexico, looking southwest, c. 1935.

Once the contracts were completed and construction came to an end, at least six of the nine boarding schools and 18 day school/community centers across Navajoland included octagonal stone hogans designed by Mayers, Murray & Phillip.[133] Collier's attempts to "improve" Diné architecture followed in the tradition of his predecessors, but never before had a commissioner of Indian Affairs gone to such lengths to validate a traditional Native American architectural form. That said, the design pioneered by Mayers, Murray & Phillip has been only rarely imitated by the Diné during the years since.

In May 1935, Superintendent Leroy F. Jackson submitted a report on how Diné students reacted to the hogans at the Fort Wingate Boarding School. According to Jackson, "the idea in constructing the three hogans was to bring out progression in the improvement of homes," but the students "more or less" preferred the second and *not* the third hogan.[134] He offered no explanation for why the more spacious and sturdy stone double-hogan fell short of the modified stacked-log hogan in the eyes of his Navajo charges. Was the double-hogan viewed as impractical because it was costly to build? Constructing a similar example would require the expertise of a skilled stonemason capable of cutting and laying ashlar blocks to create a perfect octagon with sharp, well-defined corners. Were its solidity and permanence viewed as irrelevant in a culture that has traditionally abandoned a dwelling where someone has died? Or was the building just too different from the hogans the students were familiar with?

Although Mayers, Murray & Phillip produced different designs for the hogans in Mexican Springs and for the practice hogans across the Navajo reservation, both

The Indian New Deal   153

served a similar purpose – to persuade the Diné to change their way of life. The hogan village at the soil erosion control experiment station not only housed a Diné CCC-ID crew but it also symbolized that the land-use practices being developed there were for the Navajo tribe. However briefly, Mexican Springs expressed the government's vision of a utopian landscape for the Navajo. As it turned out, that vision was unacceptable to most of the tribe, and ultimately, the government's efforts failed. The OIA used practice hogans to demonstrate new health practices intended to address trachoma and tuberculosis on the reservation and improve the general well-being of the Diné. It is unclear whether Collier meant to present the octagonal stone hogans as prototypes for the Diné to imitate. It is also possible that he requested Mayers, Murray & Phillip to create a hogan that would harmonize with the stone masonry Pueblo-Spanish Revival-style buildings that comprised most of the new day school/community centers on the reservation. Or he may have intended to unite the tribe through the construction of a pan-Navajo hogan – a single design that synthesized the architecture of the stone hogan and the octagonal stacked-log hogan.[135]

The next chapter will examine how John Collier promoted a new pedagogical approach – Progressive Education – through the use of a revolutionary new architectural design: the hogan school. Progressive Education, as applied on the reservation, sought to ground a Euro-American–style education in the everyday life of the Diné. But the hogan schools, which combined modern Euro-American construction methods with an Indigenous building form, were challenged by a powerful opponent – the Navajo leader, Jacob C. Morgan. As we shall see, the conflict between Collier and Morgan elucidated the symbolic importance of the hogan among the Diné and demonstrated the diversity that has long characterized the tribe.

Notes

1 NNTC, July 7–8, 1933: 1.
2 Edward Spicer, *Human Problems in Technological Change* (New York: Russell Sage Foundation, 1952), 186.
3 Lawrence C. Kelly, *The Assault on Assimilation: John Collier and the Origins of Indian Policy Reform* (Albuquerque: University of New Mexico Press, 1983), 11–12.
4 Lawrence Cremin, *The Transformation of the School* (New York: Alfred A. Knopf, 1961), 60. The term "*gemeinschaft* grouse" originates from Morton Grodzins. See Stephen J. Kunitz, "The Social Philosophy of John Collier," *Ethnohistory* 18, no. 3 (Summer 1971): 213–229, for an analysis of how Collier's attitude towards community reflected the thinking of other intellectuals who expressed "the *gemeinschaft* grouse."
5 Kenneth R. Philp, *John Collier's Crusade for Indian Reform, 1920–1954* (Tucson: University of Arizona Press, 1977), 9–23.
6 Quoted in Philp, *John Collier's Crusade for Indian Reform*, 23, and see pp. 23–24.
7 Philp, *John Collier's Crusade for Indian Reform*, 24.
8 Kelly, *The Assault on Assimilation*, 131.
9 Kelly, *The Assault on Assimilation*, 278.
10 John Collier, "The Fate of the Navajos," *Sunset* 52 (January 1924): 74.
11 Collier, "The Fate of the Navajos," 11–13, 60, 62, 73–74; and Collier, "Navajos," *Survey Graphic* 51 (January 1924): 332–339, 363, 365.
12 Collier, "Navajos," 365.
13 T.M. Pearce, *Oliver La Farge* (New York: Twayne, 1972), 45.

154   *The Indian New Deal*

14 A memorandum from Collier to Ickes lists the architects who were interviewed by last name, and they included Hood, Creighton, White, Holden, Canderfeldt, Stein, and Hauheim. "Memorandum for Secretary Ickes from Commissioner [Collier]," September 7, 1933, reel 19, *JCP*. I have been unable to obtain further information about "Canderfeldt," but "Hauheim" may refer to New York architect Melville Nauheim (1889–1971). See "Obituary of Melville Nauheim," *New York Times*, October 6, 1971.

15 Raymond Hood (1881–1934) was one of the most famous American architects of the era and was involved in the design of the Chicago Tribune Tower (1924), as well as several New York City landmarks, including the American Radiator Building (1924), the New York Daily News Building (1929), the McGraw Hill Building (1931), and Rockefeller Center (1933–1937).

16 William J. Creighton (1892–1955) worked for La Farge, Clark, and Creighton from 1927 to 1930 (Oliver La Farge's father, C. Grant La Farge, was a partner in the firm). Creighton had established an independent practice by 1933. See "Wm. J. Creighton," *AAD*, 116.

17 Lawrence Grant White (1887–1956) was architect Stanford White's only child and a partner in the firm of McKim, Mead, and White. Oliver La Farge's brother, Christopher Grant La Farge, worked as an architect for McKim, Mead, and White from 1924 to 1932. See "Christopher La Farge Dies at 58; Poet Wrote Best-Selling Novel," *New York Times*, January 6, 1958.

18 Arthur Cort Holden (1890–1993) was an architect and author, whose books included *Settlement Idea: A Vision of Social Justice* (New York: Macmillan, 1922). See "Arthur C[ort] Holden," *AAD*, 252.

19 Early in his career, Clarence Stein (1882–1975) worked as an architect in the office of Bertram Goodhue, and by 1933, he was well on his way to becoming one of the most important American urban planners of the 20th century. See "Clarence S. Stein," *AAD*, 533.

20 "Telegram from [John] Collier Commissioner to Mayers Murray & Phillip," August 19, 1933, reel 19, *JCP*.

21 "Francis L[aurie] S[pencer] Mayers," *AAD*, 373. Also see Mayers' obituary, "Francis L. Mayers," *The Bridgeport Telegram*, May 26, 1970.

22 "Oscar Harold Murray," *AAD*, 397. Also see Murray's obituary, "Oscar H. Murray, an Architect, 74," *New York Times*, April 26, 1957.

23 "F. Hardie Phillip," *DSA*. Also see Phillip's obituary, "Hardie Phillip, 86, Architect, Dead," *New York Times*, October 13, 1973.

24 "Twelfth-Night in Mr. Goodhue's Office," *Pencil Points* 3, no. 2 (February 1922): 23–24.

25 This list originates from Richard Oliver, *Bertram Grosvenor Goodhue* (New York: The Architectural History Foundation, 1983), 288. Buildings designed by Goodhue and Mayers, Murray & Phillip in Hawaii are discussed in Daina Julia Penkiunas, "American Regional Architecture in Hawaii: Honolulu, 1915–1935" (PhD diss., University of Virginia, 1990).

26 Penkiunas, "American Regional Architecture in Hawaii," 172.

27 Penkiunas, "American Regional Architecture in Hawaii," 181–182.

28 "To Superintendents from Commissioner [Collier]," August 24, 1933, reel 19, *JCP*.

29 Donald C. Swain, *Federal Conservation Policy, 1921–1933* (Berkeley: University of California Press, 1963), 145.

30 According to H.H. Bennett, "the abnormal phase of soil erosion" is "that which results from the activities of man and his domestic animals in breaking down natural soil conditions and stabilizers through the complete or excessive removal of vegetation and the disruption or destruction of the normal or natural soil structure by cultivation, trampling and other means." Quoted in Swain, *Federal Conservation Policy, 1921–1933*, 145.

31 Angus McDonald, "Early American Soil Conservationists," *USDA Miscellaneous Publications*, no. 449 (October 1941), 100.

32 Swain, *Federal Conservation Policy, 1921–1933*, 144–145.

The Indian New Deal 155

33 Wellington Brink, *Big Hugh, the Father of Soil Conservation* (New York: Macmillan, 1951), 55–57.
34 Douglas Helms, "Hugh Hammond Bennett and the Creation of the Soil Erosion Service," *Journal of Soil and Water Conservation* 64, no. 2 (March–April 2009): 68A. See also Swain, *Federal Conservation Policy, 1921–1933*, 147–150.
35 Helms, "Hugh Hammond Bennett and the Creation of the Soil Erosion Service," 68A.
36 Swain, *Federal Conservation Policy, 1921–1933*, 150–151.
37 Helms, "Hugh Hammond Bennett and the Creation of the Soil Erosion Service," 68A; Swain, *Federal Conservation Policy, 1921–1933*, 150–152.
38 Swain, *Federal Conservation Policy, 1921–1933*, 152–153.
39 Brink, *Big Hugh, the Father of Soil Conservation*, 78. The ten stations were located in the vicinity of the following towns: Guthrie, Oklahoma; Hays, Kansas; Temple, Texas; Tyler, Texas; Statesville, North Carolina; La Crosse, Wisconsin; Bethany, Missouri; Zanesville, Ohio; Pullman, Washington; and Clarinda, Iowa.
40 John Collier, *From Every Zenith: A Memoir and Some Essays on Life and Thought* (Denver: Sage Publications, 1963), 238.
41 For more on the CCC-ID, see Donald L. Parman, "The Indian and the Civilian Conservation Corps," *Pacific Historical Review* 40, no. 1 (February 1971): 39–56.
42 Helms, "Hugh Hammond Bennett and the Creation of the Soil Erosion Service," 70A–71A.
43 "Establishing of Navajo Experiment Station" [memorandum from Bruno Klinger to D.S. Hubbell], April 8, 1937, Box 8, SCS-CSWR.
44 "Report of the Conservation Advisory Committee for the Navajo Reservation," July 2, 1933, 7, Box 88, CCF-RG114-NARA-CP; J.W. Hoover, "Navajo Land Problems," *Economic Geography* 13, no. 3 (July 1937): 293.
45 For more, see Donald L. Parman, *The Navajos and the New Deal* (New Haven: Yale Univesity Press, 1976), 81–82.
46 "Report of the Conservation Advisory Committee for the Navajo Reservation," 4. The report was signed by Bennett, C.K. Cooperrider of the Southwest Forest and Range Experiment Station; C.E. Ramser of the US Bureau of Agricultural Engineering, Division of Soil Erosion; L.M. Winsor of the US Bureau of Agricultural Engineering, Division of Irrigation; and H.C. Neuffer of the US Indian Service, Division of Irrigation.
47 NNTC, July 7–8, 1933, 18.
48 NNTC, July 7–8, 1933, 18.
49 NNTC July 7–8, 1933, 48–49.
50 See Richard Boke to John Collier, May 18, 1933, and "Richard Boke" [curriculum vitae], June 2, 1933, reel 11, *JCP*.
51 Helms, "Hugh Hammond Bennett and the Creation of the Soil Erosion Service," 71A.
52 "Establishing of Navajo Experiment Station" [memorandum from Bruno Klinger to D.S. Hubbell], April 8, 1937, Box 3, SCS-CSWR; "Work Progressing on Big Erosion Control Project," *Winslow* [AZ] *Mail*, May 25, 1934.
53 W.C. Lowdermilk to H.H. Bennett, November 4, 1933, Box 88, CCF-RG114-NARA-CP.
54 H.H. Bennett, "Conservation Farming Practices and Flood Control," *USDA Miscellaneous Publications*, no. 253 (October 1936): 14.
55 Richard Boke, "The Mexican Springs Erosion Control Station – An Institution of Education and Research," *Indians at Work* 1, no. 13 (February 15, 1934): 13, 15.
56 "Report of the Conservation Advisory Committee for the Navajo Reservation," July 2, 1933, 7.
57 This money was made available by the end of August.
58 Charles Collier to Richard Boke, October 20, 1933, Box 88, CCF-RG114-NARA-CP.
59 "Memorandum from W.C. Lowdermilk to Richard Boke," November 4, 1933, Box 88, CCF-RG114-NARA-CP.
60 Charles Collier to Hardie Phillip, November 2, 1933; Hardie Phillip to Charles Collier, November 3, 1933; Hardie Phillip to Charles Collier, November 6, 1933; Charles

156 *The Indian New Deal*

Collier to Hardie Phillip, November 7, 1933; Hardie Phillip to Charles Collier, November 10, 1933. All in Box 88, CCF-RG114-NARA-CP.

61 W.C. Lowdermilk to H.H. Bennett, November 15, 1933, Box 88, CCF-RG114-NARA-CP.

62 O.H. Murray to Charles Collier, November 24, 1933, Box 88, CCF-RG114-NARA-CP.

63 W.C. Lowdermilk to John Collier, December 11, 1933, Box 88, CCF-RG114-NARA-CP.

64 Hardie [Phillip] to Charles [Collier], n.d., Box 88, CCF-RG114-NARA-CP.

65 Annual Report of the Navajo Project – Soil Conservation Service Project Number 10 for the Year ending June 30, 1935, 37, Box 7, SCS-CSWR.

66 Hardie Phillip, "Report of Visit to Projects in the Southwest between February 3 and February 27, 1936," March 18, 1936; Box 14, PWA-NARA-NAB.

67 Boke had concluded that he was "not sufficiently trained or experienced to spend a quarter million dollars on an 'erosion station,'" and he became the special assistant to the director after Whitfield was appointed. See "Establishing of Navajo Experiment Station" and "Organization of the Navajo Project," February 24, 194, Box 88, CCF-RG114-NARA-CP.

68 Donald S. Hubbell, *The Legacy of Hubba the Dane* (Mountain Home, AR: New Author Publishers, 1977), 92.

69 According to Charles Collier, the station began with only "one little cabin and a shed with a tin roof." Charles Collier to John Collier, January 30, 1934, Box 88, CCF-RG114-NARA-CP.

70 Charles J. Whitfield to W.D. Lowdermilk, January 2, 1934, Box 88, CCF-RG114-NARA-CP.

71 W.C. Lowdermilk, "Memorandum for Mr. Phillips, Architect – Indian Service," January 18, 1934, Box 88, CCF-RG114-NARA-CP.

72 If Bradley's figures are correct, the six houses would have cost $43,914, and the net amount that was available from the PWA allocation was $45,000. According to a letter from Acting Secretary of Agriculture T.A. Walters to Secretary Ickes, a power plant had been constructed by December 5, 1934, although the plant is not mentioned in a building inventory in the Navajo Project's annual report for 1935. The letter is located in Box 44, PWA-NARA-NAB, and see *Annual Report of the Navajo Project – Soil Conservation Service Project Number 10 for the Year ending June 30, 1935* (USDA/Soil Conservation Service, 1935), 37, Box 7, SCS-CSWR.

73 The Soil Conservation Service was renamed the Natural Resources Conservation Service in 1994.

74 M.L. Wilson [Acting Secretary of Agriculture] to Secretary of the Interior, May 14, 1935, Box 44, PWA-NARA-NAB.

75 The specifications are located in Box 44 ("Garage and Warehouse; Machine Shop and Power House") and Box 45 ("Administration Building"), PWA-NARA-NAB.

76 The financial support for the chapter house probably came from ECW rather than PWA funds.

77 Telegram from Richard Boke to Charles Collier, November 7, 1933, Box 88, CCF-RG114-NARA-CP.

78 C.J. Whitfield to H. Phillip, February 17, 1934, Box 88, CCF-RG114-NARA-CP.

79 Charles Collier to Hardie Phillip, February 19, 1934, Box 88, CCF-RG114-NARA-CP.

80 Charles Collier to Charles J. Whitfield, February 21, 1934, and Telegram from C.J. Whitfield to Charles Collier, February 22, 1934, Box 88, CCF-RG114-NARA-CP.

81 Charles Collier to Hardie Phillip, February 26, 1934, Box 88, CCF-RG114-NARA-CP.

82 Mayers, Murray & Phillip to C.J. Whitfield, March 9, 1934, Box 44, PWA-NARA-NAB.

83 "Navajos Celebrate Erosion; Dedicate New Chapter House," published in the *Gallup Independent* on June 11 described the building to be "of simple construction and sturdy." The dedication of the chapter house was part of a larger celebration dedicating the Mexican Springs erosion project. See "Indians Dedicate Mexican Springs Erosion Project," *Gallup Independent*, June 8, 1934.

84 "3 Indian Schools to be Built – $150,000 Projects for Navajos and Zunis Authorized," *Albuquerque Journal*, July 31, 1934; "$190,000 Building Program Begins on Zuni, Navajo Lands," *Gallup Independent*, August 1, 1934.

The Indian New Deal   157

85 For more about the Mexican Springs Trading Post, see Klara Kelley and Harris Francis, *Navajoland Trading Post Encyclopedia* (Window Rock, AZ: Navajo Nation Heritage and Historic Preservation Department, 2018), 259–260.

86 M.E. Musgrave, "Nursery at Naka Bito: A Harbinger of Tomorrow," *The Land Today and Tomorrow* [Official Bulletin of the Soil Erosion Service] 2, no. 3 (March 1935): 2–3.

87 Hugh G. Calkins, "Progress Report of the Livestock Demonstration Conducted by Operations in Cooperation with the Navajo Experiment Station with Brief Reference to the Research Program" (USDA Soil Conservation Service Region 8), 3, Box 27, RLR-NARA-D.

88 Hugh Hammond Bennett, *Soil Conservation* (New York: McGraw-Hill, 1939), 789.

89 The Norcross Dam was Project DD1. See "Project Report – Engineering Division, February 8 to April 30" (Navajo Experiment Station, May 2, 1934), Box 7, SCS-CSWR.

90 For more on the diversion dams at Mexican Springs, see M.E. Musgrave, "Distribution and Utilization of Flood Waters," *Science* 82, no. 2133 (November 15, 1935): 461–462.

91 "Corn of Navajos Wins High Merit – Possibilities Seen by Henry Wallace," *Gallup Independent*, November 18, 1935; *Indians at Work* 3, no. 2 (September 1, 1935): 1; Parman, *The Navajos and the New Deal*, 81; "First Navajo Boundary Hearing at Gallup, Aug. 17," *Albuquerque Journal*, August 11, 1936; "Officials Visit," *Southwest Tourist News*, May 27, 1937; W.G. McGinnies to Hugh G. Calkins, December 3, 1936, Box 4, NDF-NARA-D. Archibald MacLeish is quoted in Russell Lord, *Behold Our Land* (Boston: Houghton Mifflin Company, 1938), 281.

92 *SOC*, Part 34, 17955.

93 *SOC*, Part 34, 18019.

94 *SOC*, Part 34, 17958.

95 NNTC, July 9–11, 1943, 98.

96 NNTC, July 9–11, 1943, 103; David Aberle, *The Peyote Religion Among the Navaho* (New York: Wenner-Gren Foundation for Anthropological Research, 1966), 75.

97 E.R. Fryer, interview with Morris Burge, July 21, 1970, American Indian Oral History Transcripts, Center for Southwest Research, University of New Mexico, accessed August 26, 2012, at http://econtent.unm.edu/cdm/ref/collection/navtrans/id/370.

98 A pictorial report compiled in 1939 labeled a picture of a cylindrical stone hogan with a domical roof as "the typical hogan" at Mexican Springs. See *The Navajo Experiment Station* (US Soil Conservation Service, 1939), collection of the author.

99 William F. Zimmerman to Ivan F. Albers, stamped January 11, 1934, Box 70, CSF-NARA-R. There is an undated and (probably) earlier budget at the National Archives which totals $1,598,000 and includes a sum of $20,000 for the practice houses and hogans. See "Construction Resulting in Immediate Needed Provision and Ultimate Annual Saving," n.d., Box 165, CCPW-NARA-R.

100 John Collier to Mayers, Murray & Phillip, June 4, 1934, Box 51, PWA-NARA-NAB.

101 Hardie Phillip to Commissioner of Indian Affairs, June 6, 1934, Box 51, PWA-NARA-NAB.

102 Stephen C. Jett and Virginia E. Spencer, *Navajo Architecture: Forms History Distributions* (Tucson: University of Arizona Press, 1981), 14.

103 "Catalog, Burke Navajo Vocational School, Fort Wingate, N.M.," June 1932, Box 9, LJ-HL.

104 Harold W. Foght to John Collier, June 11, 1934, Box 51, PWA-NARA-NAB. The budget for the project was $1,000. See "Home Economics Practice Homes, F.P. 295," stamped May 6, 1935, Box 51, PWA-NARA-NAB.

105 "Specifications for Hogans to be constructed at the Charles H. Burke School, Fort Wingate, New Mex.," enclosed with Harold W. Foght to John Collier, June 11, 1934, Box 51, PWA-NARA-NAB.

106 The description is based on "Specifications for Hogans" and Leroy F. Jackson to Miss [Edna] Groves, May 9, 1935, Box 51, PWA-NARA-NAB.

158   *The Indian New Deal*

107 The description is based on "Specifications for Hogans" and Leroy F. Jackson to Miss [Edna] Groves, May 9, 1935.

108 The description is based on "Specifications for Hogans" and Leroy F. Jackson to Miss [Edna] Groves, May 9, 1935.

109 "Ninth Grade Homemakers" and "Apartment News," *Shush Betoh News* VII, no. 2 (October 15, 1937): 7, Box 9, LJ-HL.

110 See Lucy Wilcox Adams, "Notes on the Principal's Meeting," November 25, 1940, Box 11, PI-ASU.

111 *Naltsos* means "book" or "paper" in Navajo.

112 "Navajo Community Centers," *The Community Center Naltsos* 1, no. 1 (September 1, 1934): 4, SMMA.

113 "Navajo Community Centers," 5.

114 "Community Work Notes," *The Community Center Naltsos* 1, no. 2 (October 15, 1934): 14–15, SMMA.

115 "Steps in Preparing for Construction of Community Hogans at Dennehotso," *Navajo Community Center Naltsos* 1, no. 4 (June 1935): 11–13, SMMA.

116 "Home Economics Practice Homes, F.P. 295." Individuals "owing work for relief food" were allowed to apply their labor "at rate of one day work for each sack of food owed."

117 From what I have observed in the practice hogans that remain standing on the reservation, there were minor variations in how the design by Mayers, Murray & Phillip was completed.

118 "Home Economics Practice Homes, F.P. 295."

119 The Keams Canyon Boarding School was known as the Moqui Boarding School for Hopis until 1925, although many of its students were Diné. A plot plan of the boarding school at Leupp, Arizona, located in the archives of the BIA Navajo Regional Office in Gallup, New Mexico, and dating from March 1945 also shows the outlines of two single hogans and a double-hogan.

120 "Monthly Report, Public Works Projects, Iyanbito Hogan," August 31, 1934, Box 140, NCCF-NARA-R.

121 This estimate is based on documents, plans, and photographs located BIA-G; Box 140, NCCF-NARA-R; MS-NNM; Box 3, DLP-CSWR; Box 51, PWA-NARA-NAB; Boxes 165 and 166, CCPW-NARA-R; Box 56, E. Navajo CCF-NARA-R; Box 2, E. Navajo SF-NARA-R; Box 58, CSC-NARA-R.

122 "The Institute for Training Navajo Nurse-Aides," *Indians at Work* 1, no. 21 (June 15, 1934): 30.

123 See Parman, *The Navajos and the New Deal*, 221–222, and Robert A. Trennert, *White Man's Medicine: Government Doctors and the Navajo, 1863–1955* (Albuquerque: University of New Mexico Press, 1998), 183–184. Sally Lucas Jean was a school nurse who worked with John Collier's first wife, Lucy Wood Collier, at the People's Institute on a study that led to the founding of the Child Health Organization in 1918. Jean became director of field work for the group which, among its accomplishments, "pioneered the modern hot lunch program." She later served as "School Health Consultant" for Metropolitan Life Insurance Company and also worked for the Cleanliness Institute. Collier considered designating Jean as assistant commissioner of Indian Affairs, but in a letter he wrote to her on May 11, 1933, he explained, "it looks as though a woman – any woman, of the whole race – could not be appointed." See Kelly, *The Assault on Assimilation*, 81–83; Suellen Hoy, *Chasing Dirt: The American Pursuit of Cleanliness* (New York: Oxford University Press, 1995), 134–135, 141. The letter from Collier to Jean is located on reel 14, *JCP*.

124 "The Institute for Training Navajo Nurse-Aides," 29.

125 "Navajo Girls Being Trained to Aid Fight on Trachoma," *The Santa Fe New Mexican*, June 12, 1934.

126 Sally Lucas Jean, "Committee Report on Supplying of Quarters for Indian Personnel for Day Schools to be Opened February 1, 1935," December 17, 1934, Box 56, E. Navajo CCF-NARA-R.

The Indian New Deal 159

127 William F. Zimmerman to Chester E. Faris, stamped June 10, 1935. Original located in the National Archives and mimeo located in Box 3, DLP-CSWR.
128 Trennert, *White Man's Medicine*, 184–185. A total of 103 students came, but "most participants came from other tribes."
129 Trennert, *White Man's Medicine*, 185. Trennert notes that by 1939, there were only six nurse's aides working at the Fort Defiance Indian Hospital and that they probably represented the sum total for the reservation.
130 Parman, *The Navajos and the New Deal*, 222–223; Trennert, *White Man's Medicine*, 181.
131 This estimate is based on documents, plans, and photographs located at BIA-G; Box 143, NCCF-NARA-R; MS-NNM; Box 3, DLP-CSWR; Box 166, CCPW-NARA-R; Box 56, E. Navajo CCF-NARA-R; Box 2, E. Navajo SF-NARA-R; Box 58, CSC-NARA-R.
132 E.J. Stenson to Dorothy G. Ellis, February 7, 1935, Box 166, CCPW-NARA-R.
133 The reservation boarding schools, c. 1934, were at Fort Defiance, Leupp, Tuba City, and Keams Canyon in Arizona and at Crownpoint, Shiprock, Tohatchi, Toadlena, and Fort Wingate in New Mexico. See John Collier, "Office of Indian Affairs," in *Annual Report of the Secretary of the Interior for the Fiscal Year Ended June 30, 1934*, ed. Harold L. Ickes (Washington, DC: GPO, 1934), 160–163.
134 Leroy F. Jackson to Miss [Edna] Groves, May 9, 1935.
135 With thanks to John R. Stein for originating the term "pan-Navajo hogan."

Reference List

Archival Sources

Manuscripts

Bureau of Indian Affairs, Navajo Regional Office, Gallup, New Mexico. Cited as BIA-G.
Central Subject Files c. 1926–1939, Records of the Eastern Navajo Agency, RG 75, Records of the BIA, National Archives and Records Administration, Riverside, California. Cited as CSF-NARA-R.
Classified Files, September 1933–October 1935, RG 114, Records of the Natural Resources Conservation Service, National Archives and Records Administration, College Park, Maryland. Cited as CCF-RG114-NARA-CP.
Correspondence Concerning Public Works Programs, 1933–1935, Records of the Navajo Indian Agency (Fort Defiance), RG 75, Records of the BIA, National Archives and Records Administration, Riverside, California. Cited as CCPW-NARA-R.
Correspondence of the Superintendent of Construction; Records of the Phoenix, AZ, Area Office, National Archives and Records Administration, Riverside, California. Cited as CSC-NARA-R.
Donald Lee Parman Papers, 1883–1994, Center for Southwest Research, University of New Mexico, Albuquerque. Cited as DLP-CSWR.
Eastern Navajo Central Classified Files, 1904–1942, RG 75, Records of the BIA, National Archives and Records Administration, Riverside, California. Cited as E. Navajo CCF-NARA-R.
Eastern Navajo Subject Files, 1904–1942, RG 75, Records of the BIA, National Archives and Records Administration, Riverside, California. Cited as E. Navajo SF-NARA-R.
Inventory of the United States Soil Conservation Service Region 8 Records, 1919–1953, Center for Southwest Research, University of New Mexico, Albuquerque. Cited as SCS-CSWR.
The John Collier Papers, 1922–1968 [microform edition]. Edited by Andrew M. Patterson and Maureen Brodoff. Sanford, NC: Microfilming Corporation of America, 1980. Cited as *JCP*.
Leroy Jackson Papers, Huntington Library, San Marino, CA. Cited as LJ-HL.
Milton Snow Collection, Navajo Nation Museum, Window Rock, Arizona. Cited as MS-NNM.

160 *The Indian New Deal*

Navajo Central Classified Files, RG 75, Records of the BIA, National Archives and Records Administration, Riverside, California. Cited as NCCF-NARA-R.

Navajo Decimal Files, 1936–1942, RG 75, Records of the BIA, National Archives and Records Administration, Denver, Colorado. Cited as NDF-NARA-D.

Peter Iverson Collection, Labriola National American Indian Data Center, Arizona State University, Tempe, Arizona. Cited as PI-ASU.

Public Works Administration Projects 1931–43, RG 75, Records of the BIA, National Archives and Records Administration, National Archives Building, Washington, DC. Cited as PWA-NARA-NAB.

Range and Livestock Records, 1949–1961, Navajo Agency – Window Rock, Arizona, RG 75, Records of the BIA, National Archives and Records Administration, Denver, Colorado. Cited as RLR-NARA-D.

St. Michael's Mission Archives, St. Michael's, Arizona. Cited as SMMA.

Published Sources

Aberle, David. *The Peyote Religion Among the Navaho*. New York: Wenner-Gren Foundation for Anthropological Research, 1966.

American Architects Directory (R.R. Bowker, 1956). Located online at http://public.aia.org/sites/hdoaa/wiki/Wiki%20Pages/1956%20American%20Architects%20Directory.aspx. Cited as *AAD*.

Bennett, Hugh Hammond. *Soil Conservation*. New York: McGraw-Hill, 1939.

Bernard, L.L. "The Significance of Lester F. Ward." *Pi Gamma Mu, International Honor Society in Social Sciences* 16, no. 4 (October 1941): 372–381.

Brink, Wellington. *Big Hugh, the Father of Soil Conservation*. New York: Macmillan, 1951.

"The Capital and Conservation Center." *Indians at Work* I, no. 17 (April 15, 1934): 27.

Collier, John. "Navajos." *Survey Graphic* 51 (January 1924): 332–339, 363, 365.

———. "The Fate of the Navajos." *Sunset* 52 (January 1924): 11–13, 60–62, 72–74.

———. *On the Gleaming Way: Navajos, Eastern Pueblos, Zunis, Hopis, Apaches and Their Land and Their Meanings to the World*. Denver: Sage Publications, 1962.

Cremin, Lawrence. *The Transformation of the School*. New York: Alfred A. Knopf, 1961.

Dictionary of Scottish Architects. Located online at www.scottisharchitects.org.uk/architect_full.php?id=206129. Cited as *DSA*.

Helms, Douglas. "Hugh Hammond Bennett and the Creation of the Soil Erosion Service." *Journal of Soil and Water Conservation* 64, no. 2 (March–April 2009): 68A–74A.

Hitchcock, Henry-Russell. *Modern Architecture: Romanticism and Reintegration*. New York: Payson & Clarke, 1929. Reprint, New York: Da Capo Press, 1993.

Hoover, J.W. "Navajo Land Problems." *Economic Geography* 13, no. 3 (July 1937): 281–300.

Hoy, Suellen. *Chasing Dirt: The American Pursuit of Cleanliness*. New York: Oxford University Press, 1995.

Hubbell, Donald S. *The Legacy of Hubba the Dane*. Mountain Home, AR: New Author Publishers, 1977.

Ickes, Harold L., ed. *Annual Report of the Secretary of the Interior for the Fiscal Year Ended June 30, 1934*. Washington, DC: GPO, 1934.

Jett, Stephen C., and Virginia E. Spencer. *Navajo Architecture: Forms History Distributions*. Tucson: University of Arizona Press, 1981.

Kelly, Lawrence C. *The Assault on Assimilation: John Collier and the Origins of Indian Policy Reform*. Albuquerque: University of New Mexico Press, 1983.

Lord, Russell. *Behold Our Land*. Boston: Houghton Mifflin Company, 1938.

McDonald, Angus. "Early American Soil Conservationists." *USDA Miscellaneous Publications*, no. 449 (October 1941).

Minutes of the Navajo Nation Tribal Council. Cited as NNTC.

Musgrave, M.E. "Nursery at Nakai Bito: A Harbinger of Tomorrow." *The Land Today and Tomorrow* [Official Bulletin of the Scil Erosion Service] 2, no. 3 (March 1935): 1–3.

Oliver, Richard. *Bertram Grosvenor Goodhue*. New York: The Architectural History Foundation/Cambridge, MA: The MIT Press, 1983.

Parman, Donald L. "The Indian and the Civilian Conservation Corps." *Pacific Historical Review* 40, no. 1 (February 1971): 39–56.

———. *The Navajos and the New Deal*. New Haven: Yale University Press, 1976.

Pearce, T.M. *Oliver La Farge*. New York: Twayne, 1972.

Penkiunas, Daina Julia. "American Regional Architecture in Hawaii: Honolulu, 1915–1935." PhD diss., University of Virginia, 1990.

Philp, Kenneth R. *John Collier's Crusade for Indian Reform, 1920–1954*. Tucson: University of Arizona Press, 1977.

Schuyler, Montgomery. "The Works of Cram, Goodhue, and Ferguson: A Record of the Firm's Representative Structures, 1892–1910." *Architectural Record* 29 (January 1911): 1–112.

Spicer, Edward. *Human Problems in Technological Change*. New York: Russell Sage Foundation, 1952.

Swain, Donald C. *Federal Conservation Policy, 1921–1933*. Berkeley: University of California Press, 1963.

Trennert, Robert A. *White Man's Medicine: Government Doctors and the Navajo, 1863–1955*. Albuquerque: University of New Mexico Press, 1998.

"Twelfth-Night in Mr. Goodhue's Office." *Pencil Points* 3, no. 2 (February 1922): 21–26.

US Senate, Committee on Indian Affairs, Subcommittee on Senate Resolution 79. *Survey of Conditions of the Indians in the United States*, Part 34. March 18 and 25, May 14–15 and 29, August 17–21, 1936. Washington, DC: GPO, 1937. Cited as *SOC*, Part 34.

Weisiger, Marsha. *Dreaming of Sheep in Navajo Country*. Seattle: University of Washington Press, 2009.

5 Jacob Morgan and John Collier
Ideology and the Navajo Hogan

Although the hogans described in the last chapter played an important role in the architecture of the Indian New Deal, the heart of John Collier's building program on the Navajo reservation was the day school/community center. When Collier became commissioner in 1933, the Office of Indian Affairs operated ten schools where Diné children could live at home and take classes. Two years later, there were nearly 50 day school/community centers in varying stages of completion.[1] While most of the new school buildings were constructed in a simplified version of the Pueblo-Spanish Revival style, the architects also conceived a design specifically for the Diné known as a "hogan school" (see Figure 5.1). The classrooms, eating facilities, and living quarters at each hogan school occupied octagonal stone hogans similar to the practice and nurse's aide hogans described in the previous chapter.

Collier's plan to build hogan schools encountered firm resistance from Jacob C. Morgan. In 1938, Morgan, a Christian Reformed missionary, became the chairman of the Navajo Nation Tribal Council. An enthusiastic proponent of assimilation, he viewed the Diné hogan as a symbol of paganism and the past. Morgan vehemently opposed the hogan schools designed by Mayers, Murray & Phillip and fought against hogan architecture on the Navajo reservation until he stepped down as tribal chairman in 1942. Although Collier relented in the short term and only four hogan schools were constructed, he continued his attempt to educate Navajo schoolchildren in hogans until his retirement from the Office of Indian Affairs in 1945.

Schools for the Diné Before 1933

The Navajo Treaty of 1868 established a reservation for the Diné encompassing 3.5 million acres in present-day New Mexico and Arizona. The Navajo Agency, where the federal Indian agent lived and where supplies were disbursed, was located at Fort Defiance, Arizona. Article III of the treaty specified that a schoolhouse be constructed at the agency, and in 1869, Presbyterian missionaries successfully petitioned the federal government to allow them to sponsor a teacher for the Diné. Efforts to offer schooling on the reservation proved to be erratic until 1883, when a large three-story stone building with a mansard roof was completed and opened at Fort Defiance (Figure 5.2).[2]

DOI: 10.4324/9781003431770-6

Figure 5.1 The new hogan school at Shonto, Arizona, looking northeast, photographed by Elizabeth Compton Hegemann in 1934. A triple-hogan teacherage is in the foreground, a double-hogan lavatory is at left, and the main classroom building, attached to a dining room and kitchen, is at center. The Shonto Trading Post is in the background, with four guest hogans lined up along its southwest side. The largest guest hogan, at the rear, was circular and constructed from stone, and the other three were many-legged hogans (see Figure 0.7c).

Figure 5.2 Postcard of Fort Defiance, Arizona, c. 1910. The boarding school is the three-story building with a mansard roof at rear center.

164   *Jacob Morgan and John Collier*

The agents and missionaries who attempted to provide schooling for Navajo children grappled with a variety of issues that would be divisive for years to come. Should Navajo students live at home with their families and attend day schools, or would it be better to place them in residential schools? What kind of education should Diné children receive? Should they be prepared to enter Euro-American society, or should they be given training in skills that would enable them to survive on their tribal homelands?

The Fort Defiance boarding school was later joined by other reservation boarding schools located at Keams Canyon, Arizona (1887); Tohatchi, New Mexico (1900); Tuba City, Arizona (1901); Shiprock, New Mexico (1907); Leupp, Arizona (1909); Chinle (*Ch'ínílį́*), Arizona (1910); Crownpoint, New Mexico (1912); Toadlena (*Tó Háálį́*), New Mexico (1913); and Fort Wingate, New Mexico (1925).[3] A number of Diné students also attended federally funded off-reservation boarding schools for Native Americans. The first of these institutions was founded in 1879 at Carlisle, Pennsylvania, and by 1900, a total of 25 were in operation across the US.[4]

During the 1920s, several new organizations, including the American Indian Defense Association, the Eastern Association on Indian Affairs, the New Mexico Association on Indian Affairs, and the Indian Welfare Division of the General Federation of Women's Clubs began working to improve the lives of Native Americans in the United States.[5] A concerted public relations campaign and a series of high-profile controversies involving the Indian Bureau led Secretary of the Interior Hubert Work to commission a survey which ultimately became known as the Meriam Report, released in 1928.[6] The authors of the report were unstinting in their critique of the Office of Indian Affairs (OIA), and the document became highly influential.[7]

The Meriam Report was one of several factors that led to the resignation of Commissioner of Indian Affairs Charles H. Burke in March 1929. His departure signaled an important shift in federal American Indian policy, and Burke's successors, Charles J. Rhoads and Henry Scattergood, began to implement the recommendations of the Meriam Report.[8] Under their direction, the OIA increased the education budget for Native Americans and addressed the criticisms that had been lodged against Indian boarding schools. They improved the standards for educational personnel and underlined their commitment to reform by appointing W. Carson Ryan, Jr. as the OIA's director of Indian education in August 1930. Ryan, a noted scholar and consultant on education, had supervised the sections on Indian education in the Meriam Report. In March 1931, the OIA further expanded its support for Native American schools when Ryan's department became one of the five main administrative divisions within the Indian Service.[9]

As an exponent of the Progressive Education movement, Ryan sought to adapt schooling to the specific needs of each student. One of his first actions was to overhaul the Uniform Course of Study which mandated a standardized curriculum for all Indian schools. Ryan began by eliminating classes such as ancient history, algebra, English classics, and geometry that seemed irrelevant to the particular circumstances of American Indians. In the Meriam Report, Ryan had advocated a program of study that drew from Indigenous cultures, and as director of Indian education, he was able to create new classes for students that reinforced their Native American identity. As a result, Diné boarding schools expanded instruction in the traditional tribal arts of weaving and jewelry making.[10] Ryan also recommended using Indian designs in home economics classes and integrating them into clothing and home décor projects.[11] As we shall see, Ryan's plan aroused the hostility of critics like Jacob Morgan, who argued that "the Three Rs" were central to assimilating Native Americans and preparing them to further their education at mainstream American schools.

When Herbert Hoover left office in March 1933, Rhoads, Scattergood, and Ryan had made significant progress towards achieving the recommendations of the Meriam Report.[12] Their efforts set the stage for the changes in Indian policy implemented by the Franklin Delano Roosevelt administration. Ryan's work for the OIA continued until 1935 because Roosevelt's dynamic Indian commissioner, John Collier, retained him as director of Indian education. Together, they spearheaded the educational reforms of the Indian New Deal.

Native American Architecture for Native American Day Schools

By the time he was appointed commissioner of Indian Affairs in April 1933, John Collier had become well-acquainted with the problems facing contemporary Native Americans. His work for the American Indian Defense Association had been focused on protecting Native American rights, but in his new role, he was given the opportunity to implement the sociological theories he had embraced as a young man. Not surprisingly, some of Collier's work would address the preservation of cultural traditions by means of day school/community centers. Following the plan outlined in his 1924 articles about the Diné for *Sunset* and *Survey Graphic*, Collier set about the construction of "local headquarters," each with a clinic and a multi-faceted educational facility for adults and children. In the Southwest, these institutions would not only promote tribal arts and crafts but they would also embody them by incorporating Indigenous architectural forms.

John Collier's program to construct day school/community centers far exceeded the plans implemented by any of his predecessors in terms of both ambition and funding. As historian Davida Woerner has noted, Collier "was committed to the development of the day school as the keystone of Navajo educational progress."[13] In late 1933, his hard work paid off when the federal government allocated $2,113,000 to build new day schools for Native American students.[14]

CCC-ID crews finished the first of the Indian New Deal day schools – on the Pine Ridge and Rosebud reservations in South Dakota – by mid-September 1934 and completed the first Diné day school/community center at Burnham (*T'iis Tsoh Sikaad*), New Mexico, by March 1935.[15] As of 1941, the OIA had constructed nearly 100 facilities across the country, and about half of these were on the Navajo reservation.[16] Some of the day school/community centers designated for funding during the earliest stages of the program were never built, and additional construction projects were later added. But between 45 and 50 were serving Diné students by the time the US entered World War II. In 1933, Ryan described the importance of building day schools for Native Americans in *Indians at Work*, the monthly periodical published by the OIA.[17] Although still in its early stages, he noted the program was already "reestablishing the integrity of the Indian home and the wholesome atmosphere of a normal family as the bases for Indian community life, much of which had been destroyed under the system of boarding schools for young children."[18]

When John Collier proposed day school/community centers for Indian reservations, he envisioned buildings that would be pioneering in both function and appearance. It is clear he hoped the new architecture would validate Native American culture, and the most extraordinary examples completed by the OIA under his direction were the hogan schools designed for the Navajo reservation.

Collier's correspondence from 1933 indicates that his ideas about reservation architecture evolved over the course of several months. During the summer, his staff began work to develop construction projects that would reflect regional traditions.[19] In the September 15, 1933, issue of *Indians at Work*, Collier declared his resolve "to embody the spirit of the Indians in these Indian buildings."[20] Initially, the OIA did not plan to build "a strictly Navajo type" of architecture for the Diné.[21] But by November, Collier had specifically expressed his intention to employ the Diné hogan as part of the new building program.[22]

Several sources may have contributed to the concept of a school composed of hogans. Elizabeth Compton Hegemann, who owned and operated the Shonto Trading Post during the 1930s, suggested in her memoirs that Collier's hogan schools were inspired by the guest hogans at Shonto (*Shą́ą́' Tó*) (see Figures 0.7c and 5.1).[23] Shonto, which is located in northern Arizona, played host to tourists, archaeologists, ethnologists, geologists, and various government employees during the years before World War II, and in order to provide accommodations, Hegemann and her husband, Harry Rorick, constructed four hogans arranged in a row along the southwest side of the post.[24]

Sometime during 1933, an OIA employee who was researching potential school sites came to Shonto and stayed in one of the guest hogans. Soon after, Charles Collier's wife, Nina Perera Collier, arrived at the post. Nina Collier was an architecture student who would receive her degree from MIT in 1934.[25] According to Hegemann, Nina Collier came to Shonto to make sketches and discuss the details of the proposed hogan schools, which were planned for six different sites on the reservation at the time of the visit.

The architecture that Mayers, Murray & Phillip designed for the OIA drew from several different idioms. In the Southwest, most of the new buildings were executed in a simplified Pueblo-Spanish Revival style (Figure 5.3).

But Collier was particularly pleased with the architects' concept for a school based on the Diné hogan. He submitted a picture of the hogan school with an article about the OIA's new policies to *Good Housekeeping* magazine in January 1934.[26] The design for the new hogan schools was also featured in the February 15, 1934, issue of *Indians at Work* with an article about the government's new Native American–inspired architecture (Figure 5.4).

Figure 5.3 The day school/community center at Torreon, New Mexico, looking southeast, photographed by Milton Snow, c. 1935.

Figure 5.4 The hogan school at Cove, Arizona, architectural rendering by Mayers, Murray & Phillip, 1934.

168   *Jacob Morgan and John Collier*

The text praised the Diné hogan as "one of the most functional of Indian structures" and continued:

> This group of buildings is not a slavish copy of the old type of hogan, with its one doorway and its one aperture in the center of the roof, nor is it a "tricked up" hogan constructed with imported materials. The architects have frankly expanded the designs to fit the needs of a school, added windows to the octagonal sides to admit light and air, put chimneys where fireplaces were wanted, attached a covered walk to connect the classrooms with the dining room and kitchen units in the rear. Yet the spirit of the hogan has been adhered to, and the buildings are an integral part of the Navajo landscape.[27]

In May 1935, the same hogan school rendering appeared in *Architectural Record*, one of the top architecture magazines in the country.[28] Later, in 1937, Collier wrote about the reservation buildings designed by Mayers, Murray & Phillip in an article for *American Arts and Architecture,* and the article's illustrations included drawings and photographs of the hogan school at Shonto.[29]

There were several reasons why Collier and his staff at the OIA held high expectations for hogan-inspired architecture on the Navajo reservation. Some believed that hogan schools would persuade the Diné to be more invested in educational activities. Anthropologist Gladys Reichard gave classes on written Navajo to tribal members in a hogan at Fort Wingate, New Mexico, during the summer of 1934. She later reported that the choice of a hogan for her school was intentional because "In such an environment and in such an [sic] one only, could we expect the interest and cooperation of the 'long hairs,'" or traditional Navajos.[30] Allan Hulsizer, supervisor of secondary education on the Navajo reservation, compared the hogan schools to the Rosenwald Schools that African Americans had built as log cabins in the South. He argued that familiar architectural forms could help connect the day school/community centers with the people they were meant to serve.[31]

Other proponents of the hogan school maintained that the architecture would inspire the Diné to construct more schools. In July 1934, Walter Woehlke, a field representative on Collier's staff, claimed, "Build the hogan type of centers and gradually they would take over the direction of these centers – they would grow in momentum."[32] And some arguments for the hogan schools were of a strictly practical nature. Collier himself predicted economic advantages because the design was cheaper to construct.[33] Using local building techniques and materials meant that the Diné could erect the schools and then maintain them with stone, wood, or adobe on hand. Architect Hardie Phillip, writing in the *Gallup* [NM] *Independent*, cited the ease with which the hogan schools could be expanded to accommodate more students by attaching additional hogans to existing buildings.[34]

But critics of the new day school/community center program, such as Morris Burge of the National Association of Indian Affairs, disagreed. Burge argued that "the hogahn type" was "more wasteful and not a logical one for anything as large as a school."[35] He added that the hogan schools were built at such a high standard that the Diné would feel discouraged to imitate them. Furthermore, he interpreted the hogan schools as a misguided (if laudable) attempt to encourage members of the tribe to relinquish their transhumant lifestyle and settle down permanently.[36]

By the end of January 1934, eight hogan schools were in the planning stages at the OIA.[37] These included facilities at Beclabito (*Bitł'ááh Bitó*), Cove (*K'aabiizhii Nástł'ah*), and Pine Springs (*T'iis Íí'áhí*) in Arizona; at Pueblo Alto (*Nááwíiłbįįhí Bikan*), Alamo (*T'iis Tsoh Sikaadí*, also known as Puertocito), Chichiltah (*Chéch'il Tah*, also known as Chilchinbeto and Two Wells), and Torreon in New Mexico; and at Navajo Mountain, Utah. But only four examples were ever built. The two schools at Cove and Navajo Mountain were completed as planned, while two more were constructed at Shonto and at Mariano Lake (*Be'ak'id Hóteelí*), New Mexico.

The main building at each of the hogan schools was T-shaped and comprised two double-hogans connected by a walkway. One of the double-hogans housed two classrooms, while the other contained a dining room and kitchen.[38] All four campuses were planned so that the main building was aligned towards the east, as in traditional hogan architecture. Each school also had a triple-hogan teacherage, as well as single and double-hogans that served as washrooms and residences for the staff. The hogan schools manipulated vernacular forms and then ordered them into strict geometries. Each individual hogan consisted of a perfect octagon, and in the conjoined structures, the units were precisely aligned. Auxiliary buildings for storage and maintenance at the schools were constructed in the Pueblo-Spanish Revival style.

Jacob C. Morgan

From 1923, when he was appointed to the Navajo Nation Tribal Council, until 1942, when he stepped down as its chairman, Jacob Casamera Morgan was one of the most powerful political leaders on the Navajo reservation (Figure 5.5).

Morgan was born at Nahodishgish (*Nahodeeshgiizh*), New Mexico, in 1879 and grew up in a forked-pole hogan.[39] At the age of ten, he was sent to school at Fort Defiance. Shortly afterwards, he transferred to an off-reservation Indian boarding school at Grand Junction, Colorado, where he became a Christian.[40] By 1898, his academic accomplishments were impressive enough to enable him to enter Hampton Institute in Virginia, a prestigious boarding school for African-American and Native American students.

Morgan flourished at Hampton, where he studied carpentry and played cornet in the school band. When he graduated two years later, he returned to New Mexico and plied his trade framing buildings at the boarding school in Tohatchi.[41] As he later wrote:

> While I worked there Indians came along day after day to see how a white man built his house, and were much surprised to see me working on the same house. It was a good chance for me to show them what a white man's training can do for an Indian. I tried in every way to make them realize the wrong

Figure 5.5 Jacob C. Morgan, photographed by Milton Snow, 1938. Howard Gorman, vice-chairman of the Navajo Nation Tribal Council from 1938 to 1942, is at left, and Henry Taliman, Sr., chairman of the Tribal Council from 1937 to 1938, is at right.

they are doing their children by not sending them to school so that some day they may see their own boys doing the same work I was doing before them.[42]

By the fall of 1902, he was back at Hampton to complete postgraduate work, but poor health forced his departure in 1903.

During the years that followed, Morgan worked at a number of different jobs and began to express an interest in politics. In 1918, he was elected president of the Navajo Progressive League, a group of "returned students" who had been educated at boarding schools. The League's platform declared its support for the following:

the stimulating of interest in education among the Indians, the improvement of their live-stock [sic], the building of better and more sanitary homes, and the promotion of whatever would help the tribe to better living.[43]

At the time, Morgan was employed at the day school in Pinedale (*Tó Bééhwíísganí*), New Mexico, but in 1922 or 1923, he moved north to take a job at the boarding school in Shiprock. There, in the Northern Navajo jurisdiction, Morgan made his home and found his calling. In 1923, he became the jurisdiction's representative on the newly organized Navajo Nation Tribal Council, and in 1925, he became a missionary for the Christian Reformed Church, working under Reverend L.P. Brink in nearby Farmington (*Tóta'*).[44]

Shortly after being appointed to the Tribal Council, Morgan became the first Navajo to publish an architectural history of the hogan.[45] "The Navajo in his Home" – which appeared in the February 1924 issue of *The Christian Indian* – describes the construction of a forked-pole hogan.[46] In the article, Morgan clearly articulates the connection between the building's architecture and the "paganism" of traditional Diné religion.

Morgan described several different types of hogans, including brush shelters for warmer weather. He wrote that during the winter months, some homes are built from "stones and poles," although the "best hogans" are constructed from "good pinion poles." Morgan then recounted the procedure for constructing a forked-pole hogan of the type that he had lived in as a child. The first step was to locate a site, create a circular clearing, and collect the hogan's structural materials. Piñon pine poles were preferable, but if timber was not available, then stone and wood would be gathered. Building the hogan would then follow certain rules. As Morgan commented, "there are some very old and most peculiar customs that are being kept up and practiced by the Navahoes of today in building hogans."

According to Morgan's account, the first custom was to position the hogan's doorway towards the east. The second was to align the hogan's structural supports to the Four Sacred Mountains of the Diné:

> [T]here are always [a] certain number of beams or forked poles of pinon trees to form the main part of the hogan. The two poles support from the east, one from the south, one the west, and one from the north. Now listen! The supposed significance of these poles in the hogan are in accordance to the religion to correspond with that of the four sacred mountains known as follows: Mt. Baldy or the white shell-bead mountain to the east near Santa Fe, the oldest city in our country; Mt. Taylor, or the turquoise mountain to the south; St. Francisco peak or the pearl-shell mountain to the west, near the town of Flagstaff, Arizona. Now for a number of years, at the foot of this sacred mountain the great Southwest Bible and Missionary Conference is held annually. And lastly, the La Plata range, or the bash-zini-dzil, blackstone mountain to the north in the state of Colorado. All of these high peaks are in very plain view to the eyes, and almost fittingly surrounds the Navaho country. Hence the Navaho worships those things that are seen with their own eyes.
>
> Thus far for the building of the hogans. Now the next for its purpose. On all special and important ceremonial occasions the Navahoes offer their prayers and songs relating to these sacred mountains which are to be seen around the Navaho country as already stated above. Here one may see the strong influence and power of the medicine-men of today who are holding the whole tribe back from advancing to better light of living. So this is how our hogans are built, and they are called medicine lodge[s], where all manner of illegal and superstitious performances are being practiced.[47]

172   *Jacob Morgan and John Collier*

To Morgan, a devout Christian, the hogan was a threat to the "better light of living" in at least two ways: First, it symbolized the Diné ritual landscape, and second, it served as the site – "the medicine lodge" – for the performance of traditional ceremonies.

Over the next few years, Morgan would expand his argument against hogans and in favor of Euro-American–style houses. In at least two publications, he appropriated the rhetoric of the "Better Homes" movement, which became a national phenomenon during the 1920s. Initiated in 1921 by Marie Meloney, editor of the women's magazine *The Delineator*, the movement began as a campaign to improve housing with a countrywide model home competition. In 1923, Secretary of Commerce Herbert Hoover became the president of Better Homes in America, and an open house event in June involved 1,000 model homes as well as the dedication of "National Better Home" by President Warren G. Harding on the White House lawn.[48]

In July 1924, *The Southern Workman* reported that Jacob Morgan's "slogan" was "better homes, better sanitary conditions, better live stock [sic]."[49] Then in an article published in October 1925 in the religious magazine, *The Indian of the Southwest*, Morgan dedicated an entire section to the "Need of Better Homes." He argued that "better homes" are Euro-American–style houses which are clean and sanitary, as opposed to hogans which are unhealthy. Intertwined with this argument, a specious one at best, was the notion that a Euro-American house would prompt young Navajos to spend more time at home, rather than attending "pagan" ceremonies. As we shall see, Morgan's hostility towards the hogan did not diminish over time. In 1933, when his stature had risen even further, *The Southern Workman* printed Morgan's political platform. The fifth plank was "I believe in improvement of homes. This means more houses and less hogans."[50]

In October 1933, Commissioner of Indian Affairs John Collier presented the foundational elements of the Indian New Deal to the Navajo Nation Tribal Council. He asked them to support several major changes in the federal administration of Diné affairs, including the construction of day school/community centers that would supersede the boarding school system. The Tribal Council members, including Morgan, assented. But as plans moved forward to close the boarding schools at Chinle and Tohatchi, Morgan began to rankle. Finally, in July 1934, at the Tribal Council meeting in Keams Canyon, Arizona, Morgan initiated a full-blown confrontation with Collier, the first of many to follow.[51]

Morgan's criticisms of the day school/community center program stemmed from his own experiences at Indian boarding schools. As Morgan's biographer, Donald Parman, has noted, "he took an enormous pride in being a 'whitened' and successful Indian." To Morgan, boarding schools were worthy institutions because they were the place where "he had been rescued from the primitive ignorance of Navajo camp life by the government and he had succeeded in life because of education, living among whites, and conversion to Christianity."[52] Morgan was particularly dismayed by the prospect of having Diné students live at home and stay in hogans. During the meeting at Keams Canyon, he referred to a comment made by Senator William S. King of Utah praising day schools over boarding schools and remarked:

> I wish he were here. I would take him to a Navajo home to see what kind of home they have. These boys and girls who go to school today; what kind of home they go back to; what kind of a bed they sleep in. I bet he would decide that the boarding school was best.[53]

Donald Parman has maintained that Jacob Morgan's hatred for traditional Diné culture "at times even exceeded that of the white missionaries."[54] Two descriptions of the Diné hogan published by Morgan's Euro-American contemporaries provide a case in point. In 1921, the Reverend L.P. Brink, Morgan's supervisor at the Christian Reformed Mission in Farmington, wrote a chapter on "Bringing the Gospel to the Hogans" for a larger volume on missionary work in the Southwest. Brink had been living in Navajoland for over twenty years at the time of the book's publication and would surely have had some understanding of the hogan's role in traditional Diné religion. Even so, his account of Diné homes offers a stark contrast to Morgan's assessment, as the following passage illustrates:

> The typical Navaho hogan is an interesting piece of architecture; if you will take a rather oval-shaped orange, cut it into halves crosswise, and place both halves on the table, flat side down, you have the typical shape of two regular Navaho hogans. They are built out of stone or logs, whichever happens to be nearest at hand; when built of logs they are more of an octagon shape.[55]

Brink continued with a detailed description of hogan architecture and concluded, "It is in many respects a very sensible kind of dwelling, and there has been many a day in my missionary life when a Navaho hogan, whether occupied or not, was a more than welcome sight."[56]

Jacob H. Bosscher came to work at the Christian Reformed mission in Rehoboth, New Mexico, in 1909 and later served as a New Mexico State Senator from 1924 to 1932.[57] In February 1931, he authored an article about returned students who had rejected their boarding school education to "return to the blanket." The piece includes a photograph of a Navajo woman standing in front of a many-legged hogan with the caption:

> This is how many of the people live. No windows, the chimney is the only vent for air when the door is closed. The young woman in the center, after years of training in a mission school, had no other place to go than the old mud house where she was born.[58]

174 *Jacob Morgan and John Collier*

But rather than condemn the hogan, Bosscher adopted an attitude of benign tolerance and wrote:

> The very fact that they have no homes nor have the means wherewith to build themselves homes such as the white man has, is no disgrace. Their own hogans are HOMES to them and can be used to the glory of God as well as our homes can.[59]

Jacob Morgan, born and raised a Navajo, understood the close relationship between the hogan and "the pagan practices" of his forebears. His feelings were firmly rooted in the knowledge that the building's symbolism and ceremonial associations could pose an obstacle to converting the Diné to Christianity. As we shall see, Morgan's antipathy towards the hogan and the day school/community center program would lead to an explosive reaction to Collier's new hogan schools.

A Political Controversy

Collier unveiled his plans to build hogan schools in the February 15, 1934, issue of *Indians at Work*. But correspondence in Collier's archive indicates that he had already begun to wonder whether the design might be controversial. In late January 1934, he wrote Tom Dodge, the chairman of the Navajo Nation Tribal Council, about the advisability of adapting hogans for government architecture (see Figure 4.1). Dodge replied in a telegram:

> Hogan style architecture should be used sparingly in building day schools as Navajo have little or no respect for white people who use or imitate their attire, homes, or customs.[60]

Then on February 1, Collier contacted Oliver La Farge, president of the National Association on Indian Affairs, about building hogan-inspired schools and chapter houses, writing:

> I wired Dodge asking whether the Navajos would take offense, and he replied that they did not like imitations of their own architecture. What I meant to ask him was whether there might be some esoteric reason against [it]. I should like your quick advice on this question. There are strong advantages to using the hogan type if there are not compelling reasons to the contrary.[61]

La Farge responded the next day:

> I believe that I can safely say definitely that there is no esoteric reason why Navajo hogahn-type buildings should not be used. Care must be taken to have doors face *east*, and particularly to avoid doors, and have a minimum of windows to the *north*. . . . Some community and chapter houses put up by the Navajo and U.S. cooperation are semi-hogahn in construction,

apparently by Navajo preference. Mrs. Rorick [Elizabeth Compton Hegemann] at Shanto [sic] has had a number of guest-houses built for her by Navajos in the form of hogahns. No one of the conservative district seems to have minded.[62]

While there were instances of Diné opposition to the hogan schools designed by Mayers, Murray & Phillip, the evidence is often anecdotal. In the October 1935 edition of *Indian Truth*, the newspaper of the conservative Indian Rights Association, Matthew Sniffen wrote:

It was thought that the "hogan" type would appeal to the Navajos, but not so. They say "Hogan type all right for Navajo to live in, but we want real schools, just like the white man has."[63]

In 1939, Flora Warren Seymour, another conservative reformer, opined:

The hogan schools, with their low ceilings and dirt floors, the Navaho viewed with alternate amusement and disgust. So obvious was Diné disapproval that but four or five of these were perpetrated.[64]

In addition, Becenti Bega, a Tribal Council member, voiced his objections during a meeting in Keams Canyon, Arizona. Bega was one of the few original members in 1933 who had not attended Euro-American schools.[65] Nevertheless, he declared:

As I understand it the construction of these new day schools will be on a hogan type. I am not in favor of that. We should build houses and make them more modern than on an old type of hogan model.[66]

Bega's disapproval, however, paled in comparison to the opposition mounted by Jacob Morgan when he testified in hearings before a congressional subcommittee in February 1935.

The hearings were a response to a "Memorial by American Indians," written and submitted to the federal government by Joseph Bruner, the president of the American Indian Federation (AIF).[67] The AIF, which was organized at Gallup, New Mexico, in August 1934:

was the major voice of Native American criticism of federal Indian policies during the New Deal. [Its] members could only agree for a brief time on three general principles: that Commissioner of Indian Affairs John Collier be removed from office; that the Indian Reorganization Act be overturned; and most importantly, that the Bureau of Indian Affairs be abolished.[68]

At the meeting in Gallup, Jacob Morgan was elected first vice-president of the group.

176 *Jacob Morgan and John Collier*

The memorial, which outlined the AIF's objections to Collier and the OIA, was sent to President Roosevelt and members of Congress in December 1934.[69] Bruner then petitioned Congressman Will Rogers of Oklahoma, the chair of the House Committee on Indian Affairs, to schedule a congressional hearing to discuss it.[70] Rogers complied with Bruner's request, and the hearing began on February 11, 1935. On February 26, Jacob Morgan appeared, allowing Chairman Abe Murdock of Utah to present him as a spokesman for the Diné.[71]

Morgan began by answering several questions about the members of the 1933 Navajo Nation Tribal Council, several of whom he maintained were "elected illegally."[72] He then continued with an extended discussion of why the Diné preferred to send their children to boarding schools. Morgan assured the subcommittee's members, "the Government has every reason to be proud of these institutions for Indian students," and asserted that day schools were inappropriate for a people who were largely nomadic.[73]

Morgan then offered a disparaging description of the Navajo hogan in an attempt to demonstrate how damaging it would be to allow Diné students to live at home while attending school. After enumerating a long list of the hogan's "problems," he concluded by observing, "the condition of one of these huts is indescribable."[74] When Congressman Murdock asked whether the windowless, stone-and-log, one-room hogan was "the general rule" among the Diné, Morgan answered "yes," and when further queried as to whether there were exceptions, he declared, "very few of them have better homes than I have described."[75]

A few minutes later, Morgan turned his attention to the new hogan schools and remarked:

> I have pointed out the difference between the two types of schools and that our people cannot stay in one place. Moreover, we like to go forward; we like to see improvements among our people. We like better homes. We like to see, for example, a good type of day school constructed on our reservation, but we do not like to see the type of school now being introduced there. The type of building that is being designed is distinctly Indian.[76]

After a request for clarification, Morgan explained that "distinctly Indian" meant "a hogan-style of school" comprising "a hut with a little dome."[77] He admitted that his testimony was based on a picture of a hogan school – probably the rendering in Figure 5.4 – and conceded that the hogan schools were providing work for the Diné.[78] He then added:

> Nevertheless, we do not approve that kind of building. It seems to us that the authorities think that any old thing is good enough for the Indian. If we are going to receive any kind of desirable education, and for the sake of the boys and girls, we should have a good, clean, up-to-date schoolhouse.[79]

In his testimony before the subcommittee later on the same day, John Collier opened his remarks by referring to Morgan's testimony and stated, "there is hardly

Jacob Morgan and John Collier 177

a statement he has made that is not false. I have never known a more flagrant case of one befouling his own nest than we have seen this morning."[80]

On February 28, Morgan appeared again and launched an all-out attack on Collier and the federal government's policies towards the Diné. Collier followed Morgan and answered a long series of questions from Murdock and Congressman Usher L. Burdick of North Dakota. He then read into the record a telegram from Tom Dodge which said:

> Executive and employment committee of tribal council representing people of all six jurisdictions in meeting today declared that J.C. Morgan has no authority to speak for or represent Navajo Tribe or any portion of tribe, and that he is now in Washington solely as tool of unscrupulous white parasites and small group of non-Navajo Indian victims of such parasites.[81]

Collier subsequently offered a lengthy defense of his policies, much of which was specifically addressed to refuting Morgan's statements. With regard to the hogan schools, he confessed:

> I was flabbergasted when I heard Mr. Morgan tell about mud roofs, no windows, and a single hole in the top, because we are being hammered from the other end by people saying that we are constructing de luxe houses, putting in steel windows when we should put in wood windows, and that we are spending altogether too much money in that work.[82]

The following day, Collier continued his testimony accompanied by pictures of summer and winter hogans to illustrate how the Diné lived. During a discussion of the new day school/community centers, he presented another exhibit – an image of a hogan school – that verified that the Indian Office was not "building schoolhouses in the Navajo [reservation] without windows."[83] Morgan did not offer a rebuttal. He was clearly shocked and discomposed by Dodge's telegram and asked (without success) that it be stricken from the record.[84]

Although the hogan schools designed by Mayers, Murray & Phillip provoked a series of discussions during the hearings, by February 1935, the issue was already moot. The hogan school program had been cut back several months earlier, and tellingly, the commissioner did not take the opportunity to argue for its reinstatement. By the time the hearings began, Collier's chief objective was the passage of the Indian Reorganization Act (the centerpiece of the Indian New Deal) which was also opposed by Morgan. Morgan was a rising star; in 1938, he would become the first chairman of the tribe elected by popular vote. It seems likely that Collier was forced to pick his battles and that the hogan school program was relinquished to increase support for other federal policies, such as stock reduction.[85] Nevertheless, Collier's support for the Diné hogan did not waver. Under his leadership, the federal government would continue to promote the construction of hogans on the Navajo reservation, and his quest to build hogan schools was not over yet.

178 *Jacob Morgan and John Collier*

John Collier and Diné Architecture, 1937–1945

During the summer of 1937, E.R. Fryer, the new superintendent of the Navajo Agency, was in a dilemma: A group of returned students were establishing farms in Fruitland, New Mexico, near the San Juan River.[86] Rather than build hogans, the students were living in temporary shelters which offered little incentive to stay on their land and settle there. Fryer observed:

> These people have almost completely disassociated themselves from Navajo life as we know it. They want "white-man's houses." Being unable to afford this so-called luxury, they live in tents and shanties adjacent to their farms.

He pondered what he could do to help them and conceived an idea for "small, neat, well-built portable houses" that would be available from the government by way of a payment plan.[87] Fryer presented the scheme to Collier on July 12, but Collier's response was surprisingly evasive:

> I am advised informally that as a technical matter your idea could be carried out. But I wish you would give a little further thought and then advise me, upon this question: Is it wise for us to be offering frame shacks, even if well built, to the Navajos; ought they not to continue to build their own hogans, and to be encouraged to build them better? I think that a somewhat subtle question is involved here.[88]

Collier then advised Fryer to consult with authorities on Diné culture, including Tom Dodge and Father Berard Haile. Fryer talked to Dodge, who told him, "to the returned student the hogan has a certain symbolic significance in that it contemplates the same unprogressiveness as 'long hair and blankets.'"[89]

As superintendent of the newly consolidated Navajo Agency, Fryer was responsible for implementing the orders of the commissioner. But he also understood that some Diné, such as Jacob Morgan, rejected traditional Navajo culture. In a long, carefully wrought letter, Fryer considered how to articulate a "middle ground," writing:

> Unquestionably there is nothing more important in the Navajo program than the preservation of the Navajo as a self-sustaining and self-respecting individual. Certainly, the preservation of Navajo character, self-reliance, initiative, and self-respect are more important than anything else. To the extent that the building of hogans by the Navajos themselves contributes to this self-respect and self-reliance, I believe their construction should be encouraged. But we can hardly overlook the fact that our educational program and the pressure exerted on all sides by white culture are both anti-hogan, both tending to make the Navajo want other things and different values. Would not the self-respect, self-reliance, and initiative be best preserved among the

Navajos by allowing the men to make choices – rather than accepting, under pressure, what we with Anglo traditions, would consider aesthetic, or even suitable?[90]

It is significant that Fryer never mailed the letter; perhaps he sensed that his attempt to seek an intermediate position would be unwelcome to Collier. The next few years would certainly demonstrate that polarization rather than conciliation characterized the positions maintained by the leaders of the federal Indian Office and the Navajo Nation.

By the late 1930s, the day school/community center program was faltering in many parts of the Navajo Nation. Transportation issues were preventing students from getting to their classes, and the best solution seemed to be to create boarding facilities. As a result, informal dormitories began to appear across the reservation, and in 1941, the federal government joined forces with the Diné to organize housing for students near the day school/community centers. George A. Boyce, the director of Navajo education, called the new program "a cooperative, native housing and boarding school experiment," and six communities were chosen to participate.[91] The dormitories were operated as a partnership, with the government supplying some of the food for the students, while the communities selected a dormitory building staffed by women who lived locally.

The program was a success, and after World War II began, the federal government expanded it so that other day school/community centers could participate. But there was one additional stipulation: "If no local building was available for housing children, the community would construct a native hogan or some sort of structure within walking distance of the school."[92]

Boyce gave a radio talk about Diné education in mid-December 1941 and announced the new "community hogans," but emphasized, "I shall not press this particular proposal upon the Navajo people."[93] Not surprisingly, Jacob Morgan, who was in his final months as chairman of the tribe, was vocal in his opposition to the idea. He submitted a statement to the *Farmington Times-Hustler* in which he described the plan as "one of the rawest deal[s] ever thot [sic] of by any body." He continued:

> The idea for Indian education reached the highest mark up to 1933, and when the New Deal Administration got into power with [the] idea of hogan schools, the high aim for training Indians for good citizenship began to decline and [is] still going down.

He queried, "Why encourage dirt, filth, sickness and death among the children? Why encourage unsanitary conditions of hogans in which the boys and girls [are] to stay?"[94]

Adolph Bitanny was the Diné translator for Boyce's broadcast.[95] Bitanny subsequently joined the Army Air Corps, and when he was in Washington during the autumn of 1942, he visited Boyce's supervisor, Willard Beatty, the OIA's director

180 *Jacob Morgan and John Collier*

of education, to discuss the new dormitories. Beatty later recounted the conversation in a letter to Boyce, writing:

> He discussed with me quite at length the "hogan plan" for the Navajo day schools, having received according to him a number of letters from his friends on the Navaho reservation discussing it and not being very clear about it. I gave him the picture which I got from you as to what was intended and how it was working out and told him of Jake Morgan's opposition. Adolph then said something which I think might be pertinent to you and to your problem. It was to the effect that if the term "hogan plan" is one which you have introduced and are using, it is unfortunate. He says that [the] hogan has achieved the status of a stereotype in the thinking of most Christian missionaries on the reservation as representing all that is bad and pagan in Navaho life. They think of it as insanitary and in every way undesirable. Therefore, by using the term you automatically arouse their suspicion for they will respond to the word rather than examining the idea. Adolph said that he felt that the idea was entirely sound and that if the structures which were being erected for the children around the day schools were similar to some of the first ones which were built which represent an improvement on the original type of Navaho type of hogan and if children slept in beds and were otherwise protected from dirt and infection, the plan was highly meritorious and would be so accepted by the Navaho people, but he urges a change in term in connection with the discussion of the program. I think his ideas sound and am passing them on to you because I feel that way about it.[96]

During the war, gasoline rationing and wartime shortages posed enormous challenges for Diné communities, and the Indian Office struggled to keep schools open. A pictorial article published in *Indians at Work* at the end of 1944 showed Diné schoolchildren living in a stacked-log hogan, log cabins, and a variety of repurposed buildings. But none of them resembled the practice hogans funded by the Indian Office during the mid-1930s and later recommended by Bitanny.[97]

John Collier continued to urge the construction of hogans at Diné schools until his departure from the OIA in 1945.[98] Although Collier's letter of resignation had been accepted on January 22 of that year, he held a meeting to discuss budget shortfalls in Diné education on February 5.[99] Participating in the meeting were several notable anthropologists, including Ruth Benedict, Solon Kimball, Alexander and Dorothea Leighton, John Provinse, and Collier's new wife, Laura Thompson. Boyce and James M. Stewart, who replaced Fryer as the Navajo superintendent in 1942, represented the OIA's staff from the Navajo reservation.

According to Boyce's memoirs, Collier presented a scheme developed by his "committee" of anthropologists to set up a system of small schools to be held in hogans. Each of the schools in this "native plan" were to handle between six and nine pupils taught by a Diné teacher who had "as little as three years of elementary schooling." By multiplying the number of facilities and paying the teachers a smaller salary, Collier hoped to be able to continue his day school/community center program while solving the transportation problems within the Navajo Nation. At a follow-up meeting on February 12, Boyce remembered Collier instructing him "to redirect Navajo thinking" about schools in line with "the native plan." Boyce observed, "Collier had been a great pleader of 'respect for Indian culture.' However, to impose primitiveness upon a people seemed to be as undemocratic as to impose assimilation."[100] Boyce seriously considered resigning his position. But the situation was resolved when William A. Brophy was appointed commissioner of Indian Affairs on March 15, 1945.

Educating Diné students in "hogan schools" is no longer a source of friction today, but how did other members of the tribe regard them during the 1930s? According to Donald Parman:

> Morgan's objections won little sympathy from the mass of Navajos. Most tribesmen, it seems clear, reacted to Collier and his programs on totally materialistic grounds. They cared little about the abstract question of assimilation versus cultural pluralism. Instead, they worried about whether Collier would allow them to keep their sheep and goats, whether they would obtain relief jobs, and whether their children would be fed, clothed, and housed nine months of the year in government boarding schools.[101]

While it is impossible to gauge how most Diné felt about the design for Collier's original hogan school, one report offers an interesting anecdote. In February 1934, government officials visited Navajo Mountain to assess local opinion about the hogan school that was slated for construction there. Arizona State Superintendent of Indian Education R.M. Tisinger later wrote Collier:

> I note from your letter of February 2 that there is a question concerning the construction of the hogan type of school. In this connection I would like to report that some weeks ago a group of Indians at the Navajo Mountain told me specifically that they would prefer the white man's type of school rather than one built of the hogan type. A few days later Mr. Phillip, the architect wired asking if it would be possible to use the hogan style of architecture in this location. Superintendent Balmer and I made a special trip in the Navajo mountain country and held a meeting with the Indians to see if they would approve this style of architecture after seeing the architect's pencil sketch. At this meeting the hogan school was explained in full and there was a unanimous vote in favor of the plan. On numerous occasions the architect's pencil sketch has been shown to Indians, and so far I have had no unfavorable reactions to the plan.[102]

The history of the hogan schools designed by Mayers, Murray & Phillip for the Navajo reservation offers a compelling example of the power of architectural symbolism. John Collier endeavored to create an architectural form where Navajo students could receive a "Progressive Education." His plan included the creation of day schools that offered instruction geared to the specific circumstances of the Diné. To Collier, the

182   *Jacob Morgan and John Collier*

hogan schools, which incorporated Navajo architecture, made excellent sense for the kind of community institution that he envisioned, but to Jacob Morgan, the hogan was a threat to the "better light of living." Even though Collier engaged an elite firm of New York City architects to design the hogan schools and equip them with the latest amenities, Morgan fought tooth and nail to assure the construction of "white man's schools" for Navajo students. Morgan never wavered in his disdain for the hogan. In 1938, the state of New Mexico was making plans to celebrate the 400th anniversary of the arrival of the Spanish explorer, Francisco Vásquez de Coronado. Morgan proposed that the tribe participate in the festivities and sponsor a housing exhibit, "showing the progressiveness of his people and their complete adaptability to progress."[103] The theme was to be "the evolution of Navajo architecture," similar to the housing exhibit constructed at the Kinlichee chapter house in 1931 (see Figure 2.6). But in this case, the sequence of buildings would begin with a hogan, continue with a "crude adobe house," and culminate in a "present day modern house." Anecdotal evidence indicates that the battle between Collier and Morgan was too esoteric to be of interest to most Diné, but as we shall see in the next chapter, by the late 20th century, it became clear that many Navajos had a compelling interest in schooling children in "hogan schools," and new educational facilities on the Navajo reservation during the 21st century often employ some form of hogan-inspired architecture.

Notes

1 There were 46 day schools/community centers in operation during fiscal year 1935–1936, and construction was underway at Thoreau and Twin Lakes, New Mexico, *SOC*, Part 34, 17588; 17921–17922. The table on 17921–17922 of *SOC* Part 34 also lists Cedar Creek as a Navajo school but likely refers to the day school at Cedar Creek near the Fort Apache reservation in Arizona.
2 Davida Woerner, "Education Among the Navajo: An Historical Study" (PhD diss., Columbia University, 1941), 23–35.
3 Ruth Underhill, *Here Come the Navaho!* (Lawrence, KS: Haskell Institute, 1953), 227.
4 Margaret Connell Szasz, *Education and the American Indian: The Road to Self-Determination Since 1928*, 3rd ed. (Albuquerque: University of New Mexico Press, 1999), 9–10.
5 The Indian Welfare Division of the General Federation of Women's Clubs was founded in 1920, the Eastern Association on Indian Affairs and the New Mexico Association on Indian Affairs were founded in 1922, and the American Indian Defense Association was founded in 1923.
6 For more on these controversies, see Randolph C. Downes, "A Crusade for Indian Reform," *The Mississippi Valley Historical Review* 32, no. 3 (December 1945): 331–354.
7 Lawrence C. Kelly, *The Navajo Indians and Federal Policy, 1900–1935* (Tucson: University of Arizona Press, 1968), 139.
8 Szasz, *Education and the American Indian*, 27.
9 Szasz, *Education and the American Indian*, 28–29.
10 Szasz, *Education and the American Indian*, 32. By February 1932, there were Diné instructors teaching rug weaving at every Navajo boarding school, and there were also instructors in metalsmithing at some these schools. W. Carson Ryan, Jr. and Rose K. Brandt, "Indian Education Today," *Progressive Education* 9, no. 2 (February 1932): 84. And see Federal Bulletin 61631, "New Schools for Indian Children" (Washington, DC: US Department of the Interior, n.d.), SMMA.

11 See Federal Bulletin 55911, "The Use of Indian Designs in Government Schools" (Washington, DC: US Department of the Interior, n.d.), SMMA.

12 Szasz, *Education and the American Indian*, 36.

13 Woerner, "Education among the Navajo," 133.

14 "Press Release," n.d., but probably October 1933, Box 58, CSC-NARA-R.

15 "The First Navajo PWA Day School is Completed," *Indians at Work* 2, no. 14 (March 1, 1935): 31–32.

16 Szasz, *Education and the American Indian*, 62.

17 *Indians at Work* began publication on August 1, 1933, and was funded by the OIA and the CCC. It was edited by Mary Heaton Vorse and had a circulation of 12,000. See Kenneth R. Philp, *John Collier's Crusade for Indian Reform, 1920–1954* (Tucson: University of Arizona Press, 1977). 122.

18 W. Carson Ryan, Jr., "Community Day Schools for Indians," *Indians at Work* 1, no. 8 (December 1, 1933): 8.

19 David C. Trott and Roy H. Bradley, "Suggested Procedure to be Followed for School Construction under Public Works' Program" [attachment to] David C. Trott and Roy H. Bradley to William Zimmerman, August 15, 1933, Box 58, CSC-NARA-R.

20 John Collier, "At the Close of Eight Weeks," *Indians at Work* 1, no. 3 (September 1, 1933): 3.

21 David C. Trott and Roy H. Bradley, "Suggested Procedure to be Followed for School Construction under Public Works' Program."

22 John Collier to Roy H. Bradley, November 23, 1933, Box 58, CSC-NARA-R.

23 Elizabeth Compton Hegemann, *Navaho Trading Days* (Albuquerque: University of New Mexico Press, 1963), 379.

24 Hegemann, *Navaho Trading Days*, 292.

25 See Nina Perera Collier, "A Community Center, Day-School, and Clinic for Old Laguna, New Mexico" (Bachelor's thesis, MIT, 1934). On page 24 of the thesis, Collier acknowledged Mayers, Murray & Phillip for their "assistance in supplying material, their cooperation and advice." She also acknowledged the OIA's Construction and Education Departments. For more on Nina Collier's role in the federal government during the Indian New Deal, see Susan L. Meyn, *More than Curiosities: A Grassroots History of the Indian Arts and Crafts Board and its Precursors, 1920–1942* (Lanham, MD: Lexington Books, 2001), 73–74.

26 The submission to *Good Housekeeping* is mentioned in John Collier to Messrs. Mayers, Murray, and Phillip, January 20, 1934, reel 19, *JCP*. Vera Connolly published "The End of a Long, Long Trail," an article on Collier's work, in the April 1934 issue of *Good Housekeeping* (see pp. 50–51, 249–252).

27 "Indian Architecture and the New Indian Day Schools," *Indians at Work* 1, no. 13 (February 15, 1934): 31–33.

28 "Portfolio of Public Works," *Architectural Record* 77 (May 1935): 331–333. This article also included a rendering of a log day school/community center that Mayers, Murray & Phillip designed for the Navajo at Sawmill, Arizona.

29 John Collier, "Indian Reservation Buildings in the Southwest," *American Architect and Architecture* (June 1937): 34–40.

30 Gladys Reichard, "Report on Hogan School, June 1–August 31, 1934," September 29, 1934, mimeo located in Box 2, DLP-CSWR.

31 Allan Hulsizer to W. Carson Ryan, June 16, 1934, mimeo located in Box 2, DLP-CSWR.

32 Walter Woehlke, quoted in the transcript of "A Special Conference held by the Commissioner of Indian Affairs at Kearns Canyon, Arizona," July 13, 1934, reel 16, *JCP*.

33 John Collier to Oliver La Farge, February 1, 1934, reel 19, *JCP*.

34 Hardie Phillip, "Architect Plans Schools for The Diné as Center of Indians Community Life," *Gallup* [NM] *Independent*, August 28, 1934.

35 Morris Burge, "Community Schools on the Navajo Reservation, July 8–July 17," signed July 29, 1935, 3, mimeo located in Box 2, DLP-CSWR.

184 *Jacob Morgan and John Collier*

36 Burge, "Community Schools on the Navajo Reservation," 6.

37 Tabulated from a set of records dated January 26, 1934, and attached to R.M. Tisinger to W. Carson Ryan [stamped February 9, 1934], Box 70, CCF-NARA-R.

38 At Mariano Lake, the largest of the hogan schools, the main T-shaped main building included a craft shop and sewing room connected to the two classrooms, while the kitchen and dining room were located in a free-standing double-hogan. See Burge, "Community Schools on the Navajo Reservation," 5.

39 Donald L. Parman, "J.C. Morgan: Navajo Apostle of Assimilation," *Prologue* 4, no. 2 (Summer 1972): 83; J.C. Morgan, "The Story of Mission Work Among My People," unattributed manuscript, c. 1948, mimeo located in Box 3, DLP-CSWR.

40 Parman, "J.C. Morgan," 84.

41 Parman, "J.C. Morgan," 84n3; Jacob C. Morgan, "A Retrospect," *The Southern Workman* 62 (1933): 79, mimeo located in Box 3, DLP-CSWR.

42 J.C. Morgan, "Out in the Southwest," *Talks and Thoughts*, January 1902, mimeo located in Box 3, DLP-CSWR.

43 *The Southern Workman* 47, no. 12 (December 1918): 608, mimeo located in Box 3, DLP-CSWR.

44 Parman, "J.C. Morgan," 87. As early as 1911, Brink was the feature of an article in a nationally published magazine describing his efforts to translate the Bible into Navajo. See John L. Cowan, "Playing Cadmus to the Navajos," *Overland Monthly* 58, no. 4 (October 1911): 327–333.

45 J.C. Morgan, "The Navajo in His Home," *The Christian Indian*, February 1924, mimeo located in Box 3, DLP-CSWR.

46 *The Christian Indian* was founded in 1922 as the monthly magazine of the Christian Reformed Board of Missions. L.P. Brink edited and published *The Christian Indian* in Farmington, New Mexico, from 1922 until his death in 1936. Although Morgan would not become an assistant to Brink until 1925, he had clearly established a relationship with the Christian Reformed Church by the time of the article's publication.

47 J.C. Morgan, "The Navajo in His Home."

48 Karen E. Altman, "Consuming Ideology: The Better Homes in America Campaign," *Critical Studies in Mass Communication* 7 (September 1990): 286–287; Janet Hutchison, "Building for Babbitt: The State and the Suburban Home Ideal," *Journal of Policy History* 9, no. 2 (April 1997): 193; "National Move for Better Homes to be Opened by President Harding—Model Dwelling on the White House Lawn—Large Number of Demonstration Houses Throughout the Country will be Open to Public All Week," *New York Times,* June 3, 1923.

49 *The Southern Workman* 53 (July 1924), mimeo located in Box 3, DLP-CSWR.

50 Jacob C. Morgan, "A Retrospect," 81.

51 Donald Parman, *The Navajos and the New Deal* (New Haven: Yale University Press, 1976), 199.

52 Parman, *The Navajos and the New Deal*, 69–70. As Parman notes, when teachers on the Navajo reservation began to implement the principles of Progressive Education, many former boarding school students became even more resistant to the new day school/community centers. See *The Navajos and the New Deal*, 199.

53 NNTC, July 10–12, 1934, 3.

54 Parman, *The Navajos and the New Deal*, 69.

55 L.P. Brink, "Bringing the Gospel to the Hogans," in *Bringing the Gospel in Hogan and Pueblo*, ed. John Dolfin (Grand Rapids, MI: The Van Noord Book and Publishing Company, 1921), 144.

56 Brink, "Bringing the Gospel to the Hogans," 145. Although Brink clearly considered "modern houses" to be superior, he also noted, "Then there are log houses built in the shape of Uncle Tom's Cabin, and stone houses built in the same shape, sometimes with

more than one room; most of these are poorly ventilated, and on that account are no improvement over the regular hogan" (145).

57 "Jacob Bosscher" [obituary], *Gallup Independent*, March 19, 1974.

58 Jacob Bosscher, "Senator Bosscher of the Rehoboth School Writes About Fruits of the School," *Missionary Monthly Reformed Review* 34 (February 1931): 60, Box 3, DLP-CSWR.

59 Bosscher, "Senator Bosscher of the Rehoboth School," 60.

60 "Telegram from Thomas H. Dodge to John Collier," January 30, 1934, Box 56; PWA-NARA-NAB.

61 John Collier to Oliver La Farge, February 1, 1934, reel 19, *JCP*. The Eastern Association on Indian Affairs was renamed the National Association on Indian Affairs in 1933.

62 Oliver La Farge to John Collier, February 2, 1934, reel 15, *JCP*.

63 Matthew K. Sniffen, "Navajo Chaos," *Indian Truth*, October 1935: 4. At that time, Sniffen was the secretary of the Indian Rights Association. The group had broken away from supporting Collier in his reform efforts by March 1934, and in that month's issue of *Indian Truth,* Sniffen "issued a stern warning against" the Wheeler-Howard bill, (or the Indian Reorganization Act), the centerpiece of the Indian New Deal.

64 Flora Warren Seymour, "Thunder Over the Southwest," *Saturday Evening Post*, April 1, 1939: 72. Seymour, a fascinating figure, became the first woman to serve on the Board of Indian Commissioners in 1922 and was still a member when the Roosevelt administration abolished the Board in 1934. According to Kenneth Philp, "Collier and [Secretary of the Interior] Ickes wanted to end the Board's existence for political reasons, because it was controlled by Republicans and conservatives who favored assimilation policies associated with the Dawes General Allotment Act." See Philp, *John Collier's Crusade for Indian Reform, 1920–1954,* 119.

65 Young, *A Political History of the Navajo Tribe*, 77. For more about Bega, see his obituary in the *The Santa Fe New Mexican,* April 20, 1936.

66 NNTC, July 10–12, 1934, 90.

67 For more on the AIF, see Laurence M. Hauptman, "The American Indian Federation and the Indian New Deal: A Reinterpretation," *Pacific Historical Review* 52, no. 4 (November 1983): 378–402; Parman, *The Navajos and the New Deal*, 70–72; and Philp, *John Collier's Crusade for Indian Reform, 1920–1954,* 170–173, 200–202.

68 Hauptman, "The American Indian Federation and the Indian New Deal," 378.

69 Hauptman, "The American Indian Federation and the Indian New Deal," 385n20.

70 The text of the memorial and Bruner's letter to Rogers are reprinted on pages 19–21 and 24–25 in USHR.

71 USHR, 315.

72 USHR, 317.

73 USHR, 319.

74 USHR, 320.

75 USHR, 320.

76 USHR, 322.

77 USHR, 322.

78 See figure 4.9. The article in which the rendering was published ("Indian Architecture and the New Indian Day Schools," *Indians at Work* 1, no. 13 (February 15, 1934): 31–33, was introduced as Exhibit J during the hearings. See USHR, 887.

79 USHR, 322.

80 USHR, 335–336.

81 Telegram from Thomas H. Dodge to John Collier, February 5, 1935, Box 10, JCP-NARA-NAB (and see USHR, 357).

82 USHR, 359.

83 USHR, 363.

84 USHR, 379.

186 *Jacob Morgan and John Collier*

85 For more about the Indian Reorganization Act (also known as the Wheeler-Howard bill), see Parman, *The Navajos and the New Deal,* 51–80.
86 Fruitland was the site of an Irrigation Resettlement project for returned boarding school students. For background on the project, see Parman, *The Navajos and the New Deal,* 117–121.
87 E.R. Fryer to John Collier, September 15, 1937, Box 4, NDF-NARA-D.
88 John Collier to E.R. Fryer, August 5, 1937, Box 4, NDF-NARA-D.
89 E.R. Fryer to John Collier.
90 E.R. Fryer to John Collier.
91 The communities were Steamboat, Wide Ruins, Kinlichee, and Dennehotso in Arizona and Crystal in New Mexico. See George A. Boyce, *When Navajos Had Too Many Sheep: The 1940s* (San Francisco: The Indian Historian Press, 1974), 114.
92 Boyce, *When Navajos Had Too Many Sheep: The 1940s*, 115.
93 George Boyce, "Transcript of Radio Broadcast on KTGM, Window Rock, December 13, 1941," Box 25, NSF-NARA-R.
94 J.C Morgan, "Navajo Tribal Council Election on September 12," *Farmington Times-Hustler*, August 28, 1942.
95 Bitanny worked with anthropologist Gladys Reichard and later became known as an artist. For more about his life, see Nancy Mattina, *Uncommon Anthropologist: Gladys Reichard and Western Native American Culture* (Norman: University of Oklahoma Press, 2019).
96 Willard Beatty to George Boyce, [stamped] October 5, 1942, mimeo located in Box 3, DLP-CSWR.
97 See George A. Boyce, "War-Time Education on the Navajo Reservation," *Indians at Work* (November–December 1944): 23–26.
98 According to Donald Parman, "Collier was ousted from office in 1945 by an Oklahoma congressman who refused to approve the Indian Service budget unless the commissioner 'resigned'." See *The Navajos and the New Deal*, 289.
99 Philp, *John Collier's Crusade for Indian Reform*, 1920–1954, 211; Boyce, *When Navajos Had Too Many Sheep: The 1940s*, 149–150.
100 Boyce, *When Navajos Had Too Many Sheep: The 1940s*, 152.
101 Parman, *The Navajos and the New Deal*, 61–62.
102 R.M. Tisinger to Commissioner of Indian Affairs, February 14, 1934, Box 56, PWA-NARA-NAB.
103 Jack Vandermeyer, "Navajo Tribal Council Chairman Morgan Pledges Support to the Coronado Cuarto Centennial," *Farmington Times-Hustler*, December 9, 1938.

Reference List

Archival Sources

Central Classified Files, 1907–1939, RG 75, Records of the BIA, National Archives and Records Administration, National Archives Building, Washington, DC. Cited as CCF-NARA-NAB.

Central Classified Files, c. 1926–1939, Navajo Area Office, RG 75, Records of the BIA, National Archives and Records Administration, Riverside, California. Cited as CCF-NARA-R.

Correspondence of the Superintendent of Construction, Records of the Phoenix, AZ, Area Office, RG 75, Records of the BIA, National Archives and Records Administration, Riverside, California. Cited as CSC-NARA-R.

Decimal Files, 1936–1942, RG 75, Records of the BIA, National Archives and Records Administration, Denver, Colorado. Cited as NDF-NARA-D.

Donald Lee Parman Papers, 1883–1994, Center for Southwest Research, University of New Mexico, Albuquerque. Cited as DLP-CSWR.

The John Collier Papers, 1922–1968 [microform edition]. Edited by Andrew M. Patterson and Maureen Brodoff. Sanford, NC: Microfilming Corporation of America, 1980. Cited as *JCP*.

Miscellaneous Correspondence from Commissioner Collier's Office, Office Files of Commissioner John Collier, 1933–1945. RG 75, Records of the BIA, National Archives and Records Administration, National Archives Building, Washington, DC. Cited as JCP-NARA-NAB.

Navajo Subject Files, RG 75, Records of the BIA, National Archives and Records Administration, Riverside, California. Cited as NSF-NARA-R.

Public Works Administration Projects 1931–43, RG 75, Records of the BIA, National Archives and Record Administration, National Archives Building, Washington, DC. Cited as PWA-NARA-NAB.

St. Michael's Mission Archives, St. Michael's, Arizona. Cited as SMMA.

Published Sources

Altman, Karen E. "Consuming Ideology: The Better Homes in America Campaign." *Critical Studies in Mass Communication* 7 (September 1990): 286–307.

Bosscher, Jacob. "Senator Bosscher of the Rehoboth School Writes About Fruits of the School." *Missionary Monthly Reformed Review* 34 (February 1931): 59–60.

Boyce, George A. "War-Time Education on the Navajo Reservation." *Indians at Work* (November–December 1944): 23–26.

———. *When Navajos Had Too Many Sheep: The 1940s*. San Francisco: The Indian Historian Press, 1974.

Brink, L.P. "Bringing the Gospel to the Hogans." In *Bringing the Gospel in Hogan and Pueblo*, edited by John Dolfin, 140–160. Grand Rapids, MI: The Van Noord Book and Publishing Company, 1921.

Collier, John. "At the Close of Eight Weeks." *Indians at Work* 1, no. 3 (September 1, 1933): 1–4.

———. "Indian Reservation Buildings in the Southwest." *American Architect and Architecture* (June 1937): 34–40.

"The First Navajo PWA Day School is Completed." *Indians at Work* 2, no. 14 (March 1, 1935): 31–32.

Hauptman, Laurence M. "The American Indian Federation and the Indian New Deal: A Reinterpretation." *Pacific Historical Review* 52, no. 4 (November 1983): 378–402.

Hegemann, Elizabeth Compton. *Navaho Trading Days*. Albuquerque: University of New Mexico Press, 1963.

Hutchison, Janet. "Building for Babbitt: The State and the Suburban Home Ideal." *Journal of Policy History* 9, no. 2 (April 1997): 184–210.

"Indian Architecture and the New Indian Day Schools." *Indians at Work* 1, no. 13 (February 15, 1934): 31–33.

Kelly, Lawrence C. *The Navajo Indians and Federal Policy, 1900–1935*. Tucson: University of Arizona Press, 1968.

Minutes of the Navajo Nation Tribal Council. Cited as NNTC.

Morgan, J.C. "Out in the Southwest." *Talks and Thoughts* [Hampton Institute], January 1902.

———. "The Navajo in His Home." *The Christian Indian*, February 1924.

———. "A Retrospect." *The Southern Workman* 62 (1933): 76–81.

———. "A Navajo Dissenter." *Christian Century* 51 (October 1934): 1379–1380.

Parman, Donald L. "J.C. Morgan: Navajo Apostle of Assimilation." *Prologue: The Journal of the National Archives* 4 (Summer 1972): 83–98.

188 *Jacob Morgan and John Collier*

———. *The Navajos and the New Deal*. New Haven: Yale University Press, 1976.

Philp, Kenneth R. *John Collier's Crusade for Indian Reform, 1920–1954*. Tucson: University of Arizona Press, 1977.

"Portfolio of Public Works." *Architectural Record* 77 (May 1935): 331–333.

Ryan, W. Carson, Jr. "Community Day Schools for Indians." *Indians at Work* 1, no. 8 (December 1, 1933): 7–9.

Ryan, W. Carson, Jr., and Rose K. Brandt. "Indian Education Today." *Progressive Education* 9, no. 2 (February 1932): 81–86.

Seymour, Flora Warren. "Thunder Over the Southwest." *Saturday Evening Post*, April 1, 1939: 23, 71–72, 74, 76.

Smith, Hoke, ed. *Annual Report of the Secretary of the Interior, 1896,* vol. II (Washington, DC: GPO, 1896).

Sniffen, Matthew K. "Navajo Chaos." *Indian Truth*, October 1935: 1–8.

Szasz, Margaret Connell. *Education and the American Indian: The Road to Self-Determination Since 1928*, 3rd ed. Albuquerque: University of New Mexico Press, 1999.

Underhill, Ruth, *Here Come the Navaho!* Lawrence, KS: Haskell Institute, 1953.

US House of Representatives, Subcommittee on General Bills of the Committee on Indian Affairs. *Indian Conditions and Affairs: Hearings before the Subcommittee on General Bills of the Committee on Indian Affairs on HR 7781 and Other Matters*, 74th Cong., 1st sess., February 11, 1935. Cited as USHR.

US Senate, Committee on Indian Affairs, Subcommittee on Senate Resolution 79. *Survey of Conditions of the Indians in the United States*, Part 34. March 18 and 25, May 14–15 and 29, August 17–21, 1936. Washington, DC: GPO, 1937. Cited as *SOC,* Part 34.

Woerner, Davida. "Education Among the Navajo: An Historical Study." PhD diss., Columbia University, 1941.

Young, Robert W. *A Political History of the Navajo Tribe*. Tsaile, AZ: Navajo Community College Press, 1978.

6 The Stacked-Log Hogan Becomes an Architectural Type

Over the preceding chapters, we have seen how builders since the late 19th century adapted the Diné hogan for new purposes in non-traditional contexts. In almost every case, this architecture resembled the hogans the Diné were constructing on the Navajo reservation. Even when the function of those buildings departed dramatically from the hogan's original use, the hogan's traditional form was retained. Architectural theorists have invented a term – "model" – to describe a building that has been closely reproduced to create a new architectural design. According to the French architectural theorist Quatremère de Quincy, a building that serves as a "model" for an architectural design is "a thing to copy or imitate completely."[1]

But we have also looked at a few building designs that differed from traditional hogan forms. The concrete-plastered hogans at Rimmy Jim's motel, discussed in Chapter 3, and the masonry hogans designed by Mayers, Murray & Phillip, discussed in Chapters 4 and 5, represent the beginning of something new in Navajo-inspired architecture. In those instances, the architects and builders preserved only the most distinctive aspects of the stacked-log hogan – namely, its polygonal shape and corbelled dome. In this way, they were able to experiment with new designs that people would still interpret as "Navajo." These buildings illustrate the development of an architectural "type" for buildings with a distinctly Diné identity.

In the *Encyclopédie Méthodique*, published in 1825, Quatremère explained the difference between model and type. "Type," according to Quatremère, is "the idea of an element which ought itself to serve as a rule for the model." To put it differently, a type is a characteristic aspect of a particular category of architecture that a designer can rework to generate new designs that clearly belong to the same category. A type offers the flexibility that architects need to create buildings that meet specific requirements while providing those works with an underlying consistency that distinguishes them as part of a larger group. In this chapter, we will look at how architects over the last century have employed the octagon and the corbelled dome as types to be used for museums, meeting halls, schools, senior centers, chapter houses, and other architecture intended to convey an association with the Diné hogan.[2]

DOI: 10.4324/9781003431770-7

Model and Type

According to Anthony Vidler, the concept of type first entered architectural theory during the late 18th century in the work of French writers, such as Quatremère.[3] Scholarly discourse about architectural types developed further during the 19th century but came to a halt after World War I. The architects and influencers who shaped the early years of the Modernist movement insisted on abandoning the paradigms offered by historic buildings, leading to a rejection of the use of type as a design principle.[4]

During the 1960s, a new generation of architects and critics began to reconsider the concept of type and argue for its value in contemporary design. In 1963, architect Gian Carlo Argan published an article in which he restated Quatremère's definition of type and then described how a type may be produced and used in architectural practice. According to Argan, the process begins by "comparing and superimposing individual forms" and analyzing their similarities. This produces "a common root form," in which "particular characteristics of each individual building are eliminated and only those remain which are common to every unit of the series." The type thus generated "contains the possibility of infinite formal variation."[5]

Later, in an influential article published in 1978, architect Rafael Moneo also explored using Quatremère as a theoretical basis. Moneo defined a model as "the mechanical reproduction of an object" and a type as "a concept which describes a group of objects characterized by the same formal structure."[6] According to Moneo, architectural types embrace the past while creating the potential for new designs that are present and alive. As he explained:

> the architect can extrapolate from the type, changing its use; he can distort the type by means of a transformation of scale; he can overlap different types to produce new ones. He can use formal quotations of a known type in a different context, as well as create new types by a radical change in the techniques already employed. The list of different mechanisms is extensive – it is a function of the inventiveness of architects.[7]

As modernity began to impact the Navajo reservation, the hogan worked well as a model for new architecture. Almost all of the buildings we have encountered so far were reproduced on a domestic scale and were roughly the same size as a traditional hogan. But during the 1920s, an interest arose in constructing larger buildings for the Diné, and finding types that evoked the hogan became increasingly important.

As we have seen, the hogan can take many different forms. But creating archtitectural types that were distinctive to the Diné favored the stacked-log hogan as a source over all others. The forked-pole hogan is not amenable to enclosing large spaces and bears a resemblance to the Plains tipi, the most famous of all Native American buildings. Roundness, the common characteristic of female hogans, is not unique to Navajo architecture either. But the stacked-log hogan is almost always hexagonal, heptagonal, or octagonal in plan, and none of these shapes has been universally adopted as a signifier for other categories of architecture on this continent.

The Stacked-Log Hogan Becomes an Architectural Type 191

Although architects occasionally use the hexagon in large-scale buildings on the Navajo reservation, the octagon has become the preferred type for specifically referencing the Navajo hogan. There are several possible explanations for how this came about. Hexagonal buildings quickly lose a sense of being rounded as they gain in size and their sides become longer. Heptagons are not radially symmetrical, and it is particularly tricky to integrate them into larger buildings possessing a rectilinear floor plan. Octagons, however, are completely symmetrical, and octagonal buildings preserve a sense of being rounded even when their size is significant. It is also true that an octagonal hogan can be oriented so that four of its eight walls face the cardinal directions and the four Sacred Mountains so that the building's connection to the Diné ethnoscape is unambiguously expressed. I suspect that these are some of the reasons why the octagon became the preeminent type employed in large-scale architecture for the Diné during the early part of the 20th century.

A second distinctive aspect of Diné hogans is the corbelled dome traditionally found in female hogans. Large corbelled domes constructed from wood must be carefully engineered and are expensive to build, and so all of the octagonal buildings we will survey in this chapter have either flat or pyramidal roofs. But on the interior, a number of the octagonal spaces we will see have a decorative log ceiling that evokes the corbelled dome. Although corbelled domes can be found on other types of female hogans, its appearance over octagonal rooms signals a direct connection with the stacked-log hogan, and it may be deemed as a second architectural type found in Navajo-inflected buildings.

Today, the rapid pace of global change has led some designers to question whether architectural types are still useful.[8] But across the Navajo reservation, a place occupied by thousands of octagonal hogans, the landscape maintains a continuity with the past and serves as a constant reminder of the source for the octagonal type. And although the Diné embrace a great deal of cultural diversity, their ethnicity and shared history create a strong sense of collective identity fueling the meaning behind the architecture to be discussed in the following pages.

The Navajo House of Religion, 1929–1937

The Navajo House of Religion, now the Wheelwright Museum of the American Indian, was one of the first projects to adapt the Diné hogan to large-scale public architecture. Mary Cabot Wheelwright, a wealthy heiress who grew up in Boston, originated the idea for the museum during the mid-1920s. Wheelwright first traveled to the Southwest in 1897 and later became a regular visitor to New Mexico and Arizona, where she developed a special interest in the sacred ceremonialism of the Diné.

Sometime around 1920, Wheelwright met Arthur and Franc Newcomb, proprietors of a trading post on the Navajo reservation.[9] The Newcombs introduced Wheelwright to the famed Diné medicine man and ritual practitioner, Hastiin Klah, and the two established a friendship that would endure until Klah's death in 1937. Traditional Diné religion includes a set of elaborate healing rituals that address different illnesses. During the late 1920s and early 1930s, professional anthropologists, including Leland Wyman, Clyde Kluckhohn, and

192   *The Stacked-Log Hogan Becomes an Architectural Type*

Gladys Reichard, investigated and documented many of these rituals. But when Wheelwright first began touring Navajoland, the tribe's religion had received sparse attention.

Wheelwright's interest in Diné religion developed into a fascination during a period when many people believed that Native American culture was about to disappear. Although she had no academic training, Wheelwright's substantial financial resources gave her the ability to make extended stays on the Navajo reservation, where she attended a variety of different ceremonies and began a concerted effort to document the myths, rituals, and art associated with them.

In 1923, Wheelwright purchased an old hacienda near Alcalde, about 30 miles north of Santa Fe and renovated it to serve as a summer residence. Wheelwright soon became involved with civic affairs in Santa Fe and befriended several members of the Santa Fe art colony, including William Penhallow Henderson, an artist and builder, and his wife, the poet Alice Corbin. According to Wheelwright's biographer, Leatrice Armstrong, the couple had established a friendship with Wheelwright by 1925.[10] At that time, Henderson was working on the design and construction of buildings at an estate in Santa Fe belonging to two sisters, Elizabeth and Martha White, heirs to a newspaper fortune.

As Wheelwright's collection of materials grew in breadth and significance, she became increasingly aware of the need to curate and conserve it. So in October 1927, when a new project for a "Museum and Laboratory of Anthropology" was incorporated with plans for headquarters in Santa Fe, Wheelwright saw an opportunity to find a home for the items she had gathered during her research.

Wheelwright first contacted Alfred Kidder, the chair of the project's Board of Trustees, and offered to finance a building to house her collection in late 1927. Kidder responded enthusiastically.[11] Wheelwright wanted the building "as much as possible to conform to the type of the Hogahn" and engaged William Penhallow Henderson to design it. In her memoirs, Wheelwright described him as "not only an artist but a mystic, deeply interested in primitive lore." This, combined with Henderson's interest in architecture, made him an ideal collaborator for the building she envisioned.[12]

With funding from the Rockefeller family, the Laboratory's Board of Trustees made plans to construct a million-dollar campus on 50 acres located on the southeast side of Santa Fe. In September 1929, a Building Committee, serving in an advisory capacity to the Board, formalized an architectural scheme for the project, soon to become known as the Laboratory of Anthropology. The building complex was to include research facilities for bacteriology, biology, zoology, meteorology, geology, and ethnology as well as residences and an exhibit hall. Perhaps the most unusual aspect of the new Laboratory was to be "a small building devoted to Navajo arts," funded by Wheelwright and called "the Navajo Hogan."[13]

The Building Committee organized an architectural competition for the design of the Laboratory and invited five different architectural firms to participate, including Henderson; Ralph Adams Cram and Frank Ferguson of Cram & Ferguson in Boston; Arthur Addison Fisher and William Ellsworth Fisher of Fisher & Fisher in Denver; William Templeton Johnson in San Diego; and the eventual winner, John Gaw Meem in Santa Fe. The program for the project clearly stated that the main buildings comprising

The Stacked-Log Hogan Becomes an Architectural Type 193

the Laboratory were to be designed in the Pueblo-Spanish Revival style, known also as the Santa Fe style. A blueprint of Henderson's design for a "Navajo Hogan" was also enclosed in the packet that the Building Committee sent to the competitors.

From the outset, it was clear that the Navajo Hogan was not representative of the Santa Fe style. The building was dominated by a large octagonal volume measuring 50′ wide by 65′ long, with a main entrance located in a rectangular room extending 10′ from the octagon's eastern end. Windowless walls created a parapet around the building's octagonal truncated pyramidal roof, giving the structure a total height of 40′ 4″.[14] And a large exhibition hall on the building's top floor was lit by a skylight mounted on the east side of the building's roof.

The architects in the competition were left in a quandry. The Navajo Hogan could certainly be plastered in color and texture to match the other buildings at the Laboratory. But the program emphasized that the buildings were to be mostly single-story, and the Hogan was roughly three stories tall. While the specifications they had received clearly stated, "Large window openings are not in the style," the Hogan's roof included a prominent skylight, measuring approximately 8′ by 4′.[15] A "List of Features to be Avoided" appended to the program discouraged bilateral symmetry either in the individual buildings or in the overall plan for the Laboratory. But of course, on this count, Henderson's design also defied the Building Committee's guidelines. The architects were to include the Hogan in their proposals for the Laboratory, but they were also told:

> Should it fail to harmonize with the general group, its exterior appearance may be modified insofar as this competition is concerned or it should be located in the composition so as not to prejudice the appearance of the Laboratory as a whole. No change should be made in its interior size or method of lighting. The characteristics of a Navajo Hogan should be retained and accentuated, if possible.[16]

The challenge posed to the architects thus became the following: What are the characteristics of a Navajo hogan?

Henderson's notebooks offer few hints about the design process for the Hogan, making it necessary to rely on Wheelwright's memoirs, written years later.[17] What is plain is that both within and without, the building she intended was to be much more than a museum. In fact, the overriding concern for both patron and architect was to provide visitors to the building with a sense they were entering a sacred space. According to Wheelwright:

> Willie Henderson's plan of an entrance to the main exhibition hall on the upper part of the building with the working part of the museum on a lower level, was to give the feeling of an approach not directly but to give the feeling of a Medicine Hogahn where, over the door are always hung four blankets, which must be put aside in order to enter. These typify to them the Four Worlds, and Willie's design, by which you go down a flight of steps and then come up into the central hall, was to separate the everyday world from a place somewhat

194   *The Stacked-Log Hogan Becomes an Architectural Type*

isolated, with light coming from one opening in the roof to the east, to give somewhat of the feeling of the aloofness and quiet of a Medicine Hogahn that is being used for a ceremony. Our idea was, if possible, to create a sense of surprise and wonder in spectators coming by this circuitous route, face to face with the strange world of the Navajo religion. . . . I felt so definitely that I wanted to have something different from an ordinary museum that at first we called it the House of Navajo Religion.[18]

The ceiling of the exhibition hall was constructed from 16 tiers of logs layered on top of each other and arranged in a pyramidal shape to provide the semblance of a corbelled dome. As the design evolved, Wheelwright and Henderson consulted an expert in Diné ceremonialism, their friend Hastiin Klah. Wheelwright would later recall, "Klah knew all about the plan of the museum and approved it entirely."[19]

Jesse Nusbaum was appointed as the Laboratory's first director in December 1929 and served as one of the five judges for the competition.[20] Although Nusbaum had managed the construction of Diné hogans at the Panama-California Exposition in 1915 and supervised the creation of a village showcasing different varieties of Navajo architecture at Mesa Verde in 1925, he was not in favor of including Henderson's Navajo Hogan at the Laboratory. As a work of architecture based on its own merits, Nusbaum found Henderson's design to be beautiful.[21] But he felt that the Laboratory should exhibit a consistent style.

Months of wrangling between Wheelwright, Henderson, and the Building Committee ensued. In October 1930, Henderson produced another model as a response to the committee's criticisms (Figure 6.1a). But although the first floor had been dropped to make the building less prominent, the design was virtually identical to the version that Henderson had submitted in 1929.[22] Nusbaum was livid, writing to Kidder, "[It] is ultra-modern from every external angle and I might add, violates every fundamental of the so-called Santa Fe type of architecture." The spiritual dimensions of the design, which contrived to induce a sense of religious awe, also offended Nusbaum, who felt that an "emotional gift" from Wheelwright would be incompatible with the Laboratory's mission as "a serious, scientific project."[23]

In September 1931, a new model of the Navajo Hogan created by Nusbaum, Meem, and artist Carlos Vierra was presented to Wheelwright (Figure 6.1b). The model had a flat roof and a wall that obscured the skylight and helped harmonize the Hogan with the Santa Fe–style buildings at the Laboratory.[24] Wheelwright accepted the changes in the model but later reconsidered her decision. During a meeting with the Building Committee the following month, she emphasized her intention, "to give to the Navajo and to the public something transcending a mere museum – something that would catch the spirit of Navajo philosophy and give to [non-Native] people perhaps their first clear idea of the importance of Indian myth and ritual." She listed what she considered to be "the three essential features of a Navajo ceremonial hogan," namely:

1. The entrance to the East
2. The sloping and unobstructed skylight facing the East
3. The five ceremonial logs above the doorway (a design that Wheelwright later attributed directly to Hastiin Klah)[25]

The Stacked-Log Hogan Becomes an Architectural Type   195

a.

b.

c.

Figure 6.1 The Navajo House of Religion, Santa Fe, New Mexico: a. Model by William Penhallow Henderson, October 1930; b. Model showing the size and orientation of the proposed Navajo House of Religion in relation to the Laboratory of Anthropology, by Jesse Nusbaum, John Gaw Meem, and Carlos Vierra, 1931; c. The Navajo House of Religion, looking southwest, photographed by Ernest Knee, c. 1937.

196   *The Stacked-Log Hogan Becomes an Architectural Type*

But while the entrance in the model created by Nusbaum, Meem, and Vierra retained an eastern orientation, the wall concealing the skylight ensured that the sunrise would no longer shine into the interior. And the doorway design, which had originated with Hastiin Klah, now featured only two logs.[26] Although Sylvanus Morley, the chair of the Building Committee, expressed his willingness to be flexible about points 1 and 3, he would not budge about the skylight under any circumstances.[27]

The committee had lodged objections to the Hogan because of its design and its "emotional" content. But in May 1932, Kidder contacted Wheelwright to tell her that the Executive Committee of the Board of Trustees had chosen to refuse the Hogan because it lacked an endowment.[28] On June 7, Wheelwright wrote Kidder, informing him that she was withdrawing her offer.[29]

Things took a new turn when Elizabeth White deeded Mary Wheelwright a parcel of land adjoining the Laboratory of Anthropology.[30] Wheelwright worked to secure funding and then proceeded with the construction of the Navajo House of Religion. It was ritually blessed on November 22, 1937, by a Diné medicine man and then opened a week later (Figure 6.1c). In April 1938, the Architectural League of New York awarded the building an honorable mention in the category of Works of Major Importance "for its simple dignity and original design."[31]

A brochure distributed by the museum at the time of its opening explained,

> The form of the building is a synthesis of the two types of ceremonial hogahns now in use – its projecting entrance and the skylight above from the older type, and the octagonal shape from the more modern type.[32]

Five years later, in 1942, Father Berard Haile published "Why the Navaho Hogan?" in which he documented that the Diné were using two kinds of ceremonial hogan: the forked-pole (or male) hogan and the *yadah'askání* (a term he used for female hogans). He noted that roundness characterizes the *yadah'askání* – in fact, the term translates as "round below" – and that the building can take several forms. But the hogan that illustrates the *yadah'askání* in the article is a polygonal stacked-log hogan, confirming that the design by Henderson was accurate in its inspiration.[33]

The Navajo Nation Council Chamber, 1934–1935

The Navajo Nation Tribal Council, the governing body for the Navajo tribe, originated in 1922. In that year, the federal government established a three-man "Business Council" to ensure that new oil and gas leases within the reservation could be approved by a group speaking for Navajo interests. But the organization of the Business Council fell short of providing the breadth of representation required by law. So the following year, the government laid the foundations for another governing body that would be "tribal in scope." The new Navajo Nation Tribal Council held its first meeting at Toadlena, New Mexico, in July 1923. The group exercised a fraction of the power it would later come to hold, but men from across the reservation served as delegates, and as historian Robert W. Young has observed, the

The Stacked-Log Hogan Becomes an Architectural Type   197

formation of the Tribal Council "marked a turning point in the political history of the Navajos."[34]

After his appointment as federal commissioner of Indian Affairs in 1933, John Collier began to implement his plans to improve the welfare of Native Americans. As we have seen previously, he worked to enhance health care, promote soil conservation, and increase educational opportunities for the Diné. Collier was also interested in expanding the political power wielded by the tribe, and to that end, he asked Mayers, Murray & Phillip to design the Navajo Nation Council Chamber, a building that would provide a meeting place for the Tribal Council and serve as a symbol of Navajo sovereignty.[35]

Collier's interest in developing a type for new hogan architecture on the Navajo reservation was evident in his correspondence with Oliver La Farge, discussed in the last chapter. La Farge counseled the importance of keeping building entrances facing east and the need for minimizing the number of openings facing north, the direction "where evil and danger dwell," according to traditional Diné religion.[36] A few months later, in August 1934, Collier published "The First Tribal Capital," which contains a detailed description of how the new Council Chamber would be specifically Diné:

> It has the traditional octagonal shape of the Navajo hogan. No doors or windows open on its north side, and the entrance door faces east. Traditionally too it will be made of the materials which the Navajos have always used – adobe, stone, sticks and logs. Natural stone from the surrounding cliffs and logs of native pine will make the main building. The roof will be adobe, with wood canales (hollowed tree logs) to carry off the rain. The interior decoration and the furniture will be Navajo; Navajo artists will contribute their paintings and Navajo craftsmen their rugs and basketry. It will be built by all Indian labor – 60,000 man-hours of it.[37]

As we have seen, during this period, the Navajo hogan took a number of different forms on the reservation, but Collier and his architects chose the octagonal stacked-log hogan as the basis for a type to develop new kinds of public architecture.

The design by Mayers, Murray & Phillip (Figure 6.2) comprises a single large space created from two octagonal volumes stacked on top of each other. The building is roughly 30′ tall, and the ground floor measures 70′ across. The upper volume forms a clerestory illuminating the interior and is covered with a flat roof disguised by a parapet. Two smaller octagonal buildings containing committee rooms were to have been constructed on the northwest and southwest sides of the main chamber, but the costs exceeded the funding available.[38]

One of the most distinctive aspects of the Council Chamber is the group of eight large timbers that radiate from its clerestory. The timbers pass through large piers and then project beyond the building. Their resemblance to the *vigas* common in Pueblo and Pueblo-Spanish Revival architecture has been noted by scholars including Rachel Leibowitz.[39] It is certainly true that the timbers help to harmonize the Council Chamber's design with the 50 or so other buildings at Window Rock,

Figure 6.2 The Navajo Nation Council Chamber, Window Rock, Arizona, looking southwest, photographed by Burton Frasher in 1935.

which were executed in Mayer, Murray & Phillip's version of the Pueblo-Spanish Revival (see Figure 5.3). But the *viga*-pier constructions also bear an uncanny resemblance to flying buttresses, a characteristic feature of Gothic architecture. Mayers, Murray & Phillip were specialists in Gothic Revival architecture, and it seems clear to me that they drew from their training and background to give the Navajo Nation Council Chamber a truly unique architectural design.

Interestingly, the building's dimensions are very similar to those of the Navajo House of Religion, and it is tempting to wonder whether the architects knew of it.[40] Although the Navajo House of Religion was not completed until 1937, Ralph Adams Cram, Bertram Goodhue's partner from 1890 to 1914, competed for the Laboratory of Anthropology commission and produced a design that included William Penhallow Henderson's scheme.[41] Were Mayers, Murray & Phillip familiar with Cram's work? Whether or not there is a direct link between the two projects, the Navajo House of Religion and the Navajo Nation Council Chamber demonstrate that by the mid-1930s, the octagon was emerging as a type that could be adapted for large buildings and serve as an architectural symbol for the Diné.

John Carl Warnecke's Projects for the Navajo Nation, 1958–1977

Funding for new construction within the Navajo Nation diminished after the mid-1930s. But by the late-1950s, the tribe's financial situation had sufficiently improved to enable Diné leaders to hire San Francisco architect John Carl Warnecke to design the first large-scale architecture on the reservation since the Indian New Deal.

The Stacked-Log Hogan Becomes an Architectural Type   199

Warnecke received his architectural training at Harvard's Graduate School of Design, where he studied under Walter Gropius. He established his own practice in 1950, and fame came in 1956, when he received a commission to work on the US Embassy to Thailand. Warnecke would later describe the building, perched atop slender white stilts, as "in a 'floating pagoda' style, modern in design yet suggesting an ancient Thai palace." Although never constructed, the project demonstrated a particular sensitivity to its setting, and Warnecke would become especially known for the "contextualism" of his work. In 1960, he landed the commission to design a new state capitol for Hawaii (completed in 1969), and there, too, he introduced several elements evoking the building's physical and cultural environment.

During the early 1960s, he worked closely with John F. Kennedy and his wife, Jacqueline. Warnecke was commended for his efforts to restore Lafayette Square, located on the north side of the White House, where he was able to successfully integrate two new office buildings with the square's early 19th-century architecture. After Kennedy's assassination, the architect was chosen to design the president's grave in Arlington National Cemetery. During the 1970s, John Carl Warnecke and Associates grew dramatically, and by 1977, the firm had emerged as the largest in the country, with projects ranging in size from a 40-story Hilton Hotel in San Francisco to a trailer for the king of Saudi Arabia.[42]

But in 1958, when Warnecke began working with the Diné, his practice was much smaller in scale. Warnecke was able to attend meetings with the Navajo Nation Tribal Council, and he cultivated a personal relationship with Diné leaders. By mid-1959, Warnecke's office, in association with Livingston and Blaney, a city and regional planning firm, had begun work on four projects to be located at the Navajo capital in Window Rock. They had also been commissioned to complete sketch plans for several towns, and by the end of July 1960, the architects and planners had completed a reservation-wide, long-range planning program and begun work on a housing program and conservation planting program for the tribe.[43] The latter project was developed in collaboration with Lawrence Halprin, widely regarded as one of the most important American landscape architects of the 20th century.

Warnecke created three different schemes for a new Council Chamber in Window Rock. The first was octagonal while the second was circular in plan but with a two-tiered roof featuring a cross-shaped structure that separated the roof into eight sections.[44] The architects, probably in consultation with the Navajo Nation Council's Planning Committee, developed a third scheme into the model that was presented to the Tribal Council. According to the architects' proposal, this building was meant "to reflect the many sided form of the traditional Navajo hogan," with an eastern-facing main entrance and a hexadecagonal (16-sided) plan.[45] Centrally located above the building's main meeting space was a domed skylight separated into eight pie-shaped segments. The Chamber's roof radiated from the skylight in 16 scalloped sections – two extending from each of the skylight's segments. The roof was supported by 16 pillars and created a portico surrounding the chamber. The pillars were connected with bow-tie-shaped braces, and behind them, a patterned screen surrounded a cylindrical volume enclosing the building's interior spaces.

200 *The Stacked-Log Hogan Becomes an Architectural Type*

The Chamber, along with a new administration building, were to have been located in Window Rock immediately to the south of the old Council Chamber and the capitol complex designed by Mayers, Murray & Phillip during the 1930s. By choosing three different plans based on the number eight, Warnecke acknowledged the octagonal architecture of the old Council Chamber while offering a design that was clearly contemporary and similar to the New Formalist architecture of Edward Durell Stone, Philip Johnson, and Minoru Yamasaki.[46]

Meanwhile, the architects produced plans and drawings for a new community for between 2,500 and 3,000 residents at Tohdilto, later renamed Navajo, New Mexico, located 17 miles north of Window Rock. The town was to be the site of a new sawmill intended to complement and eventually replace the facility constructed in 1939 at Sawmill, Arizona, located nine miles to the west.[47] On March 31, 1960, the architects were authorized to proceed on a development plan for a town covering about 750 acres.[48]

Warnecke's plan for Navajo, New Mexico, created two residential neighborhoods on either side of an existing highway with a total of 487 housing units, including single-family homes, apartments, and teachers' housing. Streets curved around buildings and open spaces with special attention given to accommodating "the traditional Navajo extended family pattern," with "a number of clusters of adjoining homesites arranged around turn-arounds at the end of cul de sac streets, around semi-circular drives, and around short stub drives."

The town center was located on the northwest side of the plan, near to the sawmill (Figure 6.3). The building complex encompassed 26,500 square feet laid out as an octagon containing shops, a post office, library, restaurant, and a clinic arranged around an octagonal plaza, "paved in a traditional Navajo design." The entrance was on the east side, and an octagonal community building with a pyramidal roof was located across the plaza to the west. The complex's size and location by the main street leading to the mill clearly identified it as being "at the heart of things."[49]

Although the project had been authorized in March 1960, all work on the Navajo, New Mexico, project was halted on July 6 due to a boundary dispute.[50] Later that month, all of Warnecke's work on the reservation was paused due to a funding shortfall and was never resumed as the Council turned to other matters.[51] During the June 1961 meeting of the Navajo Nation Tribal Council, Robert Krause, the first head of the newly formed Navajo Nation Design and Construction Department, was introduced, and later during the same session, the Tribal Council decided to have Krause's department handle the Navajo, New Mexico, project.[52] Finally completed in 1969, it became the first planned town on the reservation.[53]

Peter MacDonald was elected the new chairman of the Navajo Nation in 1970. The following year, he began implementing plans to move the Navajo capital out of Window Rock and engaged Warnecke's firm to begin work on selecting a site. But MacDonald was unable to raise the money necessary to move forward, and Warnecke and his colleagues were forced to discontinue work on the project.[54] Meanwhile, Warnecke began developing a completely different project for the tribe. In June

The Stacked-Log Hogan Becomes an Architectural Type 201

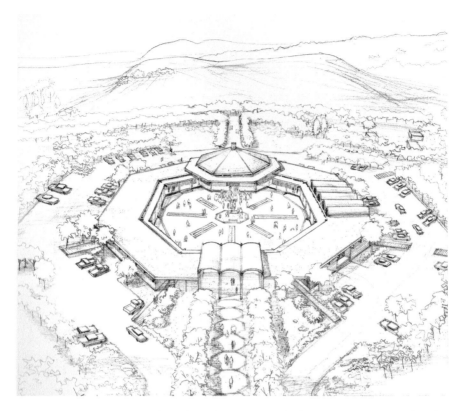

Figure 6.3 Navajo, New Mexico, view of town center, looking west. Architectural rendering dated November 11, 1960, by John Carl Warnecke and Associates.

1973, Martin Link, the director of the Navajo Nation Museum, announced plans to build a Navajo Heritage Center at Tse Bonito Park, located a mile south of the capitol complex in Window Rock (Figure 6.4).

Link conceptualized the design for the center as an interpretation of the Place of Emergence symbol found in Navajo sand paintings. Warnecke then developed a presentation booklet with a rendering and plans.[55] In those plans, the single-story building is arranged around an octagonal rotunda with a pool at its center, representing the "mystical lake" where the Diné ascended into this, the Glittering World. The rotunda opens on to four courtyards extending towards the cardinal directions, each paved with a pattern representing the four sacred plants in traditional Diné religion. The building itself was to have had four wings located between the courtyards containing the museum's galleries, a library and conference room, an auditorium, and administrative offices with a basement beneath three of the wings providing additional space. According to the booklet, "the east-facing entrance and octagonal plan recall the traditional Navajo hogan which still plays such a significant role in the religious life of the people."[56]

202 *The Stacked-Log Hogan Becomes an Architectural Type*

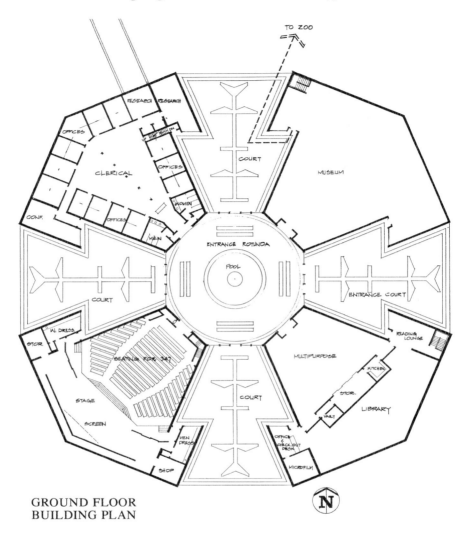

Figure 6.4 The Navajo Heritage Center, ground floor plan, c. 1973.

The Navajo Heritage Center project became associated with the country's bicentennial birthday celebration, and the federal government made funding available for the project.[57] A groundbreaking ceremony was held on October 1, 1974, during which three medicine men and a medicine woman blessed the site for the new building.[58] But the budget to construct it, originally projected to be $2 million, increased to more than $4 million three years later. Hopes had been high that a grant from the Economic Development Agency would help finance construction, but the tribe directed the monies they received elsewhere, bringing plans for the Navajo Heritage Center to an end during the summer of 1977.[59]

Education and Tribal Self-Determination: Rough Rock Demonstration School and Navajo Community College

The previous chapter of this book recounted the efforts of the Office of Indian Affairs to incorporate the hogan into educational facilities on the Navajo reservation during the 1930s. But even though most of the programs associated with the Indian New Deal had wound down by the beginning of World War II, the community-based ethos promoted by John Collier never entirely disappeared. Even during the war, when funding for schools and fuel for school buses were in short supply, many Diné contributed their time and money to building dormitories at day schools and doing what they could to ensure that their children could continue to receive an education.[60] During the 1950s and 1960s, interest grew in providing communities with a voice in how Navajo schools were being operated. For example, Lisbeth Eubank, who taught at Navajo Mountain, Utah, from 1942 until 1964, helped create a school board for the parents of her students.[61] But the person who became most associated with the rise of Navajo and, indeed, Native American self-determination in education was Robert Roessel. Roessel first began teaching on the Navajo reservation in 1951, and during the 1960s, he became a central force behind the founding of Rough Rock Demonstration School, "the first Indian-directed, locally controlled school" in the nation, and Navajo Community College, the country's first Native American community college (now known as Diné College).[62] At both campuses, Diné decision-makers worked with Euro-American architects to design a variety of octagonal buildings intended to represent the hogan.

The demonstration school program on the Navajo reservation was a collaborative effort between Roessel, the Bureau of Indian Affairs (BIA), the federal Office of Economic Opportunity (OEO), and Diné leaders, including Raymond Nakai, chairman of the Navajo Nation Tribal Council.[63] During the 1965–1966 school year, a demonstration school supervised by the BIA and OEO was set up at Lukachukai (*Lók'aa' Jígai*), Arizona, but failed in short order. A decision was quickly made to try again at another location, but this time, the BIA would turn over control of the school to a nonprofit organization, DINE (Demonstration in Navaho Education), Inc. The OEO made a grant "for intensive experimentation and demonstration" that more than doubled the budget that a typical BIA boarding school would receive. For its part, the federal government offered a newly completed but yet to be occupied school at Rough Rock (*Tsé Ch'ízhí*), Arizona, for the project. In September 1966, the demonstration school opened with Roessel as its director under the supervision of a Diné school board and a Diné board of directors.[64]

When the Rough Rock Demonstration School began, it accommodated grades one through six. But by 1969, the school had added grades seven and eight and was prepared to expand to include a high school.[65] In August 1970, faculty and students from MIT, including Chester Sprague, met with Diné from

204 *The Stacked-Log Hogan Becomes an Architectural Type*

Rough Rock to discuss how a plan for a new high school could be developed.[66] A small team spent several weeks interviewing the people of Rough Rock and helping them to produce a design that reflected traditional Navajo architecture and spatial patterns. The spatial qualities valued by the community included the following:

- No interior corridors, no limiting exterior walkways – looseness, openness
- Varied shapes and relationships between buildings and space
- Awareness of relationship of interior spaces to land, including easy access to the outdoors and the ability to see important places in the landscape
- Buildings in sympathetic relationship to the land through colors, textures, forms, dimensions, [and] scale, all of which are intended to harmonize with the surroundings[67]

Sprague and his team from MIT discovered that the community wanted to incorporate hogan architecture into the new school and that "those activities of the school similar to Navajo domestic life were thought to be particularly well housed in hogan-like forms." The site plan produced by the MIT architects for Rough Rock included several octagonal spaces, including a childcare center, a free-standing arts and crafts classroom, and an auditorium building. Two classroom buildings laid out on a rectangular plan also featured projecting bays in the shape of a half octagon. But the Rough Rock Diné felt that other spaces would be "inappropriate for certain functions," such as athletics and industrial arts, and the two buildings housing those activities were laid out without any reference to the hogan.[68] Unfortunately, the MIT plan had to be altered in a compromise with the BIA, and the hogan forms were not included in the new high school.[69] But the work that had been done to develop appropriate uses for new hogan architecture articulated a pattern that would continue for years to come.

By the end of the 1950s, the Tribal Council had begun to take steps to address the high dropout rate among Diné college students.[70] Then, with the creation of the OEO in 1964, it became possible to seriously consider building the first truly Native American institution of higher learning, one that would be solely under the control of the Diné. The BIA lent its support, and with funding from the OEO, the tribe, and a private foundation, Navajo Community College was founded in July 1968 and began offering classes in January 1969 at an existing BIA boarding school at Many Farms (*Dá'ák' eh Haláni*), Arizona.[71]

An all-Navajo board of regents worked with Roessel, who left Rough Rock to become the college's first president. After the first year, Roessel was appointed the college's chancellor, and Ned Hatathli succeeded him as president. In December 1971, Congress passed the Navajo Community College Act, enabling construction to begin for a new campus on a 1,200-acre site at Tsaile (*Tsééh yíli*), Arizona, 40 miles northeast of Window Rock.[72]

The architecture at Tsaile resulted from a collaboration between the Board of Regents, a Diné advisory group composed of Diné medicine men and tribal elders, and Chambers, Campbell, Isaacson and Chaplin, an architectural firm based in Albuquerque.[73] According to architect Douglas Campbell, the master plan mirrored the arrangement of a hogan's interior during a traditional healing ceremony. The campus is circular, and the students are housed in dormitories to the northwest, the direction where the patient in a ceremony sits. The dining hall – an analog for the hogan's hearth – is situated in the central part of campus. The classroom building was originally planned for the southwest side, the direction where the healer is usually located, but was ultimately constructed to the southeast.[74] The hogan's doorway on the east side is represented by the Navajo Culture Center, now known as the Ned Hatathli Center (Figure 6.5).

All of the hogan-inspired buildings discussed in this chapter have an entrance facing to the east, but the decision made at Tsaile to employ Diné religious thought as the basis for arranging all of the major elements in a site plan was unprecedented. The college's Board of Regents also requested that all of the buildings at the community college be shaped like a hogan.[75] But funding was limited, and in the 1972 master plan, only the cafeteria, the library, and the campus's ten dormitories were octagonal. Those buildings, which house domestic functions, including eating and sleeping, as well as introspective activities, such as studying, reiterated the pattern developed for the Rough Rock High School. Similarly, the architecture at Tsaile was intended to closely relate to the surrounding landscape; according to Campbell, the designers "used as many windows as possible."[76] In later years, octagonal forms were used to design faculty housing at Tsaile, and the college's student family housing is located in an octagonal park with an octagonal hogan at its center. An

Figure 6.5 The Ned Hatathli Culture Center, Tsaile, Arizona, looking south, photographed by Elisa Leonelli in 1985.

206   *The Stacked-Log Hogan Becomes an Architectural Type*

octagonally shaped parking lot surrounding the park emphasizes the relationship between the homes located there, which are rectilinear in plan, and the hogan.

The first phase of construction included a classroom building, a gymnasium (designed on a circular plan), the cafeteria, and the dormitories. These buildings opened at the beginning of October 1973.[77] The next phase was already under development at the time and included the Navajo Culture Center, a building that college officials described as "the hub of the campus."[78]

A booklet published by the college in July 1972 emphasized the important role the Navajo Culture Center would play in reservation life. The authors envisioned the building as a monument to Diné culture comparable to the White House and the memorial architecture located along the Mall in Washington, DC. It would provide a location for study and research; there would be a museum, and the Navajo Studies program would hold classes there. But the Center was also to be "a living shrine" that would unify the Diné and "embody, in a visible as well as a symbolic manner, the hopes and aspirations of the Navajo Nation."[79]

The text acknowledged that the Navajo Nation Council Chamber "perhaps comes closer than any other to beginning to fill a void among the Navajos." But the authors argued the need for a new building that originated from the Diné. The drawings in the booklet illustrate an octagonal building with five floors and a basement. An earthen berm concealed most of the first floor, while the upper stories were to be encased by a glass curtain wall. The basement included lecture and work areas, while the heart of the building was on the first floor, which included a central octagonal sanctuary surrounded by areas dedicated to six major Diné ceremonies: the Emergence Chant, the Lightning Chant, the Wind Chant, the Mountain Top Chant, the Blessing Chant, and the Night Chant. The founding metaphor for the Navajo Cultural Center was the hogan belonging to Changing Woman, one of the most important of the Navajo Holy People. The walls of the sanctuary would reproduce the walls of Changing Woman's hogan, which were constructed from white shell to the east, turquoise to the south, abalone to the west, and jet to the north.[80] A ramp ascended from the first floor to the top of the building, encircling an atrium and containing an exhibit displaying the history of the Diné. More exhibits about the Diné and other Native Americans were planned for the second floor. The third and fourth floors were laid out to accommodate classes in Navajo and Native American studies, while arts and crafts classrooms were to be located on the fifth floor.

The construction of the Navajo Cultural Center took longer than expected, and the effort to finance the Navajo Heritage Center in Window Rock during the same years may have been a complicating factor.[81] By the time the building was completed during the summer of 1976, its budget had risen to over $4 million. The final plan eliminated the atrium, which was filled in with floor space, while "an eternal flame" was located within the sanctuary below a chimney rising to the roof.[82] The mirrored curtain wall on the center's exterior reflected and merged with the building's environment, even though its structural materials – primarily steel, concrete, and glass – were anything but "natural."

At the same time, the center's abstract design was an interesting choice to represent an otherworldly building – Changing Woman's hogan. Carl Todacheene, president of the college's Board of Regents, explained:

> By blending the architectural form of the hogan with modern glass and concrete, we stress the fact that Navajo culture is a living and moving stream which embraces not only what we were in the past, but also our dynamic present and boundless future.[83]

Now known as the Ned Hatathli Center, the building is the tallest in the Navajo Nation and vies with the Navajo Nation Council Chamber and the Navajo Nation Museum – to be discussed shortly – as the reservation's most prominent work of public architecture.

The Navajo Hogan and Public Architecture During the 1970s and 1980s

Between the end of World War II and the early 1980s, the federal government and the tribe built many new public buildings across the Navajo Nation. A detailed survey of those projects has yet to be done, but 16 years of archival research and field work around the Four Corners region have led me to conclude that almost all of this architecture was indistinguishable from the architecture being constructed off the reservation. There were a few exceptions. We have already discussed the schools at Rough Rock and Tsaile. In 1973 and 1974, two hogan-shaped child day care centers were constructed in Fort Defiance and Chinle, Arizona, and the community at Cove, Arizona, completed a large brick and wood hogan for selling arts and crafts.[84] More significantly, between 1975 and 1980, the Diné at Pinehill, New Mexico, located about 40 miles southeast of Gallup, succeeded in building a school campus serving grades 1–12. The architectural firm of Hirshen, Gammill, Trumbo & Cook, based in Berkeley, California, drew up an imaginatively conceived design containing rectangular and octagonal buildings arranged in an octagonal pattern.[85]

But these projects were unusual, and nowhere was this more obvious than in Window Rock. In August 1981, Kee Yazzie Mann wrote a letter to the *Navajo Times* in which he criticized "the "monstrosities in the Navajo capital that reflect the poor taste of modern American construction."[86] Over the previous three decades, the town had expanded to include an International-style law enforcement building, and a motor inn and FedMart shopping center, each in a generic style that would have been appropriate anywhere in the country.[87] A new tribal administration building came in for Mann's particular ire. The 40,000-square-foot project then under construction and located about half a mile to the southwest of the Council Chamber was shortly to become the largest government building in Window Rock. Square in plan, its exterior was dominated by metal, brick, concrete, and glass with sloping berms planted with grass and trees located at

208 *The Stacked-Log Hogan Becomes an Architectural Type*

each corner. It was the first of four identical buildings planned for the capital.[88] Mann wrote:

> One would think that this building would be a masterpiece of construction incorporating traditional Navajo themes and design, but this is not the case. It is yet another concrete box, in the style found all over White America. Why isn't this building being constructed around Navajo designs? The building should stand with Navajo pride, but it doesn't.[89]

Mann was apparently not alone, and within the next few years, there was a shift towards adapting the hogan to public architecture in Window Rock. Between 1984 and 1986, two new octagonal office buildings were constructed: the headquarters for DNA Legal Services, Inc., and the Navajo Educational Center.[90] It is telling that the *Navajo Times*, the major newspaper serving the Navajo Nation, specifically referred to both of these projects as "hogan-shaped." The Educational Center was designed by Hemsley M. Lee, the first licensed Diné architect. It contains 35,000 square feet within two separate octagonal buildings connected by a rectangular foyer.[91] Lee studied architecture and construction at Arizona State University and, in 1972, passed his board exams in Arizona, after which he opened an architectural office in the Phoenix area.[92]

The Indian Self-Determination and Education Assistance Act was signed into law in 1975 and granted the tribes more control over how programs funded by the federal government were administered. According to Diné architect David Sloan, who was licensed to practice in New Mexico in 1984, it took a while for the tribe to take full advantage of the power that the Self-Determination Act conferred.[93] But by the mid-1980s, Navajo chapters were independently commissioning new chapter houses and being given the latitude to exercise "Indian preference" in hiring architects. For their second project, Sloan and his new office designed a multipurpose center with a large octagonal volume at Alamo, the tribe's most distant satellite reservation, located 70 miles southwest of Albuquerque. The contract was finalized in 1985, and construction was completed in 1987. According to Sloan, the Alamo chapter requested a hogan shape to symbolically connect the building with the Navajo Nation Council Chamber in Window Rock.[94]

Studio Southwest: The Navajo Nation Museum and New Schools for the Diné

In 1991, the tribe began planning a visitor center with a museum to be constructed on the site originally intended for the Navajo Heritage Center.[95] By mid-June 1992, tribal officials had chosen Design Collaborative Southwest (now known as Studio Southwest), based in Albuquerque, as the architects for the $6 million project.[96] The Navajo Nation Museum, Library, and Visitor's Center was completed in January 1995, although financial issues delayed the opening of the building until August 1997 (Figure 6.6).[97]

The Stacked-Log Hogan Becomes an Architectural Type   209

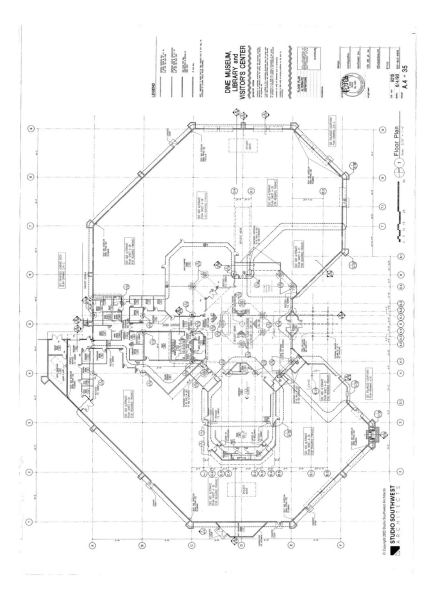

Figure 6.6 The Diné Museum, Library, and Visitor's Center, Window Rock, Arizona, floor plan dated June 4, 1993, by Studio Southwest Architects (west is up).

210   *The Stacked-Log Hogan Becomes an Architectural Type*

J. David Dekker, the lead designer for the project, worked alongside a team of architects, including Loren Miller (Diné) and David Riley (Hopi and Laguna).[98] Robert Roessel and his wife, Ruth (Diné), organized meetings with tribal elders, and the final design emerged from a collaborative process. According to Dekker and project manager Del Dixon, some of the Diné they consulted were clear that the Navajo Culture Center in Tsaile "was not their favorite building," and there was some "pushback" about whether the new museum should resemble it.

The design that eventually emerged was based on an abstracted octagon with a section of the east side cut away to create a sheltered plaza in front of the main entrance. The lobby is lit by a large octagonal oculus, symbolizing a hogan's smoke hole and surrounded by an octagonal pyramidal roof. On the interior, each facet of the pyramidal ceiling was clad with rows of logs evoking the appearance of a traditional corbelled dome. The octagonal theme is carried down to the floor, where an octagonal information desk occupies the center of the lobby.

The late 1990s signaled the beginning of "the replacement era" in BIA school construction. For about a decade or so, the BIA significantly increased its budget for building new schools in an effort to replace older facilities, many of which were in poor condition.[99] During this period, the upsurge in funding enabled architects to be particularly creative and Studio Southwest was one of several firms to design replacement schools for the Navajo reservation featuring a variety of octagonal spaces.

The main entrance to the elementary school at Indian Wells (*Tó Hadadleeh*), Arizona, completed in 2002 and designed by Dixon, opens into an octagonal lobby with a pyramidal ceiling covered in natural wood and containing a central skylight.

This space, meant to suggest the interior of a hogan with a corbelled ceiling and smoke hole, emphasizes to students and visitors alike that Indian Wells is a Diné school. The building's major circulation route follows the outline of the building's rectangular plan, and four more octagonal spaces are located at each corner where the corridor turns. On the exterior, the pyramidal roof over the lobby dominates the building's front elevation, and three of the lobby's eight walls jut forward to create a three-dimensional façade (Figure 6.7).

The 3/8 octagon visible on the exterior of the lobby evokes a hogan and has become a common motif in architecture across the reservation, both in public buildings and as an addition to homes that would otherwise lack Diné cultural associations. At Indian Wells, the motif appears twice on each of the two wings that flank the front entrance so that the façade includes five 3/8 octagons in total. The pattern is reinforced by a sunken octagonal seating area located directly in front of the building.

The two most common locations for octagonal spaces within the new replacement schools are at the main entrance and in the common room associated with dormitories at boarding facilities. The design by Studio Southwest for the community school at Dilcon (*Tó 'Áłch'įdí*), Arizona (2009), includes two entrances, each located in a 3/8 octagon on the east and west ends of the building. The library inside the west end is crowned by a hexagonal pyramidal roof tying the three wings that extend from the space together. In the dormitory at Dilcon, the students' common area features a 3/8

The Stacked-Log Hogan Becomes an Architectural Type 211

Figure 6.7 The elementary school at Indian Wells, Arizona, looking west, by Studio Southwest Architects.

octagon on the exterior and is topped by an octagonal pyramidal roof on an octagonal drum, but the facets of the octagon are of three different sizes in a ratio of 4:2:1, giving it an elongated appearance. These are but two of the more imaginative instances demonstrating how architects combined different permutations of the octagon to produce a variety of new school buildings in Navajoland during these years.

In the most dramatic examples of octagonal design, such as the Seba Dalkai Boarding School in Arizona, architects used the shape as a basis for the entire campus site plan. Completed in 2002, the school's design was inspired by the "Beauty Way," a central concept in Diné religion (Figure 6.8).

The east entrance and classrooms within the school's main building and the sleeping areas for younger children in the school's dormitory are all octagonal with ceilings of natural wood and pyramidal roofs containing an opening at the apex. The faculty housing units on the northeast side of the school also incorporate octagonal entry areas which are expressed on the exterior with a pyramidal roof and a 3/8 octagon.

According to Dekker, who was the lead designer for Seba Dalkai:

The hogan-inspired classrooms [on the south side, for grades one through six] are a cultural baseline meant to evoke the comfort of home with the opportunity of education. The art, science, computer, and seventh and eighth

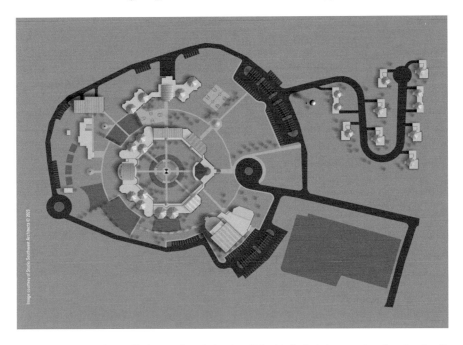

Figure 6.8 The Seba Dalkai Boarding School at Seba Dalkai, Arizona, site plan, by Studio Southwest Architects (north is up).

grade classrooms [on the north side] are more traditional school configurations in acknowledgement of the transition from Seba Dalkai to high school and ultimately contemporary life in the modern world.[100]

For the designers at Studio Southwest, the forward motion implied by these spaces expresses the idea of "Walking in Beauty" and carries students through the different stages of their education, while the school's octagonal plan transforms the entire campus into a hogan and keeps them firmly rooted in Diné traditional culture.

Leon Shirley: Public Housing for the Diné and a Senior Center for Twin Lakes

Leon Shirley became the second licensed Diné architect in 1973, a few months after Hemsley Lee was licensed to practice in Arizona. During the same year, Shirley also became the first Native American architect to be licensed in New Mexico. He graduated with his architecture degree from the University of New Mexico in 1968, briefly worked for the Navajo Nation Design and Construction Department, and then served his internship with architect Ralph Phillip in Farmington. After opening his own office in Albuquerque, Shirley began working with the Navajo Nation as an independent architect. All of his work has been for the tribe and

The Stacked-Log Hogan Becomes an Architectural Type   213

has chiefly consisted of public housing projects. Still in practice at the age of 81, Shirley estimates that he has completed about a thousand housing projects over the course of a 50-year career.[101]

Although there have been a few attempts to develop the hogan into public housing on the Navajo reservation, all of Shirley's projects contain houses based on a rectilinear plan. As discussed in the last chapter, in 1937, Navajo Superintendent E.R. Fryer and Commissioner of Indian Affairs John Collier had differing views about what types of housing should receive public financing from the government. Fryer argued that tribal members who had returned to the reservation after receiving a boarding school education preferred to live in houses, while Collier insisted on the importance of promoting hogan architecture among the Diné.

During the 1950s, the Navajo Nation constructed houses but not hogans for tribal employees in Window Rock, Crownpoint, and Shiprock.[102] Then around 1960, the tribal government commissioned John Carl Warnecke and Associates to produce a housing program for the reservation.[103] The architects worked up the design for an octagonal "Navahogan" as part of this program, although the plans for it apparently never progressed beyond the development phase.[104] Between 1958 and 1962, when Warnecke was working for the Navajo Nation, the tribe purchased 250 pre-fabricated houses for Navajo welfare recipients and then built 40 pre-fabs at Navajo, New Mexico, using timber from the tribal sawmill.[105] An article in the *Navajo Times* published on January 3, 1962, explained:

> The Navajo people are in a state of transition as to housing. A half century ago most Navajos were content to dwell in the traditional hogan but today the younger generations at least favor frame dwellings and as a result of continuing education and outside contacts desire more comforts, space and conveniences than ever before.[106]

That year, the tribe established the Navajo Housing Authority (NHA), and construction began on the first residential subdivisions on the reservation comprising 258 houses in Window Rock and Fort Defiance.[107]

In 1981, Kee Yazzie Mann would have cause to complain, "the houses built by the Navajo Housing Authority look like cracker boxes found everywhere in Middle America."[108] And today, little has changed. David Sloan, who is now the chair of the NHA's board of commissioners, told me that proposals to incorporate hogans into public housing projects on the reservation have been suggested but that there are none presently planned.[109] The expense associated with building and maintaining octagonal buildings is a major factor. According to Diné architect Dyron Murphy:

> The cost of framing a home in an octagonal shape is generally higher than framing a conventionally designed rectangular home with pre-engineered trusses. And housing entities do not enjoy having to maintain home roofs on hogan-shaped houses because of the unique geometries that may cause leaking at each change in plane.[110]

214 *The Stacked-Log Hogan Becomes an Architectural Type*

These problems have prevented the NHA from building hogans for low-income families living in the Navajo Nation, but there have been efforts to make hogans easier to purchase. Several entrepreneurs have established companies making prefabricated hogans. Perhaps the earliest dates from 1968, when Allan L. Lemley contracted with the tribal sawmill to produce octagonal hogans.[111]

Although Leon Shirley has concentrated on designing public housing for most of his career, he has also produced plans for other projects, including shopping centers, chapter houses, and the senior center at Twin Lakes (*Tsé Nahazoh*), New Mexico, completed in 2002 (Figure 6.9).

During the building's design phase, Shirley interviewed members of the Twin Lakes Chapter, some of whom had moved back to the reservation after their retirement. According to Shirley, several people told him, "We want a hogan – we lived in a box all our lives – we want to go back to the way it was."[112] He complied with their request and produced a design for a large octagonal stacked-log hogan measuring 28′ on each side. The exterior walls of the building are clad with logs, and it features a pyramidal roof with an oculus. A large recreation area is located at the center of the interior below a ceiling constructed from timbers arranged in a corbelled pattern.[113] A kitchen, dining room, arts and crafts spaces, and other rooms are located around the perimeter of the recreation area. The building is the only

Figure 6.9 The Senior Center at Twin Lakes, New Mexico, looking west, designed by Leon Shirley.

The Stacked-Log Hogan Becomes an Architectural Type   215

example in this chapter that does not use the octagon as a type. In this instance, the program for the building was to reproduce a hogan large enough for senior citizens living in the Twin Lakes Chapter to meet together, and so Shirley used the stacked-log hogan as a model, which is to say, as "a thing to copy or imitate completely."[114]

Dyron Murphy: A Diversity of Hogan-Inspired Designs

Dyron Murphy graduated from the University of Arizona School of Architecture in 1988 and opened an architectural office in Albuquerque in 2001. He has since become the most successful Diné architect working today. His firm, Dyron Murphy Architects (DMA), has completed a wide variety of projects, including schools, such as the Baca/Dlo'ay Azhi Community School (2003), New Mexico's first LEED-certified building and the first LEED-certified building constructed by the US Department of the Interior. The firm's designs for dormitories at the Ch'ooshgai Community School (2009) in Tohatchi, New Mexico, and the Rough Rock Demonstration School (2011) have influenced other dormitories across the reservation. The buildings at Tohatchi and Rough Rock are based on a cross-shaped plan with four wings containing sleeping rooms tied together by an octagonal common area. Murphy, who finds that octagonal spaces are particularly appropriate for homelike settings, also organized the Chinle Warrior's Home around a central octagon – "the 'heart' of the building" – with a fireplace for gatherings and holding traditional ceremonies.[115] When completed, the building will become the first retirement home specifically planned for veterans on a Native American reservation.

The veterans' center in Thoreau (Dlǫ́'í Yázhí), designed by DMA, includes octagonal architecture as a defining feature. The sense of "home" conveyed by this building, located on the east side of the Navajo Nation in New Mexico, is multilayered. Murphy intended "to foster a sense of belonging and offer solace" to veterans who have left the reservation to be indoctrinated into mainstream American military culture. Many of these former soldiers will have traveled abroad, been wounded, and lost comrades. The building is thus meant to possess a healing quality, as expressed in its main octagonal meeting room. The light-filled space with its wood-paneled ceiling, large central oculus, and color scheme emphasizing the four cardinal directions helps to create "the nurturing haven" that Murphy and his colleagues envisioned.[116]

Several Navajo chapters have commissioned DMA to design chapter houses and multi-purpose centers. During the development phase of an architectural design, Murphy and his team collaborate with chapter members to determine the building's program and appearance. He has found there is a correlation between a chapter's location and the interest its members express in constructing a project with specific cultural references. Chapters in more isolated areas of the reservation where there are fewer jobs tend to be more "elder-oriented" and likely to prefer hogan-inspired architecture. A recent project at Tonalea (Tó Nehełííh, formerly known as Red Lake), Arizona, completed in 2022, serves as a case in point (Figure 6.10).

DMA's design contains 7,725 square feet and includes an octagonal entrance area facing east. The ceiling of the entrance area is covered with wood in a pattern

216 *The Stacked-Log Hogan Becomes an Architectural Type*

Figure 6.10 The Chapter House at Tonalea, Arizona, looking southeast, designed by Dyron Murphy Architects.

evoking a corbelled dome, while a central oculus provides illumination. The chapter assembly room is located immediately to the west of the entry area, while the rest of the building includes offices and service areas, as well as spaces for local businesses to rent. On the exterior, the building's main façade takes the shape of a 3/8 octagon with an octagonal clerestory rising above it.

From Murphy's perspective, hogan-inspired designs are especially appropriate for buildings related to Diné culture, one example being DMA's project for the new Navajo Arts and Crafts Enterprise (NACE) headquarters.[117] The origins of the NACE date back to 1936, when Commissioner of Indian Affairs John Collier established the Indian Arts and Crafts Board (IACB). As historian Donald Parman has observed, "The encouragement of Indian handicrafts had always been a central aim of Collier's administration; indeed, perhaps no single subject fulfilled his aspirations quite so directly." The new federally funded program sought to revitalize traditional tribal arts and crafts and support Native American artisans by expanding the market for their products. In 1940, the IACB sent anthropologist John Adair to research how conditions could be improved for the manufacture of high-quality items on the Navajo reservation. Adair's report inspired the creation of the Navajo Arts and Crafts Guild in 1941. Initially based in a warehouse in Gallup, the program was given a budget to provide silver, turquoise, and wool for accomplished silversmiths and weavers across the reservation. The Guild then purchased the jewelry and rugs that the artisans created at a substantial profit.[118]

In 1941, the Navajo Arts and Crafts Guild moved into a new headquarters in Window Rock. The log building, dating from 1932, had been relocated from Crystal (*Tó Niłts'ílí*), New Mexico, where it was part of a Civilian Conservation Corp-Indian Division camp.[119] By late 1960, plans were underway to replace the building, and Ken Martinez, a Diné tribal employee, created a design for a flat-roofed, windowless rectangular building constructed from cinder blocks and containing about 7,700 square feet. The austerity of the design was alleviated by a series of eight buttresses along the front façade separating panels decorated with projecting blocks arranged in Navajo rug designs.[120]

The Guild was renamed the Navajo Arts and Crafts Enterprise in 1972, and as this book goes to press, the NACE is still housed in the building dedicated in 1961. But in 2023, the tribe approved plans by DMA for a new 33,000-square-foot facility in Window Rock that will quadruple the space of the present building (Figure 6.11).[121]

The first floor is to include a store area containing over 7,000 square feet, a 2,425-square-foot conference room, a small auditorium with seating for 50, a café, stock room, and spaces for artisans to work. Most of the administrative offices will occupy the second floor. The main entrance to the building opens to the east from a large octagonal volume accentuated with stone buttresses and topped with a pyramidal roof. Half of the octagon extends forward into a plaza decorated with a Navajo wedding basket design. The store area inside will be visible through a bank of windows, while on the second floor, the NACE's executive offices will have access to a balcony overlooking the plaza in front of the building.

But in at least one of DMA's projects for the reservation, the tribe deemed hogan architecture to be inappropriate. The Navajo Tribal Utility Authority (NTUA) insisted that DMA's design for its new headquarters (2018) in Fort Defiance be "a modern building" without the hogan symbolism that an octagonal plan would have provided. According to Murphy, the management at NTUA was wary of offending tribal elders.[122] The new multi-story office building, which encompasses 80,000 square feet, alludes to Diné culture in other ways, primarily through its color scheme, use of

Figure 6.11 The Navajo Arts and Crafts Enterprise building, architectural model, by Dyron Murphy Architects.

218 The Stacked-Log Hogan Becomes an Architectural Type

natural materials, and a large abstract design located by the front entrance composed of stacked chevrons referencing the traditional Diné motif for corn.

Creating a Diné Sacred Place: The Senator John Pinto Library in Shiprock, 2009–2011

Over the last century or so, architects and designers have used the octagon and the corbelled dome as types for museums, schools, chapter houses, senior centers, arts and crafts workshops, a nursing home, veteran's centers, and government buildings at the capital in Window Rock. These buildings have drawn upon the hogan's role as the preeminent form of Diné architecture and as the tribe's traditional home. But the hogan is also the place where Diné ceremonies are held, and the building's sacred aspect has inspired its use for Christian architecture on the reservation. Hogan churches offer a familiar and even welcoming appearance that seems to support the tribe's culture, although the religious rituals that occur inside of them must, of necessity, redefine Diné ceremonialism and intentionally or not subvert it.

But recently, the tribe has constructed a new building that takes an innovative approach to acknowledging the hogan's centrality in traditional Navajo religion. During the 1990s, Diné College began the planning process for a new campus at Shiprock. In 2009, the Phoenix office of DLR Group produced a plan for a library on the campus, now known as the Senator John Pinto Library (Figure 6.12a). The lead designer, Karl Derrah, and the project team, which included Diné architect Richard K. Begay, carried out a lengthy consultation process.[123] The library, completed in 2011, has received extensive attention from the press and is now the most famous contemporary building on the Navajo reservation.

The library's single-story design encloses about 20,000 square feet. The southeast façade, which contains the main entrance, is dominated by two windowless frustrums (truncated cones) (Figure 6.12b). The north frustrum narrows towards the top, while the south frustrum is upended in the same manner as Frank Lloyd Wright's Solomon R. Guggenheim Museum in New York City. The west side of the building has a rectilinear plan, but the addition of an enormous butterfly roof with a fold down the middle has been used to transform it into something with a great deal more drama.

The curving forms along the southeast façade, and the butterfly roof would individually have distinguished the library as one of the most visually arresting buildings in the Four Corners region. But the architects incorporated yet another extraordinary feature: A translucent octagonal volume sheathed in blue that rises from the floor of the library through the roof to create a shimmering tower (Figure 6.12c). The tower evokes the architecture of the Ned Hatathli Center and provides a visual connection to Diné College's main campus in Tsaile.

The tower encloses the library's Storytelling Room, which Derrah describes as a place "where the Elders can go and teach and talk."[124] The symbolism of the blue color relates to the sky and water but also to smoke, and inside the octagon, cushions surround a sandpit symbolizing a hearth. Colored panels on

The Stacked-Log Hogan Becomes an Architectural Type   219

a.

b.

c.

Figure 6.12 The Senator John Pinto Library, Shiprock, New Mexico, designed by the DLR Group: a. View of southwest façade; b. View of southeast façade; c. Detail of tower.

220   *The Stacked-Log Hogan Becomes an Architectural Type*

the walls in white, turquoise, yellow, and black indicate the four cardinal directions. Steel columns arranged around the octagon symbolize the reed grass stems that oral histories relate the Diné climbed when they emerged into this, the present world. The tower's roof is translucent, reinforcing the connection between earth and sky.[125]

A circular dropped ceiling separates the blue walls of the octagon from the rest of the library's interior. Lights and fiber optics in the dropped ceiling illustrate the Diné night sky and depict *Náhookos Bi'aadii* (Cassiopeia) and *Náhookos Bika'ii* (the Big Dipper), signifying the mother and the father who safeguard the hogan. They rotate around *Náhookos Biko'* (the North Star) which represents the fire at the center of a hogan according to Navajo astronomy. A vertical slit in the eastern wall of the library further accentuates the building's relationship with celestial phenomena. The slit is oriented so that light shines directly into the octagon as the sun rises between late August and late May – the beginning and the end of the school year.[126]

Richard K. Begay describes the Storytelling Room as a "sacred Center Place." It is highly unusual to find a religious space at the heart of an academic library. But the purpose of this architecture is to "inspire students to share their excitement for knowledge and education in a modern, hi-tech environment while still honoring the traditional Navajo ways."[127] The hogan schools designed by Mayers, Murray & Phillip 75 years earlier during the Indian New Deal were based on a similar idea. But the octagon has now become a type and achieved a symbolic power capable of conveying the essence of the Diné hogan in the absence of any other architectural elements.

Notes

1 Quatremère de Quincy, "Type," *Oppositions* 8 (1977): 148. Originally published in *Encyclopédie Méthodique*, Architecture, vol. III, pt. 2 (Paris, 1825).
2 Quatremère de Quincy, "Type," 148.
3 Anthony Vidler, *The Writing of the Walls: Architectural Theory in the Late Enlightenment* (Princeton: Princeton Architectural Press, 1987), 149–154.
4 Rafael Moneo, "On Typology," *Oppositions* 13 (Summer 1978): 28–35.
5 Giulio Carlo Argan, "On the Typology of Architecture," *Architectural Design* 33, no. 12 (December 1963): 564–565.
6 Moneo, "On Typology," 23, 28.
7 Moneo, "On Typology," 27.
8 Moneo, "On Typology," 41, 44.
9 Leatrice Armstrong, *Mary Wheelwright: Her Book* (Santa Fe, NM: Wheelwright Museum of the American Indian, 2016), 8.
10 Armstrong, *Mary Wheelwright*, 225.
11 A.V. Kidder to Mary C. Wheelwright, December 6, 1927, 89LA3.043.1a, LA.
12 Mary C. Wheelwright, "Journey Towards Understanding" (unpublished, undated manuscript), typescript, 48, CSWR.
13 "Competition for the Selection of an Architect for the Museum and Laboratory of Anthropology at Santa Fe, New Mexico," signed September 23, 1929, 89LA3.011a, LA.
14 "Notes to be saved on hogan structure as designed by W.P. Henderson," n.d., 89LA3.011b, LA.
15 These are the measurements for the skylight in the building that was eventually constructed in 1937 and, according to Wheelwright's memoirs, followed Henderson's

The Stacked-Log Hogan Becomes an Architectural Type   221

1929 design. See Amy Stone Ford, "Wheelwright Museum of the Indian," November 1990 [National Register of Historic Places listing #90001917], Section 7, page 6.

16 "Competition for the Selection," 4–5.

17 Henderson's papers are located in the Archives of American Art in Washington, DC.

18 Wheelwright, "Journey Towards Understanding," 49–50.

19 Wheelwright, "Journey Towards Understanding," 49.

20 Jesse Nusbaum to John D. Rockefeller, Jr., December 14, 1929, Box 95, OMR, Series H, RAC.

21 Mary Wheelwright to Jesse Nusbaum, October 11, 1930, 89LA.043.1b, LA; Jesse Nusbaum to A.V. Kidder, October 18 (possibly 28), 1930, 89LA.043.1b, LA.

22 Sylvanus G. Morley to Alfred V. Kidder, October 24, 1930, 89LA.043.1b, LA.

23 Jesse Nusbaum to A.V. Kidder, October 18 (or 28), 1930, 89LA.043.1b, LA.

24 Jesse Nusbaum to A.V. Kidder, May 12, 1931; Sylvanus Morley to Jesse Nusbaum, October 14, 1931, both 89LA3.043.1c, LA.

25 "Copy" [minutes by Kenneth Chapman of an informal meeting of the Building Committee on October 15, 1931], 89LA3.043.1c, LA.

26 Wheelwright mentioned Hastiin Klah's involvement with the design of the Navajo Hogan in her unpublished memoirs, "Journey Towards Understanding," and on page 49, wrote, "In fact, the design over the front door and at the east end of the exhibition hall on the level with the ground, were very definitely his idea."

27 Sylvanus Morley to Francis Ingersoll Proctor, November 12, 1931, 89LA3.043.1c, LA.

28 A.V. Kidder to Mary C. Wheelwright, May 24, 1932, 89LA3.043.1d, LA.

29 Mary C. Wheelwright to Dr. Kidder, June 7, 1932, 89LA3.043.1d, LA.

30 Armstrong, *Mary Wheelwright*, 231.

31 Award certificate, Box 4, WPH.

32 "The House of Navajo Religion, Incorporated, 1937, Santa Fe, New Mexico" [brochure], Box 18, OMR, Series E, RAC.

33 Berard Haile, "Why the Navaho Hogan?" *Primitive Man* 15, nos. 3–4 (July–October 1942): 39–56.

34 Robert W. Young, *A Political History of the Navajo Tribe* (Tsaile, AZ: Navajo Community College Press, 1978), 58–62.

35 John Collier and Mary Heaton Vorse, "The First Tribal Capital," *Indians at Work* 1, no. 24 (August 1, 1934): 5–6.

36 Gladys Reichard, *Navaho Religion: A Study of Symbolism* (New York: Bollingen Foundation, 1950), 194.

37 Collier and Vorse, "The First Tribal Capital."

38 Sarah Burt, "Navajo Nation Council Chamber National Historic Landmark Study," October 24, 2002, 7.

39 See Leibowitz, "The Million-Dollar Play House: The Office of Indian Affairs and the Pueblo Revival in the Navajo Capital," *Buildings and Landscapes* 15 (Fall 2008): 11–42.

40 The Council Chamber is 70 feet in diameter and 30 feet high, Burt, "Navajo Nation Council Chamber National Historic Landmark Study," 4.

41 Mimeographed copies of Cram's drawings for the competition may be found in his papers at the Boston Public Library (the collection has yet to be processed as of this writing).

42 "BD & C's Giant Firms," *Building Design & Construction* (July 1977): 41; John Carl Warnecke, FAIA, Architects, "Biography of John Carl Warnecke, FAIA," c. 1970, WAA; William Grimes, "John Carl Warnecke, Architect to Kennedy, Dies at 91," *New York Times*, April 22, 2010.

43 Lester Gorsline, "Navajo Projects," July 12, 1950; Lawrence Livingston, Jr. to G. Warren Spaulding, July 29, 1960; "Job Memorandum No. 24," January 27, 1960, WAA.

44 Plans for these two schemes, dated April 5, 1959, are located at WAA.

45 John Carl Warnecke and Associates, "Navajo Tribe Council Chamber, Administration Building and Window Rock Lodge," July 30, 1959, WAA.

222 *The Stacked-Log Hogan Becomes an Architectural Type*

46 For more on New Formalism, see Marcus Whiffen, *American Architecture since 1780: A Guide to the Styles* (Cambridge, MA: MIT Press, 1969), 261–266.
47 Navajo Forest Products Industries, "Navajo Pine Progress," [booklet], c. 1970; Lester Gorsline, "Prospective Client Contacts, September 17, 1959," WAA.
48 Lawrence Livingston, Jr. to G. Warren Spaulding, July 29, 1960; Livingston and Blaney/John Carl Warnecke and Associates, "Navajo, New Mexico Development Plan," November 11, 1960, WAA.
49 "Navajo, New Mexico Development Plan."
50 Lester Gorsline, "Navajo Projects." Interestingly, John Collier, former commissioner of Indian Affairs, was cc'd on this memorandum.
51 Lawrence Livingston, Jr., to Lawrence B. Moore, June 8, 1960; Gorsline, WAA.
52 NNTC, June 5 through June 30, 1961, 491, 993.
53 Navajo Forest Products Industries, "Clean Up Drive Nets Cans by the Hundreds," *Navajo Times*, September 3, 1970.
54 Peter MacDonald to Joseph M. Montoya, December 15, 1972; John S. Lynd to Peter MacDonald, January 19, 1973, WAA.
55 "Tribe Will Seek Funds for Museum," *Gallup Independent*, June 28, 1973.
56 John Carl Warnecke and Associates, "The Navajo Heritage Center," c. 1974.
57 "Navajo '76 Plans Total $20 Million," *Albuquerque Tribune*, July 10, 1974
58 "Navajo Rites Held at Site of New Center," *Arizona Republic*, October 2, 1974.
59 "Heritage Center is Cut," *Gallup Independent*, July 5, 1977.
60 See George A. Boyce, "War-Time Education on the Navajo Reservation," *Indians at Work* 12, no. 4 (November–December 1944): 23–26.
61 Randy Eubank, interview with author, May 19, 2009.
62 Szasz, *Education and the American Indian*, 155; T. Gregory Barrett and Lourene Thaxton, "Robert A. Roessel, Jr. and Navajo Community College: Cross-Cultural Roles of Key Individuals in its Creation, 1951–1989," *American Indian Culture and Research Journal* 31, no. 4 (2007): 28.
63 John Collier, Jr., "Survival at Rough Rock: A Historical Overview of Rough Rock Demonstration School," *Anthropology and Education Quarterly* 19, no. 3 (September 1988): 257. The Office of Indian Affairs became the Bureau of Indian Affairs in 1947.
64 Broderick H. Johnson, *Navaho Education at Rough Rock* (Rough Rock, AZ: Rough Rock Demonstration School, 1968), 15–26.
65 Teresa L. McCarty, *A Place to be Navajo: Rough Rock and the Struggle for Self-Determination in Indigenous Schooling* (Mahway, NJ: Lawrence Erlbaum and Associates, 2002), 123.
66 Chester L. Sprague, "American Indian Communities: Toward a Unity of Life and Environment," *Technology Review* 74, no. 8 (July–August 1972): 22.
67 Sprague, "American Indian Communities," 25.
68 Sprague, "American Indian Communities," 24–25.
69 Carol Herselle Krinsky, *Contemporary Native American Architecture: Cultural Regeneration and Creativity* (New York: Oxford University Press, 1996), 180–181.
70 Barrett and Thaxton, "Robert A. Roessel, Jr. and Navajo Community College," 30.
71 Szasz, *Education and the American Indian*, 176–177. Navajo Community College was renamed Diné College in 1997.
72 Szasz, *Education and the American Indian*, 179.
73 *Purpose and Plans – The Navajo Culture Center, A Shrine and Living Symbol for the Navajo Nation* (Navajo Community College Press, July 1972), 41.
74 Bob Brown, "Navajo Dream Is Now Taking Shape: College at Tsaile Ariz.," *Albuquerque Journal*, October 15, 1972.
75 "Reservation College Was Long a Dream of Navajos," *Gallup Independent*, June 12, 1974.
76 Brown, "Navajo Dream."

The Stacked-Log Hogan Becomes an Architectural Type   223

77 Lloyd Lynn House, "The Historical Development of Navajo Community College" (PhD diss., Arizona State University, 1974), 104.
78 *Purpose and Plans – The Navajo Culture Center*, 41.
79 *Purpose and Plans – The Navajo Culture Center*, 41–42.
80 *Purpose and Plans – The Navajo Culture Center*, 40.
81 In "Tribe Will Seek Funds for Museum," published in the *Gallup Independent* on June 28, 1973, the director of the Navajo Nation Museum was at pains to differentiate between the two projects and was paraphrased, "the cultural center will stick mostly to religious aspects of Navajo life while the heritage center will encompass all areas dealing with the Navajos – historic, cultural, as well as religious."
82 "NCC Cultural Center is Complete," *Gallup Independent*, October 26, 1976.
83 "NCC Cultural Center Nears Completion," *Navajo Times*, November 6, 1975.
84 "New ONEO Day Care Center in Fort Defiance," *NavajoTimes*, October 25, 1973; "Chinle Dedicates New Day Care Center," *Navajo Times*, November 7, 1974 "Cove Holds Annual Craft Sale," *Navajo Times*, July 4, 1974.
85 Krinsky, *Contemporary Native American Architecture*, 181–183.
86 Kee Yazzie Mann, letter to the editor, *Navajo Times*, August 6, 1981.
87 It should be acknowledged that the Window Rock fairgrounds included a 19,000-square-foot circular exhibition hall completed in 1958 that was sometimes referred to as "the Largest Hogan in the World." See "Hall Completed," *Gallup Independent,* September 10, 1958; Petley Studios postcard, P29486, printed by Colourpicture Publishers, Inc., Boston, MA, n.d.
88 The project was designed by the Albuquerque firm of Hutchinson, Brown & Partners. See "Tribal Adminstration Complex on the Way, *Navajo Times*, July 26, 1979; "First Building of Complex Open," *Navajo Times*, April 28, 1982.
89 Mann, letter to the editor.
90 LeNora Begay, "DNA Staff Ready for New Home," *Navajo Times*, December 12, 1984; "Education Center on Schedule; But Foundation Needs More Money," *Navajo Times*, August 30, 1984.
91 "Education Center on Schedule"; Rachel Duwyenie, "Education Center: Dream Coming True," *Navajo Times*, November 14, 1984. The model pictured in Duwyenie's article shows a version of the project that included a third and significantly larger hogan-shaped building located to the rear of the two hogan-shaped buildings that were ultimately constructed.
92 "First Navajo Architect Licensed," *Navajo Times*, October 5, 1972.
93 David Sloan, e-mail to the author, June 29, 2023.
94 David Sloan, e-mail to the author, August 7, 2023.
95 Russell P. Hartman, letter to the editor, *Navajo Times*, December 24, 1991.
96 "Not Just a 'Dream' Anymore," *Navajo Times*, June 18, 1992.
97 "Navajo Museum, Library & Visitor's Center," Studio Southwest Architects, n.d.; Marley Shebala, "Navajo History is Made and Preserved," *Navajo Times*, August 14, 1997.
98 J. David Dekker and Del Dixon, conversation with the author, June 8, 2023.
99 "The First BIA Replacement Schools are Maturing to Adolescence; How Have They Been Performing," *Office of Facilities, Environmental, and Cultural Resources Management Summary* [Bureau of Indian Affairs], January 2008.
100 J. David Dekker, e-mail to the author, June 30, 2023.
101 Leon Shirley, conversation with the author, June 27, 2023.
102 "Housing Plans on the Navajo Reservation," *Navajo Times*, January 3, 1962.
103 Lester Gorsline, "Job Memorandum No. 24," January 27, 1960, WAA.
104 See Eugene Wedell to Les Gorsline, January 8, 1960, and Eugene A. Wedell to Charles Wheeler, April 20, 1960, WAA.
105 "Pre-fab Units Solve Rental Housing Snag," *Navajo Times*, September 5, 1962.
106 "Housing Plans on the Navajo Reservation."

224   *The Stacked-Log Hogan Becomes an Architectural Type*

107 "Modern Housing on Reservation Proved Popular and Necessary," *Navajo Times*, September 5, 1962.
108 Mann, letter to the editor.
109 David Sloan, conversation with the author, June 29, 2023.
110 Dyron Murphy, e-mail to the author, October 27, 2023.
111 Becky Minter, "Navajo Hogan Enterprise Halted by Loan Rates," *Arizona Republic*, October 14, 1968.
112 Leon Shirley, conversation with the author, June 27, 2023.
113 The original plans called for the entire ceiling to be corbelled, but the expense involved exceeded the budget so that the corbelling covers only part of the ceiling.
114 Quatremère de Quincy, "Type."
115 "Chinle Warriors Home," accessed October 29, 2023, at https://dyronmurphy.com/portfolio-items/chinle-warriors-home/
116 "Thoreau Veteran's Center," accessed October 29, 2023, at https://dyronmurphy.com/portfolio-items/thoreau-veterans-center/
117 Dyron Murphy, conversation with the author, May 17, 2023.
118 Parman, *The Navajos and the New Deal*, 268–270.
119 "Tribe Will Seek Funds for New Museum," *Gallup Independent*, June 28, 1973.
120 "New Home for Arts and Crafts Being Built," *Navajo Times*, January 1961.
121 "Navajo Arts and Crafts Guild Dedicates New Building May 6," *Arizona Daily Sun*, April 26, 1961; "New NACE Location," *Navajo Times*, April 14, 2016.
122 Dyron Murphy, conversation with the author, May 17, 2023.
123 Richard K. Begay, "Seeking Cultural Relevancy in Diné Communities: Finding a Center Place in Modern Diné Buildings," in *Our Voices II: The De-colonial Project*, eds. Rebecca Kiddle, Luugigyoo Patrick Stewart, and Keven O'Brien (Novato, CA: ORO Editions, 2021), 91.
124 Quoted in Joyce Malnar and Frank Vodvarka, *New Architecture on Indigenous Lands* (Minneapolis: University of Minnesota Press, 2013), 140.
125 Begay, "Seeking Cultural Relevancy in Diné Communities," 92, 95.
126 Begay, "Seeking Cultural Relevancy in Diné Communities," 92, 95.
127 Begay, "Seeking Cultural Relevancy in Diné Communities," 95; "New Diné College Library Design Connects Community and Culture," *Navajo Times*, August 20, 2009.

Reference List

Archival Sources

Center for Southwest Research, University of New Mexico, Albuquerque. Cited as CSWR.
Laboratory of Anthropology Archives, Museum of New Mexico, Santa Fe, New Mexico. Cited as LA.
Office of the Messrs. Rockefeller records, FA314, Cultural Interests, Series E, Rockefeller Archive Center, Tarrytown, New York. Cited as OMR, Series E, RAC.
Office of the Messrs. Rockefeller records, III-2-H, Friends and Services, Series H, Rockefeller Archive Center, Tarrytown, New York. Cited as OMR, Series H, RAC.
Warnecke Architectural Archive, Sonoma County, California. Cited as WAA.
William Penhallow Henderson Papers, Archives of American Art, Smithsonian Institution, Washington, DC. Cited as WPH.

Published Sources

Argan, Giulio Carlo. "On the Typology of Architecture." Translated by Joseph Rykwert. *Architectural Design* 33, no. 12 (December 1963): 564–565.
Armstrong, Leatrice. *Mary Wheelwright: Her Book*. Santa Fe, NM: Wheelwright Museum of the American Indian, 2016.

The Stacked-Log Hogan Becomes an Architectural Type 225

Barrett, T. Gregory, and Lourene Thaxton. "Robert A. Roessel, Jr. and Navajo Community College: Cross-Cultural Roles of Key Individuals in Its Creation, 1951–1989." *American Indian Culture and Research Journal* 31, no. 4 (2007): 25–50.

"BD & C's Giant Firms." *Building Design & Construction* (July 1977): 31–42.

Begay, Richard K. "Seeking Cultural Relevancy in Diné Communities: Finding a Center Place in Modern Diné Buildings." In *Our Voices II: The De-colonial Project*, edited by Rebecca Kiddle, Luugigyoo Patrick Stewart, and Keven O'Brien, 80–95. Novato, CA: ORO Editions, 2021.

Burt, Sarah. "Navajo Nation Council Chamber National Historic Landmark Study." October 24, 2002.

Collier, John Jr. "Survival at Rough Rock: A Historical Overview of Rough Rock Demonstration School." *Anthropology and Education Quarterly* 19, no. 3 (September 1988): 253–269.

Collier, John, and Mary Heaton Vorse. "The First Tribal Capital." *Indians at Work* 1, no. 24 (August 1, 1934): 5–6.

"The First BIA Replacement Schools are Maturing to Adolescence; How Have They Been Performing," *Office of Facilities, Environmental, and Cultural Resources Management Summary.* Washington, DC: Bureau of Indian Affairs, January 2008.

Ford, Amy Stone. "Wheelwright Museum of the Indian." November 1990. National Register of Historic Places listing #90001917.

Haile, Berard. "Why the Navaho Hogan?" *Primitive Man* 15, nos. 3–4 (July–October 1942): 39–56.

House, Lloyd Lynn. "The Historical Development of Navajo Community College." PhD diss., Arizona State University, 1974.

Johnson, Broderick H. *Navaho Education at Rough Rock*. Rough Rock, AZ: Rough Rock Demonstration School, 1968.

Krinsky, Carol Herselle. *Contemporary Native American Architecture: Cultural Regeneration and Creativity*. New York: Oxford University Press, 1996.

Malnar, Joyce Monice, and Frank Vodvarka. *New Architecture on Indigenous Lands*. Minneapolis: University of Minnesota Press, 2013.

McCarty, Teresa L. *A Place to Be Navajo: Rough Rock and the Struggle for Self-Determination in Indigenous Schooling*. Mahway, NJ: Lawrence Erlbaum and Associates, 2002.

Minutes of the Navajo Nation Tribal Council. Cited as NNTC.

Moneo, Rafael. "On Typology." *Oppositions* 13 (Summer 1978): 23–45.

Parman, Donald L. *The Navajos and the New Deal*. New Haven: Yale Univesity Press, 1976.

Purpose and Plans – The Navajo Culture Center, A Shrine and Living Symbol for the Navajo Nation. Tsaile, AZ: Navajo Community College Press, July 1972.

Quatremère de Quincy. "Type." *Oppositions* 8 (1977): 147–150.

Reichard, Glady. *Navaho Religion: A Study of Symbolism*. New York: Bollingen Foundation, 1950.

Sprague, Chester L. "American Indian Communities: Toward a Unity of Life and Environment." *Technology Review* 74, no. 8 (July–August 1972): 14–25.

Stocking, Jr. George W. "The Santa Fe Style in American Anthropology: Regional Interest, Academic Initiative, and Philanthropic Policy in the First Two Decades of the Laboratory of Anthropology, Inc." *Journal of the History of the Behavioral Sciences* 18 (1982): 3–19.

Szasz, Margaret Connell. *Education and the American Indian: The Road to Self-Determination Since 1928*, 3rd ed. Albuquerque: University of New Mexico Press, 1999.

Vidler, Anthony. *The Writing of the Walls: Architectural Theory in the Late Enlightenment*. Princeton: Princeton Architectural Press, 1987.

Young, Robert W. *A Political History of the Navajo Tribe*. Tsaile, AZ: Navajo Community College Press, 1978.

Conclusion
The Stacked-Log Hogan Becomes a Cultural Icon

In December 1958, *National Geographic* published "Better Days for the Navajos," the magazine's first article to focus on the tribe. Author Jack Breed based the article's text on research collected while driving across the Navajo Nation from Tuba City, in the northwest corner, to Gallup on the southeast side. "Better Days for the Navajos" features photographs of three polygonal stacked-log hogans, each with a corbelled dome. The caption under the largest photograph, printed across two pages, describes the building as "the trademark of the Navajos."[1]

I'm not sure when, exactly, the stacked-log hogan became so closely associated with Diné identity, but by 1965, it had been transformed into an icon decorating a dress photographed for the *Navajo Times* (Figure 7.1). The dress was to be part of a fashion show at that year's Navajo Tribal Fair in Window Rock.

The stacked-log hogan lends itself to being abstracted in this way. A semi-circle on top of a rectangle quickly calls the building's profile to mind, and a series of horizontal lines suggest its stacked-log walls. The icon pictured on the dress is now commonly found on Navajo weavings, jewelry, billboards, and advertising logos. When the recent pandemic was at its height, the Navajo Nation government issued a poster urging tribal members to stay at home and the artist chose the stacked-log hogan as the most powerful image for conveying this message (Figure 7.2).

The House Blessing myth, as narrated by Diné ritual specialists who practice the Blessingway, an important Navajo ceremonial, often includes a description of the first ancestral hogan. Several versions were recorded before World War II, and when the details of the first hogan are included in these accounts, they describe the architecture of the forked-pole (or male) hogan.[2] But when anthropologist Charlotte Frisbie summarized the myths recounted by 14 medicine men between 1950 and 1967, a transition seemed to be underway: Five of those narratives mentioned the male hogan, but two described an originary female hogan.[3]

The beauty of oral traditions is their flexibility. Religious texts that are transmitted by spoken word can adapt to changes in our world and help ensure that our lives remain meaningful, even though our circumstances may have radically altered. Franc Newcomb lived at a trading post in Navajoland between 1914 and 1935, where she met Mary Wheelwright and worked with Hastiin Klah. Although not academically trained as an anthropologist, she made significant contributions towards documenting Diné ceremonialism. Before leaving the reservation,

DOI: 10.4324/9781003431770-8

Conclusion 227

Figure 7.1 Roberta La Rose models a two-piece afternoon dress, pictured in the September 9, 1965 edition of the *Navajo Times*.

Newcomb collected a set of folk tales, including one that recounted the origins of the stacked-log hogan. The story tells of the First People who consulted birds, mammals, and insects to develop the design for the First Hogan.[4]

In 1970, the Bureau of Indian Affairs reprinted Newcomb's text in *Homes for the Diné* (1970), part of a series of books intended for first-grade students at reservation schools. Then in 2009, the San Juan County School District, which includes the area of the Navajo reservation located in Utah, produced yet another version of the tale. This time, *The Story of the First Hogan* was retold by Diné author Don Mose, Jr., and illustrated by Diné artist Charles Yanito. As with the two earlier versions, First Woman and First Man draw from the wisdom of animal guides to construct the First Hogan. Eagle advises, "I like to build my home with short poles. I construct it in a tight circle, representing the sun." Cliff Swallow shows the couple how to apply mud plaster to keep their dwelling warm in the winter and cool in the summer. Later, Beaver counsels, "The logs of the roof must be placed in circular layers. Then mud and bark and small sticks must be packed between the logs to fill

228 *Conclusion*

Figure 7.2 Public Notice, posted in Tribal Administration Building #1, Window Rock, Arizona, June 2021.

all the holes. This is how you get the dome shape." The cover of the book illustrates the building that resulted, an octagonal stacked-log hogan (Figure 7.3).

Published in both Navajo and English, *The Story of the First Hogan* seems to me to present itself as a teaching tool, as a text that one would read to young people to impart knowledge about the traditions of the tribe.

More recently, Diné ritual specialists have begun to interweave the octagonal stacked-log hogan with the tribe's sacred narratives. In 2014, *Leading the Way*, a monthly magazine devoted to Diné culture, printed "The Creation of the Hogan," as told by Hastiin Bééshłigai, a Diné medicine man and Blessingway practitioner. The account describes how the Holy People gave the Beaver People the responsibility to design the forked-pole hogan. In Hastiin Bééshłigai's narrative, everyone was pleased with the forked-pole hogan, but since it was "a ceremonial home," they felt it necessary to provide another place for everyday activities, such as eating and sleeping. First Man declared, "You need to build a home with the logs stacked upwards," and so they constructed a second hogan in the shape of an octagon. Its exterior was covered with dirt, and the floor was of dirt as well to keep

Figure 7.3 Cover of *The Story of the First Hogan*, Charles Yanito, artist.

the Diné close to Mother Earth. While "The Creation of the Hogan" acknowledges the significance of the forked-pole hogan, it also provides an account of the mythic origins of the octagonal stacked-log hogan.

According to Hastiin Bééshłigai:

> The hogan is a place of love, security, togetherness, development, planning, learning, and teaching. It is the center of every blessing of life: happy births, childhoods, puberty ceremonies, marriage, and old age. This is where parents, grandparents, children, and everyone's belongings live. It is a place where our clan system, language, and cultural heritage are nurtured. The hogan is the foundation for a long life of happiness, *sa'įh naagháí bik'eh hóshóón*. It is the foundation for the Navajo way of life.[5]

Today, the octagonal stacked-log hogan is a familiar sight across Navajoland. It appears frequently in the tribe's visual culture and serves as the archetype for octagonal lumber hogans and new public buildings. For the Diné, it has become a symbol of the hogan and all that the hogan entails, just as it unifies the landscape and imbues the reservation with an identity that is unquestionably Navajo.

230   *Conclusion*

Notes

1 Jack Breed and Charles W. Herbert, "Better Days for the Navajos," *National Geographic Magazine* 114, no. 6 (December 1958): 822–823.
2 See, for example, Berard Haile, "Why the Navajo Hogan?" *Primitive Man* 15, no. 3/4 (July–October 1942): 41; Edward Sapir and Harry Hoijer, "The Building of the First Hogan," in *Navaho Texts* (Iowa City: Linguistic Society of America, 1942), 108–109; Aileen O'Bryan, *The Diné: Origin Myths of the Navaho Indians*, Smithsonian Institution Bureau of Ethnology, Bulletin 163 (Washington, DC: GPO, 1956), 13–14 [transcription of a version narrated in November 1928].
3 Charlotte Johnson Frisbie, "The Navajo House Blessing Ceremonial: A Study of Cultural Change" (PhD diss., University of New Mexico, 1971), 49–51, 323–337. See also Leland Wyman, *Blessingway* (Tucson: University of Arizona, 1970), 11–13.
4 Franc Johnson Newcomb, *Navaho Folk Tales,* 2nd ed. (Albuquerque: University of New Mexico Press, 1990), 192–203.
5 Hastiin Bééshłigai, "The Creation of the Hogan," *Leading the Way* 12, no. 3 (March 2014): 2–3.

Reference List

Bééshłigai, Hastiin. "The Creation of the Hogan." *Leading the Way* 12, no. 3 (March 2014): 2–4.

Breed, Jack, and Charles W. Herbert. "Better Days for the Navajos." *National Geographic Magazine* 114, no. 6 (December 1958): 809–847.

Frisbie, Charlotte Johnson. "The Navajo House Blessing Ceremonial: A Study of Cultural Change." PhD diss., University of New Mexico, 1971.

Mose, Don, Jr., and Charles Yanito. *The Story of the First Hogan.* Blanding, UT: San Juan School District, 2009.

The Navajo Social Studies Project. *Homes for the Diné.* Albuquerque: Bureau of Indian Affairs, 1970.

Newcomb, Franc Johnson. *Navaho Folk Tales*, 2nd ed. Albuquerque: University of New Mexico Press, 1990.

Illustration Credits

P.1	Postcard published by Cliché Photo Hall Soudanais, collection of the author	ix
0.1	Courtesy of the Bureau of Indian Affairs	2
0.2	Courtesy of Dyron Murphy Architects	4
0.3	National Anthropological Archives, Smithsonian Institution	5
0.4	National Anthropological Archives, Smithsonian Institution	7
0.5	Photograph by the author	8
0.6	Cosmos Mindeleff, "Navaho Houses," *17th Annual Report of the Bureau of American Ethnology, 1895–1896*, Part 2 (Washington, DC: GPO, 1898), 510 and plate 89	9
0.7	Photograph by the author (top); Model created and photographed by John R. Stein (middle); Elizabeth Compton Hegemann, *Navaho Trading Days* (Albuquerque: University of New Mexico Press, 1963), 284 (bottom)	10
0.8	Palace of the Governors Photo Archives, Museum of New Mexico	11
1.1	Jewell N. Halligan, *Halligan's Illustrated World: A Portfolio of Photographic Views of the World's Columbian Exposition Carefully Selected* (Chicago: The J.N. Halligan Co., 1894), unnumbered plate	21
1.2	Hubert Howe Bancroft, *The Book of the Fair*, vol. II (Chicago: The Bancroft Company Publishers, 1895), 62	21
1.3	Hubert Howe Bancroft, *The Book of the Fair*, vol. I (Chicago: The Bancroft Company Publishers, 1895), 14	24
1.4	Collection of the author	27
1.5	Detroit Publishing Company "Phostint" postcard, collection of the author	28
1.6	University of Arizona, Special Collections	30
1.7	St. Louis Public Library, Special Collections	32
1.8	Detroit Publishing Company "Phostint" postcard, National Anthropological Archives, Smithsonian Institution	33
1.9	Northern Arizona University, Cline Library Special Collections	34
1.10	Postcard published by the Indian Crafts Exhibition, collection of the author	36
1.11	Autry Museum of the American West	36

232   *Illustration Credits*

1.12	University of Arizona, Special Collections	37
1.13	Photograph by Jesse Nusbaum. Palace of the Governors Photo Archives, Museum of New Mexico	40
1.14	Photograph by Jesse Nusbaum. Palace of the Governors Photo Archives, Museum of New Mexico	41
1.15	Sanborn Fire Insurance Map, San Francisco, 1914, Sheet 7	43
1.16	University of Arizona, Special Collections	44
1.17	Postcard published by Fred Harvey, collection of the author	44
1.18	Denver Public Library, Western History Collection	46
1.19	MEVE_307_3052_[id9268], National Park Service Technical Information Center, Denver, Colorado (top and middle); Courtesy of Mesa Verde National Park Archives (bottom)	48
1.20	Collection of the author	51
1.21	Courtesy of Wallace O. Chariton	52
1.22	*Santa Fe Railway Indian Village, Chicago Railroad Fair* [exhibit guide] (Santa Fe Railway, 1948)	53
1.23	Periscope Film #34452	54
1.24	Photograph by the author	55
2.1	Alice Fletcher, *Historical Sketch of the Omaha Tribe in Nebraska* (Washington, DC: Judd & Detweiler, 1885), unnumbered plate	69
2.2	*The Red Man* [Carlisle Indian School] 6, no. 5 (January 1914): cover image	71
2.3	Postcard published by the Native American Press, US Indian School, Phoenix, Arizona, collection of the author	72
2.4	Josephine Phelps Brodhead, "A Navajo Hōghän," *Home Mission Monthly* 18, no. 4 (February 1904): 84–85	74
2.5	Courtesy of Harvey Leake	77
2.6	National Archives and Records Administration, College Park, Maryland	84
2.7	Arizona State Library, Archives and Public Records, History and Archives Division, Phoenix	85
3.1	Leslie J. Hansen, "An Appraisal of the Value of the Property Known as Painted Desert Park," December 14, 1956, courtesy of Petrified Forest National Park Archives	93
3.2	Postcard published by J.M. Young, collection of the author	93
3.3	Collection of the author	96
3.4	Collection of the author	96
3.5	Pomona Public Library, Special Collections	98
3.6	Collection of the author	100
3.7	Collection of the author	101
3.8	Pomona Public Library, Special Collections	102
3.9	Pomona Public Library, Special Collections	103

Illustration Credits   233

3.10	H.B. Embach, "Appraisal Report, All of Section 10, T 19 N, R 24 E," March 21, 1957 (top); Frank Kelly, "Appraisal Report," August 15, 1957 (bottom), courtesy of Petrified Forest National Park Archives	106
3.11	Collection of the author	107
3.12	Pomona Public Library, Special Collections	107
3.13	Collection of the author	109
3.14	Courtesy of the Guadagnoli Collection	110
3.15	Copyright Ralph Camping – USA TODAY NETWORK	111
3.16	Pomona Public Library, Special Collections	112
3.17	Postcard published by H.T. Tammen (top); Unprovenanced postcard, collection of the author (bottom)	114
3.18	Postcard published by Gifford Gillaspy (Colorado Springs), collection of the author	115
3.19	Pomona Public Library, Special Collections	118
3.20	Collection of the author	118
3.21	Unprovenanced postcard, courtesy of the North Adams Historical Society (top); Postcard published by Tichnor Bros., collection of the author (bottom)	120
4.1	Bettman Archive	130
4.2	National Archives and Records Administration, College Park, Maryland (top); Collection of the author (bottom)	137
4.3	Courtesy of the Bureau of Indian Affairs	138
4.4	National Archives and Records Administration, Riverside, California	144
4.5	Milton Snow Collection, Navajo Nation Museum	144
4.6	Periscope Film #46754	145
4.7	Periscope Film #46754	148
4.8	National Archives and Records Administration, Riverside, California	152
5.1	Elizabeth Compton Hegemann, *Navaho Trading Days* (Albuquerque: University of New Mexico Press, 1963), 385	163
5.2	Postcard published by the Feicke-Desche Printing Co., collection of the author	163
5.3	Milton Snow Collection, Navajo Nation Museum	167
5.4	"Indian Architecture and the New Indian Day Schools," *Indians at Work* 1, no. 13 (February 15, 1934): 32	167
5.5	National Archives and Records Administration, Riverside, California	170
6.1	William Penhallow Henderson Papers, Archives of American Art, Smithsonian Institution (top); Wheelwright Museum of the American Indian (middle and bottom)	195
6.2	Pomona Public Library, Special Collections	198

234 *Illustration Credits*

6.3 Livingston and Blayney, City and Regional Planners, and John Carl Warnecke and Associates, Architects and Planning Consultants, "Navajo, New Mexico Development Plan," November 11, 1960, plate, courtesy of the Warnecke Architectural Archives 201

6.4 "The Navajo Heritage Center," courtesy of the Warnecke Architectural Archives 202

6.5 Elisa Leonelli Collection, Claremont Colleges Library, Special Collections 205

6.6 Courtesy of Studio Southwest 209

6.7 Courtesy of Studio Southwest 211

6.8 Courtesy of Studio Southwest 212

6.9 Photograph by the author 214

6.10 Courtesy of Dyron Murphy Architects 216

6.11 Courtesy of Dyron Murphy Architects 217

6.12 Photographs by John R. Stein 219

7.1 Courtesy of the *Navajo Times* 227

7.2 Navajo Nation 228

7.3 Don Mose, Jr., and Charles Yanito, *The Story of the First Hogan* (Blanding, UT: San Juan School District, 2009), cover 229

Index

1867 Exposition Universelle in Paris 19
1884 World's Industrial and Cotton Centennial Exposition in New Orleans 25, 69
1897 New England Sportsman Show 35
1898 Trans-Mississippi International Exposition in Omaha 60n105
1900 Exposition Universelle in Paris 35
1901 Pan-American Exposition in Buffalo 35, 60n105
2002 Winter Olympics in Salt Lake City 54–55

Aaron, John 113
Acoma Pueblo 29, 31, 42; *see also* Panama-California Exposition; Pueblo architecture; Pueblo architecture, reproductions of
adobe architecture 11, 26, *27*, 28–29, *28*, 66, 81, 95, 100, *100*, 136, 147, 149, 150, 168, 182, 197
Ahennabah 100
Ah-He-He-Bah 121
Ahkeah, Sam 45, 47, 60n115
AIDA *see* American Indian Defense Association
AIF *see* American Indian Federation
Akimel O'odham (Pima) architecture 70, 79
Alamo Multi-Purpose Center 208
Alamo, New Mexico 169; *see also* Alamo Multi-Purpose Center
Albright, Horace 45–46
Albuquerque Citizen 27
Albuquerque Journal 12, 140
Albuquerque, New Mexico 20, 28, 29, 205, 208, 212, 215, 223n88; *see also* Alvarado Hotel
Alcalde, New Mexico 192
Althouse, John and Tillie 116–117

Alvarado Hotel 20, 26, 32, 33, 35, 39, 42, 53, 56, 99; first Indian village 26–28, *27*; Indian and Mexican Building 26, 28; Indian Museum 26; second Indian village 28–29, *29*, *30*; truncated cone-shaped structure constructed from vertically placed boards at Indian village 58n42, 125n91
American Arts and Architecture 168
American Indian Defense Association 131, 164, 165, 182n5
American Indian Federation 175–176
Antonio Apache 20, 22–24, 35, *36*, 37, 59n82
Apache architecture 52, *53*, 70, 79; *see also* Panama-California Exposition
Apache tribe 52; *see also* Chiricahua Apache tribe; Jicarilla Apache tribe
Arapaho tribe 31
Architectural League of New York 196
Architectural Record 168
Argan, Gian Carlo 190
Arizona Republic 110, *111*
Armstrong, Leatrice 192
Art Deco architecture 51
ash hopper 23
assimilation 14, 19, 25, 67, 69, 70, 79, 82, 162, 181, 185n64
Atchison, Topeka and Santa Fe Railroad (later Atchison, Topeka and Santa Fe Railway) 13, 25–26, 28, 95, 99, 113; influence on Gallup Inter-Tribal Ceremonial headquarters 108–109; plans for Century of Progress Exposition 49–50; *see also* Alvarado Hotel; Chicago Railroad Fair; Grand Canyon; Panama-California Exposition; Panama-Pacific International Exposition; United States Land and Irrigation Exposition

236 *Index*

Atkinson, Jake and Leroy 102–103, *102*
Atlantic and Pacific Railroad 25
Australian Outback ix
Aztec Ruins National Monument, New
  Mexico 9
Aztec Sun Fête 70, *72*

Babbitt Brothers Trading Company 98
Baca/Dlo'ay Azhi Community School 215
Bagota, Hosteen 25
Baker, Herbert viii
Bamako, Mali viii, *ix*
Bancroft, Hubert Howe 23
Bank of Hawaii 133
Barboane, Frank 119–121, *120*
Barney, John Dean 141
Beasley, Arthur 105
Beatty, Willard 179–180
Beauvoir, Simone de 92, 95, 103
Beaux-Arts architecture 20, *21*, 29
Beclabito, Arizona 169
Beecher, Catherine 68
Bééshłigai, Hastiin 229–230
Bega, Becenti 175
Begay, David 55
Begay family 31
Begay, Kinnie 100
Begay, Richard K. 15, 218, 220;
  see also DLR Group
Bella Coola art 22
Benedict, Ruth 180
Bennett, Hugh H. 133–136, 141
BIA *see* Bureau of Indian Affairs
Bigay, Mr. and Mrs. Nee-yo 37
Bitanny, Adolph 179–180, 186n95
Bitsui, Dineh Chili 100
Bitsuie, Roman 4–5
Blackhorse, Taft 5
Blanca Peak, Colorado viii
Bodie, Nelson 119–121, *120*
Boke, Richard 135–136, 139, 140
Book of the Fair (Bancroft) *21*, 23, *24*
Bosque Redondo, New Mexico 66, 70
Bosscher, Jacob H. 173–174
Bowman, John H. 67
Boyce, George A. 179–181
Boyd, Harry 101
Brink, L.P. 171, 173, 184n44, 184n46,
  184n56
British Guiana 22
Brodhead, Josephine 73, *74*
Broker, Joseph 70
Brophy, William A. 181

Brown Derby restaurant 94
Brown, Wally 55, *55*
Bruner, Joseph 175–176
Buchanan Amendment 134
Buffalo Bill's Wild West 25, 92
Burdick, Usher 177
Bureau of Indian Affairs 203, 210, 227
Burge, Morris 168
Burke, Charles H. 82–83, 164
Burnham, New Mexico 165
butabu viii

Cadman, Frank 135, 141–142
California Institute of Technology 133
Campbell, Douglas 205; *see also*
  Chambers, Campbell, Isaacson and
  Chaplin
Canyon de Chelly, Arizona 17n33
Carleton, James H. 66
Carlisle Indian School 70, 164; *The
  Carlisle Arrow* 70; *The Red Man* 70, *71*
Casa del Navajo *see* Crafts del Navajo
Catron, Frank 135
CCC *see* Civilian Conservation Corps
CCC-ID *see* Civilian Conservation
  Corps-Indian Division
A Century of Dishonor 116
Century of Progress Exposition in Chicago
  20, 39, 49–50, *51*
Chacoan Civilization 9, 22, 39, 113
Chaco Canyon, New Mexico 9, 12
Chaco Culture National Historical Park *see*
  Chaco Canyon
chaha'oh see summer hogans
Chambers, Arizona 103, *103*
Chambers, Campbell, Isaacson and Chaplin
  204–206, *205*
Changing Woman's hogan 206–207
Chapline, William Ridgely 134
Chapman, Kenneth 39
check dams 135, 141
Cheeno 22
Cheyenne tribe 31
Chicago, Illinois 108; as eastern terminus
  of Route 66 94; along Santa Fe Railway
  108; *see also* Century of Progress
  Exposition; Chicago Railroad Fair;
  Rockefeller Memorial Chapel; United
  States Land and Irrigation Exposition;
  World's Columbian Exposition
Chicago Railroad Fair 19, 41, 52–54, *53*, *54*
Chicago Tribune 23, 37–38
Chichiltah, New Mexico 169

Index   237

Chilchinbeto *see* Chichiltah, New Mexico
Chincilli 51
Chinle, Arizona 207; *see also* Chinle Warrior's Home; Navajo boarding schools
Chinle Warrior's Home 215
Chippewa tribe 22, 31, 70
Chiquita 22
Chiricahua Apache tribe 22; *see also* Apache architecture
Choctaw tribe 22
Ch'ooshgai Community School 215
Christian Indian 171, 184n46
Church of St. Vincent Ferrer 132
Civilian Conservation Corps (CCC) 46–47, 134; *see also* Civilian Conservation Corps-Indian Division
Civilian Conservation Corps-Indian Division (CCC-ID) 129, 134, 135–136, 139, 153, 165, 217
"The Closing of the American Frontier" 25
Coahuila tribe 22
Cochiti Pueblo 50
Cole, Fay-Cooper 49–50
Coliseum (Chicago) 37
Collier, Charles 14, *130*, 132, 134, 136, 140
Collier, David 38
Collier, John 14, 129, *130*, 203, 213; and AIF 175; articles in *Sunset* and *Survey Graphic* (1924) 131, 165; background 129–130; on building homes at Fruitland 178–179; and day school/community center program 149, 153, 162, 165–166, 168; and design for Navajo Nation Council Chamber 197; at February 1935 Congressional hearings 176–177; and Indian Arts and Crafts Board 216–217; as Indian rights activist 82–83; and Louisa Wetherill 131; "native plan" for hogan schools 180–181; and New Deal hogan schools 166, 168, 174–175, 182; and New Deal nurse's aide hogans 151; and New Deal practice hogans 143, 152–153; presents the Indian New Deal 172; resignation 180; and soil erosion 134; visit to Taos Pueblo 131; work in New York City 130
Collier, Nina Perera 166, 183n25
Colorado Springs, Colorado 113, *115*, 116
Colter, Mary Jane Elizabeth 26, 32, 39
Columbus, Christopher 20
The Community Center Naltsos (later *Navajo Community Center Naltsos*) 149

community hogans (as part of 1941 dormitory program) 179–180
conical forked-pole hogans 8, 12, 15n12, 19, 50, 55, 56, 98, 121, 190; at Chicago Railroad Fair 52, *54*; and "The Creation of the Hogan" 228–229; criticized by Josephine Brodhead 73, *74*; at first Alvarado Hotel Indian village 26–27; inspiration for Navajo House of Religion 196; and Jacob Morgan 169, 171–172; at Kinlichee Chapter House dedication 84, *84*; at Louisiana Purchase International Exposition 31, *32*; at Mesa Verde National Park 45, *46*; and Navajo House Blessing 226; origins and construction of 6, *7*; at second Alvarado Hotel Indian village *28*, 29, *30*; at World's Columbian Exposition 23, *24*
Coolidge, Dane and Mary Roberts 12
Coolidge, New Mexico *see* Crafts del Navajo
corbelled arch 11
corbelled dome 1, 2, *5*, 14, 15, 95, 121–122, 124n48; as basis for an architectural type 189–191; at Century of Progress Exposition *51*; at Chicago Railroad Fair *53*, *54*; at Crafts del Navajo *101*; at Discover Navajo Pavilion *55*; in the First Hogan 227–228; at Fort Wingate boarding school 145–149, *145*, *146*, *148*, 152; at Gallup Inter-Tribal Ceremonial headquarters *109*; at Garden of the Gods Curio Company *114*; at Grand Canyon *33*, *34*; at Indian Crafts Exhibition 35, *36*; at Kinlichee Chapter House dedication 84, *84*; Louisa Wetherill's "Big Hogan" 76, *77*; at Mesa Verde National Park 47, *48*; at Mexican Springs 136, 140, 142; at the Navajo Indian Village *103*; at Navajo rug stands *96*; in New Deal nurse's aide hogans *152*; in New Deal practice hogans designed by Mayers, Murray & Phillip 143, *144*; origins and construction of 8–9, *10*, 11; at Panama-California Exposition 39, *41*; at the Panama-Pacific International Exposition *44*; at Rimmy Jim's *112*; at Stateline Trading Post *102*; surveyed by Corbett 12; at Texas Centennial Exposition *52*; *see also* log ceiling constructed to appear corbelled
corbelled-log hogans 8–9, *10*, 11, 12
corbelled vault 11

238   *Index*

Corbett, John M. 12
Corbin, Alice 192
Coronado Cuarto Centennial 182
Cove, Arizona *167*, 169, 207
Crafts del Navajo 99–102, *100*, *101*
Cram & Ferguson 192
Cram, Ralph Adams 192, 198
Cree tribe 22
Creighton, William J. 132, 154n16
Crownpoint, New Mexico 80, 88n56, 213;
    see also Navajo boarding schools
Crow tribe 22
Crystal, New Mexico *144*, 186n91, 217

Dahl, George 51
Dakota tribe 31
Dallas Morning News 51
Dallas, Texas *see* Texas Centennial
    Exposition
Da Pah 100, *101*, 121
day school/community centers 129, 131,
    140, 143, 149, 150, 151, 152, 153, 162,
    163, 165–166, *167*, 180–182, 182n1;
    and Jacob Morgan 172–174; and
    transportation problems 179; *see also*
    community hogans (as part of 1941
    dormitory program); New Deal hogan
    schools; New Deal nurse's aide hogans;
    New Deal practice hogans
de Beukelaer cookie company 28
Dekker, J. David 210–212
The Delineator 172
demonstration hogans *see* New Deal
    practice hogans
Dennehotso, Arizona 17n33, 150, 186n91
Denver and Rio Grande Railroad 113
Derrah, Karl *see* DLR Group
Dietz, William H *see* Lone Star
Dilcon, Arizona *see* Navajo boarding schools
Diné College *see* Navajo Community
    College
Discover Navajo Pavilion 54–56
Disney, Walt 19
Dixon, Del 210
DLR Group 218, *219*, 220
DNA Legal Services, Inc. 208
Dodd, Theodore H. 66
Dodge, Chee *130*
Dodge, Mabel 131
Dodge, Tom *130*, 174, 177, 178
Dory, William 76
double-hogans: Gallup Inter-Tribal
    Ceremonial headquarters 13, 108–109,

109; the Hogan Station 109–110, *110*; at
    Mexican Springs 136, *138*; the Navajo
    Hogan (Colorado Springs) 113, *115*,
    116; at New Deal hogan schools *163*,
    169, 184n38; New Deal practice hogans
    143, *144*, 145, *146*, 147, 150–151, 152,
    158n119
Downing, Alexander Jackson 68
Drolet, J. Marshall 51
dry painting 41, 51, 53, 100, 119, 201
Dudley, L. Edwin 67
Dyron Murphy Architects *15*, 215–218,
    216, *217*

Earth lodge *see* Omaha architecture
East Charlemont, Massachusetts 119–121,
    120
Eastern Association on Indian Affairs (later
    National Association on Indian Affairs)
    77, 164, 182n5, 185n61
Eastern Navajo Agency 80–81, 88n56, 150
Edsitty, Fred 141
Edwards, Herbert R. 78
Eliot, Jared 133
Elkus, Charles de Young and Ruth C. 101
Elle of Ganado 27–28, 33, 37–38, *37*
Ellis, Dorothy 151
El Navajo Hotel 108
El Tovar Hotel *see* Grand Canyon National
    Park, Arizona
Emergency Conservation Work program
    see Civilian Conservation Corps-Indian
    Division
*An Essay upon Field Husbandry in
    New-England* 133
ethnic tourism 94
*Ethnologic Dictionary of the Navajo
    Language* 12
ethnoscape ix 191
Eubank, Lisbeth 203
Evergreen Tree 50

Fagergren, Fred 105
Farmington, New Mexico 97, 171, 173, 212
Farmington Times-Hustler 179
Fathy, Hassan viii
female hogans 6, 8, 15n12, 19, 35, 56, 66,
    76, 121, 143, 190–191, 196, 226;
    see also corbelled-log hogans;
    many-legged hogans; palisaded hogans;
    stacked-log hogans; stone hogans
fences on the Navajo reservation 135, 142
Ferguson, Frank 192

Index 239

Fisher & Fisher 192
Fisher, Arthur Addison and William Ellsworth Fisher 192
Flagstaff, Arizona 94, 171
Flanders, Alice 117, 119, 121
Fleer Bubblegum Company 28
Fletcher, Alice 68–70, *69*, 76, 87n14
Foght, Harold W. 143, 145
Fontecchio, Nicolas 113
forked-pole hogans *see* conical forked-pole hogans
Fort Defiance, Arizona 23, 31, 67, 85, 88n56, 162, *163*; *see also* Navajo boarding schools; Navajo Tribal Utility Authority headquarters
Fort Wingate, Arizona *see* Navajo boarding schools
Fowler, Don 31
Fowler, Orson Squire 98
Franciscan Fathers 12; *see also* Haile, Father Berard
Francis, Harris 97
Franke, Betty 47
Fred Harvey Company 29, 113; El Navajo Hotel 108; as employer of Charles Strausenback 113; founding and history 25–26; founding of the Indian Department 26; plans for Century of Progress Exposition 49–50; *see also* Alvarado Hotel; Chicago Railroad Fair; Grand Canyon; Panama-California Exposition; Panama-Pacific International Exposition; United States Land and Irrigation Exposition
French, Wilfred 119
Frisbie, Charlotte 101, 226
Fryer, E. Reeseman 139, 142, 178–179, 180, 213

Gaastra, T. Charles 113, 125n89
Gallup Independent 95, 101, 108, 168
Gallup Inter-Tribal Ceremonial 119; *see also* Gallup Inter-Tribal Ceremonial headquarters
Gallup Inter-Tribal Ceremonial headquarters 13, 108–109, *109*, 116
Gallup, New Mexico 1, 2, 17n33, 25, 39, 81, 97, 99, 119, 125n92, 134, 135, 150, 175, 207, 216, 227; *see also* El Navajo Hotel; Gallup Inter-Tribal Ceremonial headquarters; Hogan Station
Ganado, Arizona 27, 39, 134; *see also* Presbyterian mission to the Navajo

Ganado News Bulletin 86
Garden of the Gods 113, *114*
Garden of the Gods Curio Company 113, *114*
Gebhard, David 94
gemeinschaft grouse 130
General Federation of Women's Clubs 131, 164, 182n5
Gerken, Edna 151
Gheno, Caesar 113
Giddings, James "Rimmy Jim" 111–112
giren 11
Glittering World 55, 201
Goerke, Curt 113
Good Housekeeping 166
Goodhue, Bertram Grosvenor 132–133, 198
Good Luck family 31
Goodluck, Hosteen 113
Gorman, Howard *170*
Gothic Revival architecture 132–133, 198
Grand Canyon National Park, Arizona 32–35, 56, 75; El Tovar Hotel 32, *34*; Hopi House 32, *34*; influence on "Grand Canyon of Arizona Replica" 42; influence on representations of the Indian Crafts Exhibition 35, *36*; Navajo architecture 32–35, *33*, *34*
"The Grand Canyon of Arizona Replica" *see* Panama-Pacific International Exposition
Grand Junction Indian School 169
Grants, New Mexico 94
Grant, Ulysses S. 66–67
Graumann's Chinese Theatre 94
Gropius, Walter 199
Gudis, Catherine 94–95
A Guide Book to Highway 66 112

Hackley, Ed 54–55
Haida art and architecture 22, 35
Haida tribe 22; *see also* Haida art and architecture
Haile, Father Berard 4, 178, 196
Hallahan, Edna 119–121
Hall, Sharlott 98–99
Halprin, Lawrence 199
Hampton, Edgar Lloyd 116
Hampton Institute, Virginia 68–69, 169–170
Haskanaya 100, 101
Hatathli, Ned 204
Hawaiian style architecture (Goodhue and Phillip) 133

240   *Index*

Hawaii *see* Bank of Hawaii; Hawaiian style architecture (Goodhue and Phillip); Hawaii State Capitol; Honolulu Academy of Arts; Oahu College
Hawaii State Capitol 199
Hayzlett, G.W. 67
Hegemann, Elizabeth Compton *10*, *163*, 166, 175
Hemet, California 116–117
Henderson, William Penhallow 192–194, *195*, 196, 198
heptagonal architecture 105, 108, 112, 190–191
Hewett, Edgar 39
hexagonal architecture 81, 82, 104, 109, 121, 190–191, 210
The Hidden Inn 113
Higgins, C.A. 25
Highway 666 (later US Route 491) 2, 135
Hirshen, Gammill, Trumbo & Cook 207
Ho-Chunk architecture 50
Hoffman, Frederick L. 77
The Hogan (San Jacinto, California) 117, *118*, 119
Hogan Station 109–110, *110*
Holden, Arthur C. 132, 154n18
home economics hogans *see* New Deal practice hogans
A Home for All 98
Home Mission Monthly 73, *74*
Homes for the Diné 227
Honolulu Academy of the Arts 133
Hood, Raymond 132, 154n15
hooghan: etymology 4; meaning 4–5
hooghan nímazí 6
Hoopa tribe 50
Hoover, Herbert 83, 165, 172
Hopi architecture, reproductions of: float at Aztec Sun Fête 70, *72*; *see also* Panama-California Exposition
Hopi House *see* Grand Canyon National Park, Arizona
Hopi reservation 22, 25, 42, 50, 52, 75, 78, 88n56; *see also* Pueblo architecture
Houck, Arizona 97, 105
House, Donna 55
House, Jimmy 104
House of Navajo Rugs (Lupton, Arizona) 95
Hubbell, Donald S. 139
Hubbell, Lorenzo 27, 33, 39
Huckel, J.F. 39, 49, 60n97
Hull, Daniel R. 45
Hulsizer, Allan 168

Hunter, John G. 81, 83–84, 109
Huntington, Henry E. 35

Ickes, Anna Wilmarth 102
Ickes, Harold 102, 132, 139, 142, 185n64
iglu *see* Inuit architecture
Indian Arts and Crafts Board 216–217
Indian Bureau *see* Office of Indian Affairs
Indian Crafts Exhibition at Eastlake Park in Los Angeles 35–37
Indian New Deal 122, 143, 149, 162, 165, 172, 175, 179, 198, 203, 220; *see also* Civilian Conservation Corps-Indian Division; community hogans (as part of 1941 dormitory program); day school/community centers; Indian Reorganization Act; Mexican Springs Soil Erosion Control Experiment Station; Navajo Nation Tribal Council; New Deal hogan schools; New Deal nurse's aide hogans; New Deal practice hogans
Indian Office *see* Office of Indian Affairs
The Indian of the Southwest 172
Indian Plaza 119–121, *120*
Indian Reorganization Act 175, 177, 185n63, 186n85
Indian Rights Association 25, 175, 185n63
Indians at Work 166, 174, 180, 183n17
Indian Self-Determination and Education Assistance Act 208
Indian Service *see* Office of Indian Affairs
The Indian Traders 98
Indian Truth 175
Indian Wells, Arizona *see* Indian Wells community school
Indian Wells community school 210–211, *211*
International style architecture 207
Inter Ocean 23
Interstate 40, 97, 105
Inuit architecture 11
Inuit tribe 22; *see also* Inuit architecture
Iroquois architecture 22
Iroquois tribe 22
Irvine, Alex G. 67
Iyanbito, New Mexico *144*, 151, *152*

Jackson, Helen Hunt 116
Jackson, Leroy F. 152
Jacobs, Charlie and Loretta *93*, 94, 103–106, *103*, *106*
Jacobs, Paul and Betty 103
Jean, Sally Lucas 151, 158n123

Jemez Pueblo 50, 52
Jett, Stephen C. 11
Jewett, New Mexico 85
Jicarilla Apache tribe 31; *see also* Apache architecture
Johnson, Philip 200
Johnson, William Templeton 192
Jose family 31

Katz, Curtis L. 52
Kayenta, Arizona 17n33; *see also* Wetherill Trading Post
Keams Canyon, Arizona 88n56, 172–173, 175; *see also* Navajo boarding schools
Kelley, Klara 97
Kickapoo tribe 31
Kidder, Alfred 192, 194, 196
Kimball, Solon 180
Kimizin 22
kinaaldá 1
King, William S. 173
Kinlichee, Arizona 186n91; *see also* Kinlichee Chapter House
Kinlichee Chapter House 84, *84*, 182
Kiowa reservation 82
ki see Apache architecture
kivas 9; reproductions of 39, *40*, 52, *53*, 113, *114*
Klah, Hastiin 100, 123n33, 191, 194, 196, 221n26, 226
Kluckhohn, Clyde 191
Krause, Robert 200
Kwakiutl tribe 22

Laboratory of Anthropology 39, 53, 198; *see also* Navajo House of Religion
La Farge, C. Grant 132, 154n16
La Farge, Christopher Grant 154n17
La Farge, Oliver 132, 174–175, 197
Laguna Pueblo 29, 52
Lakota architecture 50; *see also* tipi
Lakota tribe 22, 50; *see also* Lakota architecture
Land Show *see* United States Land and Irrigation Exposition
La Plata Range *see* Mount Hesperus, Colorado
La Rose, Roberta *227*
Leading the Way 228
Lee, Eddie 104
Lee, Hemsley 15, 208, 212
Leibowitz, Rachel 197
Leighton, Alexander and Dorothea 12, 180

Leupp, Arizona *see* Leupp Navajo Agency; Navajo boarding schools
Leupp Navajo Agency 81, 83, 88n56
Link, Martin 201
Livingston and Blaney 199
Locke, Harry and Hope 112
Logan, Charles J. 73
log cabin architecture 13, 21, 24, 69, *69*, 70, *71*, 75, 79, 122, 139, 168, 180, 184n56
log ceiling constructed to appear corbelled; at Indian Wells community school 210; at Navajo Hogan (Colorado Springs) 113, *115*, 116; at Navajo House of Religion 194; at Navajo Nation Museum 210; at Seba Dalkai boarding school 211; at Thoreau Veteran's Center 215; at Tonalea Chapter House 216; at Twin Lakes Senior Center 214
Lone Star 70, *71*
The Long Walk (*Hwéeldi*) 66
Lorimer, Robert 132
Los Angeles 20, 116, 117; and Route 66, 92, 94; and Santa Fe Railway 26, 108; *see also* Indian Crafts Exhibition at Eastlake Park in Los Angeles; Los Angeles Public Library
Los Angeles Herald 28
Los Angeles Public Library 132–133
Los Angeles Times 116, 117
Los Pinos Phase 8
Louisiana Purchase International Exposition 19, 29–32, 41, 55; Anthropology Villages and Indian Village 29, 31–32; Model Indian School 29–31; Navajo architecture 31, *32*
Lowdermilk, Walter C. 136
Lukachukai, Arizona 203
lumber hogans 1, 2, *4*, 230; at the Navajo Hogan (Colorado Springs) 113, *115*, 116; at the Painted Desert Tower 105, *106*
lumber hogans clad with log siding 2; at The Hogan (San Jacinto, California) 117, *118*, 119; at the Hogan Station 109–110, *110*; at the Twin Lakes Senior Center 214–215, *214*
Lupton, Arizona 95, 102, *102*, 105, 110, *111*, 123n48
Lutyens, Edwin viii

MacDonald, Peter 200
Mackendrick, Marda 76
MacLeish, Archibald 141

242 *Index*

male hogans *see* conical forked-pole hogans
Manitou Cliff Dwellings 113
Manitou Springs, Colorado 11, 119
Mann, Kee Yazzie 207–208, 213
Many Farms, Arizona 204
many-legged hogans 20; at Century of Progress Exposition 50; at first Alvarado Hotel Indian village 27, *27*, 28, 35; at Indian Crafts Exhibition 35, *36*; at Mesa Verde National Park 45, *46*; at Navajo Indian Village 104; origins and construction of 6, 8, *9*; at Panama-California Exposition 39, *41*; surveyed by Corbett 12; at United States Land and Irrigation Exposition 37–38, *37*
Mapel Public School 81–82
Mariano Lake, New Mexico 169, 184n38
Maricopa tribe 31
Marietta 22
Mark, Mary Louise 79
Martinez, Ken 217
Maryboy, Nancy 55
Matthews, Washington 12
Mayan architecture *see* Puuc Maya architecture
Mayers, Francis L.S. 132; *see also* Mayers, Murray & Phillip
Mayers, Murray & Phillip 14, 129, 152, 162, 189, 200, 220; background 132–133; and day school/community centers 166, *167*; at Mexican Springs 136, *137*, 139, 140; and Navajo Nation Council Chamber 196–198, *198*; and New Deal hogan schools *163*, 166, *167*, 168–169, 175, 177, 181; and New Deal nurse's aide hogans 151–152, *152*; and New Deal practice hogans 143, *144*, 145, 151, 153; and Nina Collier 183n25
McCowan, Samuel M. 31
McDonald, Angus 133
McGee WJ 29–31
McKinley County, New Mexico 1
McNitt, Frank 98, 99
Medical Problems of Our Indian Population 77
Meem, John Gaw 192, 194, *195*, 196
Meloney, Marie 172
Menominee tribe 22
Meriam, Lewis 78
Meriam Report 77– 79, 83, 164, 165
Meritt, Edgar 75, 79–80, 82

Mesa Verde National Park, Colorado 9, 39, 45–48, *46*, *48*, 56, 194
Mexican Springs, New Mexico *see* Mexican Springs Soil Erosion Control Experiment Station
Mexican Springs Soil Erosion Control Experiment Station 14, 129, 135–142, *137*, *138*, 152–153
Miguelito 27–28, 39, 41, *41*
Mi'kmaq architecture 92
Miller, Harry E. "Indian" 103
Miller, Julia Grant 103
Miller, Loren 210
Miller, Wick 50
Mindeleff, Cosmos 6, *9*, 99
Mission Revival architecture 26, 29, 42, *44*
MIT (Massachusetts Institute of Technology) 166, 203–204
Mitchell, Frank 4–5
model 189–191, 215
model hogans: John Collier at the Wetherill trading post 131; Kinlichee Chapter House dedication *84*; Louisa Wetherill's "Big Hogan" 76–77, *77*, 131, 143; Mapel Public School 81–82; at Navajo boarding schools 79–82; sponsored by the Presbyterian Mission at Ganado 84–86, *85*; *see also* New Deal practice hogans
Mohawk Trail 119
Moneo, Rafael 190
Morgan, Jacob Casamera 14, 153, 162, *170*; author of "The Navajo in his Home" 171–172; background 169–171; compared to other Christian Reformed missionaries 172–174; and Coronado Cuarto Centennial 182; at February 1935 Congressional hearings 175–177; at July 1934 Tribal Council meeting 172; response to New Deal hogan schools 171–181
Morgan, Thomas H. 25
Morley, Sylvanus 196
Morris, Gouverneur 102
Morris, Ruth Wightman 102, 123n42
Mose, Jr., Don 227
Mount Baldy, New Mexico 171
Mount Hesperus, Colorado ix, 171
Mount Taylor, New Mexico viii, 171
Murdock, Abe 176
Murphy, Dyron 213; *see also* Dyron Murphy Architects

Murray, Oscar Harold 132; *see also* Mayers, Murray & Phillip
Myths and Memories of the Nation ix

Nahodishgish, New Mexico 169
Nakai, Raymond 203
Naranjo, Lupita *114*
Naschitti, New Mexico 17n33, 51
National Association on Indian Affairs 132, 168, 174, 185n61
National Geographic 226
National Old Trails Road 95
National Park Service 39, 45–47, 105
Native American boarding schools 25; *see also* Carlisle Indian School; Grand Junction Indian School; Hampton Institute; Navajo boarding schools; Phoenix Indian School
T*he Native American see* Phoenix Indian School
Natural History 76
Navajo Arts and Crafts Enterprise building 217–218, *217*
Navajo Arts and Crafts Guild (later Navajo Arts and Crafts Enterprise) 216–217
Navajo astronomy 220
Navajo boarding schools 131, 159n133; Chinle 164, 172; Crownpoint 81, 150, 164; Dilcon 210–211; Fort Defiance 150, 162, *163*, 164, 169; Fort Wingate (Charles H. Burke Indian School) 143–149, *145*, *146*, *148*, 152, 168; Keams Canyon 150, 158n119, 164; Leupp 81, 158n119, 164; Seba Dalkai 211–212, *212*; Shiprock 81, 150, 164, 170; Toadlena 164; Tohatchi 150, 164, 169, 172; Tuba City 150, 164
Navajo chapter houses *138*, 140, 174; *see also* Alamo Multi-Purpose Center; Kinlichee Chapter House; Tonalea Chapter House
Navajo chapters 81, 109, 141, 142, 150, 208, 214–215
Navajo Community College (later Diné College) 203–207, *205*, 218
Navajo Culture Center (later Ned Hatathli Center) 205–207, *206*, 210, 218
Navajo Educational Center 208
Navajo Emergence myth 55, 201, 220
Navajo Heritage Center 201–203, *202*, 206

Navajo Hogan (Colorado Springs) 113, *115*, 116
Navajo House Blessing 6, 101, 226
Navajo House of Religion (later Wheelwright Museum of the American Indian) 14–15, 191–196, *195*, 198
"Navajo Houses" (Mindeleff) 6, *9*
Navajo Housing Authority 213–214
The Navajo Indians (Dane and Mary Roberts Coolidge) 12
Navajo Indian Village (Chambers, Arizona) 103–105, *103*
Navajoland Trading Post Encyclopedia 97
Navajo Legends (Matthews) 12
Navajo metalwork: demonstrations at anthropology villages 26, 31, 33, 42; instruction in metalwork at Navajo boarding schools 165, 182n10; sale and demonstrations along Route 66 100, *101*, 104; sale and demonstrations at Indian Plaza 119
Navajo Mountain, Utah 151, 169, 181, 203
Navajo Nation Council Chamber 99, *198*, 206, 207, 208; design and construction 196–198; proposed designs by John Carl Warnecke 199–200
Navajo Nation Design and Construction Department 200, 212
Navajo Nation Museum 207, 208–210, *209*
Navajo Nation Tribal Council 14, 176; history 203–204; and Jacob Morgan 162, 169, 170, 174; and John Carl Warnecke 199–200; July 1933 meeting 129, 135; July 1934 meeting 172, 175; July 1943 meeting 142; and Navajo Community College 204; October 1933 meeting 172; and Rough Rock Community School 203; Sam Ahkeah as chairman 45; and Tom Dodge 174, 177
Navajo, New Mexico 200–201, *201*, 213
Navajo Progressive League 170
Navajo rug stands 13, 95–97, *96*
Navajo Times 207–208, 226–227, *227*
Navajo transhumance 5, 66–68
Navajo Treaty of 1868 162
Navajo Tribal Utility Authority (NTUA) 217
Navajo Tribal Utility Authority headquarters 217–218
Navajo weaving: at the 1884 World's Industrial and Cotton Centennial Exposition in New Orleans 25; as architectural ornament 95, *95*, *107*, *120*, 217; decorated with stacked-log

244 *Index*

hogan icon 226; demonstrations at anthropology villages 22, 26, 31, 32, 35, 37, *37*, 42, 45, 51, 55; and Elle of Ganado 27, 33, *37*; on float at Aztec Sun Fête 70, *72*; instruction in weaving at Navajo boarding schools 165, 182n10; at Navajo Nation Council Chamber 197; sale and demonstrations along Route 66 94, 95–96, 100, *102*, 103, 108; supported by the Navajo Arts and Crafts Guild 217

Navajo wedding basket pattern 217, *217*
Nazca Desert ix
Nebraska State Capitol 132
Ned Hatathli Center *see* Navajo Culture Center
Newcomb, Arthur 191
Newcomb, Franc 191, 226–227
New Deal 129; *see also* Civilian Conservation Corps; Indian New Deal; Public Works Administration; Works Progress Administration
New Deal hogan schools 129, 162, *163*, *167*, 174–175, 177; architecture 166–169; and Becenti Bega 175; and Flora Warren Seymour 175; and Jacob Morgan 175–177, 182; and Matthew Sniffen 175; *see also* Mayers, Murray & Phillip
New Deal nurse's aide hogans 129, 151–153, *152*
New Deal practice hogans 129, 143–151, *144*, *146*, 152–153
New Delhi, India viii
New Mexico Association on Indian Affairs 164, 182n5
New York City 68, 130, 132, 218
New York Times Sunday Magazine 116
Nez, "Big Maggie" 104
NHA *see* Navajo Housing Authority
North Adams Transcript 119
Northern Navajo Agency 81, 84–85, 88n56, 150
Norwegian villa architecture 32
NPS Branch of Plans and Design 46–47
NPS *see* National Park Service
Nuntah Beah 39, 41, *41*
Nusbaum, Aileen 45
Nusbaum, Jesse: architecture at the Laboratory of Anthropology 194, 196; background 39; at Mesa Verde National Park 45–47, *46*; plans for Century of Progress Exposition 49–50; at the Panama-California Exposition 39

Oahu College 133
octagonal shape as an architectural type 189–191
octagon house movement *see* Fowler, Orson Squire
OEO *see* Office of Economic Opportunity
Office of Economic Opportunity 203–204
Office of Indian Affairs (OIA, later Bureau of Indian Affairs) 13, 14, 80, 110, 129, 132, 203; and the American Indian Federation 175; and day school/community centers 162, 164, 165, 166, 168, 169, 176, 179, 180; and Indigenous architecture 75, 82–83, 84–85; interactions with the Navajo during the 19th century 66–67; and New Deal nurse's aide hogans 151, 153; and New Deal practice hogans 110, 143, 149, 150; and reservation model hogans 79–82
OIA *see* Office of Indian Affairs
Omaha architecture 69–70, *69*
Omaha Reservation, Nebraska 68
Onset Wigwam 92, *93*, 94
Osage (Wajiji) tribe 31
The Outlook 75–76

Pacific Monthly 28
Page, Gordon B. 13
"The Painted Desert" *see* Panama-California Exposition
Painted Desert Park 92, *93*, 94, 95, 103, 104, 105
Painted Desert Tower 105, *106*
Palace of the Governors 39, 51, 62n44, 100
palisaded hogans 20; at the Navajo Indian Village 104; origins and construction of 8; at the Panama-California Exposition 39, *41*; at the Stateline Trading Post 102, *103*; at Wonderview Wood 105, *107*
Palmer, William Jackson 113
Palos de la Frontera, Spain 20
Panama-California Exposition 20, 194; "Acoma Pueblo" 39, *40*; Apache architecture 39, *40*; history 38; "Hopi Pueblo" 39, *40*; Navajo architecture 39–41, *40*, *41*; "Taos Pueblo" 39, *40*, *41*; "The Painted Desert" 38–41; "Zuni Pueblo" 39, *40*
Panama Canal 38
Panama-Pacific Exposition *see* Panama-Pacific International Exposition

Panama-Pacific International Exposition 20, 41–44; electric railway 42; Navajo architecture 42, *44*; plan view *43*
Papago architecture *see* Tohono O'odham architecture
Papago tribe 22; *see also* Tohono O'odham architecture
Paredes, Cesar and Ellouise 55
Parezo, Nancy 31
Parman, Donald L. 172, 181, 216
Passamaquoddy tribe 22
Patterson, Florence 78–79
Pawnee tribe 31
Penkiunas, Daina 133
Penobscot architecture 22
Penobscot tribe 22
Peshlakai family 31
Peshlakai, Hosteen Begay 100
Peshloki 22
Peshoki 25
Peter, W.W. 151
Petrified Forest National Monument, Arizona (later Petrified Forest National Park) 92, *93*, 105, *106*
Phillip, F. Hardie: background 132–133; on design for hogans at Mexican Springs 136, 139–140; on design for New Deal hogan schools 168; see also Mayers, Murray & Phillip
Phillip, Ralph 212
Phoenix Indian School 70, *72*
Pike's Peak, Colorado 113, *114*
Pima architecture *see* Akimel O'odham (Pima) architecture
Pima tribe 31; *see also* Akimel O'odham (Pima) architecture
Pinedale, New Mexico 170
Pinehill, New Mexico 207
Pine Ridge reservation 50, 165
Pine Springs, Arizona 169
Plans and Specifications for Indian Homes and Improvements 82
Plummer, Edwin H. 25
Pomo tribe 31
Post, Emily 34
pre-Columbian art and architecture 11, 25, 104, 113; reproductions of 117; *see also* Chacoan Civilization; kivas; Panama-California Exposition; Puuc Maya architecture
Presbyterian mission to the Navajo 84–86, 162
Prescott, Arizona *see* Warren D. Day House
Preston, Samuel 98–99

programmatic architecture 94
Progressive Education 153, 164–165, 181
Provinse, John 180
public housing 212–214
Public Works Administration (PWA) 134, 136
Pueblo Alto, New Mexico 169
Pueblo architecture 29, 47, 79
Pueblo architecture, reproductions of 197; at Century of Progress Exposition 49–50, *51*; at Chicago Railroad Fair 52, *53*, *54*; at Garden of the Gods Curio Company 113, *114*; at Grand Canyon 32, *34*; at Indian Crafts Exhibition 35; at Manitou Cliff Dwellings 113; at Panama-Pacific International Exposition 42, *43*; at second Alvarado Indian village *28*, 29; *see also* Hopi architecture, reproductions of; Panama-California Exposition
Pueblo-Spanish Revival architecture 45, 53, 60n110, 110, 113, 117, *118*, 119, 125n101, *138*, 139, 140, 153, 166, *167*, 169, 193–194, *195*, 197–198; *see also* Palace of the Governors
Puertocito *see* Alamo, New Mexico
Putnam, Frederic Ward 22–23
Puuc Maya architecture 11, 39; reproductions of 21–22, 49, 117
PWA *see* Public Works Administration
pyramidal roof 1, 2, *4*, 191; at Dilcon boarding school 210–211; at Fort Wingate boarding school 147, *148*; at Indian Wells community school 210; at Navajo Arts and Crafts Enterprise headquarters *217*; at The Navajo Hogan 113, *115*, 116; at Navajo Indian Village 103–104, *103*; at Navajo Nation Museum 210; in New Deal practice hogans 143, *144*; at Onset Wigwam *93*; at Painted Desert Park *93*; at Painted Desert Tower 105, *106*; at Seba Dalkai boarding school 211; at Tonalea Chapter House *216*; at Twin Lakes Senior Center 214, *215*; at V.J. Holmes Trading Post *107*, 108

Quatremére de Quincy, Antoine-Chrisostome 189–190

Rainbow Bridge 75
Ramona (novel) 116–117
The Ramona Pageant 116–117

246 *Index*

Red Lake, Arizona *see* Tonalea Chapter
  House
The Red Man see Carlisle Indian School
Rehoboth, New Mexico 173
Reichard, Gladys 27, 101, 168,
  186n95, 192
Reliquary and Illustrated Archaeologist 28
"replacement era" 210
Repp, Thomas Arthur 104, 108
Rhoads, Charles J. 83, 164–165
Riley, David 210
Rimmy Jim's 111–112, *112*, 121, 189
Ripley, Edward 38
Rittenhouse, Jack 112
Roanhorse, Pony 104
Roberts, W.O. 81
Rockefeller family 192
Rockefeller Memorial Chapel 132–133
Roessel, Robert 203–204, 210
Roessel, Ruth 210
Rogers, Will (comedian) 101
Rogers, Will (congressman) 176
Roosevelt, Franklin D. 82, 102, 129, 165, 176
Roosevelt, Theodore 27, 75–76, 131
Rorick, Harry 166
Rosebud reservation 165
Rosenwald Schools 168
Rough Rock, Arizona *see* Rough Rock
  Demonstration School
Rough Rock Demonstration School
  203–204, 205, 207, 215
Route 66: Romance of the West 104
Rush, James Lowery 109–110
Ryan, J. Carson 164–165, 166

Sage Memorial Hospital School of
  Nursing 85, 89n81
Sahghy, Hosteen Deete 25
sa'íh naagháí bik'eh hóshóón 229
Salish architecture 22
Salsbury, Clarence 85
San Diego, California *see* Panama-California
  Exposition
San Diego Union 38
sand painting *see* dry painting
San Francisco, California *see*
  Panama-Pacific International
  Exposition
San Francisco Peaks, Arizona viii–ix, 171
San Ildefonso Pueblo 121
San Jacinto, California 116–119, *118*
Sanostee, New Mexico 151
Santa Clara Pueblo 31, 113

Santa Fe, New Mexico 117; *see also*
  Laboratory of Anthropology; Navajo
  House of Religion; Palace of the
  Governors
Santa Fe Railway *see* Atchison, Topeka and
  Santa Fe Railroad
Santa Fe style *see* Pueblo-Spanish Revival
  architecture
Santo Domingo Pueblo 29, 149
San Ysidro, New Mexico 50
Saturday Evening Post 102
Sawmill, Arizona 183n28, 200
sawmills 67, 83–84, 200, 213, 214
Scattergood, J. Henry 83, 164–165
Schweizer, Herman 26, 28, 33, 34, 39, 49
Schwemberger, Simeon *5, 7,* 12
Scientific American 31
Seba Dalkai, Arizona *see* Navajo boarding
  schools
Selig, William N. 37
Senator John Pinto Library 218–220, *219*
Sesser, William F. 41–42
Seymour, Flora Warren 175, 185n64
Shepard, Mrs. F.O. 81–82
Shippey, Lee 116–117
Shiprock, New Mexico 81, 88n56, 134,
  213; *see also* Navajo boarding schools;
  Senator John Pinto Library
Shirley, Leon 15, 212–215, *214*
Shonto, Arizona *10, 163,* 166, 168, 169, 175
Shonto Trading Post *10, 163,* 166, 175
Silvertongue, Chief 50
Simpson, W.H. 49
Six, Billie P. 84
Sloan, David 15, 55, 208, 213
Smith, Anthony ix
Smith, Frank 31
Smith Lake, New Mexico 101
Sniffen, Matthew 175, 185n63
Soboba Hot Springs 116–117
Soil Conservation Service *see* US Soil
  Conservation Service
Soil Erosion: A National Menace 134
soil erosion, definition 133–134, 154n30
soil erosion control experiment stations in
  the US 134, 155n39
Soil Erosion Service *see* US Soil Erosion
  Service
Solomon R. Guggenheim Museum 218
Southern Navajo Agency 83, 88n56, 109,
  150, 151
The Southern Workman 172
Southwest Tourist News 108

Index 247

Spanish mission architecture 42, 51
Spencer, Virginia E. 11
Sprague, Chester 203–204
Stacher, Samuel 79–81
stacked-log hogans viii, 1, 2, *5*, 20; as basis
 for an architectural type 189–191; at
 Century of Progress Exposition 50, *51*;
 at Chicago Railroad Fair *52*, 53, *54*; at
 Crafts del Navajo 99–102, *100*, *101*; as
 cultural icon 226–229, *227*, *228*, *229*;
 at Discover Navajo Pavilion 54–55, *55*;
 at the Fort Wingate boarding school
 145–149, *145*, *146*, *148*, 152; at Gallup
 Inter-Tribal Ceremonial headquarters
 108–109, *109*; at Garden of the Gods
 Curio Company 113, *114*; at Grand
 Canyon 33–35, *33*, *34*; at Indian Plaza
 119–121, *120*; as influence on hogans
 designed by Mayers, Murray &
 Phillip 15, 143; as inspiration for the
 Navajo House of Religion 196; at
 Kinlichee Chapter House dedication
 84, *84*; at Mesa Verde National Park 45,
 60n115; at Mexican Springs 14, 136,
 137, *138*, 139, 140; as model for the
 Twin Lakes Senior Center 214–215;
 at Navajo Indian Village 103–104,
 103; at Navajo rug stands 95–97, *96*;
 origins 3, 11, *11*, 12; at Panama-Pacific
 International Exposition 42, *44*; at
 Presbyterian Mission at Ganado 85,
 85; at Presbyterian Mission at Tselani
 86; at Rimmy Jim's 112, *112*; at second
 Alvarado Indian village *28*, 29; at
 Stateline Trading Post 102, *103*; at
 Texas Centennial Exposition 51, *51*; at
 V.J. Holmes Trading Post 105, *107*, 108
Stacy-Judd, Robert 116–117
Staples, Berton and Rebecca 99–102, 121
Stateline Trading Post 102–103, *102*
Steamboat, Arizona 186n91
Steamboat Canyon, Arizona 17n33
Stein, Clarence 132, 154n19
Stenson, E.J. 151
Stephen, Alexander 6, 12
Stewart, James M. 180
St. Louis, Missouri see Louisiana Purchase
 International Exposition
St. Michaels, Arizona *7*, 12
Stone, Edward Durell 200
stone hogans *8*; at Arizona port of entry at
 Lupton 110, *111*; as influence on hogans
 designed by Mayers, Murray & Phillip

15, 143; at Mesa Verde National Park
 46–47, *48*; at Navajo Indian Village
 103–104, *103*; origins and construction
 of 6; at Painted Desert Park 92, *93*, 94;
 surveyed by Corbett 12; as "typical"
 hogan around Mexican Springs 142;
 see also New Deal hogan schools; New
 Deal nurse's aide hogans; New Deal
 practice hogans
The Story of the First Hogan 227–228, *229*
Strausenback, Charles 113
Studio Southwest 208–212, *209*, *211*, *212*
summer hogans 177; at Century of
 Progress Exposition 50, *51*; at Chicago
 Railroad Fair 53, *53*, *54*; as described
 by Jacob Morgan 171; documented by
 Alexander Stephen 6; at Gallup Inter-
 Tribal Ceremonial headquarters 108;
 at The Hogan Station 109–110, *110*; in
 the Indian and Mexican Building at the
 Alvarado 26; at Indian Crafts Exhibition
 36, 59n82; at Navajo Indian Village
 103–104, *103*; at Navajo rug stands
 96–97, *96*; at Painted Desert Park 104;
 at Painted Desert Tower 105, *106*; at
 Panama-California Exposition 41, *41*; at
 the Stateline Trading Post 103, *102*; at
 World's Columbian Exposition 23
Sunset 76, 131
Supai tribe 42
Survey of Conditions 83
Swiss chalet architecture 32

Taft, President William Howard 75
Tahe, Benny 135
Taliman, Sr., Henry *170*
Tanabah 100
Taos family 31
Taos Pueblo 121, 131; *see also* Pueblo
 architecture; Pueblo architecture,
 reproductions of
Texas Centennial Exposition 50–52, *52*, 53
Thompson, Laura 180
Thoreau Veteran's Center 215
tipi 22, 23, 35, 50, 92, 117, 121, 190
Tisinger, R.M. 181
Tlingit art 22
Toadlena, New Mexico 196; *see also*
 Navajo boarding schools
Todacheene, Carl 207
Tohatchi, New Mexico *see* Navajo boarding
 schools; Ch'ooshgai Community School
Tohdilto *see* Navajo, New Mexico

248 *Index*

Tohono O'odham architecture 70, 79
Tolani Lakes, Arizona 17n33
Tomes, Nancy 73
Tom of Ganado 27–28, 33, 37–38, *37*
Tonalea, Arizona *see* Tonalea Chapter House
Tonalea Chapter House 215–216, *216*
Torreon, New Mexico 151, *167*, 169
trachoma 13, 66, 73, 76, 78, 86, 149, 151, 153
trading post guest hogans 99, *163*
trading posts 50, 51, 97–99, 140; *see also*
    Crafts del Navajo; Shonto Trading
    Post; Stateline Trading Post; trading
    post guest hogans; trading posts in
    anthropology villages; Tuba Trading
    Post; V.J. Holmes Trading Post;
    Wetherill Trading Post
trading posts in anthropology villages 31,
    39, *40*, 53–54, *53*
Treasury of Atreus 16n21
Trennert, Robert A. 20, 73, 151
Tribal Administration Building #1
    207–208, *228*
Troncoso, Vizente 6
Troutman, John 31–32
trulli 11
Tsaile, Arizona *see* Navajo Community
    College
Tselani, Arizona 86
Tsimshian art 22
Tsosie, Hotine 31
Tuba City, Arizona viii, *55*, 88n56, 98–99,
    98; *see also* Navajo boarding schools
Tuba Trading Post 97–99, *98*
tuberculosis 13, 66, 73, 75, 78, 86, 149, 153
Turner, Frederick Jackson 25
Twin Lakes, New Mexico *see* Twin Lakes
    Senior Center
Twin Lakes Senior Center 214–215, *214*
Two Wells *see* Chichiltah, New Mexico
type 14, 189–191, 215

United Mine Workers 113
United States Land and Irrigation
    Exposition 37–38, 49, 50
US Board of Indian Commissioners 66–67,
    185n64
USDA *see* US Department of Agriculture
US Department of Agriculture 134, 139
US House Committee on Indian Affairs
    176–177
US Route 491 *see* Highway 666
US Senate Committee on Indian Affairs
    78–79, 83–84, 141–142

US Soil Conservation Service (later
    US Natural Resources Conservation
    Service) 13, 129, 134, 139
US Soil Erosion Service (later US Soil
    Conservation Service) 135, 136, 139, 142

Valentine, R.G. 75, 80
Vidler, Anthony 190
Vierra, Carlos 194, *195*, 196
Vitruvius 11
V.J. Holmes Trading Post 105, *107*, 108

Warnecke, John Carl: background 199; design
    for Hawaii State Capitol 199; designs for
    Navajo Nation 199–203, *201*, *202*, 213
Warren D. Day House 98
Washi, Mr. and Mrs. Nas-tin 37
Water! Grass! The Navajos' Eternal Quest
    (film) 145, *145*, *146*, 147, *148*, 149
West Bank ix
Western Navajo Agency 78, 88n56, 150
Weston, Mary 92
Wetherill, John 75–76
Wetherill, Louisa 75–76, *77*, 131, 143
Wetherill Trading Post 75–76, 131
Wheeler, Burton 83–84
Wheeler-Howard bill *see* Indian
    Reorganization Act
Wheelwright, Mary Cabot 191–196, 226
Wheelwright Museum of the American
    Indian *see* Navajo House of Religion
White, Elizabeth 192, 196
White, Fred 54
White, Lawrence G. 132, 154n17
White, Martha 192
White Sands National Monument, New
    Mexico 51
Whitfield, Charles J. 139–140
Whittlesey, Charles 26, 32
Wichita tribe 31
Wide Ruins, Arizona 186n91
wigwam 50, 92, 119
wikiup *see* Apache architecture
Willoughby, W.F. 78
Wilson, M.L. 139
Window Rock, Arizona 141, 199–200,
    213, 226; *see also* DNA Legal Services,
    Inc.; Navajo Arts and Crafts Enterprise
    building; Navajo Educational Center;
    Navajo Heritage Center; Navajo
    Nation Council Chamber; Navajo
    Nation Museum; Tribal Administration
    Building #1

Index 249

Winnebago architecture 50
Winnebago tribe 22, 50, 69
Winslow Mail 100
Wittick, Ben 11, *11*
Woehlke, Walter 168
Woerner, Davida 165
Wonderview Wood 105, *107*
Woodard, M.L. 108
Work, Hubert 78, 164
Works Progress Administration (WPA) 110
World's Columbian Exposition 19, 41, 50,
   55v; and boarding schools 25; Convent
   of Santa Maria de la Rábida (exhibt) 20,
   21, 24; Court of Honor 20, *21*; log cabins
   21, 24; Model Indian School 20, *21*, 22,
   25; Navajo architecture 22–24; Outdoor
   Ethnographical Exhibit (anthropology
   village) 20, *21*, 22–25; "The Ruins
   of Yucatán" (exhibit) 21–22, *21*;
   Smithsonian exhibit 23, *24*; South Pond
   20, *21*; summer hogan 23; "The Volcano
   of Kilauea" (exhibit) 42; "Working man's
   Model Home" (exhibit) 68
woven hogans *see* corbelled-log hogans
WPA *see* Works Progress Administration
Wright, Frank Lloyd 218

Wright, Gwendolyn 68
Wyman, Leland 100–101, 191
Wyman, Paula 101

Yadah' askání 196
Yamasaki, Minoru 200
Yanabah 100
Yanito, Charles 227, *229*
Yaqui tribe 22
Yazza, Isko 51
Yazza, Pishliki 100
Yazzi, Fred 12
Yei Bichei 6, *9*, 46, 47
Yellowhorse, Anna 105
Yellowhorse, Frank 105
Yenne, Herbert C. 108
Yil Habah 100
Youngblood, Bonney 99
Young, Robert W. 15, 196

Zega, Michael 25
Zia Pueblo 50
Zuni Pueblo 22, 25, 42, 52; *see also*
   Pueblo architecture, reproductions
   of; Panama-California
   Exposition